Explainable Artificial Intelligence and Interpretable Machine Learning in Education

A Researcher's Guide to Data Science

Editor:
Myint Swe Khine
Curtin University, Australia

CRC Press
Taylor & Francis Group
Boca Raton London New York

CRC Press is an imprint of the
Taylor & Francis Group, an **informa** business
A SCIENCE PUBLISHERS BOOK

First edition published 2027
by CRC Press
2385 NW Executive Center Drive, Suite 320, Boca Raton FL 33431

and by CRC Press
4 Park Square, Milton Park, Abingdon, Oxon, OX14 4RN

CRC Press is an imprint of Taylor & Francis Group, LLC

Library of Congress Cataloging-in-Publication Data (applied for)

ISBN: 978-1-041-14901-9 (hbk)
ISBN: 978-1-041-17391-5 (pbk)
ISBN: 978-1-003-71337-1 (ebk)

DOI: 10.1201/9781003713371

Typeset in Times New Roman
by Prime Publishing Services

Preface

Today, education is being transformed by data-driven tools like explainable artificial intelligence (XAI) and interpretable machine learning (IML). These methodologies are becoming essential in educational research because they help make teaching and learning more transparent, efficient, and innovative. As educators and researchers increasingly seek to harness the immense power of these tools, the necessity of understanding their practical applications has become a matter of critical importance. This volume is crafted to provide a comprehensive and definitive guide for those dedicated to enhancing educational processes through the lens of XAI and IML. The primary goal of this work is to bridge the gap between complex AI methodologies and real-world educational practices. For too long, high-performing machine learning models have operated as "black boxes," providing outputs that, while accurate, remain opaque to the human users who must implement them. In an educational context, where decisions impact student trajectories and learning outcomes, clarity is paramount. This book delves into how XAI and IML can be harnessed to analyze vast educational datasets, assess student performance, and design adaptive learning environments, all while ensuring that these systems remain interpretable and ethically deployed.

The necessity for such a guide is underscored by the current landscape of the science of learning. As data science becomes more embedded in the classroom, there is a rising demand for trustworthy XAI educational applications that prioritize human understanding. The contributors to this volume recognize that for AI to be truly effective in education, it must be human-centered, catering not just to data scientists but also to non-expert users who are on the front lines of teaching. By focusing on human-centered explainability, this book addresses the opportunities and challenges presented by emerging technologies, including Large Language Models (LLMs), which are rapidly changing the educational landscape. The scope of this volume is intentionally broad, reflecting the diverse ways in which XAI and IML can be applied across different domains of education. This book is a result of global collaboration, featuring contributions from scholars at prestigious institutions. This international breadth ensures that the insights provided apply to a wide range of educational contexts and cultural settings.

Ultimately, this book encourages a move toward a future where AI does not replace the educator but rather empowers them with actionable, understandable insights. It emphasizes collaboration and encourages contributors and readers alike to address the emerging trends and challenges of the field. By prioritizing transparency and interpretability, we can ensure that the next generation of educational tools is not only innovative but also accountable, ethical, and aligned with the fundamental goals of human learning. This book is the result of a significant interdisciplinary collaboration involving educators, researchers, and data scientists from across the globe. I am deeply grateful to the community of scholars who have generously contributed their findings and practical experiences to this volume.

Myint Swe Khine
Perth, Australia

Contents

List of Contributors

Abdullah Tariq Choudhry is an honors undergraduate student pursuing a BS in Computer Science with a minor in Data Science at the University of the Pacific, graduating in December 2025. His research interests consist of artificial intelligence and deep learning applications in computational biology, educational technology, autonomous vehicles, and environmental conservation. In 2024, he completed an internship as a Performance Engineer at NVIDIA, focusing on deep learning (DL) and high-performance computing (HPC).

Agron Chaushi is an Associate Professor at the Faculty of Business and Economics, South East European University (SEEU) in Tetovo, North Macedonia. He earned his PhD in Economic Sciences from SEEU and completed postgraduate studies in Information Systems at Indiana University's Kelley School of Business. His research interests encompass information systems, e-government, and the application of artificial intelligence in education. Dr. Chaushi has authored over 30 publications and actively contributes to the academic community through research and teaching in information systems and educational technology.

Amanda Barany is a postdoctoral fellow at the Penn Center for Learning Analytics (PCLA) at the University of Pennsylvania Graduate School of Education. Her research interests include the design and implementation of play-based learning experiences (games, digital platforms) to foster achievement, motivation, and identity development in learners, expanding traditional pedagogical approaches. She also focuses on refining methods to automate qualitative data analysis, including the use of large language models for coding and codebook development. Additionally, she applies Quantitative Ethnographic techniques to analyze complex data. Amanda earned her PhD from Drexel University, specializing in game-based learning interventions.

Andrea Marconi is an Italian expert in European project management with a PhD in Human and Fundamental Rights from the University of Camerino. With a background in international and diplomatic sciences, he has over 15 years of experience leading complex national and EU-funded initiatives in local development, education, and social innovation. His research focuses on participatory governance and deliberative democracy. Andrea currently serves as Research Manager at the University of Camerino, where he supports strategic academic and policy projects aimed at fostering inclusive growth and community resilience across Europe.

Andrea Seveso is a Research Fellow at the University of Milano-Bicocca, working at the intersection of labor market intelligence, machine learning interpretability, and large language models (LLMs). His research focuses on two main fronts: developing innovative methods to assess the linguistic and cultural competence of LLMs, and advancing explainability techniques to make AI decision-making more transparent. Through this work, Andrea contributes to the development of a more culturally aware and interpretable AI, supporting the responsible deployment of AI in real-world settings. He has authored numerous publications and participates in EU projects bridging AI research with policy and societal impact.

Anita Montagna is an R&D expert in education and career development, with extensive experience as Scientific Director of national and European projects focused on career guidance, inclusive education, and STEM learning. She holds an MSc in Developmental and Educational Psychology and a PhD in Biomedical Engineering. Her work bridges psychopedagogical expertise and interdisciplinary innovation. She oversees trainer training programmes and leads the development of EdTech tools supporting e-guidance and inclusive educational practices.

Blerta Abazi Chaushi is an Associate Professor at the Faculty of Business and Economics, South East European University (SEEU) in Tetovo, North Macedonia. She holds a PhD in Economic Sciences from SEEU and Master's degree in Information Systems from Indiana University's Kelley School of Business. Her research focuses on digital transformation, enterprise systems, and the application of AI in education, particularly explainable AI. She also serves as a national expert for UNDP and contributed to numerous EU-funded projects in entrepreneurship, digital innovation, and education reform. She has authored over 40 scholarly publications and actively contributes to the advancement of educational technology and digital governance.

Brittany Ho is an AI/ML researcher and performance engineer with expertise in high-performance computing, machine learning, and deep learning performance optimization. Her work spans natural language processing, data science, and ML infrastructure development.

Burcu Kutlu is an English Language Teacher with a professional focus on Lifelong Learning and the integration of Artificial Intelligence in educational contexts. Her academic interests lie in the intersection of digital pedagogy, language acquisition, and educational innovation. She has conducted research on the implications of AI-driven tools in enhancing learner autonomy and inclusivity across various stages of adult education.

Erik Cambria is a Professor of Artificial Intelligence at Nanyang Technological University, where he also holds the appointment of Provost Chair in Computer Science and Engineering, and a Visiting Professor at MIT Media Lab. His research focuses on neurosymbolic AI for interpretable, explainable, and trustworthy affective computing in domains like mental health, climate resilience, and socially responsible investing. He is ranked in Clarivate's Highly Cited Researchers List of World's Top 1% Scientists, is recipient of many awards, e.g., IEEE Outstanding Early Career, was listed among the AI's 10 to Watch, and was featured in Forbes as one of the 5 People Building Our AI Future. He is an IEEE Fellow, Associate Editor of various top-tier AI journals, e.g., *Information Fusion and IEEE Transactions on Affective Computing*, and is involved in several international conferences as keynote speaker, program chair, and committee member.

Faisal Peer Mohamed is an Electrical Engineer specializing in high-voltage engineering and the application of artificial intelligence in power systems. His research focuses on the intersection of machine learning and diagnostics in high-voltage insulation systems, partial discharge analysis, and intelligent condition monitoring.

Florije Ismaili is a Full Professor in the Faculty of Contemporary Sciences and Technologies at South East European University (SEEU) in Tetovo, North Macedonia. She earned her PhD in Computer Science from the Technical University of Sofia, Bulgaria. Her research interests include data science, distributed systems, web programming, and the semantic web. Dr. Ismaili has authored over 50 publications and has contributed to projects in AI, IoT, and educational technology. She also serves as SEEU's Advisor for Academic Planning and Digitalization, leading initiatives such as the AI @ SEEU project.

Georgios Makridis is a researcher at the University of Piraeus specializing in explainable AI and interpretable machine learning, with a focus on human-centered approaches and applications. He has co-developed "XAI for ALL", leveraging a custom GPT model to democratize AI explainability for non-experts, and "VirtualXAI", a GPT persona-driven framework that combines quantitative metrics with 'virtual' user-centric qualitative assessments for AI interpretability. Beyond research, he is developing "FairyLandAI", a platform that exemplifies fair, inclusive, and transparent AI in educational storytelling.

Jeff Ginger is a Research Scientist and educator at the University of Illinois at Urbana-Champaign. Over the years he has worked on several state and federally funded research projects related to community engagement, informal learning and technology education. He is currently engaged with the NSF National AI Institute for Inclusive Intelligent Technologies for Education (INVITE) and helps to lead Project WHIMC, What-If Hypothetical Implementations in Minecraft. Jeff has also taught students ages 8 to 25 in camps, workshops and semester classes for over 15 years, primarily in areas of STEAM education. Prior to his current role Jeff served as the director of the CU Community Fab Lab.

Laurence Capus is a Professor of Computer Science at Laval University. She has contributed to the advancement of artificial intelligence applied to education and continues to actively pursue this line of research. Her work includes the development of intelligent tutoring systems and adaptive learning platforms that personalize education for individual learners. She seeks to understand and integrate the needs of various stakeholders—teachers and students alike—to enhance their experience and foster educational innovation.

Lorenzo Malandri is an Assistant Professor at the University of Milano-Bicocca, where his research spans natural language processing (NLP), explainable artificial intelligence (XAI), and large language models (LLMs), with a focus on applications in labor economics, healthcare analytics, and financial decision-making. He has contributed to numerous European and national research initiatives in areas such as digital transformation, skill intelligence, and AI for public policy, often serving as senior technical expert or project coordinator. His work combines methodological innovation with applied research, fostering collaborations with public institutions and industry. He is also active in academic teaching and advanced training in AI and data science.

Luc Paquette is an associate professor in the Department of Curriculum and Instruction at the University of Illinois Urbana-Champaign. His research focuses on the usage of machine learning, data mining and knowledge engineering approaches to analyze and build predictive models of the behavior of students as they interact with digital learning environments such as MOOCs, intelligent tutoring systems, and educational games. He is interested in studying how those behaviors are related to learning outcomes and how predictive models of those behaviors can be used to better support the students' learning experience.

Lynda Dib, PhD in Computer Science, is a researcher specializing in explainable artificial intelligence and model interpretability, currently conducting advanced research at Université Laval. Her work focuses on adapting local interpretability methods, such as LIME, to enhance the transparency and usability of predictive models, with particular attention to the refinement of generated explanations. Through an interdisciplinary approach, she bridges machine learning techniques with practical applications in various domains, including education. Her objective is to contribute to the ethical and equitable use of AI by developing interpretable tools that support personalized interventions, model accountability, and the empowerment of practitioners and end users.

Maria Cristina Popa is a lecturer and Head of the Teacher Training Department at Lucian Blaga University of Sibiu (ULBS), Romania. With over 15 years of experience in education—ranging from early childhood teaching to higher education—she holds a PhD in Educational Science. Her academic work is closely linked to international research and development projects, in which she has served as coordinator or researcher, focusing on pedagogical innovation, inclusive education, and the integration of digital tools in teaching and learning. She is the author and editor of academic volumes and research studies, and has organized numerous national and international conferences and events in the field of education. Certified as a trainer and mentor, she plays a central role in shaping future educators, building academic partnerships, and promoting a strategic vision of teacher education grounded in quality, innovation, and adaptability to contemporary educational challenges.

María Jesús Cardoso Moreno, PhD in Psychology, has worked as a university professor since 2002. She currently collaborates with the Good Project at Harvard University and coordinates various European projects. She has participated in over twenty research projects funded by national and international public calls. She has published over a hundred papers in national and international psychology journals and books, and has conducted research at several foreign institutions. She is currently a professor in the Department of Psychology and Sociology at the Faculty of Health Sciences at the University of Zaragoza.

Marica Magagnini is a PhD candidate in Computer Science and Mathematics at the International School of Advanced Studies, University of Camerino. Her research explores optimization problems for explainable and interpretable machine learning methods. She focused on counterfactual explanations for the k-Nearest Neighborhood classifier and recently investigated the construction of diverse sparse (generalized) linear models. Before starting her PhD, she completed her Master's thesis in the Operation Research group at the University of Seville, a collaboration that continues to this day. Her work bridges optimization and AI transparency, contributing to the development of trustworthy systems.

Mirka Saarela is a tenure-track Assistant Professor of Educational Technology and an Academy of Finland Research Fellow in the Faculty of Information Technology at the University of Jyvaskyla (JYU/IT), Finland. She holds a doctoral degree in Mathematical Information Technology (JYU/IT, 2017). Her research lies at the intersection of learning analytics, machine learning, education, and artificial intelligence. She is especially interested in Explainability and fairness in algorithmic decision-making. Her research on explainable AI was supported and awarded by several foundations, such as the Otto A. Malm Foundation, the Finnish Foundation for Share Promotion, the K.H. Renlund Foundation, and the Ulla Tuomisen Foundation.

Mustafa Kutlu is a researcher with a background in control engineering and a specialized focus on rehabilitation technologies and artificial intelligence. His interdisciplinary work bridges engineering principles with machine learning to develop intelligent systems for health and educational applications. He has contributed to projects involving human-in-the-loop control systems, adaptive rehabilitation interfaces, and explainable AI in assessment tools.

Navid Nobani is an Assistant Professor of Computer Science at the University of Milano-Bicocca, specializing in AI, big data, and web intelligence. With a PhD in Computer Science and dual Master's degrees in Management Engineering and Big Data Analytics, he combines academic insight with industry experience. He previously led data science and behavioral analytics teams, building large-scale machine learning pipelines and web data systems. His research focuses on natural language processing, scalable data engineering, and explainability in AI. Nobani is also active in teaching and scientific committees, contributing to top conferences such as ACL, EMNLP, and COLING.

Professor Dr. Myint Swe Khine earned an MS (Ed) from the University of Southern California (USA), an MSc (Ed) from the University of Surrey (UK), and an EdD from Curtin University (Australia). He previously served as Professor and Chair of the Assessment and Evaluation Centre at the Emirates College for Advanced Education in the United Arab Emirates. A prolific scholar, he has contributed extensively to peer-reviewed journals and edited numerous academic volumes. His latest book, *Future of Learning with Large Language Models: Applications and Research in Education*, was published by CRC Press, Taylor & Francis. He currently serves as Editor-in-Chief of the *International Journal of Science of Learning*, published by De Gruyter-Brill in the Netherlands, and teaches at Curtin University, Australia.

Qianhui (Sophie) Liu is a PhD candidate at the University of Illinois Urbana-Champaign. Her research focuses on applying data mining methods in combination with learning science theories and expert knowledge to help improve the efficiency of teaching and learning. She has been working on projects related to various educational settings, including computer science education and Minecraft-based educational games. She is interested in closing the loop of machine learning to humans for actionable insights through explainable AI methods and interpretable machine learning models.

Raluca Mihaela Bârsan is passionate about educational design and research. She coordinates the activities in the first Design Thinking center formally introduced in a Romanian university called ULBS D-School and unlike other schools around the world it first started offering semester courses for higher education teachers in Lucian Blaga University of Sibiu and only later also for students as a means to adapt curriculum design through active research, not just by introducing new teaching methods. She has a PhD in Engineering and Management with an interdisciplinary topic focused on continuous improvement in engineering and continuous improvement in higher education using design thinking.

Renato De Leone received his degree summa cum laude from the University of Napoli (Italy) in 1981. From 1984 to 1993 he was Research Associate, Lecturer, and Visiting Professor at the University of Wisconsin–Madison (USA). In these years he performed research in Mathematical Programming and Optimization and taught various courses in the areas of Applied Mathematics and Operations Research. Since 1994, he is Full Professor. Since 1994 he served, among others, as Chairman of the Mathematics and Computer Science Department, Coordinator of the Bachelor and Master courses in Mathematics, Vice Director of the School of Science and Technology, and Rector Delegate for Erasmus International Mobility (also at present). From January 2007 to December

2011 he was President of AIRO (Associazione Italiana di Ricerca Operativa), the Italian Association of Operations Research. His current research areas are Optimization and Mathematical Programming, Mathematical Modelling, Machine Learning with special interest in Classification problems using Support Vector Machines, and Decision Support Systems (DSSs).

Rudy Milani is a Postdoctoral Researcher at the University of the Bundeswehr Munich, affiliated with the Institute for Theoretical Computer Science, Mathematics and Operations Research. He obtained his Ph.D. from the same university in 2025. His research interests lie primarily in the fields of operations research, artificial intelligence and data analytics, particularly focusing on reinforcement learning and the explainability of AI-driven decision-making systems.

Sachini Gunasekara received her MSc degree in Information Technology from the Sri Lanka Institute of Information Technology (SLIIT) in 2018. She is currently a PhD student in Educational Technology and Cognitive Science in the Faculty of Information Technology at the University of Jyväskylä (JYU/IT), Finland. Her research interests include machine learning, learning analytics, and data mining.

Saša Brdnik is a Assistant Professor at the University of Maribor, Faculty of Electrical Engineering and Computer Science. Her research focuses on user evaluation and comparison of explainable artificial intelligence (XAI) techniques, with additional focus on human-centered machine learning, learning analytics, and the role of XAI in digital learning environments.

Her research focuses on user evaluation and comparison of explainable artificial intelligence (XAI) techniques, with additional focus on human-centered machine learning, learning analytics, and the role of XAI in digital learning environments.

Sašo Karataktič is an Associate Professor at University of Maribor, specializing in fair and explainable AI. His work emphasizes reducing bias in ML and ensuring fairness across applications. He leads international research projects, including Horizon, Erasmus+, NATO, and national ARIS initiatives, applying AI to finance, healthcare, education, and transportation.

Sojen Pradhan holds a Ph.D. in Computer Science and is an educator and researcher passionate about leveraging technology for social impact. With extensive teaching experience in courses such as Information Systems, Business Intelligence, Data Analytics, Business Processes, and Innovation and Entrepreneurship, Sojen bridges technical expertise with practical application. His research explores the intersection of artificial intelligence, social innovation, digital platforms, and community development, focusing on how emerging technologies can drive inclusive and sustainable change. A strong advocate for experiential education, Sojen also develops and studies innovative work-integrated learning models in higher education, helping students connect academic knowledge with real-world challenges. Through a combination of research, teaching, and community engagement, he aims to advance digital transformation that empowers communities and fosters innovation-driven social progress.

Vivek Pallipuram is an Associate Professor in Electrical and Computer Engineering and Program Chair of the Electrical Engineering, Computer Engineering, and Engineering Physics programs at University of the Pacific. His teaching bridges engineering and computer science, with favorite courses including Computer Systems, high-performance computing (HPC), and Digital Image Processing. His research group, comprising undergraduate and graduate students, explores machine learning, natural language processing (NLP), HPC, and Cloud computing to support domain scientists. Notable frameworks include *A2Cloud* for Cloud resource selection and *ChatReview* for survey data analysis, serving chemists, physicists, educators, and medical professionals.

William Cain, PhD, is Associate Professor of Learning, Design, and Technology at the University of Wyoming, where he also serves as a Faculty Fellow with the School of Computing. His research focuses on the ethical and pedagogical implications of generative AI in education, with an emphasis on prompt engineering, human-centered design, and the cognitive and critical thinking practices that support intentional, reflective engagement with AI tools. He is the creator of the EPICC framework, which guides users in structuring iterative, purpose-driven interactions with AI. His recent work explores AI-enhanced learning experience design and ethical approaches to instructional practice in AI-mediated contexts.

Zaid M. Altukhi is a PhD candidate in Information Systems at the University of Technology Sydney, Australia. His research focuses on Explainable Artificial Intelligence (XAI) in higher education, aiming to increase trustworthiness in AI-based systems. He holds an M.S. in Data Analytics Engineering from George Mason University (USA) and a B.S. in Computer Information Systems from Taibah University (Saudi Arabia). He is also a lecturer who teaches computer science and information systems courses. His research interests include XAI, human–AI interaction, educational data mining, and the ethical development of AI systems.

1 Explaining Explainability in Education
Integrating Data Science, Interpretation, and Human Understanding

Myint Swe Khine[1*]

1. Introduction

Over the past decade, artificial intelligence (AI) has evolved from a laboratory innovation into a pervasive infrastructure shaping how students learn, teachers teach, and institutions make decisions. Algorithms are now integrated into online learning platforms, plagiarism detectors, adaptive assessment tools, and intelligent tutoring systems. In recent years, large language models (LLMs) and generative systems have amplified these transformations by making AI conversational, contextual, and increasingly humanlike in its interactions. Yet as algorithms grow more powerful, their inner workings grow less visible. This opacity raises ethical and epistemological questions: How can learners trust feedback they cannot interpret? How can educators justify grades or predictions that even developers struggle to explain? Explainable Artificial Intelligence (XAI) has emerged as both a technical discipline and a moral obligation that responds to these challenges. In its simplest form, XAI seeks to make machine reasoning intelligible to human understanding (Tripathy & Seetha, 2024). But in the educational domain, explainability transcends code visualization or feature attribution—it touches the essence of learning itself. Education has always been a dialogue between evidence and meaning, between demonstration and reflection. To educate is to explain. Thus, when AI becomes an actor within this process, its outputs must not only be accurate but also interpretable, contestable, and pedagogically sound.

This volume—*Explainable Artificial Intelligence and Interpretable Machine Learning in Education: A Researcher's Guide to Data Science*—was conceived to meet precisely this intersection of inquiry, practice, and ethics. It is not simply a compendium of technical methods; it is a guidebook for understanding how data science can be aligned with educational purposes. The chapters together demonstrate the importance of explainability and interpretability, and ongoing dialogues between data, theory, and human judgment. Each contribution situates AI within the lived realities of classrooms, universities, and research laboratories, showing how interpretability enriches educational reasoning, and decision making (Khine, 2024a). This volume brings together a diverse group of scholars and

[1] Curtin University, Bentley, Australia.
* Corresponding author: m.khine@curtin.edu.au

DOI: 10.1201/9781003713371-1

practitioners who share a common vision: that explainability is not an accessory to educational AI but its ethical and epistemic foundation. The chapters included in the book traverse a rich landscape of ideas, from conceptual frameworks for trust and fairness to technical innovations in explainable modeling. The chapters reveal how transparency, interpretability, and human-centered design can transform AI from a black box into a shared understanding.

This volume is divided into three parts. While Part I introduces the overview of the volume.

Part II, Conceptual and Human-Centered Foundations of Explainable AI in Education, establishes the theoretical and ethical groundwork. It articulates the principles that should govern educational AI, trust, fairness, user agency, and accountability and introduces frameworks that embed these values into the design of AI systems. Part III, Applied and Computational Innovations in Educational XAI, complements this foundation by presenting concrete applications of explainable methods such as SHAP, LIME, and knowledge-based neural networks across contexts ranging from automated grading to affective computing. Together, these sections chart a dual trajectory: from philosophical reflection to computational implementation, and from human intention to algorithmic insight.

2. Conceptual and Human-Centered Foundations of Explainable AI in Education

The opening chapter by Altukhi and Pradhan in Chapter 2 lays the conceptual cornerstone for trustworthy XAI in education. The proposed *C-XplainEd* framework integrates affordance theory and trust theory to design explainable systems that resonate with users' cognitive and emotional expectations. The authors argue that trustworthiness emerges not from algorithmic accuracy alone but from relational transparency—how systems communicate uncertainty, respond to inquiry, and adapt to feedback. The four-stage evaluation methodology (pre-explanation, during, post, and overall system assessment) ensures that explainability is experienced as a continuous interaction rather than a static output. This cyclical model exemplifies participatory design, transforming users from passive recipients into co-interpreters of AI reasoning.

In Gunasekara and Saarela's contribution in Chapter 3, the focus shifts to one of the most contentious issues in educational AI: fairness. Drawing on the Open University Learning Analytics Dataset, the study compares random forest and artificial neural network models to explore the interplay between predictive performance, fairness, and explainability. The analysis reveals an ethical paradox—models that maximize accuracy may simultaneously amplify bias. By applying fairness metrics such as equal opportunity difference and statistical parity difference, and pairing them with local explanations, the authors uncover how algorithmic success can conceal structural inequity. The chapter reminds readers that fairness and explainability are not technical endpoints but ongoing negotiations requiring contextual interpretation. For educational stakeholders, this insight underscores the need for transparency not only about how predictions are made but also about who benefits from them (Khine, 2024b).

In Chapter 4, Makridis extends the discussion to LLMs, whose generative power introduces new forms of opacity. Unlike traditional machine-learning algorithms that operate on fixed features, LLMs generate text dynamically, creating an illusion of understanding that can mislead both students and educators. The chapter outlines a framework for human-centered LLM deployment that balances innovation with safety. By combining retrieval-augmented generation, reasoning constraints, and continuous human supervision, the author demonstrates how institutions can harness LLMs responsibly. Particularly compelling is the notion of virtual persona testing—simulating diverse learner profiles to identify potential bias and misunderstanding in AI responses. The chapter calls for a shift from static transparency to dynamic accountability, where explainability evolves through dialogue, context, and iterative refinement.

Cain's *EPICC* framework (Effective Prompting through Iterative Content Knowledge and Critical Thinking) in Chapter 5 represents a paradigm shift from explainable models to explainable *use*. Recognizing that full model transparency may remain unattainable, Cain situates interpretability within user practice, specifically, within the craft of prompting. Through design-based studies in instructional design and AI literacy workshops, EPICC structures prompt design as an iterative cycle of reflection and evaluation. In this process, learners articulate intentions, critique outputs, and reconstruct queries to refine understanding. Explainability thus becomes an epistemic habit, teaching users how to think critically with AI rather than about it. The author's contribution redefines transparency as an act of pedagogical empowerment, enabling teachers and students to become co-designers of meaning in algorithmic spaces.

In Chapter 6, Cambria and colleagues highlight the experience of non-expert users—students, parents, and educators who encounter AI explanations without technical training. The chapter argues that explanation quality depends not only on content accuracy but also on communicative accessibility. Drawing from Human-Computer Interaction and cognitive psychology, the authors introduce adaptive strategies such as layered explanations, multimodal cues, and narrative analogies that adjust to users' mental models. The result is a vision of explainability as dialogue rather than data. By transforming explanations into conversational exchanges, AI systems can support curiosity and self-efficacy. This human-centered perspective stresses that an explanation's ultimate test is not whether it satisfies the engineer, but whether it enlightens the learner.

Chaushi and her colleagues in Chapter 7 present a comprehensive evaluation framework that integrates both developer and end-user perspectives. The proposed dual-perspective model defines six dimensions of explainability—transparency, faithfulness, robustness, actionability, clarity, and ethical alignment and operationalizes them through measurable rubrics. Using SHAP-based analysis of GPA prediction models at South East European University, the chapter demonstrates how interpretability can serve multiple stakeholders simultaneously:

developers gain diagnostic insight, educators receive actionable feedback, and administrators obtain governance tools. The authors' approach bridges the gap between conceptual ideals and institutional practice, offering a pragmatic template for accountability in AI-enhanced education. Collectively, these chapters form the philosophical and ethical backbone of the volume. They position explainability as a relational construct that depends on mutual trust between human and machine, and as a moral compass guiding the responsible design of educational technology.

3. Applied and Computational Innovations in Educational XAI

Part III begins with Kutlu and the team's study (Chapter 8), in which the principles of transparency are operationalized in an engineering education context. Automated grading systems have revolutionized assessment, but also raised concerns about bias and opaqueness. Using laboratory performance data, the authors apply SHAP analysis to deconstruct how machine learning models weight technical versus narrative elements in grading. The results reveal that algorithmic systems often privilege quantifiable data, overlooking qualitative reasoning. By embedding SHAP into the grading pipeline, educators can interrogate model logic, verify its alignment with course objectives, and ensure fairness in assessment. The study exemplifies how explainability restores human oversight to automated evaluation, reinforcing trust and pedagogical integrity.

In Chapter 9, Brdnika and her colleagues venture into the realm of non-cognitive traits, applying XAI to measure grit—a student's perseverance and passion for long-term goals—through sentiment analysis. The innovation lies in replacing self-report surveys with natural-language reflections analyzed through multilingual models. By mapping emotional dimensions such as trust, anticipation, sadness, and joy, and interpreting their influence via SHAP and partial dependence plots, the study unveils intricate emotional predictors of perseverance. The results not only advance computational psychology but also humanize educational analytics: models become tools for empathy, capable of recognizing the affective nuances of learning. The chapter stands as an example of how XAI can merge emotional intelligence with analytical precision.

Lynda Dib and Laurence Capus, in Chapter 10, address a key methodological gap: the tendency of local explanation methods to produce fragmented insights. By integrating LIME with clustering techniques, the study elevates interpretability from the individual to the collective level. This approach generates clusters of explanatory features that reveal group-level learning dynamics, such as differences between students in fundamental sciences and those in computer science. Teachers can use these insights to identify collective misconceptions, design targeted interventions, and promote equity across cohorts. The authors' work marks an important methodological step in the evolution of XAI—one that recognizes that learning is social and that explanations must account for community-level patterns, not just individual predictions.

Chapter 11 by Choudhry and his colleagues provides a comprehensive pedagogical entry point into the world of explainability. By demonstrating SHAP and LIME with accessible Python code, the author transforms abstract concepts into teachable tools. The chapter bridges two audiences: educators seeking practical methods to audit AI systems and students learning to interpret data-driven decisions. By framing explainability as both a technical skill and a cognitive disposition, the authors encourage a broader educational transformation where algorithmic literacy becomes part of foundational learning. The contribution positions XAI not only as a mechanism for accountability but as a curriculum for critical thinking.

Finally, Sophie Liu and her team's study (Chapter 12) offers a striking synthesis of symbolic and data-driven reasoning through a knowledge-based neural network (KBANN) applied in a creative learning setting. In a *Minecraft* Mars-habitat design activity, the KBANN integrates domain knowledge about habitat engineering into its architecture, producing interpretable models that evaluate student designs. By comparing rules extracted from the KBANN with SHAP-derived attributions, the authors demonstrate how expert knowledge and machine learning can complement each other. The study blurs the boundary between assessment and exploration: explanations become feedback loops that reveal how students internalize scientific principles. This model epitomizes how XAI can enrich learning environments that emphasize creativity, experimentation, and reflection. The five chapters of Part II translate abstract principles into tangible applications. They showcase how explainability can permeate every layer of educational practice—from grading and analytics to design, creativity, and self-assessment.

Conclusion

The emergence of XAI in education reflects a broader historical trajectory of technological integration in learning environments. Early computer-assisted instruction in the 1960s promised to personalize the learning paths. Expert systems of the 1980s introduced rule-based transparency but lacked adaptability. Machine learning in the 2010s brought unprecedented predictive power, yet at the cost of interpretability. Now, the integration of deep learning and LLMs compels education to confront both extremes: inscrutable intelligence and human vulnerability to automation bias (Vishwarupe et al., 2022). As this volume makes a scholarly contribution, it also calls for action. Explainable AI represents more than a set of algorithms; it embodies a cultural shift toward openness, reflection, and shared responsibility in education. Across all chapters, a collective vision emerges: that the true measure of intelligence, human or artificial, lies in its capacity to explain itself.

References

Khine, M.S. (2024a). *Artificial Intelligence in Education: A Machine-generated Literature Overview.* Springer.

Khine, M.S. (2024b). *Machine Learning in Educational Sciences: Approaches, Applications, and Advances*. Springer.

Tripathy, B. and Seetha, H. (2024). *Explainable, Interpretable, and Transparent AI Systems.* CRC Press.

Vishwarupe, V., Joshi, P.M., Mathias, N., Maheshwari, S., Mhaisalkar, S. and Pawar, V. (2022). Explainable AI and interpretable machine learning: A case study in perspective. *Procedia Computer Science*, *204*, 869–876.

2 C-XplainEd
A Conceptual Framework for Trustworthy XAI Educational Applications

Zaid M. Altukhi[1] and Sojen Pradhan[2]

This study presents a conceptual framework for designing a trustworthy explainable Artificial Intelligence (XAI) system within an educational context, by integrating affordance theory and trust theory as foundational components. The framework is user-centred, targeting end-users and developers of XAI systems in the higher education sector. It addresses trustworthiness by mitigating technical complexity and providing explainability through established Human-Computer Interaction (HCI) principles. Given the opacity of advanced machine learning models (i.e., black boxes), users with no technical background often struggle to interpret their outputs, highlighting the importance of providing accessible explanation methods. To address these challenges, we propose the development of user-friendly XAI system interfaces that conform to HCI best practices and are designed specifically for non-technical users, allowing them to interact, explore, and control the system outputs. The framework also emphasises end-users' involvement in the evaluation and validation processes. The evaluation methodology comprises four stages: pre-explanation, during explanation, post-explanation, and overall system performance assessment. This multi phase evaluation ensures alignment with end-user needs and expectations.

1. Introduction

Explainable AI (XAI) is an increasingly prominent area of academic research due to its significant potential to provide various benefits among the rapid advancement of artificial intelligence (AI) technologies (Mathew et al., 2025). XAI is a technique that explicitly explains the machine learning (ML) models' process and the output they produce (Longo et al., 2024; Miller, 2019). In educational settings, the integration of advanced ML models, known as black-box models, offers powerful predictive capabilities, but their lack of transparency and interpretability limits trust by educational end-users (Michalik, 2025). Black-box models are complex and advanced ML models that provide highly accurate predictions, but are not explainable (Qamar & Bawany, 2023; ŞAHiN et al., 2025). This gap between black-box models' predictions and understanding emphasises the need for XAI

[1,2] University of Technology Sydney, New South Wales, Australia.
* Corresponding author: zaid.m.altukhi@student.uts.edu.au

DOI: 10.1201/9781003713371-2

that aligns with educators' needs and expectations to increase trust in the AI-based systems (Hassija et al., 2024; Saeed & Omlin, 2023). These models hinder the end-users' ability to trust and interpret the outcome of the ML models (Choi et al., 2025; Wiener, 2019). Conceptually, trust is defined as a psychological state in which the trustor (end-user) expects that the trustee (XAI system) will carry out a particular action that is beneficial for attaining a specific objective, particularly in situations characterised by risk or uncertainty (Chen, 2021).

XAI methods are employed in higher education (HE) AI-based systems to perform various tasks, such as to interpret student performance predictions and to identify students at-risk of academic failure (Choi et al., 2024a, 2024b). These methods support educational end-users and system designers (XAI system developers) in discerning the underlying factors that influence student achievement and underperformance by providing various types of explanations. According to Donoso-Guzmán et al. (2023), the XAI-generated explanations consist of four elements: 1) Explanation generation: the process to identify and select causes; 2) Explanation abstraction: XAI-generated explanation contents; 3) Explanation format: the way that the explanation is provided to the end-user, such as textual or visual; 4) explanation communication: focusing on how the end-user interacts with XAI-generated explanations. In prior work (Altukhi & Pradhan, 2024), we identified the challenges that hindered the integration of XAI in educational. To address these challenges, we propose a conceptual framework that helps end-users and AI-based HE application developers understand factors contributing to making these applications trustworthy and transparent by utilising XAI methods. The framework is grounded in affordance and trust theories, which guide the design of AI systems by examining how users perceive and interact with the system's features based on their goals, capabilities, and context to make them trustworthy.

1.1 Motivation

Most of the HE AI-based systems use black-box models to achieve their tasks; these models lack interpretability, transparency, and usability, which are crucial challenges in developing trustworthy AI systems (Kar et al., 2023; Mohammed, 2024).

Trust in AI-based systems is one of the most crucial variables in studies examining perceptions of AI (Cheung & Ho, 2025). Implementing XAI in AI-based systems makes them trustworthy (Brdnik et al., 2025; Kim et al., 2015; Ribeiro et al., 2016). The trust can be fostered in the XAI systems by utilising XUI, which enhances user interaction with AI-based systems (Klingbeil et al., 2024). In our previous work (Altukhi & Pradhan, 2024), we also identified trustworthiness as a major challenge of integrating XAI in educational AI-based systems. It is influenced by the explainability, technical, and HCI challenges.

This study proposed a framework to increase the end-users' trust in the educational AI-based application by integrating XAI methods to explain the AI's decisions via an explanation user interface (XUI) system, allowing educational end-users to interact with the AI's predictions and XAI-generated explanations. XUI is a broader field of XAI, focusing on designing user interfaces that effectively communicate AI explanations to end-users (Ridley, 2022).

Moreover, since the intended users are HE educational end-users, who are generally considered novice users with limited or no technical experience (Mohseni et al., 2021), explanations must be accessible, comprehensible, and designed and developed to their level of understanding to maintain their trust.

2. Background

2.1 Challenges of Integrating XAI in Education

In our previous review, Altukhi and Pradhan (2024), we identified six primary challenges associated with integrating XAI into HE applications. These challenges include: (1) Explainability, involving the necessity to produce clear and comprehensible explanations; (2) Ethical Considerations, focused on ensuring unbiased and fair outcomes by identifying and revealing potential biases; (3) Technical Complexity, highlighting the difficulties associated with embedding XAI methods within existing educational systems; (4) HCI, emphasizing the importance of developing accessible, web-based applications tailored to non-technical users; (5) Trustworthiness, requiring the combination of highly accurate predictions with interpretable explanations to foster user confidence; and (6) Policy and Guidelines, which involves establishing frameworks compliant with educational policies that are adaptable across diverse HE contexts.

2.2 XAI Stakeholders

The development and implementation of XAI systems involve several key stakeholders. Developers, including designers, are responsible for creating XAI interfaces (Colley et al., 2022; Naiseh et al., 2024). Project managers are also integral, as they oversee the operation of developing these systems (Mylrea & Robinson, 2023). End-users, who are decision-makers and professionals, will utilise these systems (Naiseh et al., 2024). Researchers, both academic and industry-based, are involved in developing and investigating the role, benefits, and pitfalls of XAI methods across various applications and domains (Khosravi et al., 2022).

2.3 XAI and Perceived Trust

Recent research by Cheung and Ho (2025) has advanced understanding of how XAI influences trust in AI-based systems by empirically examining the effect of perceived explainability on three key trust dimensions: ability, benevolence, and integrity. They demonstrated through structural equation modelling that explainability significantly contributes to each trust dimension.

2.4 XAI Human-Centred Evaluation

The evaluation in the XAI system is considered a crucial phase for measuring various aspects of the system. Hoffman et al. (2023) introduced five main dimensions that can be evaluated in an XAI system focused on end-users: user satisfaction, user mental models, curiosity, user trust, and XAI system performance.

Similarly, Donoso-Guzmán et al. (2023) proposed user-centric evaluation frameworks for recommender systems by extending the framework originally proposed by Knijnenburg & Willemsen (2015). Their framework integrated explanation properties, which include Objective System Aspects (OSA), explanation aspects, Subjective System Aspects (SSA), user experience, and interaction OSA refer to properties of the AI model and the explanation method themselves, such as accuracy, stability, and certainty. They describe how the underlying system behaves independently of users. The explanation aspects capture the quality of the XAI-generated explanations for example, whether it is complete, correct, concise, and focused on the most relevant causes. They evaluate the explanation as an artefact. SSA reflect how users perceive the explanations and the system, including whether information feels plausible, understandable, relevant, or cognitively demanding. They link system behaviour and user interpretation. User experience captures the user's overall psychological response while interacting with the system, including trust, satisfaction, curiosity, and perceived usefulness. It focuses on how explanations shape the user's mental model and confidence. Interaction shows how explanations influence users' task performance and behaviour, including efficiency, reliance on the AI, and success in decision-making. It connects explanation quality to real outcomes in use.

3. Related Works

Researchers in XAI developed various conceptual frameworks in different domains (e.g., healthcare, IoT, and financial) to make the XAI systems trustworthy by increasing user transparency, understanding, and fairness of the AI output (Colley et al., 2022; Mylrea & Robinson, 2023; Naiseh et al., 2024; Rubegni et al., 2024). Moreover, several conceptual frameworks have integrated XAI within educational contexts, aiming to improve transparency, trust and user understanding (Feldman-Maggor et al., 2025; Khosravi et al., 2022; Swamy et al., 2025). Table 1 provides an overview of these frameworks, presenting their aims, main components, domains, main stakeholders, and theoretical foundations.

To situate the proposed C-XplainEd framework within the broader literature, we compared it with frameworks in the educational field: XAI-ED (Khosravi et al., 2022), Trust-Acceptance Model (Feldman-Maggor et al., 2025), and iLLuMinaTE (Swamy et al., 2025). Table 1 above provides a structured comparison across their focus, components, stakeholders, and theoretical underpinnings, while Figure 1 illustrates a summary of their overlaps and distinctions. Together, these analyses highlight how C-XplainEd uniquely integrates affordance theory, incorporates structured evaluation, and addresses technical complexity for novice educators,

Table 1 Overview of selected XAI frameworks aims, main components, application domains, stakeholders, theoretical foundations, and key references.

Framework	*Aim*	*Main Components*	*Domain*	*Stakeholders*	*Theoretical Foundation*	*Ref.*
Calibrated XAI (C-XAI)	Calibrate the user's trust in AI systems by preventing over-trust or under-trust through tailored explainability, ensuring end-users have appropriate trust levels.	XAI interfaces, multiple stakeholders in co-design to address both technical and human factors, so that the XUI align user trust with actual AI performance.	Health care and high-stakes domains.	AI system designers and decision-makers (clinicians, analysts, etc.)	Human-centered design principles	(Naiseh et al., 2024)
Tangible XAI (TangXAI)	Increase user transparency and understanding of AI decisions (and thereby trust) by moving explanations into the tangible realm.	Data physicalisation and tangible user interfaces (TUI) to present model logic in physical forms. Developed by merging an existing XAI framework with a TUI framework.	Physical devices or IoT (robots, educational toys, etc.)	AI system designers and end-users of AI systems.	HCI and tangible interaction theory combined with XAI.	(Colley et al., 2022)
Complementarity XAI Framework	Achieve appropriate trust and adoption of AI by designing AI tools that complement human reasoning and augment human decision-making.	Feature importance explanations, counterfactual explanations, and similar case examples.	Healthcare and high-stakes decisions.	Designers and professionals	EU Trustworthy AI guidelines (transparency for trust) and human–AI complementarity (the AI should support, not override, human judgement).	(Rubegni et al., 2024)

Contd.

Table 1 *Contd.*

Framework	*Aim*	*Main Components*	*Domain*	*Stakeholders*	*Theoretical Foundation*	*Ref.*
AI Trust Maturity Model (AI-TMM)	Improve trustworthiness in AI systems by addressing factors like transparency, security, and fairness in AI system design.	Explainability, privacy, robustness, transparency, data use and design, societal well-being, and accountability.	Regulated sectors like finance, healthcare.	AI developers, project managers, and users.	User-centric requirement analysis and trustworthy AI guidelines (e.g. EU Ethics Guidelines).	(Mylrea & Robinson, 2023)
Explainable AI in Education (XAI-ED)	Increase user trust and address education-specific needs by emphasising transparency to build trust in AI systems.	Stakeholders involved, benefits of explanations, presenting explanations, AI model classes, human-centred interface design, and potential pitfalls of providing explanations.	Education	AI system designers and researchers consider how XAI can make AI decisions transparent and credible in learning contexts.	AI ethics principles (Fairness, Accountability, Transparency, Ethics) and HCI design.	(Khosravi et al., 2022)
XAI Trust–Acceptance Model for AI in Education	Improves end-users' understanding of the AI, thereby increasing their trust in the system and willingness to accept its recommendations. It addresses the lack of prior theory connecting explainability, user understanding, trust, and adoption.	Understandability, which leads to user confidence (trust), leading to the willingness to use and rely on the AI's outputs (acceptance).	Education	Educators	Trust theory in automation.	(Feldman-Maggor et al., 2025)

Contd.

Table 1 *Contd.*

Framework	*Aim*	*Main Components*	*Domain*	*Stakeholders*	*Theoretical Foundation*	*Ref.*
LLM-XAI Framework for Student Feedback (iLLuMinaTE)	Translating complex ML model outputs and human-centred explanations to build trust and improve learning outcomes by making AI models explainable and useful, and to produce easy-to-understand, actionable explanations so that users can trust and act.	Identify a causal connection in the student's performance; Explanation selection via LLM; Explanation presentation, which generates a final explanation to the user, phrased in clear language with concise, actionable suggestions for improvement.	Education	The primary end-users are students and educators as non-technical stakeholders.	Cognitive and social psychology theories of explanation.	(Swamy et al., 2025)
Conceptual XAI in Education (C-XplainEd)	Address several challenges (technical complexity, explainability, and HCI) of integrating XAI methods within AI-based applications in HE settings through using XAI system that developed based on HCI and trustworthy principles provided to the end-users in a friendly-user interface allowing them to interact, control, and understand the AI's reasoning.	The framework consists of seven components: technical complexity, explainability, HCI, end-user, XAI system, perceived trustworthiness, and evaluation process.	Education	AI developers and educators as novice users.	Trust and affordance theory.	This study

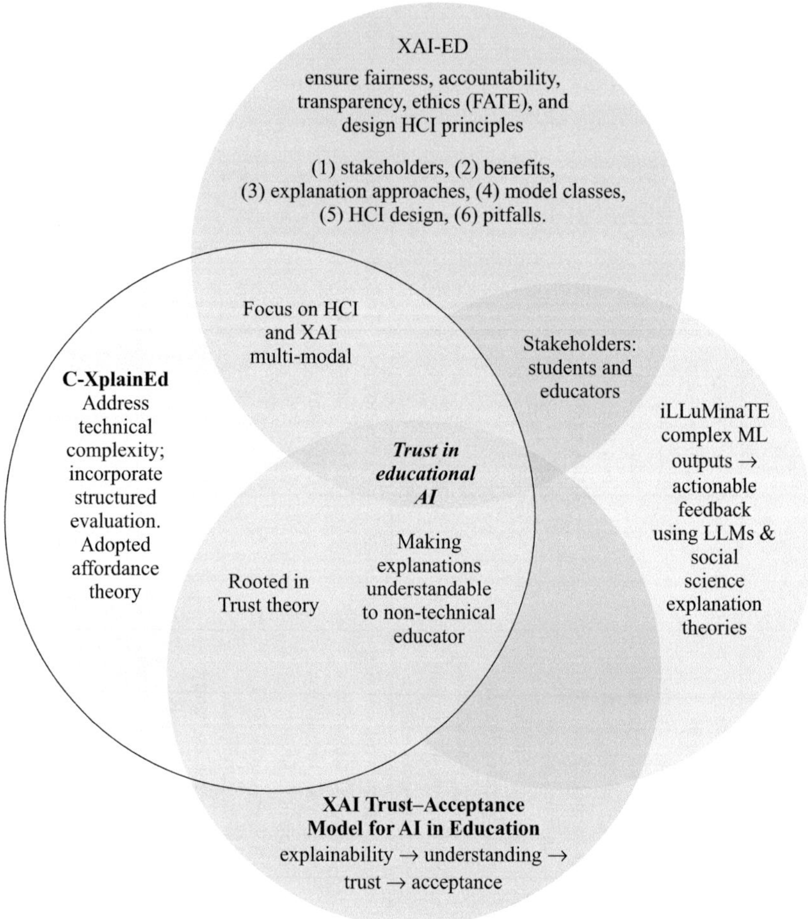

Fig. 1 Venn diagram illustrating similarities and differences between prior XAI frameworks and C-XplainEd.

while still aligning with the shared goals of explainability and trust in educational AI.

4. Theoretical Foundation

This study is grounded in two theoretical perspectives: Affordance Theory (AT), as adapted for Information Systems by Leonardi (2013) and Trust Theory (TT), based on the models of Mayer et al. (1995). While the AT explains what the system allows the end-user to have (e.g., accessibility, understanding, interaction, and confidence), the TT explains how ability, integrity, and benevolence shape trust.

4.1 Affordance Theory (AT)

AT, originally introduced by Gibson (1979) and later adapted for IS by Leonardi (2013), emphasises the actionable possibilities that technologies offer to users. In this context, affordances refer to what the AI-based system enables end-users to do, such as interpret predictions, or engage with explanations, based on how it is designed and presented (Liao & Sundar, 2022).

In IS research, affordances help conceptualise the relationship between users and technology, focusing on how system properties enable or constrain particular actions and outcomes (Leonardi, 2013; Volkoff et al., 2007). Norman (1988) defines an affordance as a relationship between the properties of an object and the ability of the user that determines how the object can be used.

Building on these foundations, the proposed framework adopts AT to model the interactions between educational end-users in HE and the XAI systems. It emphasises how the system features, such as ML prediction outputs, and various XAI explanation methods (e.g., SHAP, LIME, PDP), afford key educator actions including understanding, interpreting, interaction and exercising control over predictions. The framework highlights how these affordances support transparency and contribute to the perceived trustworthiness of the AI-enabled educational applications.

4.2 Trust Theory (TT)

This study draws on TT as articulated by Mayer et al. (1995). In this perspective, trust is defined as the willingness of a party (trustor) to be vulnerable to another (trustee) based on the expectation that the trustee will act competently, ethically, and in the trustor's interest. It identifies three keys of trust: ability, integrity, and benevolence. The ability is *"the group of skills, competencies, and characteristics that enable a party to have influence within some domain"* (Mayer et al., 1995: 717). Integrity is about whether the user believes the system adheres to principles they value. In this context, the integrity in the proposed framework reflects educators' belief that the system is transparent, accountable, consistent and non-misleading. The transparency and accountability support the perceived integrity by ensuring the explanations reveal how predictions were made and avoid hiding logic (Akhtar et al., 2024; Cheong, 2024; Park & Yoon, 2024). The consistent examines whether the input consistently leads to similar outputs or justifications (Qaadan et al., 2025). The non-misleading ensure that the explanations are not confusing or ambiguous. The benevolence refers to *"the extent to which the intents and motivations of the trustee are aligned with those of the trustor"* (Mayer et al., 1995: 719).

5. Framework Components

This section presents the framework components derived by Altukhi & Pradhan (2024), along with the affordances and trust factors, in order to support the XAI system's trustworthiness including 1) perceived trustworthiness pillars (technical complexity, explainability, and HCI); 2) the end-users; 3) the XAI system presenting the explanations; and 4) the evaluation component.

5.1 Perceived Trustworthiness

Trustworthiness in the context of XAI refers to the degree to which end-users can rely on the explanations generated by XAI methods to ensure that the AI-based system and its predictions are worthy of user trust (Deshpande & Ambatkar, 2023; Nasim et al., 2024).

5.1.1 Pillar 1: Technical Complexity

XAI is a solution to bridge the gap between the complexity of opaque AI systems and the human need for understanding and trust (Naiseh et al., 2024; Paliwal et al., 2025). Technical complexity refers to the degree of computational and algorithmic sophistication that can hinder non-experts from engaging with the system (Baskakov & Arseniev, 2021; Ding et al., 2022; Herzog et al., 2023). It also refers to the inherent complexity of ML models and the use of XAI techniques to make them interpretable (Notovich et al., 2023). It includes efforts to develop approaches usable by non-experts, and lacks insights into the internal workings of these models (Futia & Vetrò, 2020).

In the proposed framework, technical complexity is addressed by affording users access to simplified insights without requiring technical depth. This is enabled through the use of XAI techniques and mediated by HCI design. According to Arrieta et al. (2020), XAI aims to reduce the complexity of black-box models by translating their internal operations into understandable and interpretable forms for humans. In addition, Miller (2019) emphasises that explanations should be designed for the end-users' knowledge and needs, particularly for non-technical users.

The ability trust factor is supported by addressing technical complexity through XAI methods and delivering simplified insights via XAI systems. This allows users to understand ML outputs without requiring technical expertise, enhancing their perception of the system's competence. Simplified insights (or explanations) generated by XAI and delivered via HCI through XAI systems increase user understanding (Miller, 2019). Moreover, based on the definition of ability as a user's perception of a system's competence (Nothdurft et al., 2014), and the influence of explanation comprehension on trust (Leichtmann et al., 2023), it can be inferred that when users understand system outputs, they are more likely to perceive the system as capable, thereby supporting the ability dimension of trust. In other words, simplified insights increase user understanding, which enhances their perception of the system's competence, thus supporting the ability-based dimension of trust.

5.1.2 Pillar 2: Explainability

Explainability is the degree to which the AI system's prediction processes are understandable and justifiable to end-users (Arrieta et al., 2020). It affords end-users an understanding, transparency, accountability (Arrieta et al., 2020; Liao & Sundar, 2022), interpretability and fidelity (Markus et al., 2021) of the ML predictions. According to Mylrea and Robinson (2023), explainability and HCI are primary requirements that increase trust in AI systems. Table 2 shows these affordances along with their definitions and the sources that support the definitions.

Table 2 Explainability affordances and the definition of each affordance.

Affordance	*Definition*	*Source*
Understandability	The ability to make the ML model predictions understandable by end-users to understand its function, how the model works, without any need for explaining its internal structure or the algorithmic means by which the model processes the data internally.	(Colley et al., 2022; Montavon et al., 2018)
Transparency	A model that is inherently comprehensible to humans. Comprehensibility refers to the ability to understand the knowledge contained in the ML model.	(Arrieta et al., 2020; Khosravi et al., 2022; Liao & Sundar, 2022; Mylrea & Robinson, 2023)
Accountability	The system's ability to make its decisions traceable, answerable, and justifiable so that users can understand who or what is responsible for a given prediction, and on what basis that decision was made.	(Arrieta et al., 2020; Jacovi et al., 2021; Khosravi et al., 2022; Miller, 2019)
Interpretability	The ability to explain or present the AI systems in understandable terms to the end-user.	(Altukhi & Pradhan, 2024; Arrieta et al., 2020; Doshi-Velez & Kim, 2017)
Fidelity	The accuracy of an explanation is determined by providing sufficient information (completeness) and being correct (soundness).	(Markus et al., 2021)

As noted by Nothdurft et al. (2014), the ability trust factor can be influenced by how well a system's behaviour is understood. Similarly, Miller (2019) emphasises that understanding is critical to the formation of trust. Based on these insights, we map the affordances of understanding and interpretability, as provided by explainability mechanisms, to the ability trust dimension. The affordances of transparency, accountability, and fidelity in this pillar align with the integrity trust dimension. According to Arrieta et al. (2020), transparency enables users to trace the reasoning behind a model's prediction, thereby contributing to trust through responsible and accountable behaviour. Furthermore, Jacovi et al. (2021) argue that accountability and transparency mechanisms in XAI enhance the perception that the system behaves reliably and ethically, thereby reinforcing integrity-based trust. The affordance of fidelity aligns with the trust factor of integrity because it ensures that explanations that are both correct and sufficiently detailed signal that the system behaves transparently, enhancing users' perception that it operates in accordance with trust principles (Mayer et al., 1995; Nothdurft et al., 2014). Figure 2 presents the explainability's affordances mapped to the trust factors.

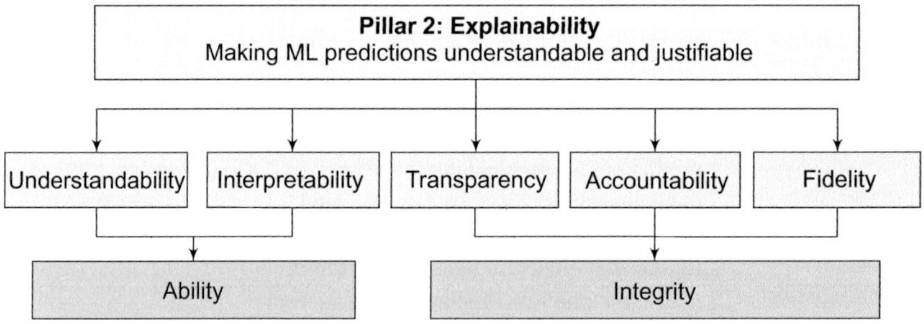

Fig. 2 Explainability affordances mapping to trust factors.

5.1.3 Pillar 3: HCI

HCI in the context of XAI refers to the design of interactive user interfaces that deliver explanations and predictions in an intuitive and accessible manner (Chromik & Butz, 2021). It focuses on the relationships between end-users and the XAI system. According to Khosravi et al. (2022), there are three main objectives of HCI: developing user-centred interfaces, promoting the creation of explainable algorithms, and integrating user feedback into the design process. Also, HCI in XAI offers reliability from the end-user perspective. In their systematic review, Al-Ansari et al. (2024) highlight how reliability is judged by users based on interface clarity, control mechanisms, and perceived system behaviour. The user reliability depends significantly on human-centred design, not just algorithmic accuracy (Bach et al., 2024). HCI enables interaction, exploration, and control over ML predictions and generated XAI explanations (Chromik & Butz, 2021). In our proposed framework, the HCI consists of three main affordances (Interaction, Exploration, and Control), as shown in Table 3, along with their definitions and sources that support these definitions.

These affordances in HCI, applied to AI outputs and XAI-generated explanations, enable users to interact effectively with the system. According to Khosravi et al. (2022) and Chromik and Butz (2021), interactive interfaces enhance user understanding and trust by supporting explainability through human-centred design. Specifically, the exploration affordance supports the benevolence trust factor when the system adapts to the user's curiosity or uncertainty, respects

Table 3 HCI affordances and the definition of each affordance.

Affordance	*Definition*	*Source*
Interaction	Engaging with the XAI-generated explanation via XUI to refine explanations or request alternative forms of explanations.	(Chromik & Butz, 2021; Hornbæk & Oulasvirta, 2017; Khosravi et al., 2022; Liao & Sundar, 2022)
Exploration	Investigating the different parts of the model's reasoning, such as how inputs affect the outputs or testing different scenarios using the explanation interface.	(Chromik & Butz, 2021; Khosravi et al., 2022)
Control	Adjusting explanation features such as choosing which explanation methods to use, selecting input features of interest or controlling the depth of explanations.	(Jacovi et al., 2021)

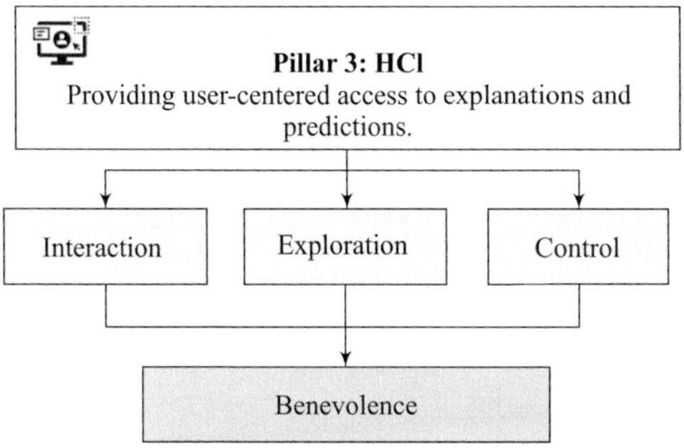

Fig. 3 HCI affordances mapping to the trust factor (Benevolence).

their need for clarity and fosters user satisfaction (Jacovi et al., 2021; Khosravi et al., 2022). Similarly, the control affordance supports the benevolence in an XAI system, when it provides user autonomy, allows explanation customisation, and shows responsiveness to users' needs and preferences (Chromik & Butz, 2021; Jacovi et al., 2021; Miller, 2019). These affordances support the benevolence trust factor, as the system is perceived to empower and respond to the user's interests (Jacovi et al., 2021; Nothdurft et al., 2014) as shown in Figure 3.

When these three pillars 1 to 3 are addressed, they lead to a trustworthy XAI system. According to Nothdurft et al. (2014), providing technical competency (pillar 1), understandability (pillar 2), and reliability (pillar 3) are key elements of trust. Moreover, showing the inner workings of the black-box models by utilising XAI methods is an important goal to make the AI-based systems more trustworthy (Hostetter et al., 2023). Moreover, according to Paliwal et al. (2025), trustworthiness in XAI encompasses transparency, interpretability, and trust. The

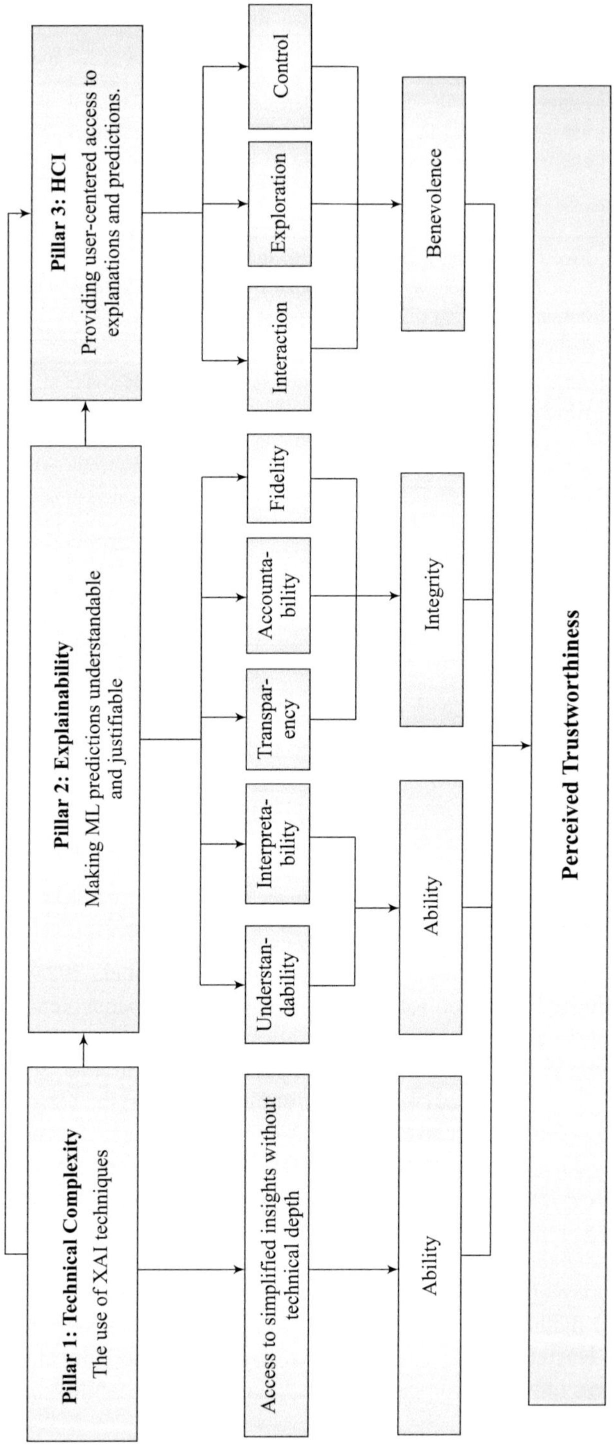

Fig. 4 The relationship between the three pillars and their affordances, and trust factors to perceived trustworthiness.

transparency contributes to clarifying the AI decisions and process behaviour the interpretability bridges the technical gap and end-users' understanding; the trust includes users' confidence and AI system reliability. Figure 4 shows all framework pillars, affordances, and the trust factors that should be included in an XAI system to perceive trustworthiness.

5.2 Education XAI System

The XAI system serves as the central artefact within the conceptual framework, integrating the core pillars (technical complexity, explainability, and HCI) to deliver an interpretable and trustworthy AI-based system to end-users. XAI systems refer to advanced intelligent systems that can explain the reasoning behind their decisions and predictions, thereby promoting greater transparency and fostering user trust (Mohseni et al., 2021). XAI systems explain the black-box model's behaviour in a way that is understandable and transparent to end-users by clarifying why these predictions were made, and support accountability and user trust (Karpagam & Varma, 2022; Severes et al., 2023). In our proposed framework, the XAI system should be designed explicitly to support educators in HE, and it should be developed by following established HCI and trustworthiness principles and refined iteratively through end-user evaluation.

The XAI system is responsible for translating complex and opaque ML processes into simplified and justifiable insights using explainability techniques (e.g., SHAP, LIME, PDP, Anchors) (Paliwal et al., 2025). These explanations are delivered via a user-friendly XUI which is a set of XAI methods that the end-user can directly interact with (Chromik & Butz, 2021). It enables interaction, exploration, and control affordances that align with users' mental models and cognitive needs (Chromik & Butz, 2021). By simplifying technical complexity and offering multiple explanation types, the system supports users' understanding and enhances their trust in AI predictions.

Trustworthiness is fostered through the XAI system's ability to provide accurate predictions alongside accessible, transparent, and accountable explanations. The XAI system integrates multiple explanation models to support the trust dimensions of ability, integrity, and benevolence, as conceptualised in trust theory (Lee & See, 2004; Mayer et al., 1995). Furthermore, the system is subject to a structured evaluation process consisting of four phases: pre-explanation, during explanation, post-explanation, and system performance evaluation. These phases enable the collection of both qualitative and quantitative feedback from users, which is used to refine the design and improve system performance and usability iteratively.

Ultimately, the XAI system acts as both the interface and the mechanism through which the technical, explanatory, and interactional elements are operationalised, supporting transparency, user interaction, and trust in AI-based educational applications.

5.3 End-users

The end-users in this framework are the domain experts, specifically, HE educators, whom the framework aims to support in developing trust in the XAI system. According to Hoffman et al. (2023), the XAI-generated explanations should be aligned with the end-user's needs, knowledge and goals. In the context of our proposed framework, the primary user need is to interpret and understand the ML predictions in educational AI-based systems. This is achieved by addressing technical complexity, delivering explanations through HCI design principles and evaluating the explanations and the XAI system. According to Arrieta et al. (2020), the primary objective of XAI in the context of domain experts is to foster trust in ML models.

5.3.1 Interaction

Educators interact with the system through a user interface grounded in HCI principles (XUI), which allows them to explore various explanation methods without engaging directly with the underlying technical complexity, as shown in Figure 5. The human-friendly design of the interface enables interaction, control, and exploration of the generated XAI explanations, thereby supporting trust formation.

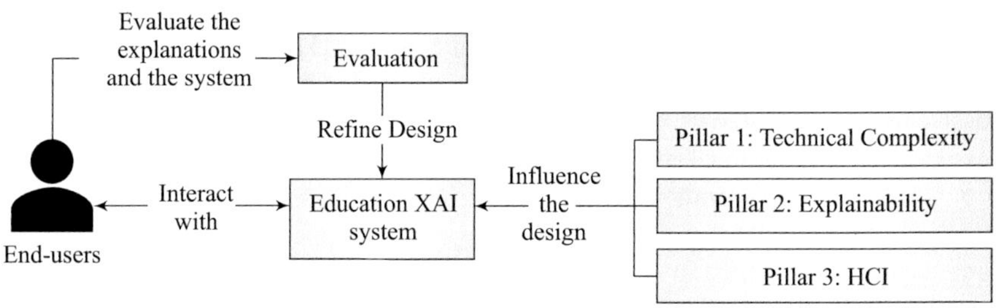

Fig. 5 End-user role within the proposed framework.

5.3.2 Evaluation

Providing explanations to end-users within an XAI system improves their transparency, interpretability, understanding, satisfaction, and trust (Brdnik et al., 2023). However, measuring these dimensions is essential to examining the XAI system's effectiveness. Hoffman et al. (2018) introduced the Explanation Evaluation Process, which begins when users receive initial instructions observing the ML decision, and then explanations are generated by an XAI system. This process enables users to assess their trust and satisfaction with the system, leading to a revision of their mental model. The refinement of this mental model contributes to forming an appropriate level of trust. A well-calibrated mental model, in turn, supports more effective interaction with the XAI system and can enhance its overall performance.

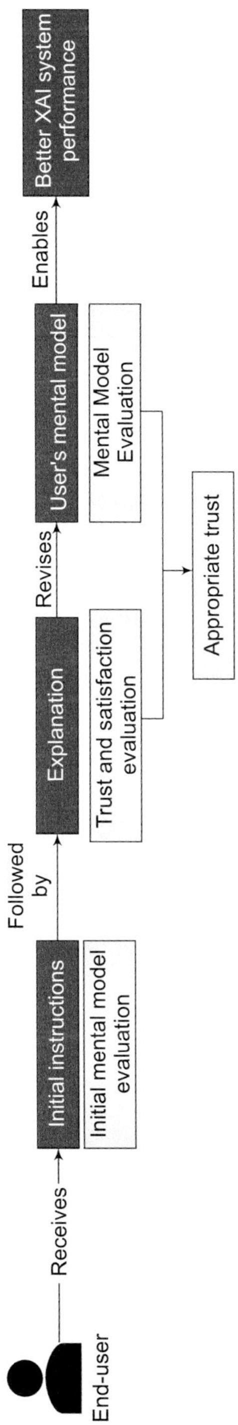

Fig. 6 XAI system and Explanations evaluation process (adapted from Hoffman et al. (2018).

The evaluation process suggested in this framework of the XAI system and explanations consists of four phases, as shown in Figure 6, to assess the impact of XAI explanations on educators' trust and understanding.

Phase 1: The pre-explanation phase (Initial instructions), participants receive only the ML prediction and respond to open-ended questions regarding their initial trust, understanding, and actionability. This phase is important to evaluate the user's level of understanding and their trust in the AI system (Donoso-Guzmán et al., 2023).

Phase 2: During the explanation phase (Explanation), participants evaluate each explanation method provided in the XAI system using Likert-scale items adapted from Hoffman et al., (2018), including the Explanation Satisfaction and Trust. In the context of an XAI system, trust describes the user's confidence that the system will successfully perform a task without unexpected outcomes (Brdnik et al., 2025). Satisfaction is defined as a posterior judgment about whether the user finds the interpretation appropriate to the context (Hoffman, 2018).

Phase 3: Post-explanation (User's mental model), this phase evaluates how the users understand the XAI system (Mohseni et al., 2021). It measures using Likert-scale questions, capturing changes in understanding, trust, and interactivity to increase trust. This approach is adopted from two previous studies (Al-Ansari et al., 2024; Mindlin et al., 2024).

Phase 4: XAI system performance employs Likert-based items to assess users' perceived trustworthiness, interactivity, and comprehensibility of the XAI system. The purpose is to gain insight into the effectiveness and reliability of the explanations in an educational context.

Consistent with Hoffman et al. (2018), performance in an XAI system refers to the extent to which the human–AI system successfully supports users in completing the task it was designed for. However, it should be noted that this conceptual model represents a strategic simplification intended to highlight key evaluation points in XAI systems. Subsequent work by Hoffman and colleagues provides more comprehensive analyses of the cognitive and social processes involved in explanation and self-explanation (Hoffman & Klein, 2017; Hoffman, Mueller, & Klein, 2017; Hoffman, Mueller, Klein, & Clancey, 2018; Hoffman, Miller, & Clancey, 2022).

6. Interdependence of Framework Components

The first component integrates three pillars (technical complexity, explainability, and HCI), which collectively contribute to perceived trustworthiness. These pillars are dedicated through the XAI system and evaluated through a structured process involving end-user interaction and feedback. Figure 8 illustrates all framework components and their interactions, aiming to establish trustworthiness in the XAI system for the end-user.

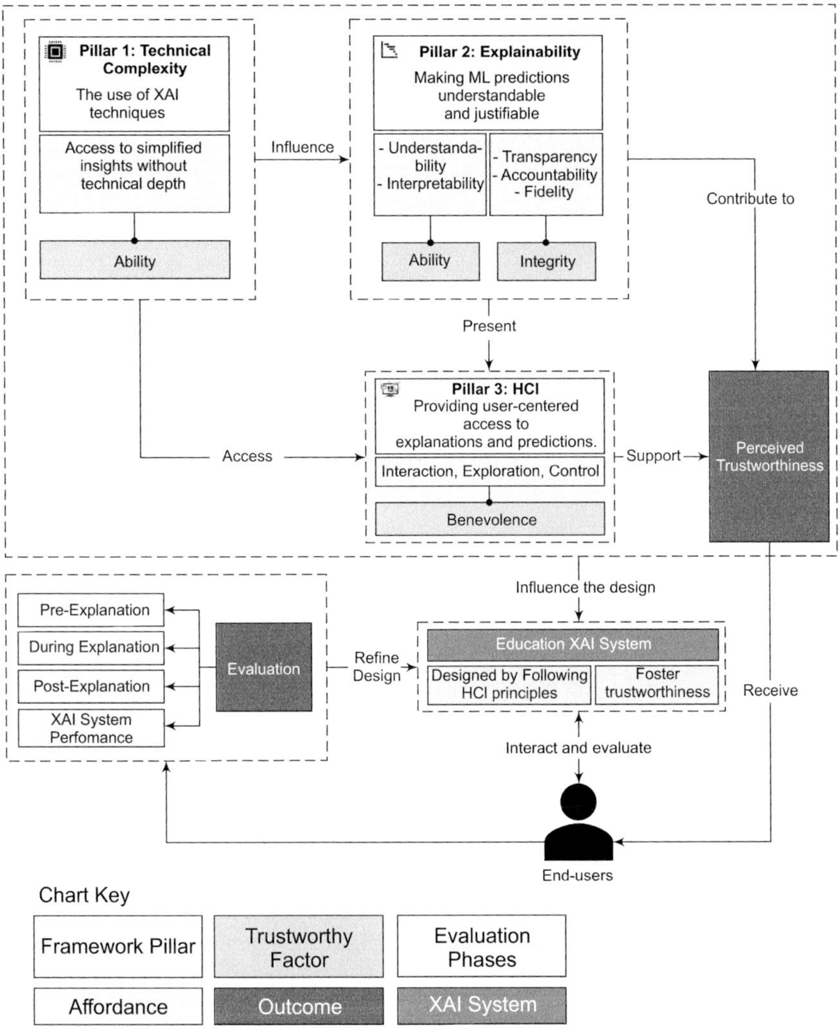

Fig. 7 Conceptual framework components and their relationships.

The first pillar Technical Complexity, is also associated with both Explainability and HCI. This explainability is influenced by necessitating the generation of understandable and justifiable insights using XAI techniques. In addition, technical complexity linked with HCI design ensuring that end-users, particularly non-experts, can access system outputs without being exposed to the full technical depth. It enables access to complex model behaviours.

The second pillar, Explainability, functions as a critical bridge between technical complexity and perceived trust, unlike the model developed by Cheung and Ho (2025), which treats explainability as a single, unified construct, without distinguishing the underlying sources or design features that lead to each trust factor. Explainability processes ML outputs and generates human-interpretable explanations through XAI methods to produce various format, such as visualisations, textual, and rule-based outputs. These explanations are designed to make the system's predictions more understandable, interpretable, and transparent. These explanations are presented through HCI design, ensuring that they are delivered in an accessible and user-centred manner. Explainability contributes directly to perceived trustworthiness, particularly by supporting the trust factors of ability and integrity.

The third pillar, HCI, plays a dual role in the framework. First, it facilitates the presentation of explanations in a manner aligned with user needs, providing interaction, exploration, and control over the XAI-generated explanations and ML predictions through XUI interfaces. Second, HCI supports the abstraction of technical complexity by acting as a mediator between complex XAI outputs and end-user understanding. As a result, HCI contributes to perceived trustworthiness, particularly through the benevolence trust factor, by ensuring the system is designed to support and empower users rather than overwhelm them.

XAI system is at the centre of this interaction, which integrates these pillars and operationalises them into a usable platform. It should be designed by following HCI principles and aims to foster end-users' trustworthiness through explanation delivery, easy access and iterative refinement based on end-user feedback.

Educational end-users engage with the XAI system by receiving ML output, explanations, interacting with the XUI interfaces and providing evaluation feedback. Through this process, end-users assess their understanding, satisfaction and trust, thereby enabling the refinement of the XAI system design and functions. The ultimate goal here is to make the end-users trust the AI decisions by incorporating all these elements into one XAI system.

Ultimately, Perceived Trustworthiness emerges as the outcome of these interactions, shaped by the user's perception of the system's Ability, Integrity, and Benevolence. The iterative evaluation and design refinement loop ensures that the system evolves in alignment with user expectations, enhancing transparency, trust, and usability in educational AI applications.

7. AT and TT Alignment

Technical complexity affords access to simplified insights without technical depth, aligning with the ability trust factor; explainability affords perceived ability and integrity, and HCI affords benevolence through interaction, exploration, and control. These dimensions inform how end-users form trust in AI-based systems and engage in risk-taking behaviour, such as intervening on AI-generated student risk predictions.

The proposed framework is grounded in AT, which serves as the theoretical lens to understand how each system component (technical complexity, explainability, HCI, and trustworthiness) affords specific actions to its users, particularly educators in HE. For example, explainability affords understanding of model decisions; HCI affords interactive engagement and usability; technical complexity could constrain and enable interpretability. Through this lens, the framework focuses on what the system enables educators to do rather than just what it is. It ensures that AI applications are technically robust, usable, meaningful, and trustworthy to educators, regardless of their technical background.

Conclusion

In this study, we proposed a conceptual framework to design and develop a trustworthy XAI system (C-XplainEd) targeted at educational end-users in HE sectors by understanding challenges that faced the AI-based HE applications while integrating XAI methods and theoretical lenses on affordance and trust theories. The challenges addressed in the proposed framework serve as pillars to any XAI system, influencing its perceived trustworthiness. Additionally, the main component of our framework is the educational end-users. Their role is to interact with, explore, and control XAI-generated explanations through XUI, and to evaluate both the explanations and the XAI system. The XAI system should be designed based on HCI and trustworthy principles to provide explanations in a format that is understandable and comprehensible to the end-users. The main aim of this framework is to increase the transparency and trustworthiness of the AI-based HE applications, allowing educational end-users to understand the ML outputs. Also, this framework also acts as a guideline for AI developers who want to develop trustworthy AI-based applications in the HE sectors.

Future Work

In future work, we recommend operationalising the proposed conceptual framework by providing XUI, which enables educational end-users to explore AI predictions and XAI explanations, thereby addressing technical complexity. To enhance the explainability, we advise providing LLM explanations in plain, simple and natural language and interactive visualisations, multi modal explanations in an XAI system to provide explanations that the educator can understand and explain the AI predictions. The system should offer the ability to interact with explanations, explore different XAI methods, upload data, conduct what-if analysis, and allow the end-user to control what explanations to view. Lastly, develop a feedback mechanism that allows educators to evaluate the explanations and performance of the XAI system. We believe these steps will operationalise the proposed conceptual framework to foster trust in the XAI systems in the educational context.

References

Akhtar, M.A.K., Kumar, M. and Nayyar, A. (2024). Transparency and accountability in explainable AI: Best practices. In: *Towards Ethical and Socially Responsible Explainable AI: Challenges and Opportunities* (pp. 127–164). Springer.

Al-Ansari, N., Al-Thani, D. and Al-Mansoori, R.S. (2024). User-Centered Evaluation of Explainable Artificial Intelligence (XAI): A Systematic Literature Review. *Human Behavior and Emerging Technologies, 2024*(1), 4628855.

Altukhi, Z.M. and Pradhan, S. (2024). *Systematic Literature Review: Explainable AI Definitions and Challenges in Education*. ResearchGate.

Arrieta, A.B., Díaz-Rodríguez, N., Ser, J.D., Bennetot, A., Tabik, S., Barbado, A., Garcia, S., Gil-Lopez, S., Molina, D., Benjamins, R., Chatila, R. and Herrera, F. (2020). Explainable Artificial Intelligence (XAI): Concepts, taxonomies, opportunities, and challenges toward responsible AI. *Information Fusion, 58*, 82–115. https://doi.org/doi.org/10.1016/j.inffus.2019.12.012

Bach, T.A., Khan, A., Hallock, H., Beltrão, G. and Sousa, S. (2024). A systematic literature review of user trust in AI-enabled systems: An HCI perspective. *International Journal of Human–Computer Interaction, 40*(5), 1251–1266.

Baskakov, D. and Arseniev, D. (2021). On the computational complexity of deep learning algorithms. In: *Proceedings of International Scientific Conference on Telecommunications, Computing and Control: TELECCON 2019*.

Brdnik, S., Karakatič, S. and Šumak, B. (2025). A comprehensive user-centric method for evaluating and comparing XAI explanations. *International Journal of Human–Computer Interaction*, 1–20.

Brdnik, S., Podgorelec, V. and Šumak, B. (2023). Assessing perceived trust and satisfaction with multiple explanation techniques in XAI-enhanced learning analytics. *Electronics, 12*(12), 2594.

Chen, M. (2021). Trust and trust-engineering in artificial intelligence research: Theory and praxis. *Philosophy and Technology, 34*(4), 1429–1447.

Cheong, B.C. (2024). Transparency and accountability in AI systems: Safeguarding wellbeing in the age of algorithmic decision-making. *Frontiers in Human Dynamics, 6*, 1421273.

Cheung, J.C. and Ho, S.S. (2025). The effectiveness of explainable AI on human factors in trust models. *Scientific Reports, 15*(1), 23337.

Choi, W.-C., Lam, C.-T., Pang, P. C.-I. and Mendes, A.J. (2025). A Systematic Literature Review of Explainable Artificial Intelligence (XAI) for Interpreting Student Performance Prediction in Computer Science and STEM Education. In: *Proceedings of the 30th ACM Conference on Innovation and Technology in Computer Science Education V. 1*.

Choi, W., Lam, C.-T. and Mendes, A.J. (2024a). Analyzing the Interpretability of Machine Learning Prediction on Student Performance Using SHapley Additive exPlanations. In: *2024 IEEE International Conference on Teaching, Assessment, and Learning for Engineering* (*TALE*).

Choi, W.C., Lam, C.-T. and Mendes, A.J. (2024b). Enhance Learning Performance Predictions with Explainable Machine Learning. In: *2024 IEEE Frontiers in Education Conference* (*FIE*).

Chromik, M. and Butz, A. (2021). Human-XAI interaction: a review and design principles for explanation user interfaces. In: *Human-Computer Interaction–INTERACT 2021: 18th IFIP TC 13 International Conference*, Bari, Italy, August 30–September 3, 2021, Proceedings, Part II 18.

Colley, A., Väänänen, K. and Häkkilä, J. (2022). Tangible explainable AI: An initial conceptual framework. In: *Proceedings of the 21st International Conference on Mobile and Ubiquitous Multimedia*.

Deshpande, R. and Ambatkar, P. (2023). Interpretable deep learning models: Enhancing transparency and trustworthiness in Explainable AI. In: *Proceeding of the International Conference on Science and Engineering*.

Ding, W., Abdel-Basset, M., Hawash, H. and Ali, A.M. (2022). Explainability of artificial intelligence methods, applications, and challenges: A comprehensive survey. *Information Sciences, 615*, 238–292.

Donoso-Guzmán, I., Ooge, J., Parra, D. and Verbert, K. (2023). Towards a comprehensive human-centred evaluation framework for explainable AI. In: *World Conference on Explainable Artificial Intelligence*.

Doshi-Velez, F. and Kim, B. (2017). Towards a rigorous science of interpretable machine learning. *arXiv preprint arXiv:1702.08608*.

Feldman-Maggor, Y., Cukurova, M., Kent, C. and Alexandron, G. (2025). The Impact of Explainable AI on Teachers' Trust and Acceptance of AI EdTech Recommendations: The Power of Domain-specific Explanations. *International Journal of Artificial Intelligence in Education*, 1–34.

Futia, G. and Vetrò, A. (2020). On the Integration of Knowledge Graphs into Deep Learning Models for a More Comprehensible AI: Three Challenges for Future Research. *Information*, *11*(2), 122. https://www.mdpi.com/2078-2489/11/2/122.

Gibson, J.J. (1979). *The theory of affordances.* In *The people, place, and space reader* (pp. 56–60). Routledge.

Hassija, V., Chamola, V., Mahapatra, A., Singal, A., Goel, D., Huang, K., Scardapane, S., Spinelli, I., Mahmud, M. and Hussain, A. (2024). Interpreting Black-Box Models: A Review on Explainable Artificial Intelligence. *Cognitive Computation*, *16*(1), 45–74. https://doi.org/10.1007/s12559-023-10179-8.

Herzog, M.H., Doerig, A. and Sachse, C. (2023). Why computational complexity may set impenetrable barriers for epistemic reductionism. *Synthese*, 202(5), 136.

Hoffman, R. R. (2018). Theory→ concepts→ measures but policies→ metrics. In: *Macrocognition Metrics and Scenarios* (pp. 3–10). CRC Press.

Hoffman, R.R., Mueller, S.T., Klein, G. and Litman, J. (2018). Metrics for explainable AI: Challenges and prospects. *arXiv preprint arXiv:1812.04608*.

Hoffman, R.R., Mueller, S.T., Klein, G. and Litman, J. (2023). Measures for explainable AI: Explanation goodness, user satisfaction, mental models, curiosity, trust, and human-AI performance. *Frontiers in Computer Science*, *5*, 1096257.

Hoffman, R.R. and Klein, G. (2017). Explaining explanation, Part 1: Theoretical foundations. *IEEE Intelligent Systems, 32*(3), 68–73.

Hoffman, R.R., Mueller, S.T. and Klein, G. (2017). Explaining explanation, Part 2: Empirical foundations. *IEEE Intelligent Systems, 32*(4), 78–86.

Hoffman, R.R., Mueller, S.T., Klein, G. and Clancey, W.J. (2018). Explaining explanation Part 4: A deep dive on deep nets. *IEEE Intelligent Systems, 33*(3), 87–95.

Hoffman, R.R., Miller, T. and Clancey, W.J. (2022). Psychology and AI at a crossroads: How might complex systems explain themselves? *American Journal of Psychology, 135*(3), 365–378.

Hornbæk, K. and Oulasvirta, A. (2017). What is interaction? In: *Proceedings of the 2017 CHI Conference on Human Factors in Computing Systems*.

Hostetter, J.W., Conati, C., Yang, X., Abdelshiheed, M., Barnes, T. and Chi, M. (2023). XAI to increase the effectiveness of an Intelligent Pedagogical Agent. In: *Proceedings of the 23rd ACM International Conference on Intelligent Virtual Agents*.

Jacovi, A., Marasović, A., Miller, T. and Goldberg, Y. (2021). Formalizing trust in artificial intelligence: Prerequisites, causes, and goals of human trust in AI. In: *Proceedings of the 2021 ACM Conference on Fairness, Accountability, and Transparency*.

Kar, S.P., Das, A.K., Chatterjee, R. and Mandal, J.K. (2023). Assessment of learning parameters for students' adaptability in online education using machine learning and explainable AI. *Education and Information Technologies*, 1–16.

Karpagam, G. and Varma, A. (2022). Understanding, visualizing, and explaining XAI through case studies. In: *2022 8th International Conference on Advanced Computing and Communication Systems (ICACCS)*.

Khosravi, H., Shum, S.B., Chen, G., Conati, C., Tsai, Y.-S., Kay, J., Knight, S., Martinez-Maldonado, R., Sadiq, S. and Gašević, D. (2022). Explainable Artificial Intelligence in education. *Computers and Education: Artificial Intelligence*, *3*, 100074. https://doi.org/10.1016/j.caeai.2022.100074.

Kim, B., Glassman, E., Johnson, B. and Shah, J. (2015). iBCM: Interactive Bayesian case model empowering humans via intuitive interaction. ResearchGate.

Klingbeil, A., Grützner, C. and Schreck, P. (2024). Trust and reliance on AI: An experimental study on the extent and costs of overreliance on AI. *Computers in Human Behavior*, *160*, 108352.

Knijnenburg, B.P. and Willemsen, M.C. (2015). Evaluating Recommender Systems with User Experiments. In: F. Ricci, L. Rokach and B. Shapira (Eds.), *Recommender Systems Handbook* (pp. 309–352). Springer US. https://doi.org/10.1007/978-1-4899-7637-6_9.

Lee, J.D. and See, K.A. (2004). Trust in automation: Designing for appropriate reliance. *Human Factors*, *46*(1), 50–80.

Leichtmann, B., Humer, C., Hinterreiter, A., Streit, M. and Mara, M. (2023). Effects of Explainable Artificial Intelligence on trust and human behavior in a high-risk decision task. *Computers in Human Behavior*, *139*, 107539. https://doi.org/10.1016/j.chb.2022.107539.

Leonardi, P.M. (2013). When does technology use enable network change in organizations? A comparative study of feature use and shared affordances. *MIS Quarterly*, 749–775.

Liao, Q.V. and Sundar, S.S. (2022). Designing for responsible trust in AI systems: A communication perspective. In: *Proceedings of the 2022 ACM Conference on Fairness, Accountability, and Transparency*.

Longo, L., Brcic, M., Cabitza, F., Choi, J., Confalonieri, R., Del Ser, J., Guidotti, R., Hayashi, Y., Herrera, F. and Holzinger, A. (2024). Explainable Artificial Intelligence (XAI) 2.0: A manifesto of open challenges and interdisciplinary research directions. *Information Fusion*, *106*, 102301.

Markus, A.F., Kors, J.A. and Rijnbeek, P.R. (2021). The role of explainability in creating trustworthy artificial intelligence for health care: A comprehensive survey of the terminology, design choices, and evaluation strategies. *Journal of Biomedical Informatics*, *113*, 103655.

Mathew, D.E., Ebem, D.U., Ikegwu, A.C., Ukeoma, P.E. and Dibiaezue, N.F. (2025). Recent emerging techniques in explainable artificial intelligence to enhance the interpretable and understanding of AI models for human. *Neural Processing Letters*, *57*(1), 16.

Mayer, R.C., Davis, J.H. and Schoorman, F.D. (1995). An integrative model of organizational trust. *Academy of Management Review*, *20*(3), 709–734.

Michalik, K. (2025). AI for Education, Education of AI: Exploring the Role of Explainable AI (XAI) Through LogosXAI. In: A.I. Cristea, E. Walker, Y. Lu, O.C. Santos and S. Isotani, *Artificial Intelligence in Education*. In: *International Conference on Artificial Intelligence in Education*, Cham.

Miller, T. (2019). Explanation in artificial intelligence: Insights from the social sciences. *Artificial Intelligence*, *267*, 1–38.

Mindlin, D., Robrecht, A.S., Morasch, M. and Cimiano, P. (2024). Measuring user understanding in dialogue-based XAI systems. In: *ECAI 2024* (pp. 1148–1155). IOS Press.

Mohammed, B. (2024). The Synergy of Explainable AI and Learning Analytics in Shaping Educational Insights. *IAENG International Journal of Computer Science*, *51*(9).

Mohseni, S., Zarei, N. and Ragan, E.D. (2021). A multidisciplinary survey and framework for design and evaluation of explainable AI systems. *ACM Transactions on Interactive Intelligent Systems (TiiS)*, *11*(3–4), 1–45.

Montavon, G., Samek, W. and Müller, K.-R. (2018). Methods for interpreting and understanding deep neural networks. *Digital Signal Processing*, *73*, 1–15.

Mylrea, M. and Robinson, N. (2023). Artificial Intelligence (AI) trust framework and maturity model: Applying an entropy lens to improve security, privacy, and ethical AI. *Entropy*, *25*(10), 1429.

Naiseh, M., Simkute, A., Zieni, B., Jiang, N. and Ali, R. (2024). C-XAI: A conceptual framework for designing XAI tools that support trust calibration. *Journal of Responsible Technology*, *17*, 100076.

Nasim, M., Ferdous, A., Rashid, A., Soshi, F.T.J., Biswas, P., Biswas, A. and Gupta, K.D. (2024). Trustworthy XAI and Application. *arXiv preprint arXiv:2410.17139*.

Norman, D.A. (1988). *The Psychology of Everyday Things*. Basic Books.

Nothdurft, F., Richter, F. and Minker, W. (2014). Probabilistic human-computer trust handling. In: *Proceedings of the 15th Annual Meeting of the Special Interest Group on Discourse and Dialogue (SIGDIAL)*.

Notovich, A., Chalutz-Ben Gal, H. and Ben-Gal, I. (2023). Explainable artificial intelligence (XAI): motivation, terminology, and taxonomy. In: *Machine Learning for Data Science Handbook: Data Mining and Knowledge Discovery Handbook* (pp. 971–985). Springer.

Paliwal, G., Kumar, A., Sharma, K.P., Bhargava, D. and Shrimal, V.M. (2025). Transformative impact of explainable artificial intelligence: Bridging complexity and trust. *Discover Artificial Intelligence*, *5*(1), 51.

Park, K. and Yoon, H.Y. (2024). Beyond the code: The impact of AI algorithm transparency signaling on user trust and relational satisfaction. *Public Relations Review*, *50*(5), 102507.

Qaadan, S., AlZamer, A., Mohamed, M., Alshare, A. and Schmuelling, B. (2025). Introducing Feature Importance Consistency (FIC) in XAI Models: A Comprehensive Evaluation using Rank Correlation Coefficients. In: *2025 IEEE International Conference on Computational Intelligence and Virtual Environments for Measurement Systems and Applications (CIVEMSA)*.

Qamar, T. and Bawany, N.Z. (2023). Understanding the black-box: Towards interpretable and reliable deep learning models. *PeerJ. Computer Science*, *9*, e1629.

Ribeiro, M.T., Singh, S. and Guestrin, C. (2016, 2016/08/13/). "Why Should I Trust You?": Explaining the Predictions of Any Classifier. KDD '16: In: *The 22nd ACM SIGKDD International Conference on Knowledge Discovery and Data Mining*.

Ridley, M. (2022). Explainable Artificial Intelligence (XAI). *Information Technology and Libraries*, *41*(2). https://doi.org/10.6017/ital.v41i2.14683.

Rubegni, E., Ayoub, O., Rizzo, S.M.R., Barbero, M., Bernegger, G., Faraci, F., Mangili, F., Soldini, E., Trimboli, P. and Facchini, A. (2024). Designing for Complementarity: A Conceptual Framework to Go Beyond the Current Paradigm of Using XAI in Healthcare. In: *International Conference on Human-Computer Interaction*.

Saeed, W. and Omlin, C. (2023). Explainable AI (XAI): A systematic meta-survey of current challenges and future opportunities. *Knowledge-Based Systems*, *263*, 110273. https://doi.org/10.1016/j.knosys.2023.110273.

ŞAHiN, E., Arslan, N.N. and Özdemir, D. (2025). Unlocking the black box: An in-depth review on interpretability, explainability, and reliability in deep learning. *Neural Computing and Applications*, *37*(2), 859–965.

Severes, B., Carreira, C., Vieira, A.B., Gomes, E., Aparício, J.T. and Pereira, I. (2023). The human side of XAI: Bridging the gap between AI and non-expert audiences. In: *Proceedings of the 41st ACM International Conference on Design of Communication*.

Swamy, V., Romano, D., Desikan, B.S., Camburu, O.-M. and Käser, T. (2025). iLLuMinaTE: An LLM-XAI Framework Leveraging Social Science Explanation Theories towards Actionable Student Performance Feedback. In: *Proceedings of the AAAI Conference on Artificial Intelligence*.

Valori, I., Jung, M.M. and Fairhurst, M.T. (2024). Social touch to build trust: A systematic review of technology-mediated and unmediated interactions. *Computers in Human Behavior*, *153*, 108121.

Volkoff, O., Strong, D.M. and Elmes, M.B. (2007). Technological embeddedness and organizational change. *Organization science*, *18*(5), 832–848.

Wiener, N. (2019). *Cybernetics or Control and Communication in the Animal and the Machine*. MIT Press.

3 | The Relation between Fairness and Explainability in Predictive Modeling of Student Performance

A Study on the OULAD

Sachini Gunasekara[1] and Mirka Saarela[2]

With the growing integration of machine learning into the education domain, the need to balance model accuracy with fairness and explainability has become critical. Using the Open University Learning Analytics Dataset, this study examines these trade-offs in the context of predicting performance among students. Two different machine learning models—RF and ANN—are evaluated for predictive performance, fairness across demographic subgroups, and explainability. While fairness is assessed using two metrics, including equal opportunity difference and statistical parity difference, model behavior is interpreted using model-agnostic local explanations. Our findings reveal these explanations can uncover hidden biases in accurate models, showing that models often rely on sensitive attributes, leading to unfair predictions for certain student groups despite their strong academic behavior. In contrast, interpretable models make it easier to identify and understand potential unfairness, even if they may come at the cost of reduced predictive accuracy. In addition, we illustrate that although fairness metrics exist to detect and reduce bias, it is mathematically impossible to optimize all of them at once, and efforts to improve fairness frequently lead to a decline in overall system performance. This study emphasizes the ethical implications of using predictive models in educational settings and the significance of context-aware model selection.

1. Introduction

Predictive modeling has become widely adopted in education as institutions seek data-driven strategies to enhance student outcomes, personalize learning pathways, and identify at-risk students early. Consequently, machine learning (ML) models are now widely used in educational technologies and policy decisions, ranging from adaptive learning systems to student admissions and retention strategies (Alwarthan et al., 2022). While these models offer many benefits, using them in important educational decisions raises concerns about fairness and explainability, especially when educators, policymakers, or students cannot easily understand how the decisions are made (Memarian & Doleck, 2023; Zhao et al., 2023).

[1,2] University of Jyväskylä Jyväskylä, Finland.
* Corresponding author: savisama@jyu.fi

DOI: 10.1201/9781003713371-3

Many state-of-the-art ML models, including deep neural networks and ensemble methods, are often described as "black boxes" because their internal mechanisms are highly complex and difficult to interpret. This lack of explainability may reduce user trust, especially when the predictions have significant social or academic significance. To address these concerns, researchers have developed post-hoc explainability techniques that provide insights into individual predictions by highlighting the most influential features. The quality of these explanations is typically assessed through metrics such as fidelity, which measures how closely a simplified, human-interpretable surrogate model replicates the outputs of the original black-box system (Craven & Shavlik, 1995; Ribeiro et al., 2016).

Although explainable AI (artificial intelligence) tools like LIME and SHAP provide valuable insights into model behavior, questions remain about whether these explanations are always fair. Differences in explanation quality—for example, lower fidelity for students with disabilities or certain genders—could inadvertently reinforce existing biases, leading users to trust predictions unequally across groups (Kizilcec & Lee, 2022). While prior research has extensively examined the trade-offs between performance and explainability or between performance and fairness (Gunasekara & Saarela, 2025a), the interaction between explainability and fairness has received limited attention in educational contexts.

To address this gap, this chapter investigates whether fidelity of post-hoc explanations varies across sensitive groups in the Open University Learning Analytics Dataset (OULAD), to clarify how fairness and explainability influence each other in predictive modeling. We train two ML models to predict student performance using demographic and behavioral features and generate instance-level explanations using the Local Interpretable Model-Agnostic Explanations (LIME). We compute fidelity scores and compare feature importance across groups, complemented by two fairness metrics to evaluate disparities. Furthermore, we apply the Equalized Odds post-processing technique to improve predictive fairness and reassess the fidelity of LIME explanations post-intervention. By systematically examining the interplay between fairness and explainability, this work provides new insights into how equitable and trustworthy predictive modeling can be achieved in education.

2. Related Works

2.1 *Fairness in Education*

Fairness has long been a fundamental concern in education, reflecting enduring debates around inequality in opportunities and outcomes (Baker & Hawn, 2022; Hutchinson & Mitchell, 2019). The rise of learning analytics and AI-driven systems has intensified these debates, as predictive models now inform decisions that directly affect students at scale. Research consistently documents systematic disparities in predictions of dropout risk (Hu & Rangwala, 2020; Kai et al., 2017;

Yu et al., 2021), course grades (Lee & Kizilcec, 2020), and academic performance (Anderson et al., 2019; Sapiezynski et al., 2017). These models often underperform for historically underrepresented groups, producing higher false positive and false negative rates (Hu & Rangwala, 2020). Despite the growing adoption of such tools, surveys show that fairness-aware methods in learning analytics remain scarce, raising concerns about their potential to exacerbate rather than reduce educational inequalities.

At the same time, the integration of AI into classrooms promises transformative opportunities. Educational technologies are promoted as tools for personalization, scalable feedback, and reduced teacher workload (Holmes & Tuomi, 2022; Schleicher, 2020; Webb et al., 2021). This potential is particularly relevant given the global challenges of unequal access to high-quality education and limited teaching resources (UNESCO, 2024; United Nations, 2023). However, when AI systems begin to support or even replace human decision-making, fairness becomes a critical safeguard (Baker & Hawn, 2022; Li et al., 2023). Unfair outcomes in high-stakes contexts—such as grading, admissions, or scholarship allocation—can have life-changing consequences for students (Akgun & Greenhow, 2021; Heaton et al., 2023; Mehrabi et al., 2022; Saxena et al., 2019; Sha et al., 2022).

The discourse on fairness in education has increasingly focused on how bias can be defined and measured. The literature distinguishes between causality-based, similarity-based, and statistical definitions of fairness (Castelnovo et al., 2022; Verma & Rubin, 2018). In practice, most educational applications rely on statistical group metrics, as they are comparatively simple to operationalize. Still, different definitions can conflict, requiring careful alignment between fairness criteria and educational goals (Dunkelau & Duong, 2022). For example, equalized odds has been proposed as a particularly suitable metric for academic performance prediction, since it accounts for disparities in both false positives and false negatives (Dunkelau & Duong, 2022). The relationship between fairness and predictive performance remains debated: some studies report no inherent trade-off (Gardner et al., 2019), while others find complex dependencies that vary across contexts and datasets (Opoku et al., 2025).

Finally, fairness in education is not solely a technical matter but also an institutional and pedagogical one. Biases in predictive models have implications for how educators identify and support at-risk students, how practitioners design algorithms that balance accuracy and inclusiveness, and how policymakers regulate the deployment of such technologies (Miao et al., 2021; Saarela et al., 2025). Growing awareness of these risks has already shaped international initiatives, such as UNESCO's Education and AI recommendations (Miao Fengchun, Holmes Wayne, Ronghuai Huang, 2021b) and recent analyses of the European AI Act's implications for education (Saarela et al., 2025). Ensuring fairness in educational AI is thus a multidimensional challenge—requiring not just technical bias mitigation, but also governance, teacher training, and a commitment to equity in the use of data-driven technologies.

2.2 *Trade-off between Fairness, Performance, and Explainability*

A growing body of work in learning analytics shows that fairness interventions often affect model performance: mitigation methods can reduce disparate impact but may also lower predictive accuracy. For an example, Raftopoulos et al. (2025) empirically compare preprocessing, in-processing, and post-processing bias-mitigation techniques on educational datasets (including OULAD) and report trade-offs between fairness and performance depending on the chosen method and dataset. Besides, a recent systematic mapping of fairness research in education by Pham et al. (2025) synthesizes trends across studies and highlights that most empirical work in education focuses on outcome fairness and mitigation strategies, making the fairness-performance trade-off a well-studied concern in learning analytics.

Explainability adds another layer to this trade-off. Recent research indicates that requiring explainability often slightly reduces performance, depending on the method used. For instance, Gomez et al. (2025) develop an interpretable model for real-time student performance prediction in serious games, achieving 77.21% balanced accuracy while ensuring interpretability via explainable AI methods. Similarly, Mai et al. (2024) present a dual-level belief rule-based approach incorporating explainability requirements, though optimization and class imbalance can make higher accuracy reduce explanation clarity. However, a systematic review of explainable student performance models (2015–2020) confirms that while studies report both performance and explainability, they often emphasize one over the other, with few providing direct quantitative trade-offs (Alamri & Alharbi, 2021).

By contrast, the question of whether explainability itself is equitable has received much less empirical attention in education. While fairness is typically examined on predictive outcomes, it is less clear whether AI-generated explanations are equally accurate or understandable across groups. Research outside education shows that explanation quality can differ across groups, so fairness in explanations cannot be assumed. An example, Angerschmid et al. (2022) show how explanations and fairness jointly influence user trust and perceived fairness in AI-assisted decision-making for health insurance and medical treatment. In controlled user studies, they found that low fairness reduced trust, while explanations consistently improved both trust and perceived fairness, regardless of explanation type. In educational contexts, this issue is especially relevant since fairness often concerns socioeconomic or learning-related attributes, and explainability also serves a pedagogical role in helping students and educators understand and act on model outputs. Studies such as Kesgin et al. (2025) demonstrate how SHAP explanations can help reveal sources of bias in student performance prediction, but they also highlight that explainability tools may not automatically improve fairness outcomes.

The conceptual framework in Figure 1 highlights this underexplored interplay between fairness and explainability. The figure emphasizes that fairness and explainability are not independent: both influence how students, educators, and developers engage with models. Future research should therefore investigate not only whether explanations are technically faithful, but also whether they are distributed equitably and interpreted fairly across different educational stakeholders.

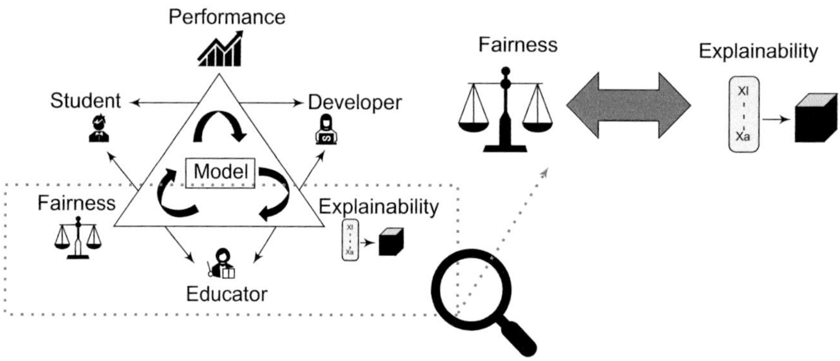

Fig. 1 Conceptual framework highlighting the interplay between model performance, fairness, and explainability in educational AI (evolved from Gunasekara, S., & Saarela, M. (2024)). The focus of this chapter is on the relationship between fairness and explainability, which remains underexplored compared to performance-focused trade-offs.

3. Background and Notation

Fairness in ML encompasses multiple perspectives on equitable decision-making (Castelnovo et al., 2022; Dwork et al., 2012; Hardt et al., 2016; Speicher et al., 2018). In educational applications, fairness ensures that predictive models do not systematically advantage and disadvantage certain students based on attributes such as *disability, gender*, or *socioeconomic* status. It can be broadly categorized into individual fairness, which ensures similar individuals receive similar predictions, and group fairness, which ensures that outcomes are equitable across predefined groups based on protected attributes (Dwork et al., 2012; Kusner et al., 2017). For instance, individual fairness would require that two students with similar study behaviors and engagement patterns receive similar predicted probabilities of course completion, whereas group fairness would aim to ensure that students with and without disabilities have comparable predicted outcomes, preventing systematic disadvantage of any group. We specifically adopt group fairness in this study because educational settings often involve structural inequities, where entire groups of students may systematically experience different outcomes. Group fairness metrics allow us to detect and address these disparities at the population level, which is critical for promoting equitable learning opportunities. In particular, we evaluate three key metrics: Statistical Parity Difference (SPD), Equality of Opportunity Difference (EOD), and Equalized Odds (EO).

Consider a structured dataset $\boldsymbol{D}$ that includes a class label and multiple attributes, some of which are protected attributes linked to fairness concerns.

Based on these protected attributes, we can partition the data into privileged and unprivileged groups—for example, male students as privileged group (***D*** = ***0***) and female students as the unprivileged group (***D*** = ***1***). Let ***Y*** denote the true outcome, where ***Y*** = ***1*** represents a positive (favorable) result, such as passing a course, and ***Y*** = ***0*** represents a negative (unfavorable) result, such as failing and $\overline{\mathbf{Y}}$ denotes the predicted outcome.

True Positive (TP): $Y = 1$ and $\overline{\mathbf{Y}} = 1$ False Positive (FP): $Y = 0$ and $\overline{\mathbf{Y}} = \mathbf{1}$
True Negative (TN): $Y = 0$ and $\overline{\mathbf{Y}} = \mathbf{0}$ False Negative (FN): $Y = 1$ and $\overline{\mathbf{Y}} = \mathbf{0}$

From these, the true positive rate (TPR) is $\boldsymbol{TPR} = \dfrac{\boldsymbol{TP}}{\boldsymbol{TP + FN}}$ and false positive rate (FPR) is $\boldsymbol{FPR} = \dfrac{\boldsymbol{FP}}{\boldsymbol{FP + TN}}$.

Consider a dataset of 100 students. Among 70 male students (privileged group), 52 are predicted to pass, of which 45 are correct ($TP = 45$) and 7 are incorrect ($FP = 7$), while 8 students who actually passed were predicted to fail ($FN = 8$). Among 30 female students (unprivileged group), 12 are predicted to pass, with 9 correct ($TP = 9$) and 3 incorrect ($FP = 3$), while 6 students who actually passed were predicted to fail ($FN = 6$).

Statistical Parity Difference (SPD)

$$\boldsymbol{SPD} = \mathbf{Pr}\ [\overline{\mathbf{Y}} = \mathbf{1} \mid \boldsymbol{D} = \mathbf{0}] - \boldsymbol{Pr}\ [\overline{\mathbf{Y}} = \mathbf{1} \mid \boldsymbol{D} = \mathbf{1}]$$

$$\boldsymbol{SPD} = \mathbf{Pr}\,[\overline{\mathbf{Y}} = \mathbf{1} \mid \boldsymbol{Male}] - \mathbf{Pr}\,[\boldsymbol{Female}] = \left(\frac{\mathbf{52}}{\mathbf{70}}\right) - \left(\frac{\mathbf{12}}{\mathbf{30}}\right) = \mathbf{0.3429}$$

SPD directly measures whether privileged and unprivileged groups receive positive predictions at similar rates, making it a simple and widely used fairness metric (Hardt et al., 2016; Mehrabi et al., 2022).

Equality of Opportunity Difference (*EOD*)

$$\boldsymbol{EOD} = \boldsymbol{TPR}_0 - \boldsymbol{TPR}_1 = \left(\frac{\mathbf{45}}{\mathbf{53}}\right) - \left(\frac{\mathbf{9}}{\mathbf{15}}\right) = \mathbf{0.249}$$

EOD focuses specifically on true positive rates, ensuring that students who actually succeed have an equal chance of being correctly identified across privileged and unprivileged groups; this makes it especially meaningful in education, where denying recognition of capable students can reinforce inequities (Hardt et al., 2016).

Equalized Odds (*EO*)

$$\boldsymbol{P}(\overline{\mathbf{Y}} = \mathbf{1} \mid \boldsymbol{Y} = \boldsymbol{y}, \boldsymbol{D} = \mathbf{0}) = \boldsymbol{P}(\overline{\mathbf{Y}} = \mathbf{1} \mid \boldsymbol{Y} = \boldsymbol{y}, \boldsymbol{D} = \mathbf{1}) \qquad \forall\, \boldsymbol{y} \in \{\mathbf{0}, \mathbf{1}\}$$

EO is a stronger fairness criterion than EOD because it requires both true positive and false positive rates to be equal across privileged and unprivileged groups, ensuring that success and failure are predicted fairly for everyone (Buijsman, 2024; Dunkelau & Duong, 2022).

3.1 Bias Mitigation

To mitigate bias and improve fairness, researchers have suggested various strategies, such as pre-processing methods that alter the input data to reduce bias (Calders et al., 2009; Calmon et al., 2017); in-processing methods that modify the learning algorithms during training (Elisa Celis et al., 2019; Kamishima et al., 2012; Zhang et al., 2018); and post-processing methods that improve outputs after the model has been trained (Friedler et al., 2019; Hardt et al., 2016).

In this study, we applied the Equalized Odds post-processing method (Hardt et al., 2016) to adjust model predictions in order to satisfy EO fairness constraints. This method is chosen based on evidence that EO is particularly effective for predicting academic performance (Dunkelau & Duong, 2022), as it addresses disparities in both false positive and false negative rates. Although EO defines the fairness criterion for our intervention, we also present SPD and EOD to provide complementary and interpretable metrics of group fairness in educational contexts.

3.2 Local Interpretable Model-agnostic Explanations (LIME)

LIME is a widely used method for interpreting predictions of any ML model, regardless of its complexity (Ribeiro et al., 2016). It works by approximating a model's behavior locally—around a single prediction—using a simple interpretable model, typically linear. In an educational model, it can, for example, explain why a student was predicted to succeed or fail, highlighting influential attributes such as engagement or submission patterns (Nnadi et al., 2024; Swamy et al., 2022). Its model-agnostic nature makes it applicable to a wide range of models, from neural networks to ensembles, offering an accessible way to understand feature contributions at the individual level. However, LIME is limited to local explanations and cannot capture the model's global behavior or complex feature interactions (Swamy et al., 2022).

3.3 Explainability Metrics

While evaluating explainability in ML goes beyond simply generating model outputs that appear interpretable, fewer studies have focused on systematically measuring it (Alamri & Alharbi, 2021; Kondo et al., 2020; Sohail et al., 2022). For an explanation to be meaningful, it should help users make informed decisions by offering clarity, relevance, and practical guidance. Explanations can take many forms and to evaluate them, researchers have proposed quantitative metrics capturing various qualities. In this study, we focus on fidelity, which measures how well an explanation reflects the model's actual behavior. For inherently interpretable models, fidelity is perfect, since explanations directly mirror predictions. By contrast, model-agnostic approaches, such as LIME depend on surrogate approximations, making fidelity a key indicator of their reliability (Carvalho et al., 2019). High fidelity indicates strong alignment between explanations and model decisions, while low fidelity suggests weaker correspondence. It can be assessed both locally—on individual predictions—and globally, across the entire dataset.

4. Methodology

The experimental pipeline was designed to evaluate models for three complementary objectives: predictive performance, fairness across student subgroups, and model explainability. In this study, we used the OULAD dataset, selecting a subset that balances student demographics and includes features such as academic records, sociodemographic data, and behavioral attributes. We framed the problem as a binary classification (pass/fail) and trained two ML models: Random Forest (RF) and Artificial Neural Network (ANN). These models were selected because they are widely used and well understood and represent diverse learning paradigms, with RF as an ensemble of decision trees, provides interpretability and robustness to noisy features (Arévalo-Cordovilla & Peña, 2024; Spoon et al., 2016), and ANN as a black-box model with strong predictive power (Baashar et al., 2022; Lau et al., 2019). Fairness was evaluated using SPD and EOD to quantify group-level disparities between privileged and unprivileged students. To test mitigation, we applied an equalized-odds post-processing method and re-computed the same two metrics for comparison. We used LIME to interpret model behavior, identify whether sensitive features contributed disproportionately to predictions, and assess whether changes in fairness after mitigation corresponded to changes in feature attributions. This joint use of fairness metrics and interpretability allowed us to connect what the models predicted with why they produced those predictions.

4.1 OULA Dataset

The OULAD is a publicly available dataset provided by the Open University, a well-established public distance learning university in the United Kingdom. It has been applied to predicting student academic performance (Alonso & Casalino, 2019; Casalino et al., 2022; Gunasekara & Saarela, 2025a), identifying at-risk students (Gupta et al., 2022; Lu et al., 2023; Qin & Boicu, 2023), evaluating the fairness in ML models (Idowu et al., 2024; Saarela, 2024), and exploring student engagement patterns (Casalino et al., 2022). OULAD includes rich information such as demographics, assessment results, course structure, and detailed learning activity logs from the Virtual Learning Environment (VLE).

In this study, we used a subsets of OULAD from (https://github.com/gogoladzetedo/Open_University_Analytics, accessed on 02 June 2025), specifically studentInfo.csv (demographics and registration), assessment.csv (assessment details), studentAssessment.csv, and studentVle.csv (online activity). Features were selected to support academic outcome prediction, fairness evaluation across groups, and interpretability with LIME. Table 1 summarizes the attributes used in our analysis.

Table 1 Description of attributes related in OULAD.

Attribute Name	*Description*
code_module	Module identification code (e.g., *AAA, BBB, CCC*) indicating the specific course to which each assessment is linked.
code_presentation	Identification code of the student presentation (*2014B, 2014J, 2013B, 2013J*)
gender	Gender of student (*F/M*)
Region	Geographic region where the student resided during the time the module was presented.
imd_band	Index of Multiple Deprivation Band Value. (*Values: 0% –100%)*
highest_education	Highest student's education level when enrolled. (*A level or Equivalent, Lower Than A Level, HE Qualification, Post Graduate Qualification, No Formal quals*)
disability	Whether the student has declared a disability. (*Y/N*)
age_band	Students' age band (*0–35, 35–55, higher than 55*)
studied_credits	Total amount of credits a student has earned for each currently enrolled module.
num_of_attempts	Total count of attempts the student has made for the module.
assessment_count	Total number of assessments the student has submitted for the module.
delay	Calculated as the average number of days between the fixed assessment date and submission date by student.
score	Scores fall between 0 and 100. Less than 40 is considered a fail.
id_site	VLE material identification number.
date	Day of the student's interaction with the material.
sum_click	The number of times a student engages with the materials on a given day.

4.2 Data Preprocessing

For preprocessing, *imd_band*, and *age_band* were converted into numeric values, with missing values in *imd_band* replaced by the mode. Binary attributes like *gender* and *disability* were encoded as 0/1, while multicategory variables (*code_module*, *region*, *highest_education*) were processed using one-hot encoding to avoid artificial rankings. The target variable was simplified from four classes to two: *Pass* (Pass/distinction) and *Fail* (Fail/Withdrawn), improving balance and interpretability. Additional features included the average number of VLE clicks per student (*sum_click*) and submission delay (*delay*), calculated from assessment timelines. Data sources were merged using *id_student* as the key, producing a final dataset of 34 features and 32,593 records, with 15,385 students labeled *Pass* and 17,208 labeled *Fail*. Out of the 34 features, *disability* and *gender* were selected as sensitive attributes. Overall, the dataset is relatively balanced, with 15,385 students passing (47.2%) and 17,208 failing (52.8%). *Gender* differences are small: 51.6% of female students failed versus 53.8% of male students. In contrast, *disability* shows a strong disparity: among students with disabilities, 61.9% failed and 38.1% passed, while students without disabilities had a nearly even split between pass (48.9%) and fail (51.1%) outcomes (see Figure 2).

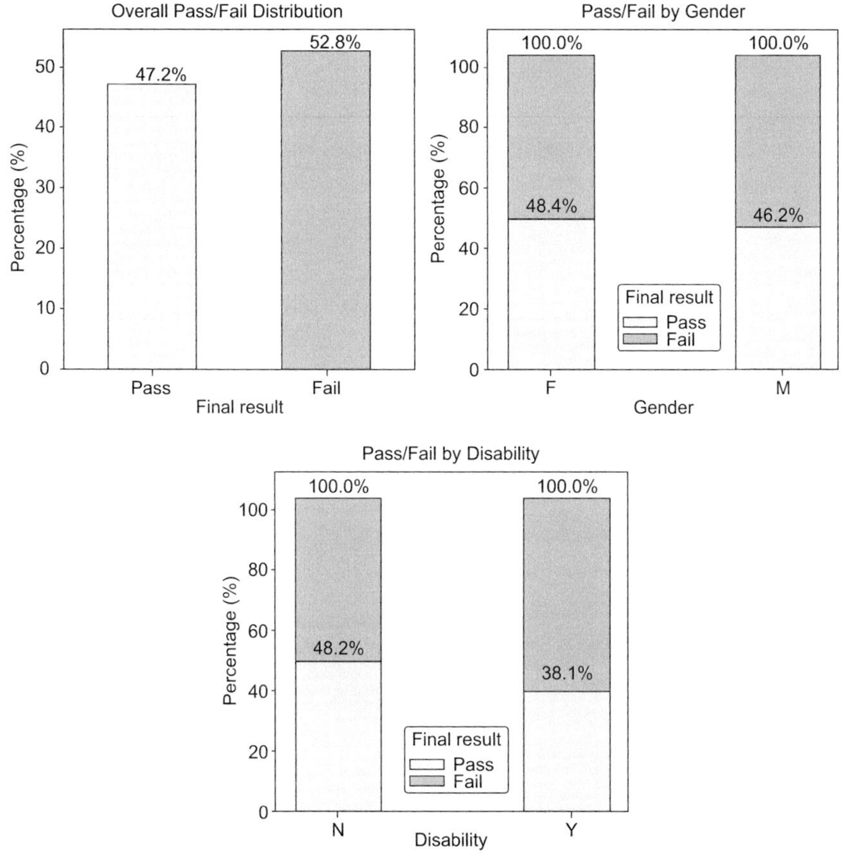

Fig. 2 Distribution of Results.

4.3 Analysis Flow and Model Evaluation

The model evaluation process, as illustrated in Figure 3, was designed to jointly assess predictive performance, fairness, and explainability of applied models. We applied two classifiers: RF and ANN. To ensure reliable results, we used five-fold cross validation, which preserves the distribution of sensitive attributes in each fold. This reduces the risk of biased results from a single train-test split while maintaining computational efficiency. Model performance was measured using

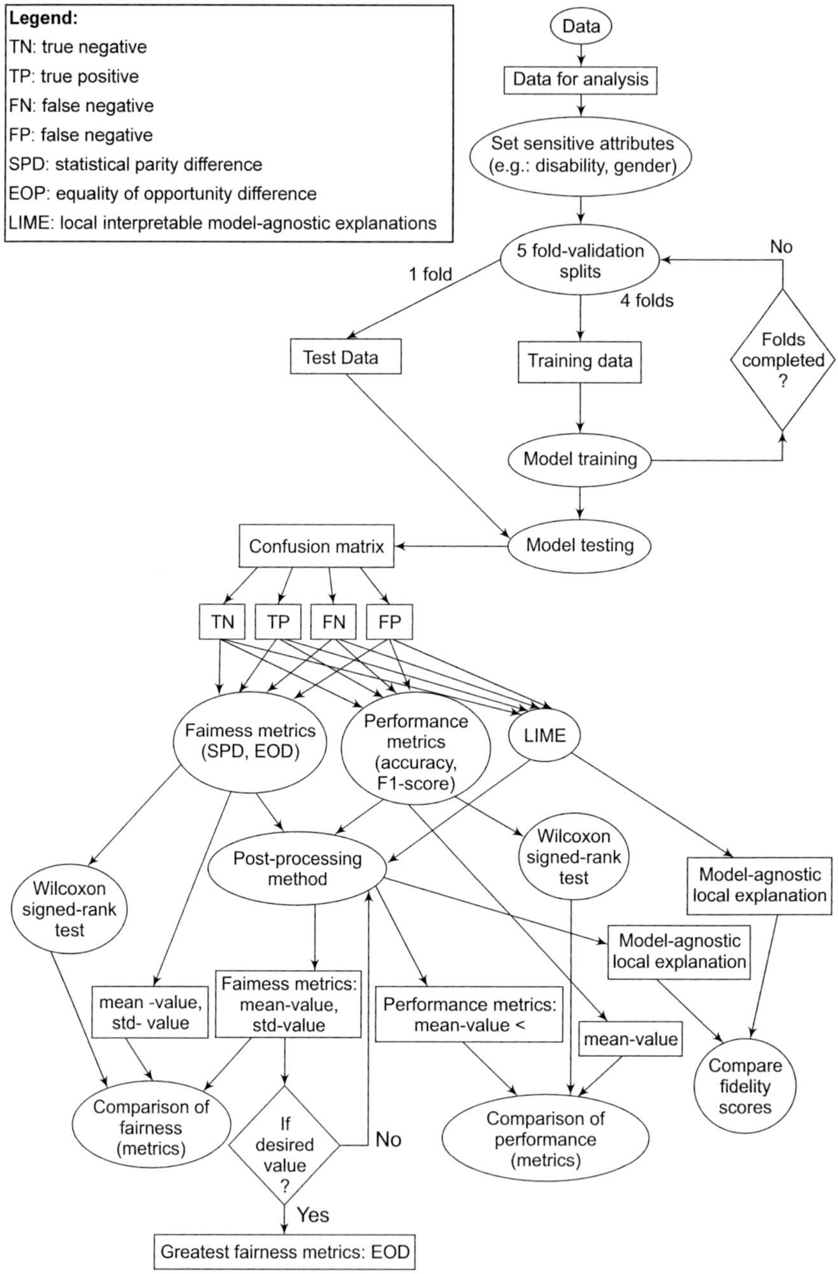

Fig. 3 Flowchart of the analysis pipeline, starting with preprocessing, model training/testing, and evaluation through performance and fairness metrics. Equalized odds post-processing and Wilcoxon tests are applied, with LIME used before and after mitigation to check whether sensitive attributes influence predictions. The process concludes with EOD identified as the most suitable fairness metric in this context.

accuracy and F-score, while fairness was evaluated with SPD and EOD to capture group-level disparities in predictions. To test fairness mitigation, we applied an equalized-odds post-processing method and re-computed SPD and EOD for comparison. For interpretability, we used LIME to analyze feature contributions at the individual level, identifying whether sensitive attributes disproportionately influenced predictions. We further examined whether improvements in fairness after post-processing aligned with changes in feature attributions. This combined use of fairness metrics and explainability provided a comprehensive understanding of both what the models predicted and why those predictions were made.

5. Results

We evaluated the predictive performance of the ANN and RF models using standard classification metrics without applying any bias mitigation techniques. The ANN model achieved an overall accuracy of 91.97% with an AUC-ROC of 0.9143. It showed balanced performance across both classes, F-score around 0.92, indicating strong but slightly less consistent performance on pass and fail classes. In contrast, the RF model performed better overall, reaching 93.90% accuracy with an AUC-ROC of 0.9675. It demonstrated with F-scores of 0.94 for the fail class and 0.94 for the pass class, highlighting its superior discriminative ability. These results indicate that both ANN and RF models are effective in predicting student success in the OULAD dataset (see Figure 4), with RF achieving the strongest overall performance, closely followed by ANN. These baseline outcomes serve as a reference point for evaluating fairness and the impact of bias mitigation.

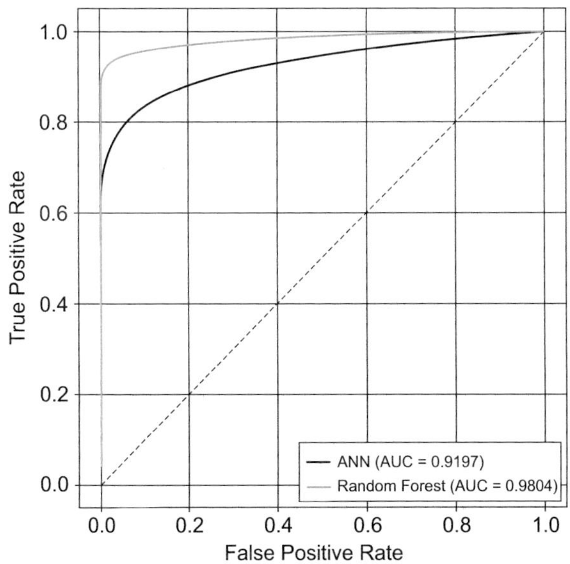

Fig. 4 AUC-ROC curves comparing the performance of two ML models.

To assess the impact of fairness mitigation, we used Wilcoxon signed-rank tests to compare predictive performance and fairness metrics before and after intervention. Non-parametric testing was chosen because metric differences were not normally distributed. We conducted all analyses using the RF model, selected as the best-performing baseline. Table 2 showed that, for both *gender* and *disability*, accuracy and F-score decreased slightly but significantly ($p < 0.005$), reflecting a modest performance trade-off. However, AUC remained unchanged ($p = 1$), indicating preserved ranking ability.

Table 2 Performance metrics (Mean ± SD) before and after mitigation for disability and gender with Wilcoxon p-values from the RF model.

Metric	*Disability*			*Gender*		
	Before	*After*	*p-value*	*Before*	*After*	*p-value*
Accuracy	0.912±0.005	0.899±0.013	0.008	0.912±0.004	0.902±0.005	0.016
F score	0.911±0.005	0.895±0.014	0.008	0.910±0.004	0.901±0.005	0.016
AUC	0.969±0.005	0.912±0.002	1.000	0.969±0.002	0.969±0.002	1.000

Table 3 presents SPD and EOD values before and after mitigation. For both *gender* and *disability*, fairness improved significantly, as reflected in reduced SPD and near zero EOD after mitigation ($p < 0.05$).

Table 3 Fairness metrics (Mean ± SD) before and after mitigation for disability and gender, with Wilcoxon *p*-values from the RF model.

Metric	*Disability*			*Gender*		
	Before	*After*	*p-value*	*Before*	*After*	*p-value*
SPD	–0.116±0.012	–0.081±0.011	0.008	–0.038±0.019	–0.019±0.013	0.016
EOD	–0.031±0.024	0.001±0.004	0.031	–0.011±0.008	0.000±0.002	0.031

Figure 5 shows the effect of equalized odds post-processing on the RF and ANN models with respect to *disability* groups. Before intervention, the unprivileged group (students with disabilities) exhibited lower true positive rates and higher false negative rates compared to the privileged group. Post-processing substantially reduced these disparities for both models. In the RF model, TPRs between groups converged and FNR differences narrowed, suggesting improved parity in predictions. The ANN model showed similar improvements, with TPR and FNR distributions becoming more balanced after intervention, although remaining disparities were slightly larger than RF.

Figure 6 illustrates the fairness evaluation for *gender* groups. In the RF model, strong disparities were evident before intervention: the privileged group achieved higher TPRs and lower FNRs, while the unprivileged group faced systematic disadvantages. After applying equalized odds, both TPR and FNR values became closely aligned across groups, indicating significant fairness improvements. In the ANN model, pre-intervention differences were less marked than in RF, but

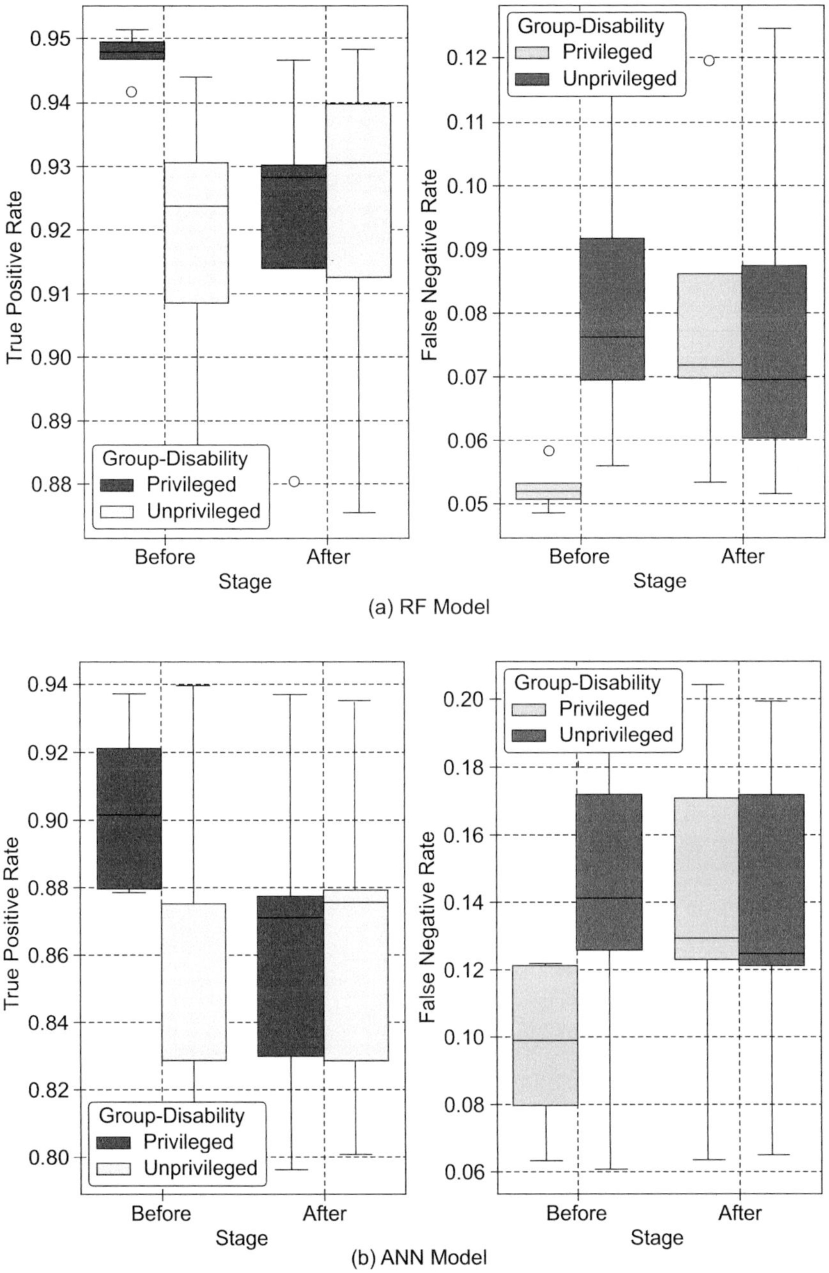

Fig. 5 TPR and FNR before and after equalized odds across two models: (a) RF, (b) ANN. The boxplots show the distribution of TPR and FNR for privileged (without disability) and unprivileged (with disability) groups. Post-processing reduces disparities between privileged and unprivileged groups, bringing TPRs closer and reducing FNR differences.

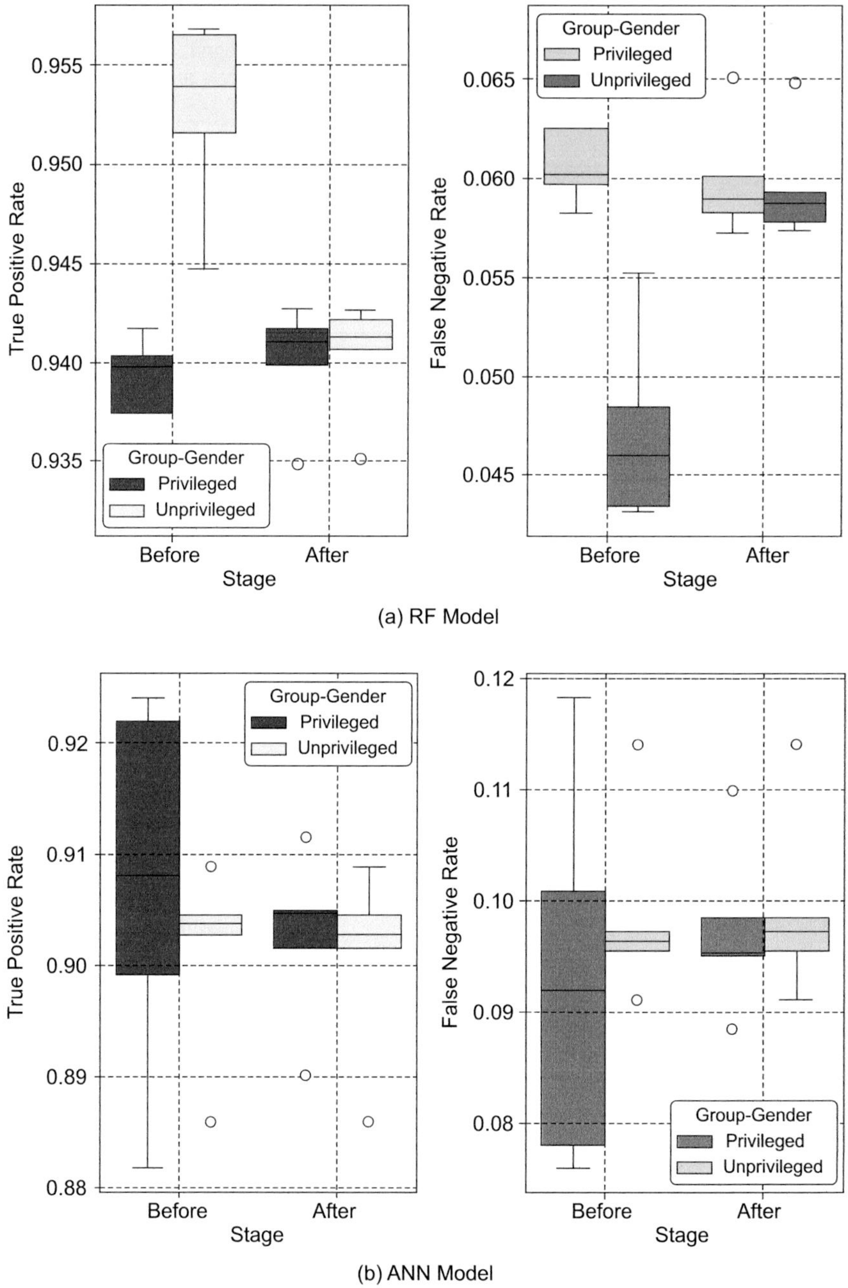

Fig. 6 TPR and FNR for privileged (male) and unprivileged (female) groups before and after equalized odds across two models: (a) RF, (b) ANN.

the privileged group still maintained an advantage. Post-processing again reduced gaps, though some minor variation remained.

Figure 7 illustrates the performance-fairness trade-off for the RF and ANN models under *disability* status. Each subplot presents mean accuracy against two fairness metrics—EOD and SPD—with standard deviation error bars across folds. Results are shown both before and after applying equalized odds post-processing. For the RF model, equalized odds resulted in a marked improvement in fairness. Both EOD and EPD values moved closer to zero after intervention, indicating reduced disparities between privileged and unprivileged groups. This improvement in fairness was accompanied by a slight decrease in accuracy, underscoring the typical trade-off between fairness and predictive performance. For the ANN model, a similar trend was observed. Post-processing substantially improved fairness metrics, particularly bringing EOD closer to zero, though SPD also showed progress.

A similar pattern is observed when considering *gender* status (Figure 8). For the RF model, equalized odds resulted in clear improvements in fairness: both EOD and SPD values shifted closer to zero after intervention, reflecting reduced disparities between male and female groups. This fairness gain was achieved with only a marginal reduction in accuracy, indicating that the RF model maintained stable predictive performance under fairness constraints. For the ANN model, a similar pattern emerged. Post-processing substantially improved fairness metrics, especially for EOD, with values moving nearer to zero. However, unlike the RF model, the ANN experienced a more noticeable decrease in accuracy, suggesting higher sensitivity to fairness adjustments across both *disability* and *gender* groups.

All analyzes examining the relationship between explainability and fairness were conducted using the RF model, which was chosen as the best-performing baseline due to its predictive performance and suitability for interpretability analyses, and EOD was selected as the fairness metrics because it performed best in balancing the performance-fairness trade-off for both RF and ANN models across *disability* and *gender* groups. Before applying the equalized odds post-processing, the RF model achieved an average LIME fidelity that varied slightly across sensitive attributes. Specifically, the average fidelity by *gender* was 0.2329 for female students and 0.2275 for male students, while the average fidelity by *disability* status was 0.2283 for non-disabled students and 0.2539 for disabled students. These differences indicate that, although the model predictions were relatively accurate, the local explanations produced by LIME were slightly biased in favor of certain groups, reflecting an inconsistency in interpretability across demographic subgroups.

After applying equalized odds post-processing, the average LIME fidelity increased for all groups and became nearly identical across sensitive attributes. The post-processed results showed an average fidelity of 0.3029 for females and 0.3048 for males, and 0.3042 for non-disabled and 0.3035 for disabled students. This indicates that fairness intervention not only mitigated predictive disparities between privileged and unprivileged groups but also enhanced the uniformity

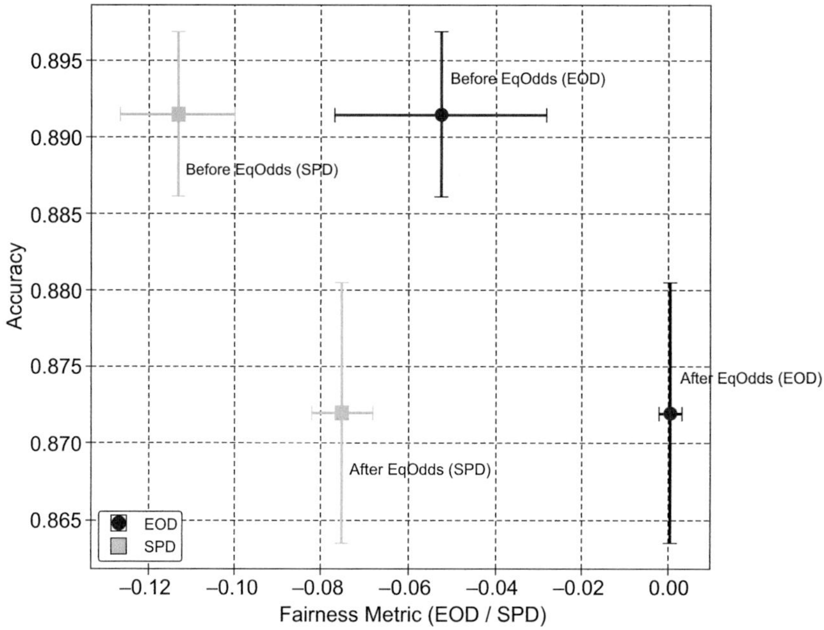

(a) ANN Model

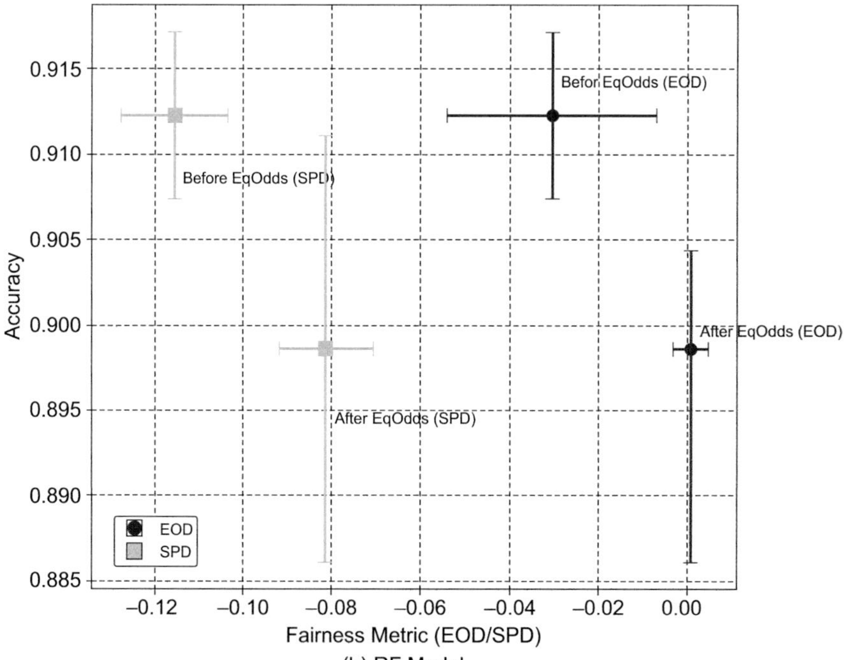

(b) RF Model

Fig. 7 Performance-fairness trade-off plots for different classifiers under disability status. Each subplot shows the mean accuracy vs fairness metrics with standard deviation error bars across folds. Results are shown before and after applying equalized odds for (a) RF, (b) ANN.

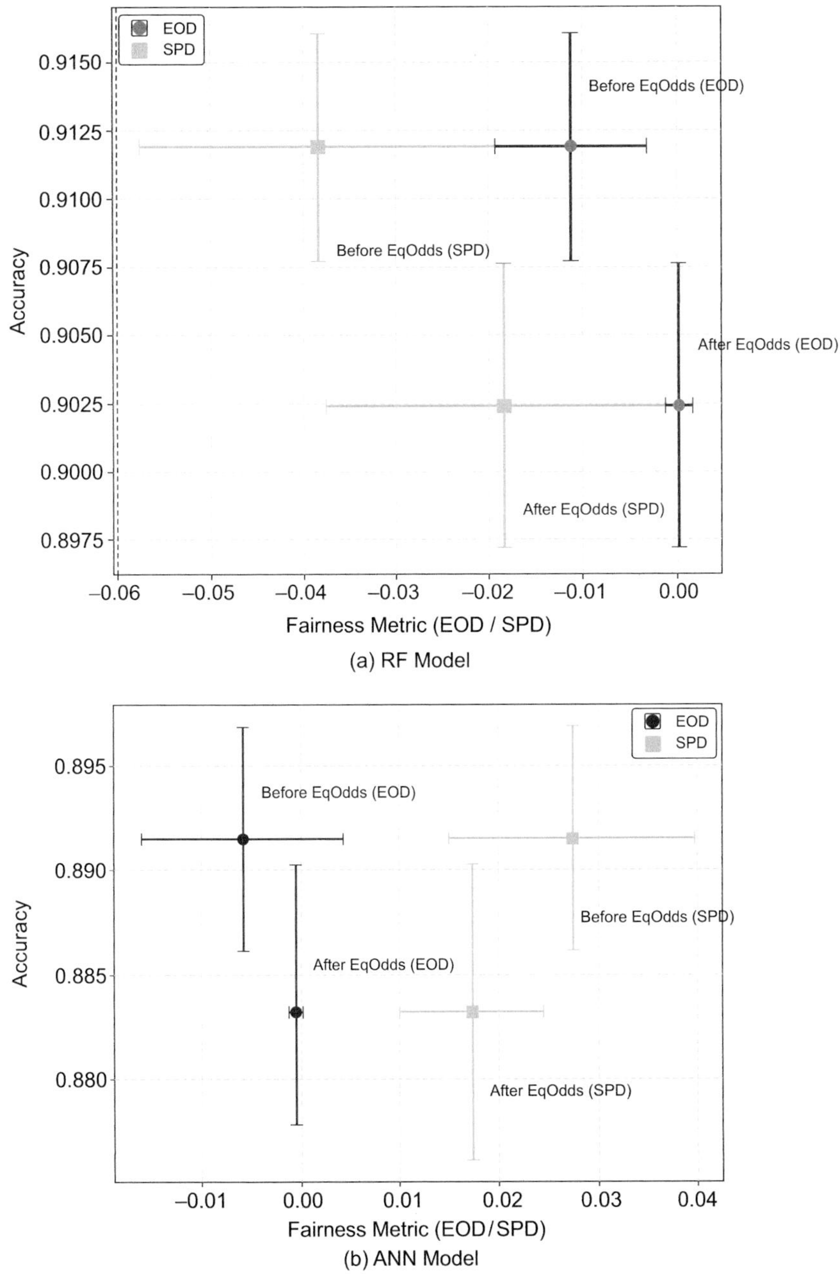

Fig. 8 Performance-fairness trade-off plots for different classifiers under gender status. Each subplot shows the mean accuracy vs fairness metrics with standard deviation error bars across folds. Results are shown before and after applying equalized odds for (a) RF (b) ANN.

and reliability of local explanations. Figure 9 illustrates the changes in LIME fidelity before and after equalized odds post-processing. For both gender and disability, fairness intervention increased overall fidelity and EOD between groups, confirming that fairness adjustments improved both predictive equity and explainability.

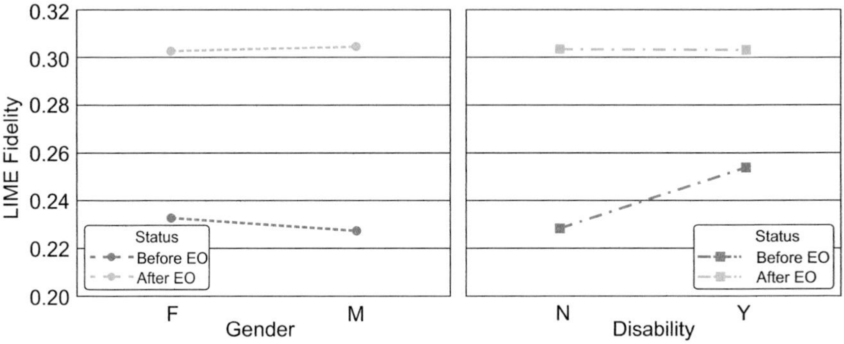

Fig. 9 LIME fidelity across sensitive attributes before and after Equalized Odds (EO) post-processing. The analysis was conducted using a Random Forest (RF) model. Left panel shows fidelity for gender (F = female, M = male), and right panel shows fidelity for disability status (N = non-disabled, Y = disabled). Post-processing improves overall fidelity and reduces disparities between privileged and unprivileged groups, indicating enhanced fairness and more consistent local explanations.

6. Discussion

In the educational domain, much research has focused on trade-offs between performance vs fairness (Jiang & Pardos, 2021; Kim & Kim, 2026; Pham, Do, et al., 2025; Raftopoulos et al., 2025), or performance vs explainability (Feldman-Maggor et al., 2025; Gunasekara & Saarela, 2025b). These studies have contributed to a better understanding of how high prediction accuracy can sometimes come at the cost of fairness or how stakeholders prefer interpretable models, even when they are somewhat less accurate. However, the connection between fairness and explainability remains largely unexplored. This gap is critical because disparities in explanation fidelity could undermine trust among marginalized populations even if predictive outcomes are considered fair. Looking at both fairness and explainability together can help build models that are accurate, fair, and transparent in educational settings.

This chapter investigates whether fidelity of post-hoc explanations varies across sensitive groups in the OULAD, aiming to clarify how fairness and explainability influence each other in predictive modeling. In this context, both ANN and RF models achieved high predictive accuracy on the OULAD dataset, with RF outperforming ANN in terms of accuracy and AUC. These strong baselines provided a meaningful reference for evaluating the effects of fairness interventions. As expected, applying equalized odds post-processing introduced a modest trade-off: accuracy and F-scores declined slightly for both *gender* and *disability* groups, while AUC remained unchanged, preserving ranking ability. This illustrates the usual trade-off between fairness and predictive accuracy, where improvements in fairness are achieved with only a slight reduction in performance.

Fairness analyzes confirmed that equalized odds post-processing substantially reduced disparities between privileged and unprivileged groups. The SPD and EOD metrics for both *disability* and *gender* shifted closer to zero, suggesting that the model's predictions became more fair and balanced. Importantly, group-level disparities in true positive and false negative rates narrowed significantly after intervention, with RF benefiting the most, and ANN showing similar but slightly less stable improvements.

The analysis of LIME fidelity before and after applying equalized odds highlights a meaningful link between model fairness and explainability. Prior to fairness interventions, the model displayed variations in fidelity across sensitive groups. For example, female students had slightly higher LIME fidelity than male students, and disabled students had notably higher fidelity than non-disabled students. This suggests that while the model's predictions were generally accurate, the local explanations—that indicate how individual features influenced predictions—were not equally reliable for all groups. Such disparities in interpretability can undermine trust, especially among marginalized populations, and reveal hidden biases in the model's decision-making process.

Following equalized odds post-processing, LIME fidelity improved overall and became more consistent across demographic groups. This indicates that fairness interventions can stabilize local model behavior, ensuring explanations are equally faithful regardless of sensitive attributes. By reducing predictive disparities between privileged and unprivileged groups, equalized odds also mitigates differences in how the model justifies its predictions for different populations. This supports the notion of equitable interpretability, where models that are fairer are inherently easier to explain in a consistent manner. These findings suggest that explainability and fairness are closely linked. While fairness interventions primarily target alignment of predicted outcomes, they can also influence local model behavior captured by interpretability methods like LIME. This underscores the importance of evaluating fairness and interpretability together: a model may be fair in its predictions but inconsistent in its explanations, which can compromise transparency and limit its utility for educators, policymakers, or students.

Moreover, fairness metrics often conflict, so they cannot all be optimized at once (Buijsman, 2024; Carey & Wu, 2023; Kleinberg et al., 2017). In addition, for this task of predicting student outcomes, EOD is most suitable because it balances true positive rates; ensuring students are not unfairly misclassified by *gender* or *disability*.

7. Limitation and Future Works

This study presents some limitations that may affect the interpretation of the results. First, the OULAD dataset may not capture the full diversity of learners across different educational contexts, limiting the generalizability of the findings to K-12 schools, traditional universities, or online platforms. Second, while we considered *gender* and *disability* as separate attributes, we could not explore their intersection (e.g., female + disabled) in depth due to strong group imbalances in the OULAD dataset (female without *disability*:13,097; female with *disability*: 1,621; male without *disability*: 16,332; male with *disability*: 1,543). Such imbalance reduces the reliability of intersectional analysis, underscoring the need for future studies with larger or more balanced samples. Third, the analysis depended on widely used fairness metrics (e.g., EOD, SPD) that, while informative, do not fully capture structural or historical biases. Moreover, because fairness metrics often conflict, simultaneous optimization is mathematically infeasible, necessitating context-specific trade-offs.

Further research should incorporate more diverse datasets, consider multiple sensitive attributes jointly, and explore a wider range of fairness-aware methods, including pre-processing and in-processing techniques. The use of explainability tools, such as SHAP and metrics—stability—would also provide deeper insights into model behavior and enable more meaningful cross-model comparisons.

Conclusion

This study highlights the importance of examining fairness and explainability together in educational predictive modeling. Using the OULAD dataset, we showed that while ANN and RF models achieve strong baseline performance, applying equalized odds post-processing reduced disparities between *gender* and *disability* groups with only modest costs to accuracy and F-score. Beyond improving fairness, the intervention also stabilized LIME fidelity across groups, suggesting that fairer models produce more consistent and trustworthy explanations. These findings demonstrate that fairness interventions can enhance both equitable outcomes and equitable interpretability. However, because fairness metrics often conflict, trade-offs remain unavoidable, and careful selection of context-appropriate metrics is essential. Overall, these findings underscore the importance of future research that jointly addresses fairness and explainability, with the aim of developing predictive models that are accurate, equitable, transparent, and supportive of all stakeholders.

References

Akgun, S. and Greenhow, C. (2021). Artificial intelligence in education: Addressing ethical challenges in K?12 settings. *AI and Ethics*, *2*(3): 431–440. https://doi.org/10.1007/s43681-021-00096-7.

Alamri, R. and Alharbi, B. (2021). Explainable Student Performance Prediction Models: A Systematic Review. *IEEE Access*, *9*: 33132–33143. https://doi.org/10.1109/ACCESS.2021.3061368.

Alonso, J.M. and Casalino, G. (2019). Explainable Artificial Intelligence for Human-Centric Data Analysis in Virtual Learning Environments. *Communications in Computer and Information Science*, *1091*(September): 125–138. https://doi.org/10.1007/978-3-030-31284-8_10.

Alwarthan, S.A., Aslam, N. and Khan, I.U. (2022). Predicting Student Academic Performance at Higher Education Using Data Mining: A Systematic Review. *Applied Computational Intelligence and Soft Computing*, *2022*. https://doi.org/10.1155/2022/8924028.

Anderson, H., Boodhwani, A. and Baker, R.S. (2019). Assessing the fairness of graduation predictions. In: *EDM 2019: Proceedings of the 12th International Conference on Educational Data Mining* (pp. 488–491).

Angerschmid, A., Zhou, J., Theuermann, K., Chen, F. and Holzinger, A. (2022). Fairness and Explanation in AI-Informed Decision Making. *Machine Learning and Knowledge Extraction*, *4*(2): 556–579. https://doi.org/10.3390/make4020026.

Arévalo-Cordovilla, F.E. and Peña, M. (2024). Comparative Analysis of Machine Learning Models for Predicting Student Success in Online Programming Courses: A Study Based on LMS Data and External Factors. *Mathematics*, *12*(20). https://doi.org/10.3390/math12203272.

Baashar, Y., Alkawsi, G., Mustafa, A., Alkahtani, A.A., Alsariera, Y.A., Ali, A.Q., Hashim, W. and Tiong, S.K. (2022). Toward Predicting Student's Academic Performance Using Artificial Neural Networks (ANNs). *Applied Sciences (Switzerland)*, *12*(3). https://doi.org/10.3390/app12031289.

Baker, R.S. and Hawn, A. (2022). Algorithmic Bias in Education. *International Journal of Artificial Intelligence in Education*, *32*(4): 1052–1092. https://doi.org/10.1007/s40593-021-00285-9.

Buijsman, S. (2024). Navigating fairness measures and trade-offs. *AI and Ethics*, *4*(4): 1323–1334. https://doi.org/10.1007/s43681-023-00318-0.

Calders, T., Kamiran, F. and Pechenizkiy, M. (2009). Building classifiers with independency constraints. In: *ICDM Workshops 2009: IEEE International Conference on Data Mining, December* (pp. 13–18). https://doi.org/10.1109/ICDMW.2009.83.

Calmon, F.P., Wei, D., Vinzamuri, B., Ramamurthy, K.N. and Varshney, K.R. (2017). Optimized preprocessing for discrimination prevention. *Advances in Neural Information Processing Systems*, *2017Decem*(NIPS), (pp. 3993–4002).

Carey, A.N. and Wu, X. (2023). The statistical fairness field guide: Perspectives from social and formal sciences. *AI and Ethics*, *3*(1): 1–23. https://doi.org/10.1007/s43681-022-00183-3.

Carvalho, D.V., Pereira, E.M. and Cardoso, J.S. (2019). Machine learning interpretability: A survey on methods and metrics. *Electronics (Switzerland)*, *8*(8), 1–34. https://doi.org/10.3390/electronics8080832.

Casalino, G., Ducange, P., Fazzolari, M. and Pecori, R. (2022). Fuzzy Hoeffding Decision Trees for Learning Analytics. In: *CEUR Workshop Proceedings*, *3380*(May).

Castelnovo, A., Crupi, R., Greco, G., Regoli, D., Penco, I.G. and Cosentini, A.C. (2022). A clarification of the nuances in the fairness metrics landscape. *Scientific Reports*, *12*(1): 1–21. https://doi.org/10.1038/s41598-022-07939-1.

Craven, M.W. and Shavlik, J.W. (1995). Extracting Tree-Structured Representations of Trained Networks. In: *NIPS 1995: Proceedings of the 8th International Conference on Neural Information Processing Systems* (pp. 24–30).

Dunkelau, J. and Duong, M.K. (2022). *Towards Equalised Odds as Fairness Metric in Academic Performance Prediction*. http://arxiv.org/abs/2209.14670.

Dwork, C., Hardt, M., Pitassi, T., Reingold, O. and Zemel, R. (2012). Fairness through awareness. In: *ITCS 2012: Innovations in Theoretical Computer Science Conference* (pp. 214–226). https://doi.org/10.1145/2090236.2090255.

Elisa Celis, L., Huang, L., Keswani, V. and Vishnoi, N.K. (2019). Classification with fairness constraints: A meta-algorithm with provable guarantees. In: *FAT* 2019: Proceedings of the 2019 Conference on Fairness, Accountability, and Transparency* (pp. 319–328). https://doi.org/10.1145/3287560.3287586.

Feldman-Maggor, Y., Cukurova, M., Kent, C. and Alexandron, G. (2025). The Impact of Explainable AI on Teachers' Trust and Acceptance of AI EdTech Recommendations: The Power of Domain-specific Explanations. *International Journal of Artificial Intelligence in Education* (Issue 0123456789). Springer New York. https://doi.org/10.1007/s40593-025-00486-6.

Friedler, S.A., Choudhary, S., Scheidegger, C., Hamilton, E.P., Venkatasubramanian, S. and Roth, D. (2019). A comparative study of fairness-enhancing interventions in machine learning. In: *FAT**

2019: *Proceedings of the 2019 Conference on Fairness, Accountability, and Transparency* (pp. 329–338). https://doi.org/10.1145/3287560.3287589.

Gardner, J., Brooks, C. and Baker, R. (2019). Evaluating the fairness of predictive student models through slicing analysis. *ACM International Conference Proceeding Series* (pp. 225–234). https://doi.org/10.1145/3303772.3303791

Gomez, M.J., Armada Sánchez, Á., Albaladejo-González, M., García Clemente, F.J. and Ruipérez-Valiente, J.A. (2025). Utilising Explainable AI to Enhance Real-Time Student Performance Prediction in Educational Serious Games. *Expert Systems*, *42*(3). https://doi.org/10.1111/exsy.70008.

Gunasekara, S. and Saarela, M. (2025a). Explainable AI in Education: Techniques and Qualitative Assessment. *Applied Sciences* (*Switzerland*), *15*(3). https://doi.org/10.3390/app15031239.

Gunasekara, S. and Saarela, M. (2025b). Quantitative Assessment of Explainability in Machine Learning Models: A Study on the OULA Dataset. In: *Proceedings of the ACM Symposium on Applied Computing* (pp. 101–103). https://doi.org/10.1145/3672608.3707815.

Gupta, A., Garg, D. and Kumar, P. (2022). Mining Sequential Learning Trajectories with Hidden Markov Models for Early Prediction of At-Risk Students in E-Learning Environments. *IEEE Transactions on Learning Technologies*, *15*(6): 783–797. https://doi.org/10.1109/TLT.2022.3197486.

Hardt, M., Price, E. and Srebro, N. (2016). Equality of opportunity in supervised learning. *Advances in Neural Information Processing Systems*: 3323–3331.

Heaton, D., Nichele, E., Clos, J. and Fischer, J.E. (2023). "The algorithm will screw you": Blame, social actors, and the 2020 A Level results algorithm on Twitter. *PLoS ONE*, *18*(7 July): 1–29. https://doi.org/10.1371/journal.pone.0288662.

Holmes, W. and Tuomi, I. (2022). State of the art and practice in AI in education. *European Journal of Education*, *57*(4), 542–570. https://doi.org/10.1111/ejed.12533.

Hu, Q. and Rangwala, H. (2020). Towards Fair Educational Data Mining: A Case Study on Detecting At-risk Students. In: *Proceedings of the 13th International Conference on Educational Data Mining, EDM 2020* (pp. 431–437).

Hutchinson, B. and Mitchell, M. (2019). 50 Years of Test (Un)fairness: Lessons for machine learning. In: *FAT* 2019*: *Proceedings of the 2019 Conference on Fairness, Accountability, and Transparency* (pp.49–58). https://doi.org/10.1145/3287560.3287600.

Idowu, J.A., Koshiyama, A.S. and Treleaven, P. (2024). Investigating algorithmic bias in student progress monitoring. *Computers and Education: Artificial Intelligence*, *7*(August): 100267. https://doi.org/10.1016/j.caeai.2024.100267.

Jiang, W. and Pardos, Z.A. (2021). Towards Equity and Algorithmic Fairness in Student Grade Prediction. In: *AIES 2021*: *Proceedings of the 2021 AAAI/ACM Conference on AI, Ethics, and Society* (pp. 608–617). https://doi.org/10.1145/3461702.3462623.

Kai, S., Andres, J.M.L., Paquette, L., Baker, R.S., Molnar, K., Watkins, H. and Moore, M. (2017). Predicting student retention from behavior in an online orientation course. In: *Proceedings of the 10th International Conference on Educational Data Mining, EDM 2017* (pp. 250–255).

Kamishima, T., Akaho, S., Asoh, H. and Sakuma, J. (2012). Fairness-aware classifier with prejudice remover regularizer. *Lecture Notes in Computer Science* (*Including Subseries Lecture Notes in Artificial Intelligence and Lecture Notes in Bioinformatics*), *7524 LNAI*(PART 2): 35–50. https://doi.org/10.1007/978-3-642-33486-3_3.

Kesgin, K., Kiraz, S., Kosunalp, S. and Stoycheva, B. (2025). Beyond Performance: Explaining and Ensuring Fairness in Student Academic Performance Prediction with Machine Learning. *Applied Sciences*, *15*(15): 8409. https://doi.org/10.3390/app15158409.

Kim, W. and Kim, H. (2026). *Counterfactual Fairness Evaluation of Machine Learning Models on Educational Datasets* (pp. 88–103). https://doi.org/10.1007/978-3-031-98284-2_7.

Kizilcec, R.F. and Lee, H. (2022). Algorithmic fairness in education. In: *The Ethics of Artificial Intelligence in Education: Practices, Challenges, and Debates* (pp. 174–202). https://doi.org/10.4324/9780429329067-10.

Kleinberg, J., Mullainathan, S. and Raghavan, M. (2017). Inherent trade-offs in the fair determination of risk scores. *Leibniz International Proceedings in Informatics, LIPIcs, 67*: 1–23. https://doi.org/10.4230/LIPIcs.ITCS.2017.43.

Kondo, N., Matsuda, T., Hayashi, Y., Matsukawa, H., Tsubakimoto, M., Watanabe, Y., Tateishi, S. and Yamashita, H. (2020). Academic Success Prediction based on Important Student Data Selected via Multi-objective Evolutionary Computation. In: *Proceedings: 2020 9th International Congress on Advanced Applied Informatics, IIAI-AAI 2020* (pp. 370–373). https://doi.org/10.1109/IIAI-AAI50415.2020.00082.

Kusner, M., Loftus, J., Russell, C. and Silva, R. (2017). Counterfactual fairness. *Advances in Neural Information Processing Systems, 2017-Decem*(*NIPS*): 4067–4077.

Lau, E.T., Sun, L. and Yang, Q. (2019). Modelling, prediction and classification of student academic performance using artificial neural networks. *SN Applied Sciences, 1*(9): 1–10. https://doi.org/10.1007/s42452-019-0884-7.

Lee, H. and Kizilcec, R.F. (2020). *Evaluation of Fairness Trade-offs in Predicting Student Success.* 1–3. http://arxiv.org/abs/2007.00088.

Li, L., Sha, L., Li, Y., Rakovic, M., Rong, J., Joksimovic, S., Selwyn, N., Gasevic, D. and Chen, G. (2023). Moral Machines or Tyranny of the Majority? A Systematic Review on Predictive Bias in Education. *ACM International Conference Proceeding Series*: 499–508. https://doi.org/10.1145/3576050.3576119.

Lu, J., Mou, J. and Li, P. (2023). Interpretive Analyses of Learner Dropout Prediction in Online STEM Courses. In: *Proceedings*: *2023 5th International Conference on Computer Science and Technologies in Education, CSTE 2023* (*2022*, pp. 72–80). https://doi.org/10.1109/CSTE59648.2023.00020.

Mai, J., Wei, F., He, W., Huang, H. and Zhu, H. (2024). An Explainable Student Performance Prediction Method Based on Dual-Level Progressive Classification Belief Rule Base. *Electronics* (*Switzerland*), *13* (22). https://doi.org/10.3390/electronics13224358.

Mehrabi, N., Morstatter, F., Saxena, N., Lerman, K. and Galstyan, A. (2022). A Survey on Bias and Fairness in Machine Learning. *ACM Computing Surveys*, *54*(6). https://doi.org/10.1145/3457607.

Memarian, B. and Doleck, T. (2023). Fairness, Accountability, Transparency, and Ethics (FATE) in Artificial Intelligence (AI) and higher education: A systematic review. *Computers and Education: Artificial Intelligence*, 5(June): 100152. https://doi.org/10.1016/j.caeai.2023.100152.

Miao Fengchun, Holmes Wayne, Ronghuai Huang, H.Z. (2021a). AI and education: Guidance for policy-makers. In: *AI and Education: Guidance for Policymakers*. https://doi.org/10.54675/pcsp7350.

Miao Fengchun, Holmes Wayne, Ronghuai Huang, H.Z. (2021b). AI and education: Guidance for policymakers. In *UNESCO*. https://doi.org/10.54675/pcsp7350

Nnadi, L.C., Watanobe, Y., Rahman, M.M. and John-Otumu, A.M. (2024). Prediction of Students' Adaptability Using Explainable AI in Educational Machine Learning Models. *Applied Sciences* (*Switzerland*), *14*(12). https://doi.org/10.3390/app14125141.

Opoku, R.A., Pei, B. and Xing, W. (2025). Unveiling Accuracy-Fairness Trade-Offs. *Investigating Machine Learning Models in Student Performance Prediction. 7750*: 1–15.

Pham, N., Do, M.K., Dai, T.V., Hung, P.N. and Nguyen-Duc, A. (2025). FAIREDU: A multiple regression-based method for enhancing fairness in machine learning models for educational applications. *Expert Systems with Applications*, *269*. https://doi.org/10.1016/j.eswa.2024.126219.

Pham, N., Pham Ngoc, H. and Nguyen-Duc, A. (2025). Fairness for machine learning software in education: A systematic mapping study. *Journal of Systems and Software*, *219* (January 2024). https://doi.org/10.1016/j.jss.2024.112244.

Qin, A. and Boicu, M. (2023). EduBoost: An Interpretable Grey-Box Model Approach to Identify and Prevent Student Failure and Dropout. In: *Proceedings*: *Frontiers in Education Conference* (*FIE*) (pp. 1–7). https://doi.org/10.1109/FIE58773.2023.10343186.

Raftopoulos, G., Davrazos, G. and Kotsiantis, S. (2025). Evaluating Fairness Strategies in Educational Data Mining: A Comparative Study of Bias Mitigation Techniques. *Electronics (Switzerland)*, *14*(9). https://doi.org/10.3390/electronics14091856.

Ribeiro, M.T., Singh, S. and Guestrin, C. (2016). "Why Should I Trust You?" Explaining the Predictions of Any Classifier. In: *NAACL-HLT 2016: 2016 Conference of the North American Chapter of the Association for Computational Linguistics: Human Language Technologies, Proceedings of the Demonstrations Session* (pp. 97–101). https://doi.org/10.18653/v1/n16-3020.

Saarela, M. (2024). On the relation of causality versus correlation-based feature selection on model fairness. In: *Proceedings of the ACM Symposium on Applied Computing* (pp. 56–64). https://doi.org/10.1145/3605098.3636018.

Saarela, M., Gunasekara, S. and Karimov, A. (2025). The EU AI Act: Implications for Ethical AI in Education. *Lecture Notes in Computer Science*, *15704 LNCS*(May): 36–50. https://doi.org/10.1007/978-3-031-93979-2_3.

Sapiezynski, P., Wilson, C. and Kassarnig, V. (2017). Academic performance prediction in a gender-imbalanced environment. In: *Proceedings of FATREC Workshop on Responsible Recommendation at ACM RecSys, Como, Italy, August* (pp. 15–18). https://doi.org/10.18122/B20Q5R.

Saxena, N.A., Radanovic, G., Huang, K., Parkes, D.C., DeFilippis, E. and Liu, Y. (2019). How do fairness definitions fare? Examining public attitudes towards algorithmic definitions of fairness. In: *AIES 2019: Proceedings of the 2019 AAAI/ACM Conference on AI, Ethics, and Society* (pp. 99–106). https://doi.org/10.1145/3306618.3314248.

Schleicher, A. (2020). The impact of COVID-19 on education: Insights from education at a glance 2020. *OECD Journal: Economic Studies*, 1–31. https://www.oecd.org/education/the-impact-of-covid-19-on-education-insights-education-at-a-glance-2020.pdf.

Sha, L., Rakovic, M., Das, A., Gasevic, D. and Chen, G. (2022). Leveraging Class Balancing Techniques to Alleviate Algorithmic Bias for Predictive Tasks in Education. *IEEE Transactions on Learning Technologies*, *15*(4): 481–492. https://doi.org/10.1109/TLT.2022.3196278.

Sohail, S., Alvi, A. and Khanum, A. (2022). Interpretable and adaptable early warning learning analytics model. *Computers, Materials, and Continua*, *71*(2): 3211–3225. https://doi.org/10.32604/cmc.2022.023560.

Speicher, T., Heidari, H., Grgic-Hlaca, N., Gummadi, K.P., Singla, A., Weller, A. and Zafar, M. B. (2018). A unified approach to quantifying algorithmic unfairness: Measuring individual and group unfairness via inequality indices. In: *Proceedings of the ACM SIGKDD International Conference on Knowledge Discovery and Data Mining* (pp. 2239–2248). https://doi.org/10.1145/3219819.3220046.

Spoon, K., Whitmer, J.C., Frazee, J.P., Bohonak, A.J., Beemer, J., Fan, J., Stronach, J. and Levine, R.A. (2016). Random Forests for Evaluating Pedagogy and Informing Personalized Learning. *Journal of Educational Data Mining*, *8*(2): 20–50.

Swamy, V., Radmehr, B., Krco, N., Marras, M. and Käser, T. (2022). Evaluating the Explainers: Black-Box Explainable Machine Learning for Student Success Prediction in MOOCs. In: *Proceedings of the 15th International Conference on Educational Data Mining, EDM 2022*. https://doi.org/10.5281/zenodo.6852964.

UNESCO. (2024). *Global Report on Teachers: Addressing Teacher Shortages and Transforming the Profession*. UNESCO. https://www.unesco.org/en/global-report-teachers.

United Nations. (2023). *The 17 Sustainable Development Goals 2030*. https://www.un.org/en/sustainable-development-goals.

Verma, S. and Rubin, J. (2018). Fairness definitions explained. In: *Proceedings: International Conference on Software Engineering* (pp. 1–7). https://doi.org/10.1145/3194770.3194776.

Webb, M.E., Fluck, A., Magenheim, J., Malyn-Smith, J., Waters, J., Deschênes, M. and Zagami, J. (2021). Machine learning for human learners: Opportunities, issues, tensions, and threats.

Educational Technology Research and Development, *69*(4): 2109–2130. https://doi.org/10.1007/s11423-020-09858-2.

Yu, R., Lee, H. and Kizilcec, R.F. (2021). Should College Dropout Prediction Models Include Protected Attributes? In: *L@S 2021*: *Proceedings of the 8th ACM Conference on Learning @ Scale* (pp. 91–100). https://doi.org/10.1145/3430895.3460139.

Zhang, B.H., Lemoine, B. and Mitchell, M. (2018). Mitigating Unwanted Biases with Adversarial Learning. In: *AIES 2018*: *Proceedings of the 2018 AAAI/ACM Conference on AI, Ethics, and Society* (pp. 335–340). https://doi.org/10.1145/3278721.3278779.

Zhao, Y., Wang, Y. and Derr, T. (2023). Fairness and Explainability: Bridging the Gap towards Fair Model Explanations. In: *Proceedings of the 37th AAAI Conference on Artificial Intelligence, AAAI 2023* (*37*, 11363–11371). https://doi.org/10.1609/aaai.v37i9.26344.

4 Human-Centered Explainable AI in Education

Opportunities and Challenges of Large Language Models

Georgios Makridis[1*]

This chapter explores the integration of eXplainable Artificial Intelligence (XAI) in educational contexts through a human-centered lens, examining how AI-driven insights can be meaningfully aligned with the diverse needs of students and educators. As large language models (LLMs) increasingly power educational technologies, their ability to provide natural language explanations presents unprecedented opportunities for personalized learning support and intuitive AI interaction. However, deploying LLM-based XAI systems in educational environments introduces complex challenges requiring careful consideration. The chapter examines the paradoxical nature of using LLMs for explainability—while these models can generate seemingly coherent explanations, their internal mechanisms remain fundamentally opaque. Drawing from human-centered design principles, this work proposes a comprehensive approach for trusted LLM implementation in educational contexts, incorporating safety guardrails, retrieval-augmented generation, advanced reasoning techniques, and virtual persona testing methodologies. The approach emphasizes continuous human oversight and stake holder involvement as essential components for responsible deployment. The chapter concludes by outlining validation strategies and future directions for ethical XAI implementation in educational settings.

1. Introduction

The emergence of large language models (LLMs) represents a paradigmatic shift in educational technology, transforming how knowledge is accessed, processed, and transmitted in learning environments (Beale, 2025). This transformation extends beyond mere technological advancement to challenge core assumptions about teaching, learning, and the nature of educational interaction itself. Since the public deployment of ChatGPT in November 2022, educational institutions worldwide have witnessed an unprecedented acceleration in AI adoption, with recent surveys indicating that over 60% of educators have integrated LLM-powered tools into their pedagogical practices (T. Wang et al., 2025).

[1] University of Piraeus, Attica, Greece.
* Corresponding author: gmakridis@unipi.gr

DOI: 10.1201/9781003713371-4

Rapid integration of LLMs in educational settings manifests itself in diverse applications that span the entire learning ecosystem. Personalized tutoring systems, such as Khan Academy's Khan migo, employ sophisticated Socratic questioning methods to guide student learning without providing direct answers, fostering critical thinking, and problem-solving skills (Troussas et al., 2023). Content generation tools help educators create assessments, develop culturally responsive lesson plans, and produce instructional materials tailored to specific learning objectives (G. Wang & Sun, 2025; Makridis et al., 2024). Advanced applications include automated essay feedback systems that provide detailed writing guidance, language learning platforms that simulate conversational practice, and adaptive learning environments that adjust difficulty to real-time performance evaluation (Labadze et al., 2023; Maity & Deroy, 2024).

Furthermore, the role of LLMs has already extended as tools for explainability, since LLMs can generate natural-language explanations both for their own decisions and for other AI models' outputs, offering an accessible way to communicate with users and support learning processes (Mavrepis et al., 2024). For example, an LLM-powered educational assistant can deliver a step-by-step explanation of a math problem in plain language, making AI guidance far more intuitive for students and teachers. This capacity to provide human-readable justifications unlocks new possibilities for student engagement and personalized instruction. However, this technological revolution introduces various challenges that threaten to undermine its potential. The 'opacity' of LLMs systems containing billions of parameters whose decision-making processes remain largely creates what we might call an "epistemic crisis" in educational contexts (Chu et al., n.d.; Yang et al., 2025). When an AI system recommends a learning path, evaluates student work, or explains complex concepts, the inability to understand its reasoning processes raises critical questions about trust, accountability, and educational validity. This opacity becomes particularly problematic when considering that LLMs can generate explanations that appear coherent and authoritative while being 'hallucinated' sounding but factually incorrect or disconnected from the model's actual computational process (Agarwal et al., 2024; Duan et al., 2024; Lee et al., 2025).

In educational contexts, the impact of hallucinations is high, as errors or biases in AI-generated content directly impact cognitive development and knowledge formation. A hallucinated math ematical explanation might create misconceptions that persist throughout a student's academic career, while biased content generation could reinforce stereotypes or disadvantage vulnerable populations (Bedi et al., 2025; Huang et al., 2025). Research has documented numerous instances where LLMs generate incorrect explanations with unwarranted confidence, potentially misleading students who lack the expertise to identify these errors (Goslen et al., 2025). Furthermore, the educational context introduces requirements that general-purpose AI systems fail to address: developmental appropriateness, cultural sensitivity, curriculum alignment, and support for diverse learners, including those with disabilities or language barriers (Clark et al., 2025; Gouseti et al., 2025).

This chapter presents a comprehensive approach for implementing explainable LLM-based systems in educational contexts, addressing these multifaceted challenges through systematic integration of safety mechanisms, transparency features, and human-centered design principles. Rather than proposing a rigid framework, we advocate for an adaptive approach that recognizes the complexity of educational ecosystems and the need for continuous refinement based on stakeholder feedback and empirical validation. Our approach emerges from extensive analysis of existing implementations, theoretical considerations from educational psychology and AI safety research, and recognition of the fundamental tension between technological capability and pedagogical responsibility.

2. The Current State of Explainable AI in Educational Applications

2.1 Evolution and Current (Run On) Landscape

The quest for explainable AI (XAI) in education has deep historical roots, originating from early expert systems and intelligent tutoring systems that employed transparent rule-based reasoning (Khosravi et al., 2022). These pioneering systems, while limited in flexibility and scope, offered complete interpretability as educators could examine the exact logical rules governing system behavior and trace decision paths from input to output. The transition to machine learning approaches brought increased capabilities but decreased transparency, creating a fundamental tension between perfor mance and explainability that continues to challenge the field (Altukhi & Pradhan, 2025; Makridis et al., 2023).

Contemporary XAI implementations in education employ various technical approaches, each with distinct advantages and limitations. Model-agnostic methods such as SHAP (SHapley Additive exPlanations) (Lundberg & Lee, 2017) and LIME (Local Interpretable Model-agnostic Explanations) (Ribeiro et al., 2016) provide common tools for explaining predictions, but struggle with the scale and complexity of modern LLMs (Bilal et al., 2025). Attention visualization techniques reveal information flow within models, but often produce noisy or counterintuitive results when applied to deep transformer architectures (Zheng et al., 2024). Saliency-based explanations identify influential input tokens through gradient computation, although their educational utility remains questionable given the difficulty of interpreting high-dimensional feature interactions (Feldhus et al., 2022; Mumuni & Mumuni, 2025; Seo et al., 2025).

The emergence of natural language explanations generated by LLMs themselves represents both an opportunity and a challenge for educational XAI. While these explanations appear to solve the interpretability problem through human-readable justifications, research has conclusively demonstrated that such explanations may have little relationship to actual model computations (Singh et al., 2024). This phenomenon of "explanation hallucination" poses particular risks in educational contexts where students may internalize incorrect reasoning patterns as valid problem-solving approaches (Maity and Deroy, 2024).

2.2 The Paradox of Self-Explanation in LLMs

The capacity of LLMs to generate explanations for their own outputs introduces a fundamental paradox, when prompted to explain their reasoning, these models produce text that sounds like logical justification but emerges from the same statistical pattern-matching process used for all text generation (Duan et al., 2024). The LLMs essentially draw upon patterns of explanation encountered in training data, producing plausible-sounding rationales that may be entirely post-hoc and disconnected from actual computational processes (Agarwal et al., 2024).

This paradox becomes particularly acute when considering that LLMs do not 'reason' in any human-recognizable sense. They perform high-dimensional pattern matching across vast parameter spaces, identifying statistical regularities to generate likely text continuations (Singh et al., 2024). The explanations they provide, while often convincing, represent learned patterns of explanatory discourse rather than genuine insights into decision-making processes (Huang et al., 2025).

Educational stakeholders often struggle to navigate this paradox, as the fluency and coherence of LLM-generated explanations can mask their fundamental unreliability. Students, particularly younger learners or those with limited domain expertise, may accept these explanations uncritically, potentially internalizing flawed reasoning patterns (Liu et al., 2024). Educators report difficulty distinguishing between genuine and hallucinated explanations, which undermines their ability to provide appropriate oversight and intervention (Chaudhry, 2023; Miller & Jing, 2024).

2.3 Unique Challenges in Educational Contexts

Educational deployment of XAI faces challenges that extend beyond general technical considerations to encompass pedagogical, developmental, and institutional dimensions. The diversity of educational stakeholders, from kindergarten students to university professors, requires explanation strategies that adapt to vastly different levels of technical sophistication and domain knowledge (Chaudhry et al., 2022).

Regulatory and ethical frameworks introduce additional complexity, as educational AI operates within environments subject to strict privacy regulations, duty-of-care obligations, and institutional accountability requirements (Bellas et al., 2025). For example, the European Union's AI Act mandates specific explainability requirements for high-stakes applications including education.

Cultural and linguistic diversity further complicates educational XAI implementation. Explanation strategies that resonate with students from one cultural background may be confusing or inappropriate for others, requiring careful consideration of cultural communication patterns, pedagogical traditions, and linguistic nuances (Türkmen, 2025). Mathematical reasoning conventions, writing styles, and conceptual frameworks vary significantly across cultures, necessitating adaptive approaches that respect and accommodate this diversity.

3. A Human-Centered Approach to Educational XAI

3.1 Conceptual Foundation

Our approach to implementing explainable AI in educational contexts emerges from a synthesis of human-centered design principles, educational theory, and cutting-edge AI safety research. Rather than treating explainability as a technical feature to be added post-hoc, we position transparency and interpretability as foundational requirements that shape all aspects of system design and deployment. This perspective recognizes that trust in educational AI cannot be achieved through technical solutions alone but requires holistic consideration of technological, pedagogical, and social dimensions.

The approach is based on five interconnected principles that guide design and implementation decisions. *Pedagogical alignment* ensures that AI capabilities serve educational objectives rather than determining them, keeping the focus on learning outcomes over algorithmic optimization. *Developmental sensitivity* requires that all system outputs, including explanations and feedback, match the cognitive and emotional developmental stages of users. *Cultural responsiveness* demands adaptation to diverse educational traditions and learning contexts rather than imposing uniform approaches. *Transparent accountability* establishes clear governance structures that allow stakeholder understanding and contestation of AI decisions. *Continuous refinement* recognizes that educational AI systems must evolve through ongoing feedback from actual classroom deployment, rather than remaining static.

These principles inform a layered architecture where each component addresses specific as pects of a trustworthy LLM deployment while maintaining systemic coherence through bidirectional information flow.

3.2 Architectural Components and Integration

The architectural design reflects the recognition that educational AI systems operate within complex sociotechnical environments where technical capabilities must align with pedagogical practices, institutional constraints, and stakeholder needs. Each layer provides specific functional ity while contributing to overall system coherence through bidirectional interactions.

3.3 Safety and Governance Foundation

The foundational layer establishes comprehensive safety mechanisms tailored to educational contexts, which extend beyond simple content filtering (Dong, Mu, Zhang, et al., 2024). Reinforcement Learning from Human Feedback (RLHF) provides baseline safety training, teaching models to refuse inappropriate requests, and avoid generating harmful content. However, educational safety requires additional considerations including protection of academic integrity, and pedagogical alignment (Dong, Mu, Jin, et al., 2024).

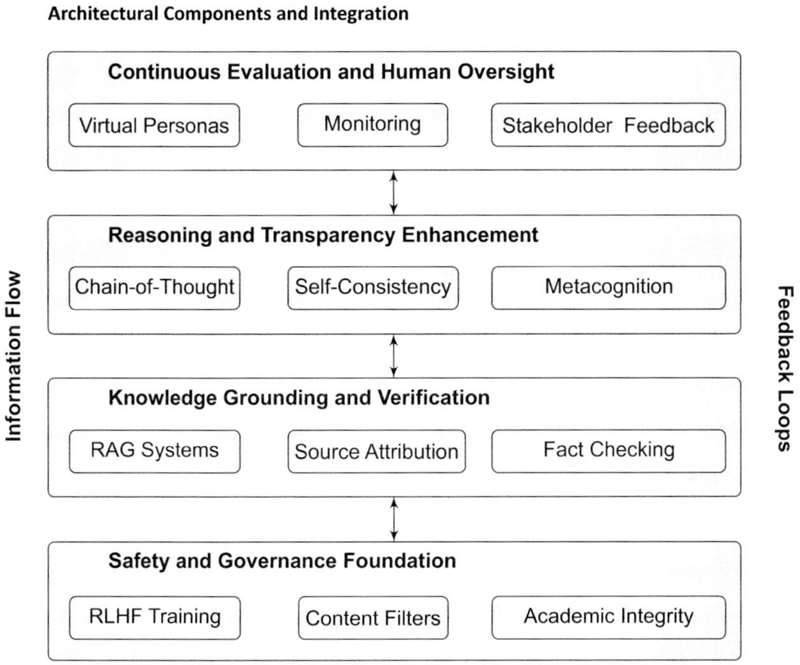

Fig. 1 Layered Architecture for Human-Centered Educational XAI Implementation.

Educational safety guardrails must navigate nuanced boundaries between appropriate support and inappropriate assistance. The system must distinguish between legitimate requests for explanation and attempts to obtain direct answers to assessments, which requires a sophisticated understanding of educational context and intent (Ayyamperumal & Ge, 2024). Age-appropriate content filtering ensures that explanations match developmental stages, preventing exposure to concepts or language that might be harmful or confusing for young learners.

Governance structures establish clear lines of accountability and oversight, enabling educators to maintain awareness and control over AI interactions in their classrooms. Real-time monitoring dashboards provide visibility into system behavior, flagged content, and usage patterns, supporting informed intervention when necessary. This way ensures that any potential issue receives appropriate human review, maintaining the primacy of human judgment in educational decision-making.

3.4 Knowledge Grounding Through Retrieval-Augmented Generation

Retrieval-Augmented Generation (RAG) transforms LLMs from closed systems based solely on training data into open architectures that dynamically access proper educational resources (Gupta et al., 2024). This capability proves essential for ensuring accuracy, currency, and alignment with specific curriculum requirements. Rather than relying on potentially outdated or biased training data, RAG-enabled systems consult curated knowledge bases containing textbooks, peer-reviewed research, validated problem sets, and institution-specific materials (Maity et al., 2024).

The implementation of RAG in educational contexts requires careful attention to source quality and pedagogical appropriateness. Knowledge bases must be continuously maintained and validated, with regular updates to ensure currency and accuracy (Tobler, 2024). Retrieval mechanisms employ semantic search capabilities that understand educational intent, distinguishing between requests for basic concepts, detailed explanations, worked examples, or assessment preparation materials (Nematov et al., 2025). At the same time, source attribution represents a critical feature for educational transparency and academic integrity. Every piece of retrieved information that influences response generation must be properly cited, modeling appropriate scholarly practices while enabling verification of accuracy (Holmes, Miao, et al., 2023).

3.5 Advanced Reasoning and Transparency Mechanisms

The reasoning layer enhances transparency by making problem-solving processes visible through structured approaches that mirror expert thinking (Wei et al., 2022). Chain-of-Thought (CoT) prompting guides models to articulate intermediate steps, transforming opaque answer generation into observable reasoning sequences. This approach serves dual purposes: improving accuracy through systematic thinking and providing educational value by demonstrating problem-solving methodologies (Cohn et al., 2024).

Beyond basic CoT, the approach incorporates subject-specific reasoning patterns that reflect best practices. Mathematical reasoning follows established proof structures, scientific reasoning employs hypothesis-testing frameworks, and literary analysis uses close reading techniques. These specialized approaches ensure that generated explanations not only reach the correct conclusions, but do so through pedagogically correct pathways.

Self-consistency mechanisms address the inherent variability in LLM reasoning by generating multiple solution paths and identifying the most reliable approach. This technique not only improves accuracy, but also provides opportunities for educational enrichment, demonstrating that complex problems often have multiple valid solutions (Lan & Zhou, 2025). Metacognitive prompting adds reflective dimensions, explicitly considering questions about problem understanding and relevant concepts (Y. Wang & Zhao, 2023).

3.6 Continuous Evaluations and Human Oversight

3.6.1 Conceptual Framework for Persona-Based Validation

The validation of educational AI systems presents unique challenges that traditional testing methodologies fail to adequately address. Real-world deployment with actual students raises ethical concerns about potential harm from untested systems, while limited pilot studies may not reveal edge cases or systematic biases that emerge only through extensive use. Virtual persona testing offers an innovative solution, enabling evaluation across diverse user scenarios without risk to actual learners. The same approach has already been incorporated into different frameworks such as Makridis et al. (2025), where virtual personas evaluated XAI approaches in a qualitative manner.

Virtual personas represent carefully constructed profiles that embody specific demographic characteristics, learning styles, cognitive abilities, and behavioral patterns representative of actual student populations following the approach presented in Moon et al. (2024). These personas, implemented through separate LLM instances programmed with detailed backstories and behavioral constraints, interact with educational AI systems in controlled experiments that reveal patterns difficult to observe through traditional testing.

The theoretical foundation for persona-based validation rests on recognition that educational AI must serve heterogeneous populations with vastly different needs, capabilities, and contexts. A system that works well for typical users might fail catastrophically for edge cases—students with learning disabilities, English language learners, or those from underrepresented backgrounds. Virtual personas enable systematic exploration of this diversity, uncovering potential failures before they impact real students.

The construction of educational virtual personas requires careful attention to authenticity and representativeness. Each persona encompasses multiple dimensions that influence educational interactions: demographic characteristics (age, gender, cultural background), cognitive profiles (working memory capacity, processing speed, prior knowledge), learning preferences (visual, auditory, kinesthetic), behavioral tendencies (persistence, help-seeking, frustration tolerance), and contextual factors (technology access, family support, educational goals).

Guided LLM-generated persona backstories provide rich context that guides interaction patterns. Consider 'Maria', a 14-year-old English language learner from a Spanish-speaking house hold, who excels in mathematics but struggles with written expression. Her persona includes specific language patterns (code-switching between English and Spanish), cultural references (preference for collaborative learning reflecting collectivist values), and behavioral traits (reluctance to ask for help due to previous negative experiences). These details enable realistic simulation of how actual students with similar profiles might interact with AI systems.

The implementation process involves programming LLM instances with persona-specific prompts that establish identity, context, and behavioral constraints. These virtual students or educators then engage in extended interactions with the educational AI system under evaluation, attempting various tasks representative of actual educational use: solving problems, asking for explanations, seeking help when confused, and even attempting to game or exploit the system. Interaction logs capture detailed behavioral data enabling further analysis of system responses across diverse user profiles.

3.6.2 Testing Dimensions and Scenarios

Virtual persona testing encompasses multiple evaluation dimensions critical for educational AI deployment. *Fairness and bias assessment* examines whether the system provides equitable support across demographic groups, identifying potential discrimination in explanation quality, feedback detail, or resource recommendations.

Developmental appropriateness testing ensures that content and explanations match cognitive developmental stages, preventing exposure to inappropriate concepts or overwhelming complexity. *Accessibility evaluation* verifies that students with disabilities receive appropriate accommodations and support.

Adversarial testing represents a crucial component, employing personas designed to probe system boundaries and exploit potential vulnerabilities. These adversarial personas simulate students attempting to extract inappropriate content, bypass academic integrity protections, or manipulate the system into providing assessment answers. Such testing reveals security vulnerabilities and helps strengthen protective mechanisms before real-world deployment where motivated students might attempt similar exploits.

Cultural sensitivity assessment uses personas representing diverse cultural backgrounds to identify potential issues with examples, explanations, or interaction styles that might alienate or confuse students from different traditions. Mathematical word problems featuring culturally specific scenarios, idiomatic expressions that don't translate across languages, or pedagogical approaches that conflict with cultural learning preferences can be identified and addressed through systematic persona testing.

3.6.3 Analysis and Iteration

The analysis of virtual persona interactions provides rich insights into system behavior across diverse scenarios. Quantitative metrics capture response accuracy, explanation quality, and safety violations, while qualitative analysis reveals patterns in how the system adapts to different user profiles. Disparities in treatment across personas highlight potential biases that require correction, while consistent failures with specific persona types indicate systemic issues that require architec tural changes.

Iterative refinement based on persona testing results enables systematic improvement before real-world deployment. Identified biases can be addressed through retraining with balanced datasets or implementing fairness constraints in response generation. Safety vulnerabilities discovered through adversarial testing inform strengthened protective mechanisms. Cultural insensitivities revealed through diverse persona testing guide development of more inclusive content and interaction patterns.

The virtual persona approach also enables longitudinal studies simulating extended use over time. Personas can be programmed to evolve, simulating learning progression, changing interests, or developing expertise. This temporal

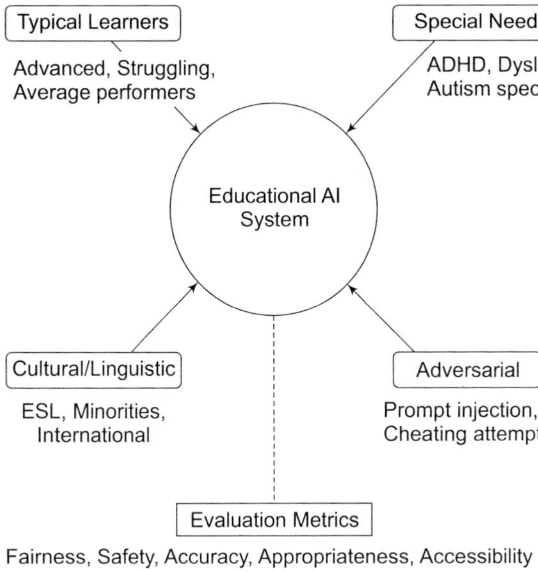

Fig. 2 Virtual Persona Testing Architecture for Educational AI Validation.

dimension reveals how well systems adapt to user growth and whether they maintain appropriate challenge levels as students advance.

3.7 Human Oversight

3.7.1 The Imperative of Human-in-the-Loop Systems

Human oversight in educational AI transcends simple monitoring to encompass active participation in system operation, evaluation, and refinement. The complexity of educational contexts, combined with the high stakes of influencing human development, demands that AI systems augment rather than replace human judgment. This perspective positions educators not as passive consumers of AI capabilities but as essential partners whose expertise, intuition, and ethical judgment remains irreplaceable.

The necessity of human oversight emerges from multiple considerations. Technical limitations of current AI systems, including hallucination tendencies and inability to truly understand context, require human validation of outputs Miller and Jing, 2024. Ethical responsibilities toward students demand human accountability for educational decisions that impact learning and development. Pedagogical expertise that encompasses understanding of individual student needs, classroom dynamics, and long-term educational goals cannot be fully encoded in algorithmic systems (Chaudhry, 2023).

Furthermore, human oversight provides essential feedback for system improvement. Educators possess contextual knowledge about what works in specific classroom settings, which explanations resonate with particular student populations, and when AI assistance helps versus hinders learning. This experiential wisdom, accumulated through years of practice, proves invaluable for refining AI systems to better serve educational goals.

3.7.2 Structured Oversight Mechanisms

Effective human oversight requires structured mechanisms that enable meaningful participation without overwhelming educators with technical complexity. Dashboard interfaces provide real-time visibility into AI system behavior, displaying key metrics about usage patterns, flagged content, and intervention points. These interfaces must balance comprehensive information provision with usability, presenting data in pedagogically meaningful ways rather than raw technical metrics.

Escalation protocols establish clear pathways for human intervention when AI systems encounter scenarios outside their competence. These protocols define trigger conditions (uncertainty thresholds, safety concerns, unusual patterns), notification mechanisms (alerts to appropriate personnel), and intervention procedures (temporary system suspension, human takeover, post-incident review). The design of escalation protocols must consider practical constraints including educator availability, technical expertise, and institutional resources.

3.7.3 Collaborative Governance Models

The governance of educational AI systems requires collaborative models that involve multiple stakeholders in oversight and decision-making. Teachers bring pedagogical expertise and class room experience, administrators provide institutional perspective and resource allocation, students offer direct feedback on system effectiveness and user experience, parents contribute concerns about child safety and development, and technical specialists ensure system reliability and security.

Collaborative governance structures might include AI ethics committees that establish policies for appropriate use, review committees that evaluate new AI tools before deployment, feedback panels that gather ongoing input from users, and incident response teams that address problems as they arise. These structures must be designed to facilitate meaningful participation while avoiding bureaucratic paralysis that prevents beneficial innovation.

4. Challenges and Future Directions

Table 1 presents the essentials for deploying explainable LLMs in education. It maps five areas—technical, pedagogical, ethical/societal, innovation, and interdisciplinarity—from today's limitations to their classroom impact and the most pragmatic research priorities. In short: extra compute/latency and integration/

privacy constraints can disrupt flow and trust; poor pedagogy risks shortcut learning; privacy, bias, and vendor lock-in threaten equity and curricular diversity; current systems remain opaque and centralized; and siloed teams slow real progress. The priorities emphasize efficient XAI-friendly pipelines, stability/faithfulness checks, teacher-centred scaffolding, routine bias/privacy safeguards, multimodal and federated designs, and genuine CS–education co-design with shared evaluation metrics.

Conclusion

This chapter has explored the complex landscape of implementing explainable AI in educational contexts, examining both the tremendous opportunities and significant challenges that LLMs present for teaching and learning. Through analysis of current approaches and their limitations, we have proposed a comprehensive strategy for deploying LLM-based educational systems that prioritizes human-centered design, systematic safety mechanisms, and continuous stakeholder involvement.

Table 1 Essentials for deploying explainable LLMs in education.

Challenge Category	Current Limitations	Educational Implications	Research Priorities
Technical & Computational	• Extra compute for reasoning/RAG • Added latency and variability • Integration and privacy constraints	• Unequal access • (cost/infra) • Disrupted class flow if slow • Trust issues if outputs vary	• Efficient/XAI-friendly pipelines • Stability & faithfulness checks • Easy, standard LMS integration
Ethical & Societal	• Privacy and data risks • Bias in models/ content • Vendor lockin	• Lifelong data exposure • Unequal outcomes • Less curricular diversity	• Privacy-preserving methods • Routine bias audits • Open, auditable options
Innovation Opportunities	• Low interpretability • Centralized pipelines • Text-only interfaces	• Opaque explanations • Higher compliance burden • Limited accessibil-ity/engagement	• Neuro-symbolic XAI • Federated/edge learning • Multimodal/AR-VR tools
Interdisciplinary Needs	• Siloed teams • Misaligned incentives • Little co-design	• Tech over pedagogy • Fragmented evidence • Poor classroom fit	• CS–education partner-ships • Shared metrics & venues • Co-design methods

The approach presented here recognizes that technical solutions alone cannot address the mul tifaceted challenges of educational AI deployment. Rather than treating explainability as a feature to be added to existing systems, we position transparency and interpretability as foundational requirements that shape all aspects of design and implementation. The layered architecture we propose—encompassing safety guardrails, knowledge grounding through retrieval-augmented generation, advanced reasoning techniques, and continuous evaluation—provides a practical pathway for institutions seeking to harness AI capabilities while maintaining educational integrity.

The virtual persona validation methodology offers a novel solution to the challenge of testing educational AI systems comprehensively without risking harm to actual students. By simulating interactions across diverse user profiles, including those with special needs, cultural minorities, and even adversarial users, this approach enables identification and correction of biases, safety vulnerabilities, and pedagogical misalignments before real-world deployment. The systematic nature of persona testing, combined with its scalability and low risk, makes it an essential tool for responsible AI development in educational contexts.

Human oversight emerges not as an optional addition but as an essential component of educational AI systems. The complexity of educational contexts, the vulnerability of student populations, and the high stakes of influencing human development demand that human judgment remains central to AI-assisted education. The structured oversight mechanisms and collaborative governance models we propose enable meaningful human participation while recognizing practical constraints on educator time and technical expertise.

The challenges facing educational XAI implementation—technical, pedagogical, and ethical—are substantial but not insurmountable. Computational requirements will decrease as tech nology advances, integration barriers will fall as standards emerge, and understanding of optimal human-AI collaboration will grow through experience and research. The key lies in maintaining focus on educational goals rather than technological capabilities, ensuring that AI serves human development rather than determining it.

Looking toward the future, the continued evolution of educational AI will require sustained commitment from multiple stakeholders. Technologists must prioritize educational needs over algorithmic elegance, developing systems that are not just powerful but appropriate for learning contexts. Educators must engage actively with AI development, contributing their expertise while remaining open to new possibilities. Policymakers must create frameworks that encourage innovation while protecting student welfare. Researchers must investigate not just immediate effectiveness, but long-term impacts on human development.

The journey toward trustworthy educational AI has only begun. The framework of safety, transparency, validation, and oversight we have outlined provides essential scaffolding, but the edifice of human-centered educational AI must be built through collective effort over time. Each classroom implementation, each student interaction, each educator insight contributes to our growing understanding of how to harness these powerful technologies responsibly. Through sustained commitment to human-centered principles, rigorous validation, and continuous refinement, we can create educational AI systems that augment human capabilities rather than replacing human connections, that promote equity rather than perpetuating bias, and that serve the fundamental purpose of education: nurturing human potential in all its diverse forms.

References

Agarwal, C., Tanneru, S.H. and Lakkaraju, H. (2024). Faithfulness vs. plausibility: On the (un) reliability of explanations from large language models. *arXiv preprint arXiv:2402.04614.*

Altukhi, Z.M. and Pradhan, S. (2025). Systematic literature review: Explainable AI definitions and challenges in education. *arXiv preprint arXiv:2504.02910.*

Ayyamperumal, S.G. and Ge, L. (2024). Current state of LLM risks and AI guardrails. *arXiv preprint arXiv:2406.12934.*

Beale, R. (2025). The revolution has arrived: What the current state of large language models in education implies for the future. *arXiv preprint arXiv:2507.02180.*

Bedi, S., Jiang, Y., Chung, P., Koyejo, S. and Shah, N. (2025). Fidelity of medical reasoning in large language models. *JAMA Network Open*, *8*(8), e2526021–e2526021.

Bellas, F., Ooege, J., Roddeck, L., Rashheed, H.A., Skenduli, M.P., Masdoum, F., Zainuddin, N.B., Gori, J.N., Costello, E., Kralj, L., et al. (2025). Explainable AI in education: Fostering human oversight and shared responsibility.

Bilal, A., Ebert, D. and Lin, B. (2025). LLMs for explainable AI: A comprehensive survey. *arXiv preprint arXiv:2504.00125.*

Chaudhry, M.A. (2023). *A Transparency Index Framework for Machine Learning Powered AI in Education*. Doctoral dissertation, UCL (University College London).

Chaudhry, M.A., Cukurova, M. and Luckin, R. (2022). A transparency index framework for AI in education. In: *International Conference on Artificial Intelligence in Education* (pp. 195–198).

Chu, Z., Wang, S., Xie, J., Zhu, T., Yan, Y., Ye, J., Zhong, A., Hu, X., Liang, J., Yu, P., et al. (n.d.). LLM agents for education: Advances and applications. *arxiv 2025. arXiv preprint arXiv:2503.11733.*

Clark, H.-B., Benton, L., Searle, E., Dowland, M., Gregory, M., Gayne, W. and Roberts, J. (2025). Building effective safety guardrails in AI education tools. In: *International Conference on Artificial Intelligence in Education* (pp. 129–136).

Cohn, C., Hutchins, N., Le, T. and Biswas, G. (2024). A chain-of-thought prompting approach with LLMs for evaluating students' formative assessment responses in science. In: *Proceedings of the AAAI Conference on Artificial Intelligence*, *38*(21), 23182–23190.

Dong, Y., Mu, R., Jin, G., Qi, Y., Hu, J., Zhao, X., Meng, J., Ruan, W. and Huang, X. (2024). Building guardrails for large language models. *arXiv preprint arXiv:2402.01822.*

Dong, Y., Mu, R., Zhang, Y., Sun, S., Zhang, T., Wu, C., Jin, G., Qi, Y., Hu, J., Meng, J., et al. (2024). Safeguarding large language models: A survey. *arXiv preprint arXiv:2406.02622.*

Duan, H., Yang, Y. and Tam, K. Y. (2024). Do LLMs know about hallucination? An empirical investigation of LLM's hidden states. *arXiv preprint arXiv:2402.09733.*

Feldhus, N., Hennig, L., Nasert, M. D., Ebert, C., Schwarzenberg, R. and Möller, S. (2022). Saliency map verbalization: Comparing feature importance representations from model-free and instruction-based methods. *arXiv preprint arXiv:2210.07222.*

Goslen, A., Kim, Y. J., Rowe, J. and Lester, J. (2025). LLM-based student plan generation for adaptive scaffolding in game-based learning environments. *International Journal of Artificial Intelligence in Education*, *35*(2), 533–558.

Gouseti, A., James, F., Fallin, L. and Burden, K. (2025). The ethics of using AI in K-12 education: A systematic literature review. *Technology, Pedagogy, and Education*, *34*(2), 161–182.

Gupta, S., Ranjan, R. and Singh, S. N. (2024). A comprehensive survey of retrieval-augmented generation (rag): Evolution, current landscape, and future directions. *arXiv preprint arXiv:2410.12837*.

Holmes, W., Miao, F., et al. (2023). *Guidance for Generative AI in Education and Research*. UNESCO Publishing.

Huang, L., Yu, W., Ma, W., Zhong, W., Feng, Z., Wang, H., Chen, Q., Peng, W., Feng, X., Qin, B., et al. (2025). A survey on hallucination in large language models: Principles, taxonomy, challenges, and open questions. *ACM Transactions on Information Systems*, *43*(2), 1–55.

Khosravi, H., Shum, S.B., Chen, G., Conati, C., Tsai, Y.-S., Kay, J., Knight, S., Martinez-Maldonado, R., Sadiq, S. and Gašević, D. (2022). Explainable artificial intelligence in education. *Computers and Education: Artificial Intelligence*, *3*, 100074.

Labadze, L., Grigolia, M. and Machaidze, L. (2023). Role of AI chatbots in education: Systematic literature review. *International Journal of Educational Technology in Higher Education*, *20*(1), 56.

Lan, M. and Zhou, X. (2025). A qualitative systematic review on AI empowered self-regulated learning in higher education. *NPJ Science of Learning*, *10*(1), 21.

Lee, S., Lee, H., Heo, S. and Choi, W. (2025). Hudex: Integrating hallucination detection and explainability for enhancing the reliability of LLM responses. *arXiv preprint arXiv:2502.08109*.

Liu, B., Li, C. and Wan, Z. (2024). Using explainable AI (XAI) to identify and intervene with students in need: A review. In: *Proceedings of the 2024 3rd International Conference on Artificial Intelligence and Education* (pp. 636–641).

Lundberg, S. and Lee, S.-I. (2017). A unified approach to interpreting model predictions. *arXiv preprint arXiv:1705.07874*.

Maity, S. and Deroy, A. (2024). Generative AI and its impact on personalized intelligent tutoring systems. *arXiv preprint arXiv:2410.10650*.

Maity, S., Deroy, A. and Sarkar, S. (2024). Leveraging in-context learning and retrieval-augmented generation for automatic question generation in educational domains. In: *Proceedings of the 16th Annual Meeting of the Forum for Information Retrieval Evaluation* (pp. 40–47).

Makridis, G., Fatouros, G., Kiourtis, A., Kotios, D., Koukos, V., Kyriazis, D. and Soldatos, J. (2023). Towards a unified multidimensional explainability metric: Evaluating trustworthiness in AI models. In: *2023 19th International Conference on Distributed Computing in Smart Systems and the Internet of Things (DCOSS-IoT)* (pp. 504–511).

Makridis, G., Koukos, V., Fatouros, G., Kotios, D., Separdani, M. M., Kyriazis, D. and Soldatos, J. (2025). Virtual XAI: A user-centric framework for explainability assessment leveraging gpt-generated personas. In: *2025 21st International Conference on Distributed Computing in Smart Systems and the Internet of Things (DCOSS-IoT)* (pp. 1034–1041).

Makridis, G., Oikonomou, A. and Koukos, V. (2024). Fairyland AI: Personalized fairy tales utilizing chatgpt and Dalle-3. *arXiv preprint arXiv:2407.09467*.

Mavrepis, P., Makridis, G., Fatouros, G., Koukos, V., Separdani, M. M. and Kyriazis, D. (2024). XAI for all: Can large language models simplify explainable AI? *arXiv preprint arXiv:2401.13110*.

Miller, T. and Jing, Z. (2024). Explanation in artificial intelligence: Insights from the social sciences. *Digital Humanities Research*, *4*(2), 90.

Moon, S., Abdulhai, M., Kang, M., Suh, J., Soedarmadji, W., Behar, E. K. and Chan, D. M. (2024). Virtual personas for language models via an anthology of backstories. *arXiv preprint arXiv:2407.06576*.

Mumuni, F. and Mumuni, A. (2025). Explainable artificial intelligence (XAI): From inherent explain ability to large language models. *arXiv preprint arXiv:2501.09967*.

Nematov, I., Kalai, T., Kuzmenko, E., Fugagnoli, G., Sacharidis, D., Hose, K. and Sagi, T. (2025). Source attribution in retrieval-augmented generation. *arXiv preprint arXiv:2507.04480*. Ribeiro, M. T., Singh, S. and Guestrin, C. (2016). "Why should I trust you?" explaining the predictions of any classifier. In: *Proceedings of the 22nd ACM SIGKDD International Conference on Knowledge Discovery and Data Mining* (pp. 1135–1144).

Seo, S., Yoo, S., Lee, H., Jang, Y., Park, J.H. and Kim, J.-N. (2025). A sentence-level visualization of attention in large language models. In: *Proceedings of the 2025 Conference of the Nations of the Americas Chapter of the Association for Computational Linguistics: Human Language Technologies (System Demonstrations)* (pp. 313–320).

Singh, C., Inala, J.P., Galley, M., Caruana, R. and Gao, J. (2024). Rethinking interpretability in the era of large language models. *arXiv preprint arXiv:2402.01761.*

Tobler, S. (2024). Smart grading: A generative AIU-based tool for knowledge-grounded answer evaluation in educational assessments. *MethodsX, 12*, 102531.

Troussas, C., Papakostas, C., Krouska, A., Mylonas, P. and Sgouropoulou, C. (2023). Personalized feedback enhanced by natural language processing in intelligent tutoring systems. In: *International Conference on Intelligent Tutoring Systems* (pp. 667–677).

Türkmen, G. (2025). The review of studies on explainable artificial intelligence in educational research. *Journal of Educational Computing Research, 63*(2), 277–310.

Wang, G. and Sun, F. (2025). A review of generative AI in digital education: Transforming learning, teaching, and assessment. *International Journal of Information and Communication Technology, 26*(19), 102–127.

Wang, T., Zhan, Y., Lian, J., Hu, Z., Yuan, N.J., Zhang, Q., Xie, X. and Xiong, H. (2025). LLM- powered multi-agent framework for goal-oriented learning in intelligent tutoring system. In: *Companion Proceedings of the ACM on Web Conference 2025* (pp. 510–519).

Wang, Y. and Zhao, Y. (2023). Metacognitive prompting improves understanding in large language models. *arXiv preprint arXiv:2308.05342.*

Wei, J., Wang, X., Schuurmans, D., Bosma, M., Xia, F., Chi, E., Le, Q. V., Zhou, D., et al. (2022).Chain-of-thought prompting elicits reasoning in large language models. *Advances in Neural Information Processing Systems, 35*, 24824–24837.

Yang, Y., Shen, Y., Sun, T. and Xie, Y. (2025). Validating the effectiveness of a large language model-based approach for identifying children's development across various free play settings in kindergarten. *arXiv preprint arXiv:2505.03369.*

Zheng, Z., Wang, Y., Huang, Y., Song, S., Yang, M., Tang, B., Xiong, F. and Li, Z. (2024). Attention heads of large language models: A survey. *arXiv preprint arXiv:2409.03752.*

5 When the Model Won't Explain Itself
EPICC as a Framework for Human-Centered Explainability in Educational AI Use

William Cain[1*]

As large language models (LLMs) continue to shape educational practice, the limits of model-level transparency—especially in terms of bias, opacity, and interpretability—necessitate a shift in focus: from explainable models to explainable use. This chapter explores Cain's (2024, 2025) EPICC framework (*Effective Prompting through Iterative Content Knowledge and Critical Thinking*) as a scalable, design-oriented solution for enabling user-centered explainability in AI-enhanced educational environments.

Assuming that current and near-future AI systems will continue to lack meaningful transparency at the algorithmic level, we argue that responsibility for interpretability must shift to the human-AI interface, where educators and learners articulate intentions, assess outputs, and guide revisions. EPICC supports this human-centered explainability by structuring prompt engineering as a reflective, iterative process that makes cognitive, ethical, and epistemic dimensions of AI use visible.

Drawing on student design and use cases from graduate-level instructional design courses and AI literacy workshops, the chapter demonstrates how EPICC equips users to critically evaluate AI outputs, recognize embedded bias or hallucination, and construct trustworthy learning experiences. By embedding explainability in user practice rather than model design, EPICC offers a pragmatic response to the inherent opacity of LLMs—supporting transparent, ethical, and pedagogically sound AI integration in education.

1. Introduction

Generative AI has become one of the most influential learning technologies in education, reshaping how learning is designed, experienced, and assessed. Educational applications of large language models (LLMs) continue to emerge and evolve—teachers employ them to draft lesson plans, students engage with them as writing partners, and administrators explore their potential for feedback, tutoring, and assessment (Yan et al., 2023; Viberg et al., 2023). Yet this integration brings forward persistent questions: whether such systems can be trusted, and whether

[1] University of Wyoming, Wyoming, USA.
* Corresponding author: wcain@uwyo.edu

DOI: 10.1201/9781003713371-5

their operations can be rendered understandable in ways that matter for teaching and learning.

One of the thorniest challenges lies in explainability. While AI (artificial intelligence) researchers have developed a range of methods to peer into the "black box" of machine learning—ranging from feature importance rankings to visualization techniques (Doshi-Velez & Kim, 2017; Guidotti et al., 2018)—these model-level explanations often fail to resonate with educators or learners. A maths teacher deciding whether to trust an AI-generated problem set is not interested in gradient-based attributions; a student revising an essay with AI support is unlikely to benefit from a heat map of token activations. In education, what people need is not technical transparency but practical clarity: the ability to understand, interpret, and act on AI outputs in the context of their goals.

This distinction between **explainable models** and **explainable use** is critical. Traditional explainable AI (XAI) aims to make the inner workings of algorithms visible, typically through technical approximations or simplified models (Ribeiro et al., 2016; Lundberg & Lee, 2017). While valuable in fields like medicine or finance, such explanations rarely translate into the kinds of insights that help educators evaluate the appropriateness, reliability, or fairness of AI in the classroom. What matters for education is not how the model works in the abstract, but how its outputs can be understood and guided within real teaching and learning practices.

This is where a shift in perspective becomes necessary. If we accept that current—and likely near-future—AI systems will remain opaque at the algorithmic level, then the responsibility for interpretability must move to the human-AI interface. It is at this interface that intentions are set, outputs are scrutinized, and revisions are made. Here, explainability becomes less about opening the black box and more about cultivating reflective practices that make AI use itself interpretable.

The EPICC framework (Cain, 2024, 2025) offers one way to anchor this shift. EPICC stands for *Effective Prompting through Iterative Content Knowledge and Critical Thinking*. At its core, the framework treats prompt engineering not as a technical trick but as a structured, reflective process. It emphasizes making intentions explicit, drawing on domain knowledge, applying critical thinking, and iterating based on results. By doing so, EPICC brings the invisible work of AI interaction into the open and makes it easier for educators and learners to explain, justify, and refine their use of generative AI.

This chapter explores EPICC as a pragmatic response to the challenges of educational explainability. Rather than chasing ever-elusive algorithmic transparency, we focus on how users themselves can create explainable practices through structured engagement with AI tools. The chapter begins with a brief overview of explainability in AI and its limits in educational contexts. It then presents the EPICC framework in detail, highlighting how its components connect with established traditions in design, learning theory, and AI literacy. Building on this foundation, we explore how EPICC supports what we call "human-centered explainability"—practices that foreground intentionality, reflection, and ethical awareness at the point of use.

To ground these ideas, the chapter draws on design cases from graduate-level learning design courses and AI literacy workshops. In these contexts, EPICC has helped both students and faculty critically evaluate AI outputs, recognize bias and hallucination, and construct trustworthy learning experiences. These examples illustrate how explainability can be embedded in everyday educational practice—not through technical transparency, but through design-oriented, reflective use.

By reframing explainability as something users do rather than something models provide, EPICC opens a new pathway for integrating AI in education. The goal is not to replace technical efforts at transparency but to complement them with human-centered practices that are accessible, actionable, and pedagogically meaningful. In the sections that follow, we build the case for this shift, argue for EPICC's role as a bridging framework, and outline its implications for research, pedagogy, and policy.

2. Background: Explainability in AI and Education

The conversation around explainability in AI often begins in the technical domain. Over the past decade, researchers have developed a variety of approaches to help illuminate how machine learning models arrive at their predictions. Some methods emphasize feature importance, highlighting which variables had the greatest influence on an output. Others use local approximation models to simplify and "stand in" for the complexity of deep networks (Ribeiro et al., 2016). Still others rely on visualization techniques that map out how inputs relate to outputs across layers of computation (Lundberg & Lee, 2017). Doshi-Velez and Kim (2017) described this pursuit as a push toward a more rigorous science of interpretability, while Guidotti et al. (2018) offered one of the earliest comprehensive surveys of techniques for making black-box models more transparent. Collectively, these efforts form what is often called *explainable AI* (XAI) or *interpretable machine learning* (IML).

From a technical standpoint, XAI methods have been valuable in high-stakes domains such as medicine, finance, and criminal justice, where regulatory requirements or ethical obligations demand some account of how predictions are made. But when we shift into education, the limitations of these methods quickly come into view. Teachers and students rarely have the time, expertise, or inclination to parse gradient maps or surrogate models. More importantly, such explanations are usually disconnected from the everyday decisions that matter in classrooms. A science teacher reviewing an AI-generated quiz does not benefit from knowing which hidden layer weights contributed most to the output. What matters is whether the quiz items are aligned with learning objectives, free from misleading errors, and appropriate for their students' developmental level.

This mismatch is what makes explainability such a stubborn problem in educational AI. Yan et al. (2023), in their scoping review of large language models in education, emphasized that technical transparency often fails to translate into practical clarity. Similarly, Wang et al. (2024) demonstrated through their classroom dialogue analysis that even when AI systems can surface structural insights about conversations, teachers still struggle to connect those insights to actionable strategies. The gap here is not just about usability but about relevance: technical explanations address the 'how' of the model's mechanics, while educators need clarity about the "so what" for learning and teaching.

This gap also has roots in the way AI first emerged into education discourse. As Cain (2023) showed in an analysis of scholarly and popular writing on AI in education, much of the early conversation was polarized: on one side, warnings about black-box opacity and risks of bias; on the other, celebratory narratives about AI's transformative potential. These formative tensions meant that educators were left with competing discourses—some framing AI as dangerously inscrutable, others as a revolutionary teaching partner. The net effect was confusion about what 'explainability' really ought to mean for classrooms. Should teachers expect to see inside the algorithm, or should they demand clarity at the level of pedagogical practice? This unsettled discourse laid the groundwork for today's challenges, where technical transparency and educational explainability remain misaligned.

Another dimension is trust. Research consistently shows that educators' willingness to adopt AI depends not only on whether systems perform accurately, but also on whether they feel understandable and trustworthy. Viberg et al. (2023), in a cross-national study of teachers' perceptions, found that explainability was a major factor in shaping trust—yet the kind of explanations teachers wanted were rarely technical. Instead, they valued domain-specific, contextually meaningful accounts. Feldman-Maggor et al. (2025) explored this more directly, showing that when AI systems offered explanations tied to specific teaching domains, teachers' trust and acceptance increased significantly. A math teacher who sees not just that an AI recommends a lesson sequence, but why that sequence builds on prerequisite concepts in algebra, is far more likely to adopt the recommendation than if offered a generic performance score.

These findings highlight a growing consensus: in education, explainability must be reframed around human needs rather than model mechanics. Teachers want to know how AI outputs connect to curriculum goals, whether they can be adapted to their classrooms, and whether hidden biases might be at play. Students, for their part, want clarity about how AI can support their learning without replacing their agency or misleading them with hallucinated facts. Technical visualizations or local approximations simply do not meet these needs.

This reframing connects closely to ongoing work in AI literacy and competency. Long and Magerko (2020) proposed an early framework for AI literacy in education, emphasizing that learners should be able to critically interpret AI outputs, question their validity, and recognize potential biases. Chiu et al. (2024) extended this work by offering a comprehensive framework for AI literacy and competency that highlights the skills needed to use AI tools effectively and responsibly. Both sets of authors converge on the point that explainability is not just about algorithms but also about equipping humans with the knowledge and practices to interpret and evaluate AI in context.

Seen this way, explainability in education becomes less a matter of decoding black boxes and more a matter of cultivating interpretive practices. Teachers must learn to ask: *What was I trying to accomplish with this AI prompt? Does the output align with my pedagogical goals? Where might biases or errors lurk? How should I adapt this material for my learners?* Students, likewise, must be encouraged to view AI as a partner that requires critical oversight rather than a source of ready-made answers.

The limitations of model-level explanations, the evidence about trust and perception, and the unsettled discourse that has shaped early adoption (Cain, 2023) all point to a shared conclusion: if AI is to be explainable in education, the focus must shift toward the human-AI interface. It is at this interface that intentions are articulated, outputs are evaluated, and revisions are guided. Technical explainability may still play a role, but it is not sufficient on its own. What is required is a framework that helps educators and learners make their use of AI itself explainable—transparent to themselves, to others, and to the learning process.

This is the rationale for moving from explainable models to explainable use. The next section introduces one such framework: EPICC, which situates explainability not in the hidden workings of AI systems but in the visible, reflective practices of those who use them.

3. The EPICC Framework

The turn from explainable models to explainable use requires more than a shift in mindset; it requires a structured way of engaging with AI that makes intentions, reasoning, and reflection explicit. This is the role of the EPICC framework. Developed and refined through classroom and research practice (Cain, 2024a, 2024b, 2025), EPICC—*Effective Prompting through Iterative Content Knowledge and Critical Thinking*—is designed to help users structure their interactions with large language models in ways that foreground explainability at the point of use.

At its core, EPICC frames prompt engineering not as a technical trick for 'hacking' AI systems, but as a design practice. Prompts are treated as moments of cognition—articulations of intent, grounded in knowledge, shaped by critical questioning, and refined through iteration. By making these elements visible, EPICC creates a process that is inherently more transparent and accountable.

3.1 Origins and Rationale

The EPICC framework first emerged in Cain's (2024a) work on prompt engineering as a transformative practice in education. That study emphasized that prompting is not simply about eliciting better outputs from AI but about shaping the very conditions of human-AI interaction. In parallel, research on AI-enhanced online learning (Cain, 2024b) highlighted how structured, intentional design processes could help faculty and students embed AI tools into learning environments in transparent and assessable ways. Taken together, these studies revealed a recurring pattern: the most meaningful and explainable uses of AI arose when prompts were crafted iteratively, anchored in domain knowledge, and interrogated critically.

In graduate-level design courses, for example, students who used AI without a structured approach often found themselves overwhelmed or misled by inconsistent outputs. Those who articulated clear intentions, documented iterations, and evaluated responses against their disciplinary knowledge achieved more useful results—and, importantly, were able to explain how they arrived at those results. These observations crystallized into the EPICC framework, which positions prompt engineering as a reflective design practice rather than a technical shortcut.

3.2 Components of EPICC

EPICC consists of four interconnected components, best represented as a circular flow (Cain, 2024a, Figure 1):

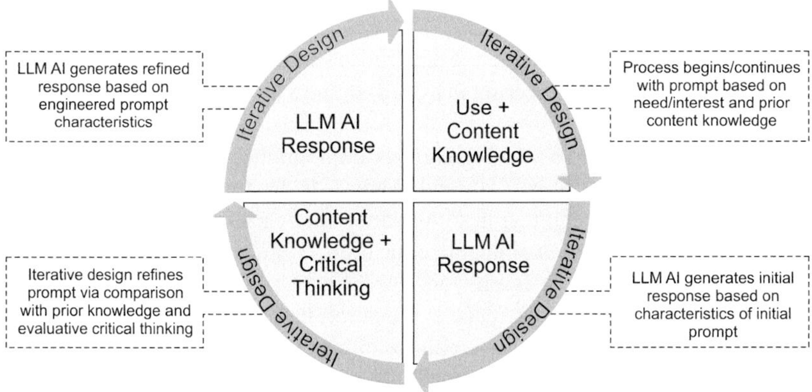

Fig. 1 The Framework for Effective Prompting through Iterative Content Knowledge and Critical Thinking (EPICC).

- **Content Knowledge:** Users bring their own expertise to bear. Rather than outsourcing judgment to AI, EPICC encourages applying disciplinary knowledge to guide prompts, evaluate outputs, identify errors, and contextualize results. This includes asking: *What is the task? What constraints or style should shape the output?* Making the purpose and background of a prompt explicit not only improves AI responses but also makes the reasoning behind the request visible to others.
- **Critical Thinking:** EPICC requires users to question the reliability, bias, and ethical implications of AI outputs. Why did the model generate this response? Where might hallucinations appear? What assumptions are embedded in the phrasing?
- **Iteration:** AI use is never a one-shot process. EPICC emphasizes cycles of prompting, receiving, evaluating, and revising. Each cycle generates

artifacts—versions of outputs and reflections—that make the trajectory of reasoning transparent.

Together, these components reinforce one another. Content knowledge establishes a grounded starting point, iteration makes the process visible through refinement, and critical thinking ensures outputs are interrogated rather than accepted at face value. In practice, effective prompting emerges from the interplay of all three, captured in EPICC's circular flow: an iterative, reflective cycle that mirrors how learners and educators construct meaning in dialogue with AI.

3.3 Contrasting EPICC with Other Frameworks

EPICC does not stand alone in recognizing the importance of prompt engineering, but its emphasis on design and explainability distinguishes it from other approaches. Federiakin (2024), for instance, frames prompt engineering as a new 21st-century skill, emphasizing its role in the broader digital skillset needed for modern work and learning. While aligned in spirit, this view tends to treat prompting as a skill to be acquired rather than a reflective practice to be cultivated. EPICC goes further by embedding prompt engineering in cycles of knowledge application and critical reasoning.

Technical frameworks also highlight prompt engineering, though often from a system-oriented perspective. Hu and Wang (2024), for example, propose the FOKE framework, which integrates foundation models with knowledge graphs to provide personalized and explainable education. Similarly, Swamy et al. (2024) developed iLLuMinaTE, a framework for using LLMs to generate actionable feedback grounded in social science explanation theories. These frameworks are powerful at the system level but remain primarily technical. EPICC, by contrast, positions itself squarely at the user level: its purpose is not to make models more interpretable but to make user practices more explainable.

3.4 EPICC as a Bridge between Design and AI Literacy

One of the reasons EPICC resonates in educational settings is its grounding in design traditions. Design thinking emphasizes iteration, empathy, and problem framing (Kolko, 2015; Norman, 2013). Instructional design models, from Merrill's (2002) First Principles of Instruction to Branch's (2009) ADDIE approach, highlight systematic processes for clarifying goals, structuring solutions, and evaluating outcomes. Cain (2024b) extended these traditions into AI-enhanced online learning, showing how intentional design and assessment frameworks can integrate AI in ways that remain transparent and pedagogically grounded. EPICC builds directly on this lineage by treating AI interaction as a form of design—where each prompt and iteration is a step in structuring learning experiences.

At the same time, EPICC aligns with emerging frameworks for AI literacy and competency. Chiu et al. (2024) argue that AI literacy requires competencies in both technical understanding and critical engagement. Long and Magerko

(2020) emphasize interpretive and ethical dimensions, urging educators to prepare students not only to use AI but to question it. EPICC bridges these literacies with design practice, providing a structured method for turning critical engagement into visible, explainable action.

3.5 Why EPICC Matters for Explainability

By structuring prompt engineering as a reflective design process, EPICC directly addresses the limitations outlined in the previous section. It shifts explainability from being a property of the model to being a property of use. When educators and students apply EPICC, they create artifacts—prompts, iterations, reflections—that make their reasoning visible. These artifacts can be shared with peers, integrated into assignments, or documented for accountability. They offer an explanation not of *how the model works* but of *how the human used the model.*

This reorientation matters for trust, ethics, and pedagogy. Trust is built when intentions and reasoning are transparent, even if the model itself remains opaque. Ethical concerns—such as bias or hallucination—become manageable when they are systematically interrogated as part of the process. Pedagogically, EPICC creates teachable moments: opportunities for students to see not just outputs but the thinking and iteration behind them.

In short, EPICC provides a structured pathway for human-centered explainability in education. It operationalizes reflection and iteration, situates AI use within disciplinary knowledge, and insists on critical engagement. As the next section will show, these practices translate into concrete strategies for making AI use explainable in real educational contexts.

4. Human-Centered Explainability through EPICC

If explainability in education cannot realistically come from model-level transparency, then it must emerge through the way humans engage with AI. EPICC provides a structured pathway for this shift, positioning explainability as something *users do* rather than something *systems reveal*. By emphasizing intentions, iteration, content knowledge, and critical thinking, the framework embeds interpretability directly into the human-AI interface. This section illustrates how EPICC operationalizes "explainable use" through three main strategies: making intentions explicit, documenting iterative cycles, and cultivating awareness of bias and hallucination.

4.1 Making Intentions Explicit

One of the simplest but most powerful moves EPICC encourages is stating intentions clearly. When users craft prompts that specify goals, constraints, and context, they generate not only better outputs but also a transparent record of what they were trying to achieve. A teacher asking an AI system to "generate three debate prompts for 10th grade students on climate change, aligned with NGSS standards, emphasizing critical thinking" is doing more than requesting content – they are making their pedagogical intent visible.

This practice echoes competencies highlighted in AI literacy frameworks (Long & Magerko, 2020; Chiu et al., 2024), where clarity of purpose is a cornerstone of responsible use. It also echoes design traditions (Norman, 2013; Kolko, 2015), where problem framing shapes the quality of solutions. In the context of explainability, explicit intentions help others—students, colleagues, administrators—understand *why* AI was engaged and how its outputs should be interpreted.

4.2 Iterating and Documenting Prompt/Response Cycles

Explainability grows stronger when users treat AI interaction as a cycle rather than a one-off exchange. EPICC's iterative component emphasizes prompting, evaluating, revising, and re-prompting, with each step leaving behind an artifact. For example, a faculty member developing case studies might begin with a broad request, receive a generic output, and then refine the prompt with discipline-specific details. Documenting each iteration creates a visible trajectory of reasoning—showing how the user guided the AI toward a more accurate or relevant result.

Kolko (2015) describes iteration as central to design thinking; Norman (2013) likewise emphasizes reflective cycles in human-technology interaction. By adopting these cycles with AI, educators generate their own form of transparency. Iterations can be shared with students as part of assignments, included in reflective journals, or integrated into portfolios. The result is a traceable record of *how* AI was used, which demystifies both the tool and the process.

4.3 Bias and Hallucination Awareness

Perhaps the most pressing challenge for generative AI in education is the risk of bias and hallucination. LLMs can reproduce stereotypes, embed cultural biases, or generate factually incorrect information while presenting it with confidence. EPICC explicitly requires critical interrogation of outputs: What assumptions are embedded in this text? Does it reflect balanced perspectives? Are any factual claims verifiable?

This aligns with emerging scholarship on ethics in AI for education. Yan et al. (2023) identify bias and misinformation as practical and ethical challenges for classroom use. Holmes et al. (2022) call for frameworks that equip educators to critically evaluate AI recommendations, rather than trusting them at face value. By embedding bias awareness into every iteration, EPICC transforms explainability into an ethical practice: users can explain not only what AI produced, but also what limitations or risks they identified along the way.

4.4 Alignment with Ethical Frameworks

Human-centered explainability does not exist in a vacuum. It connects with broader ethical frameworks that call for transparency, fairness, and accountability in educational technology. Holmes et al. (2022) outlined a community-wide ethics framework for AI in education, emphasizing that responsible use requires shared practices as well as technical safeguards. Li et al. (2025), interpreting UNESCO's global AI in education guidelines, situate explainability within sustainable development goals—arguing that transparency and accountability are prerequisites for equitable and responsible adoption worldwide.

EPICC can be read as a pragmatic pedagogy for meeting these calls. It does not solve the problem of opaque algorithms, but it equips educators and students with habits of reflection, iteration, and documentation that make their use of AI interpretable to others. In this way, explainability shifts from being an elusive technical fix to being a teachable, assessable practice.

4.5 Explainable Use as Pedagogy

The real significance of EPICC is not technical but pedagogical. By treating explainability as a human-centered practice, EPICC reframes how AI is integrated into learning environments. Instructors can design assignments that require students to show their prompt iterations alongside final outputs, encouraging transparency of reasoning. Faculty can adopt reflective journals where they document their use of AI in course preparation, making their decision-making visible to colleagues and learners. Students can be guided to critique AI-generated material, not just consume it—developing critical literacy in the process.

This move mirrors the larger point made in Cain (2025), and Kell, Kraeer, and Cain (2025): when AI is positioned as a cognitive partner, its value comes not from replacing human judgment but from catalyzing reflective and dialogic processes. EPICC operationalizes this partnership by making explainability a built-in outcome of use.

In short, human-centered explainability is less about prying open the black box of AI and more about creating transparent, reflective practices at the human-AI interface. Through explicit intentions, iterative documentation, and critical interrogation of outputs, EPICC enables educators and learners to explain *their use* of AI, even if the models themselves remain opaque. This shift reframes explainability not as an elusive technical aspiration but as a concrete pedagogical strategy - one that makes AI use visible, interpretable, and accountable within education.

5. Case Studies from Practice

The EPICC framework moves from theory into practice when applied in real educational contexts. While abstract principles of prompt engineering and explainability provide conceptual grounding, the true test is how educators and learners use these ideas in their day-to-day work. The following case studies illustrate how EPICC has been taken up in graduate-level LDT coursework, faculty development workshops, and K–12 and higher education classrooms. To protect privacy, student names have been changed and identifying details adjusted while preserving the integrity of their professional contexts. Together, these vignettes highlight the power of human-centered explainability across settings where the opacity of AI models might otherwise undermine trust and learning.

5.1 Graduate-Level LDT Courses

In a graduate-level design course, students were encouraged to apply EPICC in their projects, documenting iterations of prompts and reflecting on how they used AI. Three examples illustrate the breadth of contexts in which EPICC can create explainable practice.

- **Melissa: Organizational Development and Training** Melissa worked in corporate training and leadership development, where AI was being explored as a way to streamline LMS content and coaching resources. Initially, she approached AI with straightforward prompts such as "Generate a leadership training module ". The outputs looked polished but generic, and Melissa found it difficult to justify them to her colleagues. By applying EPICC, she reframed her process: instead of asking for ready-made content, she clarified her intent ("designing for mid-career managers in water management"), iterated prompts to refine scope, and layered her own knowledge of leadership coaching into the evaluation. Through critical thinking, she identified places where the AI's recommendations leaned on clichéd leadership models or omitted the specific organizational culture she wanted to foreground. Documenting these iterations allowed her to explain to colleagues not only what she produced but *how* she had guided the AI to produce it. For Melissa, explainability became a design asset: the process trail gave her organization confidence that the final module was not simply AI-generated but thoughtfully curated.
- **Jordan: Creative Dissemination and Gamification** Jordan came from a makerspace and STEM background and was passionate about designing creative dissemination tools such as educational board games. She saw AI as a brainstorming partner but worried that the creative process would become unexplainable—"the machine just spit this out". Using EPICC, she began each project by stating her design intention clearly (e.g., "a cooperative board game that teaches environmental sustainability to middle school students"). She then iterated prompts, asking for mechanics, narrative hooks, and playtesting scenarios, while cross-checking each suggestion against her content expertise in STEM education. Critical thinking became essential as she identified where the AI over-relied on popular culture tropes or failed to account for age-appropriate complexity. By keeping a record of iterations, Jordan was able to show her peers how AI ideas were incorporated, adapted, or rejected. Her explainability was not about the AI's algorithm, but about the *design reasoning* she applied throughout. EPICC gave her a way to make creativity both transparent and accountable.

- **Claire: Nursing Faculty in Distance Education** Claire taught nursing students in both clinical and distance settings, where clarity and trust were critical. She experimented with AI to design case studies for online learners, initially worried that AI's hallucinations might undermine credibility. Applying EPICC, she started by explicitly framing prompts around specific patient profiles, learning objectives, and ethical considerations. She iterated outputs, asking AI to revise for realism and alignment with clinical standards. Drawing on her content knowledge, Claire cross-checked every case with professional nursing guidelines, and through critical thinking, she flagged and corrected AI-generated stereotypes around mental health. Importantly, she shared her iterative prompt-output cycle with her students as part of the learning experience. Students not only engaged with the case studies but also saw *how* the materials were generated and refined. This transparency built trust, as learners recognized that their instructor was critically mediating AI rather than presenting unvetted content. For Claire, EPICC transformed AI from a liability into a teachable tool for ethical practice.

Together, these vignettes from Melissa, Jordan, and Claire illustrate how EPICC enables graduate students and professionals to make AI use explainable in diverse settings. Whether in corporate training, creative game design, or healthcare education, EPICC shifts the emphasis from what AI produces to how humans guide and refine the process.

5.2 AI Literacy Workshops

Faculty development workshops provided another venue for applying EPICC. Here, participants ranged from experienced instructors to graduate students building curricula for the first time. Two examples illustrate how human-centered explainability was fostered in these contexts.

- **Diana: Social Work Faculty in Hyflex Teaching** Diana, a faculty member in social work, had extensive experience teaching in hyflex formats but was new to integrating AI. Her concern was how to make decisions about the use of AI transparent to students, who often worried about equity and trust in hybrid learning environments. In the workshop, she applied EPICC by explicitly stating her instructional intent when prompting ("adapt a case study on child welfare for both online and in-person students"). She iterated outputs across formats, comparing how AI suggestions would play differently in face-to-face vs. online discussions. Using her content expertise in social work, she flagged where AI responses risked oversimplifying complex systemic issues. Her critical reflection centered on how AI outputs might inadvertently marginalize vulnerable groups. By documenting her process, Diana was able to show her students not only the final activity but also her reasoning in shaping it. For her, EPICC provided a method for aligning transparency with her ethical commitments as a social work educator.

- **Sophie: Curriculum Design from Scratch** Sophie, a full-time graduate student, was developing equine curriculum materials – an area with little preexisting AI training data. She found that generic prompts produced irrelevant or inaccurate material. Using EPICC, Sophie began with clear intentions ("developing a lesson on equine anatomy for beginning riders"), iterated prompts with increasing specificity, and layered her growing disciplinary expertise into each cycle. She critically assessed outputs for factual accuracy and ethical appropriateness (e.g., ensuring AI did not misrepresent animal welfare). By documenting her iterations, Sophie created a transparent pathway from vague AI output to credible curriculum materials. This not only supported her own learning but also demonstrated to peers how explainability emerges when humans guide AI into less familiar domains.

In both Diana's and Sophie's cases, EPICC supported explainability as a visible, teachable process. Faculty and students alike were able to articulate how and why they engaged with AI, providing transparency in contexts where trust and credibility were paramount.

5.3 Comparative Anchor Cases

While course projects and workshops provide vivid accounts of EPICC in practice, comparative anchor cases show how these local practices align with broader findings in the research literature.

- **Marco: K-12 Classroom Teacher and Dialogue Analysis** Marco, a third-grade teacher, used AI to analyze classroom discussions, inspired by Wang et al. (2024), who explored explainable AI in dialogue analysis. Initially, Marco asked AI to "summarize student discussion themes", but the results felt opaque—summaries lacked justification or actionable clarity. Using EPICC, Marco clarified his intent ("identify how many students are asking clarifying questions during group discussions"), iterated prompts to refine the scope, and applied his knowledge of developmental language norms to evaluate results. His critical reflection focused on where AI summaries might misrepresent student intent. Documenting iterations allowed Marco to explain to colleagues and parents how the analysis was conducted and what it did—and did not—show. In this way, EPICC helped him mirror the teacher-facing explainability strategies outlined in Wang et al.'s study (2024) while embedding them in classroom practice.
- **Ethan: Higher Education Computer Science Faculty and Domain-Specific Explanations** Ethan, a faculty member in computer science, explored AI for designing online programming exercises. He was struck by the findings of Feldman-Maggor et al. (2025), which showed that teachers' trust in AI improves when explanations are tied to their domain. Applying EPICC, Ethan began by making his instructional intent explicit ("create a debugging exercise in Python for students learning recursion"), iterated prompts to

refine complexity, and used his disciplinary expertise to evaluate outputs for accuracy and pedagogical fit. His critical reflection centered on where AI introduced inefficient or non-idiomatic code. Documenting this process provided a domain-specific explanation he could share with students: not simply "the AI wrote this code", but "here is how I refined and corrected it". The transparency of his process built trust in the exercises and aligned with Feldman-Maggor et al.'s findings (2025) on the power of domain-specific explainability.

Together, Marco's and Ethan's cases highlight how EPICC translates insights from the research literature into everyday teaching. By situating explainability at the human-AI interface, educators can operationalize practices that align with empirical findings while remaining grounded in their own contexts.

5.4 Synthesis and Takeaways

Across these case studies, a consistent pattern emerges: EPICC equips educators and students to make their use of AI explainable through intentionality, iteration, knowledge, and critical reflection. In graduate courses, Melissa, Jordan, and Claire used EPICC to turn AI from a source of opacity into a tool for transparent design. In workshops, Diana and Sophie found that documenting their processes not only improved outcomes but also made their reasoning visible to learners. In anchor cases, Marco and Ethan demonstrated how EPICC aligns with broader research, embedding domain-specific and teacher-facing explainability into practice.

These examples show that explainability in education need not rely on technical transparency at the model level. Instead, it can be cultivated through human-centered practices that leave behind visible trails of reasoning. EPICC makes these trails systematic, turning AI use into something that can be explained, justified, and shared. The case studies also underscore the versatility of EPICC: whether in corporate training, curriculum design, nursing education, social work, K-12 classrooms, or computer science, the framework adapts to diverse contexts without losing its core emphasis on reflective, iterative engagement.

Most importantly, these cases illustrate that explainable use is not an abstract aspiration but a practical pedagogy. By embedding EPICC into their work, educators and students generate transparency where models cannot provide it—building trust, supporting ethics, and fostering deeper learning.

6. Implications and Opportunities

The case studies illustrate how EPICC functions in practice, but they also point to broader implications for pedagogy, research, and policy. By shifting explainability from models to use, EPICC opens new opportunities for educators and institutions to integrate AI in ways that are transparent, ethical, and pedagogically meaningful.

6.1 Pedagogical Implications

From a teaching and learning perspective, EPICC suggests that AI should not be treated as a silent assistant operating in the background but as a tool whose use is itself part of the learning process. When instructors make their prompting strategies visible, they create a model of reflective practice that students can emulate. Assignments can require learners to document prompt iterations alongside final products, making their reasoning transparent and assessable. This moves explainability into the heart of pedagogy: the focus is no longer only on what students produce but also on how they engage with AI critically and intentionally.

Instructional design models provide a useful anchor here. Merrill's (2002) First Principles of Instruction emphasize the importance of activation, demonstration, application, and integration; Branch's (2009) ADDIE model highlights analysis and evaluation as systematic steps in design. EPICC aligns naturally with these traditions by embedding analysis (intentions), iteration (design and development), evaluation (critical thinking), and integration (reflection and sharing). In faculty development, EPICC can also serve as a scaffold for instructors who are hesitant to integrate AI, offering a clear, design-oriented pathway that foregrounds explainability rather than blind trust. Holmes et al. (2022) noted that shared ethical frameworks are needed across institutions; EPICC provides one pedagogically grounded entry point into such frameworks.

6.2 Research Implications

For researchers, EPICC offers both a conceptual and methodological lens. Conceptually, it bridges the gap between AI literacy and instructional design. Chiu et al. (2024) call for comprehensive frameworks to define the skills needed for AI use, while Federiakin (2024) positions prompt engineering as a new 21st-century skill. EPICC contributes to this conversation by showing how prompting can be structured as reflective practice rather than a technical trick. This reframing opens up opportunities for empirical work: How do students' documented iterations correlate with learning outcomes? What kinds of critical questions are most effective in surfacing bias or hallucination? How does explainable use affect trust, adoption, and long-term competency in AI-supported learning?

Methodologically, EPICC invites research designs that treat prompt-output cycles as data. Iterative prompts can be analyzed as artifacts of cognition, revealing how learners refine their goals, apply content knowledge, and interrogate AI responses. This provides a novel source of evidence for studying reflection, metacognition, and critical thinking in the age of AI. Cain's own work on generative AI in graduate design courses (2025) and in supporting online learning experiences (2024b) illustrates how EPICC-informed research can yield insights into both pedagogy and design.

6.3 Policy Implications

At the policy level, the question of explainability has become increasingly urgent. UNESCO's global guidelines for AI in education, as interpreted by Li et al. (2025), emphasize transparency, accountability, and alignment with sustainable development goals. Yet these guidelines often assume that technical solutions to explainability will emerge from AI developers. EPICC reframes this assumption: while model transparency remains limited, policy can encourage institutions to cultivate *human-centered explainability* through design frameworks like EPICC.

This has two important implications. First, policy initiatives can support professional development that trains educators in reflective prompt engineering, treating it as part of digital literacy. Second, accreditation and quality assurance processes—such as those modeled in Quality Matters or national instructional standards—can incorporate explainability as a design criterion. Rather than asking whether the AI system itself is interpretable, policies could ask whether the *use* of AI in courses is documented, transparent, and ethically guided.

6.4 Positioning EPICC in the XAI/IML Discourse

Finally, EPICC's contribution to the broader discourse on explainable AI should be understood as complementary rather than oppositional. Technical frameworks such as LIME (Ribeiro et al., 2016), SHAP (Lundberg & Lee, 2017), and surveys by Doshi-Velez & Kim (2017) or Guidotti et al. (2018) remain critical for fields that demand algorithmic accountability. But in education, where decisions hinge on pedagogy, trust, and human reasoning, EPICC fills a crucial gap by shifting attention to the interpretive practices of users.

In this sense, EPICC positions itself as a bridge: it acknowledges the importance of model-level transparency but insists that in many learning environments, the most immediate form of explainability will come from human-centered use. This positioning aligns with Cain's earlier call to examine AI's formative tensions in education (2023) and his proposal that generative AI should be understood as a cognitive partner rather than a deterministic system (2025).

Synthesis

The implications of EPICC extend beyond classroom anecdotes. They suggest a broader vision for AI in education—one where transparency comes not only from engineers but also from educators and learners who intentionally shape their interactions with AI. Pedagogically, EPICC turns explainability into a teachable skill. For researchers, it provides both a lens and a dataset for studying human-AI collaboration. For policymakers, it reframes transparency as a practice to be supported institutionally, not just a property of the model to be demanded from developers.

By embedding explainability into the human-AI interface, EPICC offers a pragmatic, scalable pathway for trustworthy AI integration. It does not eliminate the opacity of large language models, but it ensures that opacity does not have to be the final word in educational practice.

Conclusion

The challenge of explainability in AI has often been framed as a technical problem: if only models could reveal their inner workings more clearly, educators and students would know when and how to trust them. Yet as this chapter has argued, in education the real need is not for algorithmic transparency but for human-centered clarity. Teachers and learners rarely benefit from saliency maps or surrogate models. What they require is the ability to make sense of AI outputs in relation to their goals, their expertise, and their ethical commitments.

The EPICC framework responds to this challenge by shifting the focus from *explainable models* to *explainable use*. By structuring AI interaction through Effective Prompting, Iteration, Content Knowledge, and Critical Thinking, EPICC turns every engagement with AI into a process that can be documented, shared, and reflected upon. This shift does not resolve the opacity of large language models at the algorithmic level, but it does ensure that opacity need not define educational practice.

The case studies show how this shift plays out in real contexts. Melissa used EPICC to build trust in corporate training by documenting her iterative design choices. Jordan made creativity explainable by revealing how she refined game design ideas. Claire modeled transparency for her nursing students by showing how case studies were critically vetted. Diana and Sophie demonstrated that explainability can be cultivated in both faculty practice and student curriculum design. Marco and Ethan illustrated how EPICC aligns with empirical findings on teacher-facing and domain-specific explainability. Across settings, the common thread was that explainability emerged not from the AI itself but from how humans engaged with it.

The implications are significant. Pedagogically, EPICC suggests that explainability can and should be taught as part of digital and AI literacy. Research-wise, it provides a lens for studying how iterative prompt cycles reflect critical thinking and metacognition. At the policy level, it reframes explainability as a practice that institutions can support through faculty development, curricular standards, and ethical guidelines. Taken together, these implications point toward a broader vision: AI in education that is trustworthy not because it has been made transparent at the algorithmic level, but because it is used transparently at the human level.

The central claim of this chapter is thus straightforward: when the model will not explain itself, users must explain their use of the model. EPICC provides a structured, design-oriented way to make this possible. By embedding explainability in the human-AI interface, educators and learners create a culture of transparency that builds trust, addresses ethical concerns, and enhances learning.

As AI continues to evolve, technical efforts at explainability will no doubt advance. But waiting for perfect transparency risks leaving educators without the tools they need now. EPICC offers a pragmatic, immediately applicable framework—one that complements technical advances while centering the human practices that define education. In doing so, it affirms a simple but powerful principle: in education, the most important explanations are not about how models work, but about how people work with models.

References

Branch, R.M. (2009). *Instructional Design: The ADDIE Approach.* Springer.

Cain, W. (2023). AI emergence in education: Exploring formative tensions across scholarly and popular discourse. *Journal of Interactive Learning Research*, *34*(2), 239–273. https://www.learntechlib.org/primary/p/222352/.

Cain, W. (2024a). Prompting change: Exploring prompt engineering in large language model AI and its potential to transform education. *Tech.Trends*, *68*(1), 47–57. https://doi.org/10.1007/s11528-023-00896-0.

Cain, W. (2024b). Supporting AI-enhanced active online learning experiences: A framework for design and assessment. In: T. Martindale, T.B. Amankwatia, L. Cifuentes, & A.A. Piña (Eds.), *Handbook of Research in Online Learning: Insights and Advances.* BRILL. https://doi.org/10.1163/9789004702813.

Cain, W. (2025). Cognitive partners in design: Using generative AI for active online learning in a graduate-level course. *Educational Research: Theory and Practice*, *36*(1), 42–51. https://www.nrmera.org/wp-content/uploads/2025/04/ERTP_V36-1_006_Cain.pdf.

Chen, Y., Wang, Q., Xu, J., Cao, R., Fang, Y. and Lin, J. (2024). A systematic review on prompt engineering in large language models for K-12 STEM education. *arXiv preprint arXiv:2410.11123.* https://arxiv.org/abs/2410.11123.

Chiu, T. K. F., Ahmad, Z., Ismailov, M. and Sanusi, I. T. (2024). What are artificial intelligence literacy and competency? A comprehensive framework to support them. *Computers and Education Open, 6,* 100171. https://doi.org/10.1016/j.caeo.2024.100171.

Doshi-Velez, F. and Kim, B. (2017). Towards a rigorous science of interpretable machine learning. *arXiv preprint arXiv:1702.08608.* https://arxiv.org/abs/1702.08608.

Federiakin, D. (2024). Prompt engineering as a new 21st century skill. *Frontiers in Education, 9,* 1366434. https://doi.org/10.3389/feduc.2024.1366434.

Feldman-Maggor, Y., Cukurova, M., Kent, C. and Alexandron, G. (2025). The impact of explainable AI on teachers' trust and acceptance of AI-EdTech recommendations: The power of domain-specific explanations. *International Journal of Artificial Intelligence in Education.* https://doi.org/10.1007/s40593-025-00486-6.

Guidotti, R., Monreale, A., Ruggieri, S., Turini, F., Giannotti, F. and Pedreschi, D. (2018). A survey of methods for explaining black box models. *ACM Computing Surveys, 51*(5), 93. https://doi.org/10.1145/3236009.

Holmes, W., Porayska-Pomsta, K., Holstein, K., Sutherland, E., Baker, T., Buckingham Shum, S., Santos, O. C., Rodrigo, M. T., Cukurova, M., Bittencourt, I. I. and Koedinger, K. R. (2022). Ethics of AI in education: Towards a community-wide framework. *International Journal of Artificial Intelligence in Education, 32,* 504–526. https://doi.org/10.1007/s40593-021-00239-1.

Hu, S. and Wang, X. (2024). FOKE: A personalized and explainable education framework integrating foundation models, knowledge graphs, and prompt engineering. *arXiv preprint arXiv:2405.03734.* https://arxiv.org/abs/2405.03734.

Kell, C., Kraeer, B. and Cain, W. (2025). Can AI facilitate a human-centric approach to writing a problem of practice dissertation?: Insights from doctoral students. *Impacting Education: Journal on Transforming Professional Practice*, *10*(1), Article 1. https://doi.org/10.5195/ie.2025.482.

Kolko, J. (2015). Design thinking comes of age. *Harvard Business Review, 93*(9), 66–71.

Li, X., Zhou, Y. and Sun, L. (2025). Integrating AI in education: Navigating UNESCO global guidelines, emerging trends, and its intersection with sustainable development goals. *ChemRxiv.* https://doi.org/10.26434/chemrxiv-2025-67d5cbf681d2151a0281479b.

Long, D. and Magerko, B. (2020). What is AI literacy? Competencies and design considerations. In: *Proceedings of the 2020 CHI Conference on Human Factors in Computing Systems* (pp. 1–16). ACM. https://doi.org/10.1145/3313831.3376727.

Lundberg, S.M. and Lee, S.I. (2017). A unified approach to interpreting model predictions. In: *Proceedings of the 31st International Conference on Neural Information Processing Systems* (pp. 4765–4774).

Merrill, M.D. (2002). First principles of instruction. *Educational Technology Research and Development, 50*(3), 43–59. https://doi.org/10.1007/BF02505024.

Norman, D.A. (2013). *The Design of Everyday Things* (Rev. & Expanded Edn.). Basic Books.

Ribeiro, M.T., Singh, S. and Guestrin, C. (2016). "Why should I trust you?" Explaining the predictions of any classifier. In: *Proceedings of the 22nd ACM SIGKDD International Conference on Knowledge Discovery and Data Mining* (pp. 1135–1144). ACM. https://doi.org/10.1145/2939672.2939778.

Swamy, V., Romano, Y., Desikan, S., Camburu, O. and Käser, T. (2024). iLLuMinaTE: An LLM-XAI framework leveraging social science explanation theories towards actionable student performance feedback. *arXiv preprint arXiv:2409.08027.* https://arxiv.org/abs/2409.08027.

Viberg, O., Cukurova, M., Feldman-Maggor, Y., et al. (2023). What explains teachers' trust of AI in education across six countries? *arXiv preprint arXiv:2312.01627.* https://arxiv.org/abs/2312.01627.

Wang, L., et al. (2024). Using explainable AI to unravel classroom dialogue analysis. *British Journal of Educational Technology.* https://doi.org/10.1111/bjet.13466.

Yan, L., Sha, L., Zhao, Y., Li, Z., Martinez-Maldonado, R. and Gašević, D. (2023). Practical and ethical challenges of large language models in education: A systematic scoping review. *arXiv preprint arXiv:2303.13379.* https://arxiv.org/abs/2303.13379.

6 Human-Centred Approaches for Non-Expert Users in Explainable AI

Erik Cambria[1], Lorenzo Malandri[2*], Navid Nobani[3] and Andrea Seveso[4]

For an explanation to be truly effective, it must be understandable and useful to its intended audience, particularly non-expert users. The adoption of human-centric approaches to explanation, as opposed to system-centric approaches, is crucial for selecting effective and targeted mediums of explanation. In this chapter, we examine the role of human-centered design in creating explanations of AI systems that offer accessible and actionable insights to non-expert users. We will explore techniques and frameworks rooted in eXplainable Artificial Intelligence (XAI) and Human-Computer Interaction (HCI). The core objective is to investigate how interdisciplinary approaches can enhance the interpretability of explanations, build user trust, improve usability, and ultimately support informed decision-making. Special attention will be paid to methods that adapt explanations to varying user knowledge levels, foster user engagement, and facilitate critical assessment of the system's output. Through examples, case studies, and evaluations, we will illustrate these concepts and also discuss the tangible benefits and inherent challenges of implementing such human-centred strategies in real-world contexts. By placing the non-expert user at the heart of the explanation design process, it is possible to transform explanations from complex technical outputs into meaningful dialogues that empower users and foster a more responsible and effective human-AI collaboration.

1. Introduction: The Imperative of Human-Centred AI Explanations

Artificial intelligence (AI) systems are increasingly embedded in the fabric of modern life. From medical diagnostics and financial risk assessment to driverless vehicles and personalised education platforms, AI technologies are transforming how decisions are made and services are delivered. While these systems offer unprecedented capabilities, their growing complexity presents a fundamental challenge: understanding and interpreting their behaviour. Without adequate explanations, users (especially non-experts) face a "black box" problem: outputs are observed without comprehension, leaving decisions opaque and potentially

[1] Nanyang Technological University, Singapore.
[2-4] University of Milan-Bicocca, Milan, Italy.
* Corresponding author: lorenzo.malandri@unimib.it.

DOI: 10.1201/9781003713371-6

risky. The consequences of such opacity are far from hypothetical; high-profile failures in AI applications, such as misdiagnoses in healthcare, biased predictive policing, or algorithmic discrimination in lending, have demonstrated the urgent need for explanations that are not only technically accurate but also humanly intelligible (Cambria, Malandri, et al., 2024).

Historically, AI explanations have often been system-centric. Early research on interpretability and transparency focused primarily on exposing the internal workings of models, such as feature weights, decision rules, and activation patterns in neural networks. These explanations were intended mainly for developers or domain experts, emphasising fidelity to the underlying algorithm rather than end-user usability. While system-centric explanations provide insight into how models function, they frequently fail to support non-expert users in making informed judgements or in critically assessing AI outputs. For instance, providing a healthcare professional with a statistical breakdown of neural network activations may offer high technical fidelity, but conveys little actionable guidance on patient risk management. Similarly, a consumer receiving a numerical importance score for a recommendation algorithm may lack the context to understand its relevance or reliability (Cambria et al., 2023).

This gap underscores the imperative of human-centred AI explanations, an approach that puts users' needs, knowledge, and goals at the forefront. Human-centred explanations are designed to be understandable, actionable, and relevant, bridging the divide between complex algorithmic processes and human decision-making. Drawing from interdisciplinary research in Human-Computer Interaction (HCI), cognitive psychology, and eXplainable AI (XAI), this approach emphasises tailoring explanations to users' mental capacities, expertise levels, and task contexts. It prioritises not only what the model does but also why it does so, how confident the model is in its predictions, and what implications the output may have for the user's decision-making process (Ge, Mao, & Cambria, 2022).

A key principle of human-centred explanation design is adaptability. Users vary widely in prior knowledge, technical literacy, and cognitive style, making a "one-size-fits-all" explanation often insufficient. For non-expert users, effective explanations may rely on intuitive visualisations, analogies, or narrative descriptions that translate abstract model behaviour into concrete, relatable terms. Conversely, expert users may prefer detailed feature importance metrics or probabilistic reasoning outputs. Beyond user expertise, explanations must also align with the decision's context and goals. In a financial advisory scenario, for example, explanations that highlight potential risk factors and uncertainty may be more relevant than a complete technical deconstruction of the underlying model. By attending to these human factors, explanations can empower users to engage critically with AI, fostering informed and responsible decision-making.

The benefits of human-centred AI explanations extend beyond comprehension. Trust, engagement, and usability are closely tied to how explanations are designed and communicated. When users can understand and interrogate AI outputs, they are more likely to trust the system, appropriately calibrate reliance on its predictions, and detect potential errors or biases. Human-centred explanations also facilitate learning and skill development, enabling users to refine their domain knowledge and their mental models of AI behaviour. These outcomes are particularly important in high-stakes domains, such as healthcare (Han, Mao, & Cambria, 2022; Wang et al., 2025), finance (Yeo et al., 2025; Du et al., 2024; Ong et al., 2024), and HCI (Cambria, Zhang, et al., 2024; Diwali et al., 2024; Cambria et al., 2022), where misinterpretation of AI outputs can have serious consequences.

Operationalising human-centred explanations requires integrating diverse research perspectives and methodological approaches. XAI provides algorithmic tools and frameworks for interpreting complex models, ranging from feature attribution methods to counterfactual and example-based explanations. HCI contributes design principles, user-centred evaluation techniques, and insights into cognitive processing, ensuring that answers are not only accurate but also comprehensible and actionable. Cognitive psychology informs our understanding of how people perceive, process, and retain explanatory information, guiding the selection of formats, levels of detail, and interactive modalities. By synthesising these perspectives, researchers can develop explanations that are simultaneously technically sound and human-centred, balancing fidelity with interpretability and complexity with usability.

This chapter examines these considerations in detail, providing a roadmap for creating AI explanations that genuinely serve their intended audiences. We explore techniques for tailoring explanations to different user profiles, fostering engagement and reflection, and supporting critical assessment of AI outputs. We present case studies and examples illustrating both successes and challenges in implementing human-centred strategies in real-world contexts. These discussions highlight trade-offs inherent in explanation design, for instance, the tension between simplifying information for comprehension and maintaining sufficient technical fidelity, or the challenge of balancing transparency with privacy or security considerations.

By placing the non-expert user at the centre of the explanation process, human-centred approaches transform AI explanations from opaque technical outputs into meaningful, interactive dialogues. This transformation is not merely aesthetic or pedagogical; it is a practical and ethical imperative. Effective human-centred explanations empower users, enhance trust and accountability, and facilitate responsible human-AI collaboration. As AI continues to permeate critical societal, organisational, and personal contexts, ensuring that its outputs are understandable, actionable, and aligned with human needs will be essential for the responsible and equitable deployment of these technologies.

Human-centred AI explanations represent both a conceptual shift and a practical necessity. They urge a shift from system-centric metrics to user-focused explanations that are be intelligible, useful, and trustworthy. By integrating insights from XAI, HCI, and cognitive science, and by grounding explanation design in real-world user needs, we can cultivate AI systems that not only perform effectively but also communicate transparently, support informed decisions, and align with human values. The remainder of this chapter explores the theoretical foundations, practical frameworks, and empirical evidence for human-centred explanations, illustrating how interdisciplinary approaches can create AI systems that are not only powerful but also comprehensible, responsible, and truly human-centred.

2. The "Black Box" Challenge in AI and the Rise of Explainable AI

AI has made extraordinary progress in recent decades, largely driven by advances in machine learning and, more recently, deep learning and large-scale generative models. Yet, these very advances have introduced a paradox: the more powerful the systems become, the less transparent they often are. Models such as deep neural networks, gradient-boosted ensembles, or large language models operate with millions or even billions of parameters. While these architectures can capture subtle correlations in data and deliver highly accurate predictions, their internal logic is opaque to human observers. This phenomenon is commonly described as the black-box nature of AI.

For many stakeholders, the inability to see *how* an AI model arrives at a particular decision is deeply problematic. In domains such as medical diagnostics, credit scoring, or criminal justice, stakeholders are not only interested in the correctness of an outcome but also in the reasoning behind it. If a medical AI suggests a specific treatment plan, physicians and patients must understand why. If an AI denies a loan, the applicant has the right to know the rationale for the denial. Without such insight, even highly accurate models may remain unusable or distrusted in critical contexts.

3. Why Black Boxes are Problematic

The black box challenge has multiple dimensions, namely: epistemic, ethical, and practical. Each of these poses distinct obstacles to transparent and trustworthy AI.

3.1 Epistemic Concerns

Knowledge should ideally be justifiable. If AI systems provide answers without explanations, they resemble oracles rather than scientific tools. This raises questions about whether we can genuinely 'know' or 'trust' what the system outputs.

3.2 Ethical and Social Concerns

Black-box systems can embed and perpetuate biases that are invisible to users. For example, an algorithm trained on historical hiring data might systematically disadvantage women or minorities, and without transparency, these injustices remain hidden. Furthermore, opaque models complicate accountability: if harm arises from an AI-driven decision, who is responsible: the developer, the deploying institution, or the model itself?

3.3 Practical Concerns

Adoption in real-world settings is also limited. Regulators in healthcare, finance, and other high-stakes fields demand traceability of decisions. The European Union's General Data Protection Regulation (GDPR) explicitly mentions a "right to explanation" for automated decisions, underscoring that interpretability is not merely desirable but legally mandated. Companies that deploy AI systems without adequate transparency risk reputational damage, legal liability, and user resistance to unexplained outputs.

4. The Emergence of Explainable AI

The recognition of these problems has fueled the development of XAI. Although concerns about interpretability date back to early expert systems of the 1980s, the modern movement toward XAI gained momentum in the mid-2010s, particularly after the U.S. Defence Advanced Research Projects Agency (DARPA) launched a dedicated XAI programme in 2017 (Gunning & Aha, 2019). This initiative sought methods to produce high-performing, explainable machine learning models.

At its core, XAI is not a single technology but a collection of approaches and philosophies. Some researchers emphasise *intrinsically interpretable models* (for instance, decision trees, rule-based systems, or generalised linear models) that are transparent by design. Others pursue *post-hoc explanation techniques*, such as feature attribution methods (e.g., LIME (Ribeiro, Singh, & Guestrin, 2016), SHAP (Lundberg & Lee, 2017)) or visualisation tools that aim to shed light on otherwise opaque models. Still others focus on *model distillation*, where a simpler surrogate model approximates the behaviour of a more complex one.

The central tension in XAI is the trade-off between accuracy and interpretability. Simpler models tend to be more interpretable but may lack predictive power. Conversely, complex models excel at accuracy but often sacrifice transparency. Much of the research in XAI is motivated by the desire to minimise this trade-off, enabling both high performance and sufficient interpretability.

4.1 From Transparency to Human-Centred Explanations

Technical transparency is only a first step. Exposing how an algorithm works internally does not automatically yield explanations that are meaningful to those who must rely on it. Scholars assert that there is a crucial distinction between *interpretable models*, which are transparent by design, and *explainable models*, which are made understandable through post-hoc methods (Guidotti et al., 2018). This distinction highlights that explanation is not simply a property of a model's architecture, but a communicative process that connects system behaviour with human understanding. Beyond this technical distinction, Miller's review of explanation research in the social sciences (Miller, 2019) highlights that explanations must be understood as *social practices*. People do not usually seek full causal accounts; instead, they look for reasons framed in everyday terms,

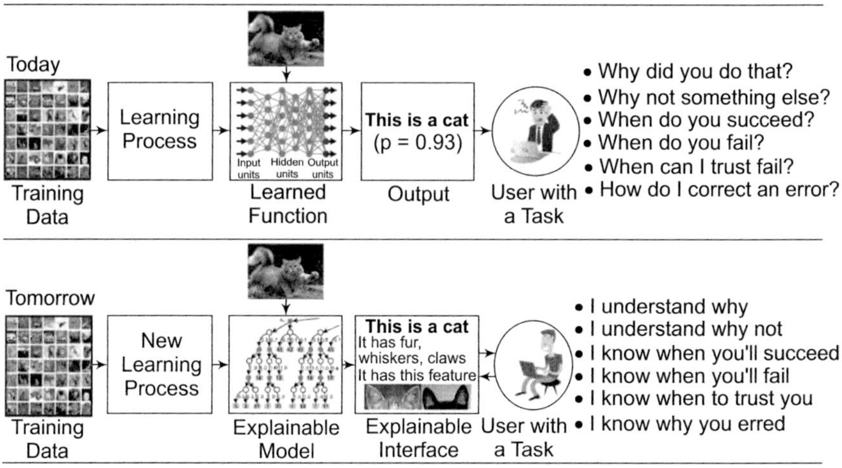

Fig. 1 The XAI Concept. From (Gunning & Aha, 2019). Comparison of an ML and an XAI framework.

often asking why one outcome occurred *rather than* another. Explanations are thus contrastive, selective, and evaluated within conversational and cognitive norms (Malandri et al., 2023). This perspective shifts the focus from merely providing technically accurate information to designing explanations that resonate with how humans naturally generate, interpret, and use them.

Other authors (Jacovi et al., 2021) extend this perspective by analysing trust in AI as a contractual relationship between humans and systems (Figure 2). They argue that trust arises when users, who are inevitably vulnerable to algorithmic outcomes, can anticipate an AI system's behaviour and believe it upholds an implicit contract. Explanations thus play a dual role: they should not only clarify how a model works, but also foster *warranted trust*, calibrating confidence to the system's actual capabilities rather than producing blind reliance.

This point is pushed further by critiquing the dominant "recommend and defend" paradigm of XAI (Miller, 2023), in which systems present a single preferred decision and then justify it. Such approaches can lead either to under-reliance (when users ignore recommendations) or over-reliance (when they accept them uncritically). The proposal of *evaluative AI* instead frames explanations as evidence *for and against* competing hypotheses, supporting the human decision-making process rather than substituting for it. This reorientation places the user's reasoning and agency at the centre of explainability.

In sum, these perspectives collectively reframe explainability from a purely technical exercise in transparency to a fundamentally *human-centred practice*. Explanations must support trust, align with human reasoning processes, and empower users to act responsibly in their own contexts. The challenge is therefore not only to open the black box, but to ensure that what is revealed is meaningful, comprehensible, and useful to the intended audience.

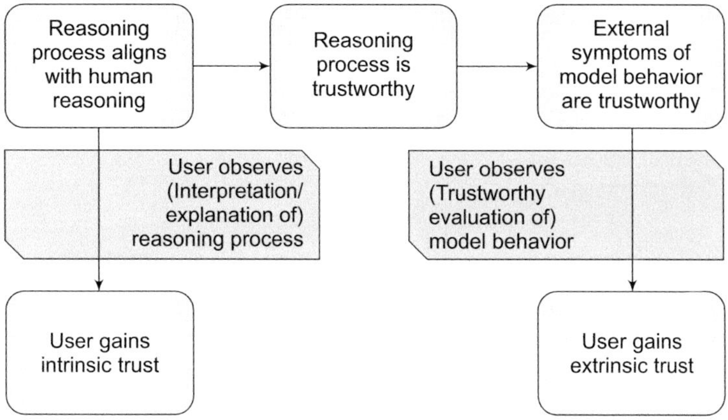

Fig. 2 A schematic of the causes of warranted trust in AI models (from Jacovi et al., 2021).

5. Foundational Disciplines for Human-Centred Explanations

Before discussing human-centred explanations we should clarify the difference between interpretability and explainability, even if such distinction is not always clear within the XAI community.

Basic Definitions

We distinguish: *interpretability* (the inherent transparency of a model's decision-making process that allows humans to understand how decisions are reached) versus *explainability* (external mechanisms and methods that make an opaque model's behaviour understandable through post-hoc analysis).

Several key distinctions should be made regarding types of interpretability and explanations:

- **By timing:** *Intrinsic* methods build models that are interpretable by design (e.g., decision trees, linear regression), while *post-hoc* methods explain an existing black-box model after training (e.g., LIME, SHAP).
- **By scope:** *Local* explanations target a prediction for a specific input instance, whereas *global* explanations summarise overall model behaviour across the entire dataset or feature space.
- **By model dependency:** *Model-agnostic* methods work with any black-box model regardless of its internal architecture, while *model-specific* methods exploit the particular internal structure of specific model types.
- **By output type:** Common explanation formats include *feature-based* explanations (highlighting important input features), *example-based* explanations (using prototypes or counterfactuals), and *concept-based* explanations (relating decisions to high-level human-interpretable concepts). (Figure 3)

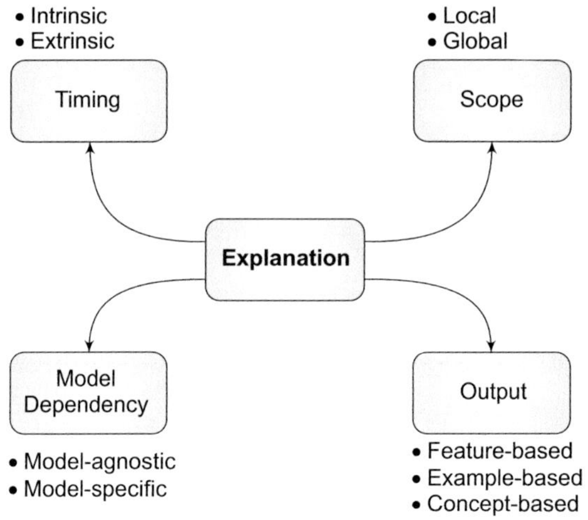

Fig. 3 A Simple taxonomy of XAI.

5.1 Evaluating Explanations

An explanation created to shed light on the inner workings of a black-box model may not add value if it is not useful to stakeholders. To ensure such utility, we should conduct a systematic evaluation to assess the quality and effectiveness of the generated explanation. The main categories of evaluation methods are as follows: Evaluation operates at three levels (Doshi-Velez & Kim, 2017).

Surrogate models

A surrogate model is a simpler, interpretable model trained to approximate the behaviour of a more complex and opaque model in a specific region of the input space. They are particularly relevant in XAI because they allow researchers and practitioners to generate explanations for predictions of black-box models. For instance, local surrogate models such as LIME learn a linear approximation around a single input instance, enabling users to inspect which features contribute most to that specific prediction. Beyond generating explanations, surrogate models are also used to *evaluate* explanations: their fidelity to the original model provides a measure of how accurately the explanation reflects the true decision process. If the surrogate reliably mimics the black box while remaining interpretable, the resulting explanations are considered both faithful and understandable, striking a balance between model complexity and human interpretability.

Human-grounded approach

This approach involves simplified tasks conducted with target users or crowd workers to assess the effectiveness of explanations in realistic scenarios. Key metrics include task accuracy, completion time, perceived cognitive workload (e.g., NASA-TLX scale), and trust calibration. Trust calibration measures whether users appropriately adjust their confidence based on model reliability. A well-calibrated user exhibits high confidence when the model is correct and appropriate caution when the model is likely to err.

Application-grounded approach

This approach evaluates explanations in realistic deployment scenarios with domain experts making actual decisions. The methodology requires pre registering research hypotheses, defining success metrics that align with domain-specific objectives, and conducting systematic ablation studies across different explanation designs. This evaluation framework ensures that explanations demonstrate practical value in their intended application context rather than merely performing well on artificial tasks.

5.2 Designing for Non-Experts

Non-expert audiences benefit from conservative, progressive, and concrete explanation designs that prioritise clarity and actionability over comprehensive technical detail.

Effective patterns

- ***Contrastive Q & A***: Present *Why* and *Why not* explanations side by side to help users understand both the reasoning behind a decision and the factors that would lead to alternative outcomes.
- ***Progressive disclosure***: Begin with a concise one-line explanation and confidence score, then enable users to drill down progressively to detailed features, similar examples, and what-if scenarios as needed.
- ***Counterfactual sliders***: Expose actionability boundaries and realistic feature ranges through interactive controls that show users how changes to input variables would affect predictions.
- ***Example galleries***: Display nearest approved and rejected cases with appropriate caveats, helping users understand decision patterns through concrete instances.
- ***Uncertainty ribbons***: Show calibrated confidence intervals with explanations displayed only when confidence exceeds a predetermined threshold, or pair low-confidence predictions with explicit warnings.
- ***Plain language templates***: Eliminate technical jargon and clearly explain units, directions of effect, and magnitudes using accessible language tailored to the target audience.
- ***Accessibility considerations***: Implement colour-safe encodings for users with visual impairments, provide comprehensive alt text for screen readers, ensure full keyboard navigation support, and offer multilingual labels where appropriate.

Anti-patterns to avoid

Common design mistakes include presenting raw saliency heatmaps without proper calibration or context; offering unbounded free-form counterfactuals that may mislead users; displaying feature importance scores that ignore correlation structures; and creating overloaded dashboards that overwhelm users with excessive information.

5.3 Risk, Governance, and Uncertainty

- **Uncertainty management** Explanations should present predictive confidence with proper calibration in mind, clearly distinguishing between aleatoric uncertainty (inherent randomness in the data) and epistemic uncertainty (model ignorance due to limited training data). Systems should offer abstention or referral to human experts when uncertainty exceeds acceptable thresholds, while explicitly explaining how uncertainty levels affect the reliability of both predictions and recommendations.
- **Appropriate reliance** To guard against over-trust and automation bias, explanation systems must implement safeguards, including contextual warnings, confidence-linked UI friction that requires additional user action for low-confidence predictions, and random spot checks that require users to justify their acceptance of model recommendations explicitly. These mechanisms help maintain appropriate human oversight and critical evaluation.
- **Fairness, privacy, and security considerations** Attribution-based explanations can inadvertently leak sensitive information about training data or enable adversarial gaming of model decisions. Counterfactual explanations must respect actionability constraints and non-discrimination principles, ensuring suggested changes are both feasible and legally permissible. Organisations should regularly audit explanations for group disparities, implement rate-limiting on explanation access to prevent abuse, and maintain comprehensive logs of explanation requests for security monitoring.
- **Documentation and audit trails** Responsible deployment requires publishing comprehensive model cards and datasheets that document system capabilities and limitations. Organisations must maintain detailed records of explanation algorithm versions, parameter configurations, and user interaction patterns to enable effective auditing and monitoring for model drift or explanation degradation over time.

6. Mini Case Studies

6.1 Credit Scoring (Tabular Data)

- **Goal:** Provide rejection reasons that satisfy regulatory requirements and enable meaningful appeals.
- **Method combination:** Calibrated probability scores paired with top-k SHAP values using correlation-aware feature grouping to avoid redundancy. Counterfactual explanations are constrained by institutional credit policies, while global Partial Dependence Plots (PDPs) illustrate key feature relationships across the population.

- **User interface:** Plain-language explanations with direct links to relevant policy documentation, complemented by what-if sliders restricted to actionable features that applicants can realistically modify.
- **Validation approach:** Comprehensive evaluation using insertion-deletion metrics for explanation fidelity, human-grounded comprehension studies with actual loan officers, and systematic fairness audits across demographic groups.

6.2 *Clinical Imaging (Computer Vision)*

- **Goal:** Provide decision support to radiologists without overstepping into autonomous diagnosis.
- **Method combination:** Grad-CAM attention maps paired with rigorous sanity checks to ensure clinical relevance, prototype tile galleries showcasing typical and atypical pattern examples, and uncertainty ribbons to communicate prediction confidence.
- **User interface:** Attention heatmaps with adjustable confidence thresholds, curated exemplar galleries for pattern recognition, and clinical rationale text that has been reviewed and validated by domain experts.
- **Validation approach:** Application-grounded studies measuring diagnostic reading time, sensitivity improvements, and trust calibration between radiologists and the AI system in realistic clinical workflows.

6.3 *Content Moderation (Natural Language Processing)*

- **Goal:** Enable consistent content triage decisions under tight time constraints while maintaining policy compliance.
- **Method combination:** Token-level attention rationales with stability testing across paraphrases, counterfactual word substitutions to identify borderline cases, and example-based contrasts that illustrate different policy violation categories.
- **User interface:** Compact text highlighting with contextual tooltips linking to specific policy clauses, plus clear escalation guidance when human review is recommended for edge cases.
- **Validation approach:** Multi faceted evaluation measuring decision accuracy, time-to-decision efficiency, inter-rater agreement among moderators, and system robustness against adversarial paraphrase attacks.

7. Choosing an XAI Method: A Checklist

When selecting appropriate explainability methods for a given application, practitioners should systematically consider the following key factors:

1. **Task type and risk level:** Identify whether the application involves prediction, ranking, triage, or recourse provision, and assess the associated

risk level (low, medium, or high stakes). Higher-risk applications require more rigorous explanation, validation, and may necessitate conservative, well-established methods.

2. **Target audience characteristics:** Determine whether users are domain experts, trained operators, or laypersons, and assess any relevant literacy constraints or cognitive load limitations. Audience expertise directly influences the appropriate complexity and technical depth of explanations.
3. **Explanation scope requirements:** Clarify whether the application needs local explanations for individual decisions, global insights into overall model behaviour, or counterfactual recourse options that show users how to achieve different outcomes.
4. **Data modality and model properties:** Consider the input data type (tabular, text, image, time series) and model characteristics such as differentiability, which constrain the applicable explanation methods and influence computational requirements.
5. **Operational constraints:** Evaluate practical limitations, including time budget per decision, computational resources, privacy requirements, and governance or regulatory constraints that may restrict certain explanation approaches.
6. **Robustness requirements:** Assess the need for explanations to remain stable under feature correlation, distribution shift, and potential adversarial manipulation, particularly in high-stakes or security-sensitive applications.
7. **Validation strategy:** Define appropriate evaluation approaches, including functionally-grounded metrics (e.g., faithfulness, stability), human-centred studies with target users, and domain-specific success criteria that align with real-world deployment objectives.

8. Strategies for Enhancing Interpretability, Trust, and Usability

Explainable AI must be judged by three tightly-coupled objectives: interpretability (the degree to which humans can form an accurate mental model of a system), trust (appropriate reliance, calibrated to the system's actual reliability), and usability (the extent to which explanations help users accomplish domain tasks efficiently, safely, and fairly). Technical progress in algorithmic explanations (such as feature attributions, saliency maps, counterfactuals, and interpretable-by-design models) has increased the number of available tools. Yet these tools succeed only to the extent that they are integrated with human-centred design, rigorous evaluation, and governance practices that address robustness, fairness, and privacy. Recent reviews and position pieces argue that XAI should be treated as a human-machine design problem, not merely an applied statistics problem; insights from the social sciences, HCI, and domain practice are therefore essential complements to algorithmic advances (Miller, 2019; Liao, Gruen, & Miller, 2020).

8.1 *Designing Explanations for Human Cognition and Decision-making*

Algorithmic correctness is necessary but not sufficient: explanations must be crafted to align with human cognitive processes, information needs, and social contexts.

Psychological desiderata: Contrastivity, selectivity, and social framing

Cognitive science shows people prefer contrastive explanations ("why X rather than Y?"), selective explanations that emphasise causes humans judge relevant, and social explanations that incorporate norms and accountability. If explanations are overly exhaustive or framed in low-level technical terms, users either ignore them or form incorrect mental models. Miller's synthesis of social science research recommends that XAI leverage these principles when designing explanation content and format (Miller, 2019).

Personalisation and role-sensitive explanations

Users differ in expertise, goals, and incentives. Clinicians need evidence-level chain-of-reasoning; regulators need auditable summaries and aggregate fairness metrics; lay users need concise, actionable guidance. A single static explanation design rarely fits all users; adaptive or multi layered explanations (short summary, deeper technical details, provenance, and uncertainty) are a practical pattern. CHI/HCI work advocates eliciting question sets from stakeholders early (question-driven design) and mapping explanation techniques to the questions they best answer.

Explanation formats and their affordances

- Textual narratives (plain-language justifications) are accessible but risk oversimplification.
- Visualisations (saliency heatmaps, partial dependence plots, decision paths) leverage perceptual strengths, but require careful calibration to avoid misleading impressions (Adebayo et al., 2018).
- Example-based explanations (prototypes and counter-examples) enable analogical reasoning. Counterfactuals/recourse map directly to user actionability and legal rights in regulated domains. Choosing format should be driven by the user question (why? why not? how to change?) and by evidence from user studies about which formats materially improve task performance (Mothilal, Sharma, & Tan, 2020).

Interaction-oriented explanations

Static explanations often fall short; inter- active tools like question-driven interfaces and "what-if" simulators let users probe models, improving understanding and joint decisions. HCI research has proposed design patterns (question banks, layered explanation panels) for matching explanations to user needs (Liao, Gruen, & Miller, 2020). Explanatory debugging (where the system explains a decision and the user provides corrective feedback that updates the model) has empirical support for improving mental model accuracy and enabling users to personalise models. Interaction enables mutual calibration: users learn about model limitations, and the model learns about user intent or constraints. Such loops are particularly valuable in personalisation and End-User Development contexts (Kulesza et al., 2015).

8.2 Reconciling Fidelity, Robustness, and Trust

Explanations must be faithful (reflect model reasoning), stable (similar inputs lead to similar explanations), and interpretable (human-comprehensible). These desiderata sometimes conflict.

- **The fidelity–simplicity trade-off** High-fidelity explanations (e.g., full local surrogate models with many features or exact contributions from subnetwork activations) can be difficult to comprehend. Simpler explanations (top-k feature lists, a single counterfactual) are easier, but they risk omitting critical nuances or leading to misleading causal inferences. A common design solution is progressive disclosure: present a compact high-level view first and allow users to drill down to more faithful representations when needed. Empirical work indicates that users often prefer a combination of confidence signals and concise explanations for decision support; however, these preferences vary by task and level of expertise (Poursabzi-Sangdeh et al., 2021).
- **Robustness, fragility, and adversarial manipulation** A substantial body of literature demonstrates that many explanation methods are fragile: small input perturbations or model changes can produce drastically different attributions, even when predictions remain unchanged. Saliency maps can be insensitive to model parameters unless they are properly tested; adversaries can manipulate post-hoc perturbation methods to conceal discriminatory behaviour. These vulnerabilities undermine trust and necessitate robustness checks (randomisation/sanity checks, sensitivity analyses) and adversarial-aware evaluation pipelines. Research proposes regularisation, stability constraints, and self-explanatory architectures to address fragility (Slack et al., 2020; Ghorbani, Abid, & Zou, 2019).
- **Trust calibration versus blind trust** The aim of explanations is appropriate trust: users should accept correct model outputs and challenge erroneous ones. Explanations that increase subjective trust without improving behavioural outcomes (e.g., users following an incorrect model more often) are harmful. Empirical studies highlight instances in which explanation visibility led to over-reliance or reduced error detection; conversely, calibrated confidence estimates (well-designed uncertainty communication) can improve decision quality. Designing explanations with explicit cues about uncertainty, scope, and limitations is therefore important (Poursabzi-Sangdeh et al., 2021).

9. Evaluation: Methods, Metrics, and Experimental Design

Rigorous evaluation is the backbone of responsible XAI. Evaluation must measure not only technical fidelity but also downstream human outcomes.

9.1 What to Measure (Multi Dimensional Evaluation)

A mature evaluation plan considers multiple, complementary outcomes (Hoffman et al., 2023; Cesarini et al., 2024), such as:

- **Model-centric metrics:** Faithfulness/fidelity measures, stability, and computational cost.
- **Human-centric metrics:** Task performance (accuracy, time), behavioural reliance (when users accept/reject model suggestions), mental model accuracy (elicitation tasks), perceived usability and satisfaction, and trust calibration (behavioural, not only attitudinal measures).
- **Societal metrics:** Fairness across groups, privacy leakage from explanations, and legal compliance.

9.2 Quantitative Experiments

Large-N experiments (varying explanation type, information quantity, or model transparency) have produced counterintuitive but essential results. For example, seeing a 'clear' model does not necessarily improve people's ability to detect model errors and can sometimes reduce corrective behaviour. Such controlled experiments should be complemented with domain-specific tasks for ecological validity (Poursabzi-Sangdeh et al., 2021).

9.3 Qualitative and Mixed-methods Evaluation

Human subjects, think-aloud protocols, and field studies reveal how explanations fit into workflows and how they affect sense-making, accountability, and trust. Mixed-methods approaches combine behavioural measures (reliance, task accuracy) with qualitative insights (mental models, workarounds) to produce rich, actionable findings for designers. Systematic reviews emphasise that XAI evaluation is currently heterogeneous; best practice is to report both standardised metrics and contextualised user outcomes (Kim, Maathuis, & Sent, 2024).

9.4 Benchmarks and Simulation vs Real Tasks

Benchmarks and synthetic tasks are useful for controlled comparisons, but conclusions about human impact require real tasks, representative users, and longitudinal deployment studies. Benchmarks should measure not only technical properties but also how explanation variants affect decisions in ecologically valid scenarios. Recent calls for "better metrics" aim to unify quantitative criteria with usage contexts (Saeed & Omlin, 2023).

10. Deployment, Governance, and Continuous Improvement

Strategies must extend beyond model training into documentation, monitoring, and organisational governance.

10.1 Documentation and Artifacting: Model Cards, Datasheets, and Fact Sheets

Structured documentation artefacts, such as model cards, datasheets for datasets, and fact sheets, support transparency across the development, procurement, and auditing stages. Model cards summarise intended use, evaluation across subpopulations, fairness constraints, and known limitations. Datasheets document data provenance and collection biases; together, they make the explanation behaviour interpretable in context (Mitchell et al., 2019).

10.2 Monitoring Explanations in Production

Operational monitoring should include explanation-level metrics, such as the stability of attributions over time, shifts in feature importance distributions, user feedback on the utility of explanations, and the detection of explanation manipulation. A/B testing of explanation variants, coupled with downstream performance metrics (task accuracy, false-positive/negative rates), provides evidence for iterating on explanation designs.

10.3 Governance, Auditing, and Multidisciplinary Review

High-stakes deployments require auditing teams with expertise in technical, legal, and domain-specific areas. Audits should review both model decisions and the fidelity of explanations (i.e., whether the explanation is consistent with the model), as well as privacy implications (whether the explanation leaks sensitive information). Embedding cross-functional review cycles (involving designers, ethicists, and domain experts) reduces the risk of misapplied explanations.

11. Synthesis and Recommendations

Strategies for enhancing interpretability, trust, and usability must be plural: human-centred design practices (question-driven, multi layered, role-sensitive interfaces), rigorous evaluation (behavioural measures, robustness testing), and governance artefacts (model cards, monitoring, audits) are all necessary components. No single algorithmic trick will suffice; the field must continue to integrate insights from machine learning, HCI, cognitive science, law, and domain disciplines to produce explanations that are faithful, actionable, and ethically sound. Continued investment in robust explanation methods, standardised and contextualised evaluation, and long-term field research will determine whether XAI moves beyond promising prototypes to dependable practice.

12. Real-World Applications and Case Studies

The adoption of AI across industries has been uneven. While technical capabilities advance rapidly, organisational uptake is often limited when systems remain opaque or fail to embed human needs. Reports from the MIT Centre for Information Systems Research stress that "algorithmic trust" is a prerequisite for pervasive adoption: without explanations, AI initiatives often stall (MIT Center for Information Systems Research, 2023). Similarly, MIT's NANDA project (MIT NANDA, 2025) found that 95% of generative AI pilots deliver no measurable returns, largely because they lack transparency and integration into human workflows.

Human-Centred AI (HCAI) addresses this gap. It focuses not only on accuracy, but also on providing understandable, actionable, and socially meaningful explanations. A recurring feature of successful HCAI applications is the use of *ad hoc* explanations anchored in concrete words, features, or criteria. Users are told not just *what* decision was made, but *why*, often through highlighting keywords or factors that shaped the outcome. This chapter reviews real-world applications across domains, emphasising how such practices enhance trust, fairness, and human agency.

13. Labour Market and Recruitment

- **LinkedIn Job Matching** LinkedIn's recommendation engine connects millions of workers with job postings. To avoid a "black box" effect, the platform highlights the skills that triggered the match. For instance, a user might see: "This position is suggested because your profile lists *Python* and *project management*." **Why human-centred?** These keyword-based explanations empower candidates to refine their profiles, strategically highlight skills, and understand how opportunities are generated. The AI becomes a partner in career building rather than an opaque filter.
- **Indeed and Glassdoor Transparency** Similar transparency practices have emerged on platforms like Indeed and Glassdoor, which display explicit match percentages or top-matching keywords: "Your profile matches 70% of this posting, especially for *SEO* and *content strategy*." **Why human-centred?** The explanation is not a technical breakdown but a direct mapping to criteria that candidates can recognise and act upon.
- **HireVue and Unilever Recruitment** HireVue initially used opaque AI scoring of video interviews, including facial and voice analysis. After strong criticism, the company removed controversial components and began issuing transparency reports and candidate-facing explanations. Similarly, Unilever's recruitment system, which combines gamified assessments with AI scoring, provides applicants with feedback on their strengths and weaknesses. **Why human-centred?** These cases demonstrate that explanations are not abstract. They are rooted in concrete factors (cognitive test results, keyword matches, skill indicators) that help candidates understand and contest outcomes.
- **Terminator Economy** The *Terminator Economy* project is an initiative to track the broader impact of AI and automation on jobs, wages, and industries. It provides dashboards accessible to unions, policymakers, and

citizens, highlighting keywords such as *automation risk*, *job displacement*, and *reskilling opportunities*. Instead of hiding labour market shifts behind abstract indices, it translates AI-driven analysis into intelligible categories. By foregrounding concrete terms and factors, it democratizes knowledge of automation's impacts and empowers collective decision-making.

13.1 Finance and Credit Scoring

- **Mastercard / Brighterion Reason Codes** In credit decisioning, users and regulators demand transparency. Mastercard's Brighterion system attaches "reason codes" to every AI-based risk score. For example: "Loan declined due to *high debt-to-income ratio* and *short credit history*." **Why human-centred?** These keyword-based factors translate technical model reasoning into human-relevant explanations, allowing applicants to understand and, if needed, challenge the outcome.
- **SHAP for Credit Risk** Banks have scaled SHAP-based explanations across entire portfolios. For a declined credit card application, an explanation might read: "Decision influenced primarily by *high card utilisation* and *low annual income*." **Why human-centred?** The explanation is grounded in recognisable attributes, moving beyond abstract accuracy metrics. By anchoring reasoning to familiar financial keywords, the system respects user comprehension and supports fairness.

13.2 Health and Medicine

- **Radiology Assistants** Systems like Philips IntelliSpace AI aid radiologists by highlighting suspicious regions in medical images and labelling them with clinical keywords such as "*lung opacity*" or "*bronchial thickening*." **Why human-centred?** These explanations align with professional vocabularies, empowering physicians to validate AI findings against their expertise. Instead of substituting judgement, the system augments human reasoning through transparent, keyword-driven cues.
- **Clinical Decision Support** Some clinical AI tools provide counterfactual feedback, e.g., "This diagnosis was suggested because symptoms matched *persistent cough* and *chest pain*." Doctors can then verify or dispute the reasoning. **Why human-centred?** By tying AI recommendations to specific medical terms, the system integrates into diagnostic workflows while preserving professional agency.

13.3 Retail and Consumer Recommendations

- **Amazon and E-Commerce** Recommendation systems often risk opacity. Amazon mitigates this by offering short, keyword-based rationales: "You are seeing this item because you searched for *running shoes*" or "Customers who bought *Harry Potter* also bought this." **Why human-centred?** These explanations reference user actions or recognisable items. Even if simplistic, they help customers trace why an option appears, reducing suspicion of manipulative or irrelevant suggestions.

- **Recommender Systems with Critiquing** Beyond Amazon, several commercial recommenders implement 'critiquing' interfaces that allow users to refine results: "How me more like this, but with *lower price* or *eco-friendly*." **Why human-centred?** Keyword-level transparency and control convert AI from passive automation to an interactive collaborator.

13.4 Public Sector and Policy

- **City of Helsinki Transparency Initiative** Helsinki has deployed AI to recommend social services to citizens. Importantly, citizens are told *why* a service is recommended: "We suggest this program because you declared *unemployment* and *need for retraining*." **Why human-centred?** The explanations explicitly reference the words citizens used in their self-declarations, ensuring transparency and reducing the risk of opaque bureaucratic filtering.

13.5 Lessons Across Domains

Across the labour market, in finance, health, retail, and governance, certain patterns emerge:

- **Explanations Anchored in Keywords:** Successful systems ground their reasoning in terms that users recognise: skills, medical symptoms, financial ratios, rather than abstract model features.
- **Transparency that Empowers:** Keyword-based rationales are not just informative but actionable: candidates update profiles, patients question diagnoses, and citizens contest services.
- **Agency and Trust:** Explanations restore agency by showing *why* and allowing humans to contest or adapt. This aligns with research showing that explanations are inherently social and contrastive: people want to know "why this instead of that".
- **Context-Sensitive Formats:** The type and form of explanations, whether textual narratives, visual heatmaps, or interactive counterfactuals, must fit the domain and align with the cognitive style of their users. Explanations are effective only when they connect naturally to how people think, decide, and act.
- **From Opaque Automation to Dialogue:** Whether in recruitment or policy, the move from silent AI to explanatory AI repositions technology as a collaborator. The system no longer dictates but converses, grounded in human language.

13.6 Conclusion

Human-Centred AI is defined not only by technical performance but by the quality of its explanations. Real-world applications, from LinkedIn to Helsinki, from Mastercard to Terminator Economy, show that when systems reveal the *keywords and criteria* behind decisions, they become trustworthy, fair, and usable.

As the MIT CISR and NANDA reports emphasise, adoption fails when AI lacks explainability and human integration. The cases reviewed here demonstrate the inverse: when explanations are specific, contextual, and grounded in language people understand, AI becomes not just accurate but meaningful. In the labour market and beyond, the future of AI depends less on opaque sophistication than on transparency that empowers.

14. Challenges and Future Directions

Despite the significant advancements in human-centred XAI, several challenges persist, shaping the trajectory of future research and development. XAI can both mitigate and introduce harms. Explanations that increase unwarranted trust, leak private attributes, or can be gamed to hide discriminatory behaviour are real threats.

14.1 Balancing Explainability and Performance

A fundamental challenge is the inherent trade-off between the complexity and accuracy of AI models and their interpretability. Highly accurate deep learning models often sacrifice transparency, making their decisions difficult to explain and understand. Finding the right balance that meets user needs for understanding without compromising model performance remains an ongoing effort. Future work must focus on developing scalable XAI techniques that can effectively explain large, complex models while maintaining high accuracy. Tailoring explanations to diverse audiences with varying levels of technical understanding is also crucial to ensure that answers are both informative and easily digestible.

14.2 Addressing Cognitive Biases and Over-Reliance

A critical concern is the potential for AI explanations to induce cognitive biases in users, leading to inappropriate trust or over-reliance on the AI system. Users may develop an "illusion of explanatory depth", believing they understand the AI's reasoning more thoroughly than they do, or they might accept AI advice passively without critical scrutiny. This can be detrimental, especially when AI recommendations are not infallible. Future directions must focus on designing XAI systems that foster calibrated trust, encouraging users to understand both the AI's capabilities and its limitations. This involves communicating the AI's confidence levels, highlighting uncertainties, and designing interfaces that prompt critical thinking and active engagement rather than passive acceptance (Poursabzi-Sangdeh et al., 2021).

14.3 Standardisation and Evaluation of Human-Centred XAI

The field currently lacks standardisation in methodologies for evaluating human-centred XAI, particularly in user studies. Many studies rely on anecdotal evidence or subjective feedback rather than robust quantitative metrics. The complexity of HCI evaluation, coupled with the diversity of user backgrounds and cognitive skills, makes objective assessment challenging. There is a pressing need for standardised evaluation frameworks that combine objective measures (e.g., task performance, predictive accuracy of user mental models) with subjective measures (e.g., perceived usability, trust, satisfaction) to assess the quality and effectiveness of explanations. This will enable more consistent cross-study comparisons and guide the XAI community toward a unified approach in human-centred explainability.

14.4 Regulatory Considerations

As AI systems become more integrated into critical decision-making processes, ethical considerations surrounding their use gain prominence. Explainability is increasingly recognised as a legal and institutional requirement for the responsible deployment of AI, as seen in regulations such as the GDPR and the EU AI Act. Future efforts must focus on ensuring that XAI systems facilitate compliance with these evolving regulatory frameworks. This includes robust bias detection and mitigation strategies, clear lines of accountability for AI decisions, and active involvement of policymakers, industry leaders, and users in the development of explainable AI systems.

14.5 Ethical and Security Challenges

Explanations of machine learning models, while crucial for transparency and trust, introduce a range of ethical and security risks. Adversarial manipulation of explanations demonstrates how models or training regimes can be engineered to retain biased or undesirable predictions while producing seemingly innocuous post-hoc explanations. To counteract this, approaches such as adversarial robustness for explanation methods, cross-validation of explanation fidelity, and governance checks that align global model behaviour with presented local explanations are essential (Slack et al., 2020).

Beyond adversarial concerns, explanations can also inadvertently compromise privacy. Fine-grained attribution methods or example-based explanations may reveal sensitive training records or subgroup statistics. Designing privacy-aware explanations, such as through aggregation or differential privacy techniques, is therefore a critical safeguard.

Furthermore, the public release of explanation interfaces can enable gaming and strategic manipulation, in which stakeholders adjust their behaviour to exploit model suggestions—such as applicants tailoring their inputs based on counterfactual recommendations from a credit scoring model. Effective mitigation requires thoughtful policy design and interface controls that provide actionable guidance without facilitating unfair advantage.

A layered defence combining robust algorithmic design, restricted feature-level disclosure, auditing, and human-centred communication could provide the most effective strategy to address these intertwined risks, ensuring that explanations improve accountability without introducing new vulnerabilities.

Conclusion

Human-centred eXplainable AI reframes explanation as a communicative practice that serves people, not merely as a technical property of models. In this chapter, we argue that effective explanations must align with users' goals, knowledge and contexts, and that doing so requires integrating methods and insights from XAI, HCI, and cognitive science. In this view, interpretability is not an end in itself, but a means to support appropriate reliance, critical assessment, and accountable decision-making.

This chapter walks us through three fundamental pillars for generating explanations that are not only useful, but also efficient and impactful. First, design for cognition and action: prefer contrastive, selective rationales; provide progressive disclosure with clear confidence signals; and privilege actionable formats such as counterfactual recourse, example-based galleries, and plain-language templates. Second, evaluate human outcomes and model fidelity: combine functionally grounded metrics with human- and application-grounded studies that measure task performance, mental model accuracy, behavioural reliance, and fairness. Third, govern explanations in deployment: document capabilities and limits, monitor explanation stability and utility, manage uncertainty explicitly, and audit for privacy leakage, security abuse and group disparities.

Real-world cases across labour markets, finance, health, retail, and the public sector illustrated that concise, keyword-anchored rationales can increase transparency and agency when they map model reasoning to familiar terms and policies. These examples also showed that explanation is most useful when it enables dialogue, that is, when users can contest, refine, and adapt system outputs rather than merely observe them.

Looking forward, the central challenge is to reconcile fidelity, robustness, and simplicity while preventing overtrust. Meeting this challenge requires standardised, context-sensitive evaluation protocols, adversarially aware, privacy-preserving explanation methods, and longitudinal field studies that test whether explanation variants improve decisions, equity, and safety at scale. The chapter's recommendations can be summarised as a compact mandate for practice: start with users' questions, layer information conservatively, quantify uncertainty, validate with people in the loop, and treat explanations as living artefacts documented, monitored, and improved over time. If followed, these practices can move XAI from promising prototypes to dependable, human-centred systems that are both powerful and meaningfully understandable.

References

Adebayo, Julius, Justin Gilmer, Michael Muelly, Ian Goodfellow, Moritz Hardt and Been Kim. (2018). Sanity Checks for Saliency Maps. *Advances in Neural Information Processing Systems*, *31*.

Cambria, Erik, Akshi Kumar, Mahmoud Al-Ayyoub and Newton Howard. (2022). Guest Editorial: Explainable Artificial Intelligence for Sentiment Analysis. *Knowledge-Based Systems*, *238*, 107920.

Cambria, Erik, Lorenzo Malandri, Fabio Mercorio, Mario Mezzanzanica and Navid Nobani. (2023). A Survey on XAI and Natural Language Explanations. *Information Processing and Management*, *60*, 103111.

Cambria, Erik, Lorenzo Malandri, Fabio Mercorio, Navid Nobani and Andrea Seveso. (2024). XAI Meets LLMs: A Survey of the Relation between Explainable AI and Large Language Models. *arXiv Preprint arXiv:2407.15248*.

Cambria, Erik, Xulang Zhang, Rui Mao, Melvin Chen and Kenneth Kwok. (2024). SenticNet 8: Fusing Emotion AI and Commonsense AI for Interpretable, Trustworthy, and Explainable Affective Computing. In: *HCI International 2024: Late Breaking Papers* (pp. 197–216). Washington DC, USA.

Cesarini, Mirko, Lorenzo Malandri, Filippo Pallucchini, Andrea Seveso and Frank Xing. (2024). Explainable AI for Text Classification: Lessons from a Comprehensive Evaluation of Post-Hoc Methods. *Cognitive Computation*, *16* (6): 3077–3095.

Diwali, Arwa, Kawther Saeedi, Kia Dashtipour, Mandar Gogate, Erik Cambria and Amir Hussain. (2024). Sentiment Analysis Meets Explainable Artificial Intelligence: A Survey on Explainable Sentiment Analysis. *IEEE Transactions on Affective Computing*, *15* (3): 837–846.

Doshi-Velez, Finale and Been Kim. (2017). Towards a Rigorous Science of Interpretable Machine Learning. *arXiv Preprint arXiv:1702.08608*.

Du, Kelvin, Rui Mao, Frank Xing and Erik Cambria. (2024). Explainable stock price movement prediction using contrastive learning. In *CIKM*, 529–537.

Ge, Mengshi, Rui Mao and Erik Cambria. (2022). Explainable Metaphor Identification Inspired by Conceptual Metaphor Theory. In: *Proceedings of the 36th AAAI Conference on Artificial Intelligence* (pp. 10681–10689).

Ghorbani, Amirata, Abubakar Abid and James Zou. (2019). Interpretation of Neural Networks is Fragile. In: *Proceedings of the AAAI Conference on Artificial Intelligence* (*33*: 3681–3688. 01).

Guidotti, Riccardo, Anna Monreale, Salvatore Ruggieri, Franco Turini, Fosca Giannotti and Dino Pedreschi. (2018). A Survey of Methods for Explaining Black Box Models. *ACM Computing Surveys* (*CSUR*), *51* (5): 1–42.

Gunning, David and David Aha. (2019). DARPA's Explainable Artificial Intelligence (XAI) Program. *AI Magazine*, *40* (2): 44–58.

Han, Sooji, Rui Mao & Erik Cambria. (2022). Hierarchical attention network for explainable depression detection on twitter aided by metaphor concept map- pings. In Proceedings of COLING, 94–104

Hoffman, Robert R., Shane T. Mueller, Gary Klein and Jordan Litman. (2023). Measures for Explainable AI: Explanation Goodness, User Satisfaction, Mental Models, Curiosity, Trust, and Human-AI Performance. *Frontiers in Computer Science*, *5*: 1096257.

Jacovi, Alon, Ana Marasović, Tim Miller and Yoav Goldberg. (2021). Formalizing Trust in Artificial Intelligence: Prerequisites, Causes and Goals of Human Trust in AI. In: *Proceedings of the 2021 ACM Conference on Fairness, Accountability, and Transparency* (pp. 624–635).

Kim, Jenia, Henry Maathuis and Danielle Sent. (2024). Human-Centered Evaluation of Explainable AI Applications: A Systematic Review. *Frontiers in Artificial Intelligence*, *7*: 1456486.

Kulesza, Todd, Margaret Burnett, Weng-Keen Wong and Simone Stumpf. (2015). Principles of Explanatory Debugging to Personalize Interactive Machine Learning. In: *Proceedings of the 20th International Conference on Intelligent User Interfaces* (pp. 126–137).

Liao, Q., Vera, Daniel Gruen and Sarah Miller. (2020). Questioning the AI: Informing Design Practices for Explainable AI User Experiences. In: *Proceedings of the 2020 CHI Conference on Human Factors in Computing Systems* (pp. 1–15).

Lundberg, Scott M. and Su-In Lee. (2017). A Unified Approach to Interpreting Model Predictions. *Advances in Neural Information Processing Systems, 30.*

Malandri, Lorenzo, Fabio Mercorio, Mario Mezzanzanica and Navid Nobani. (2023). Convxai: A System for Multimodal Interaction with Any Black-Box Explainer. *Cognitive Computation, 15* (2): 613–644.

Miller, Tim. (2019). Explanation in Artificial Intelligence: Insights from the Social Sciences. *Artificial Intelligence, 267*: 1–38.

Miller, Tim. (2023). Explainable AI is Dead, Long Live Explainable AI! Hypothesis-Driven Decision Support Using Evaluative AI. In: *Proceedings of the 2023 ACM Conference on Fairness, Accountability, and Transparency* (pp. 333–342).

MIT Center for Information Systems Research. (2023). *Building AI Explanation Capability for the AI-Powered Organization.* MIT Sloan School of Management. https://cisr.mit.edu/publication/2022_0701_AIX_SomehWixomBeath.

MIT NANDA. (2025). *The GenAI Divide: State of AI in Business 2025.* https://mlq.ai/media/quarterly_decks/v0.1_State_of_AI_in_Business_2025_Report.pdf.

Mitchell, Margaret, Simone Wu, Andrew Zaldivar, Parker Barnes, Lucy Vasserman, Ben Hutchinson, Elena Spitzer, Inioluwa Deborah Raji and Timnit Gebru. (2019). Model Cards for Model Reporting. In: *Proceedings of the Conference on Fairness, Accountability, and Transparency* (pp. 220–229).

Mothilal, Ramaravind K., Amit Sharma and Chenhao Tan. (2020). Explaining Machine Learning Classifiers through Diverse Counterfactual Explanations. In: *Proceedings of the 2020 Conference on Fairness, Accountability, and Transparency* (pp. 607–617).

Ong, Keane, Rui Mao, Ranjan Satapathy, Erik Cambria, Johan Sulaeman and Gianmarco Mengaldo. (2024). Explainable Natural Language Processing for Corporate Sustainability Analysis. *Information Fusion, 115*: 102726.

Poursabzi-Sangdeh, Forough, Daniel G. Goldstein, Jake M. Hofman, Jennifer Wortman Wortman Vaughan and Hanna Wallach. (2021). Manipulating and Measuring Model Interpretability. In: *Proceedings of the 2021 CHI Conference on Human Factors in Computing Systems* (pp. 1–52).

Ribeiro, Marco Tulio, Sameer Singh and d Carlos Guestrin. (2016). Why Should I Trust You? Explaining the Predictions of Any Classifier. In: *Proceedings of the 22nd ACM SIGKDD International Conference on Knowledge Discovery and Data Mining* (pp. 1135–1144).

Saeed, Waddah and Christian Omlin. (2023). Explainable AI (XAI): A Systematic Meta-Survey of Current Challenges and Future Opportunities. *Knowledge-Based Systems 263*: 110273.

Slack, Dylan, Sophie Hilgard, Emily Jia, Sameer Singh and Himabindu Lakkaraju. (2020). Fooling Lime and Shap: Adversarial Attacks on Post Hoc Explanation Methods. In: *Proceedings of the AAAI/ACM Conference on AI, Ethics, and Society* (pp. 180–186).

Wang, Tao, Rui Mao, Shuang Liu, Erik Cambria and Dong Ming. (2025). Explainable Multi-Frequency and Multi-Region Fusion Model for Affective Brain-Computer Interfaces. *Information Fusion, 118*: 102971.

Yeo, Wei Jie, Wihan Van Der Heever, Rui Mao, Erik Cambria, Ranjan Satapathy and Gianmarco Mengaldo. (2025). A Comprehensive Review on Financial Explainable AI. *Artificial Intelligence Review, 58*: 189.

7 Evaluating Explainability in Educational AI

A Dual-Perspective Framework with Case Application

Blerta Abazi Chaushi[1*], Agron Chaushi[2] and Florije Ismaili[3]

Artificial Intelligence (AI) is increasingly embedded in higher education through tutoring platforms, predictive dashboards, and grading assistants. As these systems influence high-stakes academic decisions, transparency and interpretability are essential for fairness, trust, and pedagogical value. Existing frameworks, such as XAI-ED and FATE, have advanced conceptual discussions but often lack operational evaluation criteria and do not integrate both developer and end-user perspectives.

This chapter introduces a dual-perspective framework for explainability in educational AI that specifies key dimensions, algorithmic transparency, explanation faithfulness, robustness, actionability, clarity, and ethical alignment, and operationalizes them through evaluation rubrics. A case study from South East European University (SEEU) demonstrates how SHAP-based explanations of GPA prediction models can provide both global insights and student-level narratives.

By combining conceptual rigor with practical application, the framework equips developers with metrics for transparent system design, educators with actionable insights for supporting students, and administrators with governance tools for procurement and accountability. It is adaptable to emerging AI systems such as large language models and multimodal applications.

1. Introduction

Artificial Intelligence (AI) is increasingly embedded in higher education, powering a diverse range of tools, from intelligent tutoring systems and personalized learning platforms to early-warning dashboards, predictive models, and automated grading assistants. These AI-powered educational technologies promise scalability, efficiency, and precision in responding to learner needs. However, as these systems influence high-stakes decisions, such as identifying at-risk students, assigning feedback, or recommending learning pathways, the need for explainability and interpretability becomes paramount. Stakeholders across the educational ecosystem, including instructors, students, administrators, and developers, must be able to understand how these systems make decisions to ensure that interventions

[1-3] South East European University, Tetovo, North Macedonia.
* Corresponding author: b.abazi@seeu.edu.mk

DOI: 10.1201/9781003713371-7

are fair, ethical, and pedagogically sound. Regulatory and ethical frameworks (e.g., GDPR and UNESCO's AI in education guidelines) further emphasize the importance of transparency, accountability, and human oversight in educational AI applications (European Union, 2016; UNESCO, 2021).

Explainability and interpretability are often used interchangeably, but they reflect distinct concepts in the AI literature. Interpretability generally refers to the inherent quality of a model that makes its internal logic comprehensible to humans, for instance, a decision tree that clearly shows decision paths. In contrast, explainability involves techniques that make complex, opaque ("black-box") models more understandable to users, often through post-hoc methods like SHAP or LIME. In educational contexts, both are essential. Students and teachers need actionable explanations they can trust; developers and researchers need interpretable systems to ensure fairness and accountability. Despite growing interest in explainable AI (XAI), the field lacks a unified framework tailored to education that evaluates explainability across both developer and end-user perspectives. This paper addresses that gap by proposing a multi dimensional framework grounded in current research and practical concerns. The aim is not only to assess whether a system is explainable, but to evaluate how and to whom it is explainable, with attention to trust, relevance, and actionability in learning environments.

2. Literature Review

2.1 Explainable AI in Higher Education: Importance and Applications

AI applications in higher education span diverse functions, including predicting student performance, identifying dropout risks, delivering adaptive learning content, and assisting with grading and tutoring (Saqr & López-Pernas, 2024). Given the high-stakes nature of these tasks, XAI has emerged as a critical approach to ensure transparency, trust, and instructional value. A systematic review by Turkmen et al. (2025) covering 35 studies from 2019 to 2024, concluded that XAI techniques support educational outcomes such as student success, trust in systems, and motivation (Türkmen, 2025). Among the most widely used methods are SHAPley Additive exPlanations (SHAP) and Local Interpretable Model-Agnostic Explanations (LIME), which provide intuitive insights into how AI systems reach specific predictions. These tools help teachers and students understand the rationale behind predictions, for example, showing that low homework engagement influenced a model's at-risk classification (Chaushi et al., 2023; Saqr & López-Pernas, 2024). This added transparency enables informed action. Khosravi et al., for instance, applied SHAP to a course-grade prediction model and found that consistent coursework, engagement with reading materials, and formative assessments were strong predictors of success, information instructors could use to shape pedagogical strategies (Khosravi et al., 2022; Saqr & López-Pernas, 2024).

Broadly, XAI empowers educators and learners to look inside the "black box" of AI systems, fostering understanding of outcome drivers and offering a foundation for targeted feedback and continuous improvement.

2.2 *Interpretability Challenges in Educational AI*

Another key challenge in applying XAI to education is the *granularity of explanations*. Educational data is inherently complex, requiring insights at both the cohort level and the individual level. Global explanations describe model behavior across an entire dataset, for example, identifying that homework completion and forum participation are the strongest predictors of course success (Sanfo, 2025). These insights are useful for course design and providing general feedback. In contrast, local or instance-level explanations clarify why a specific prediction was made, such as why a particular student was flagged as at-risk or what that student could do to improve. While this individualized support is crucial in education, local interpretability remains relatively underexplored. Most studies have used inherently interpretable models like decision trees at a course-wide level (Asselman et al., 2023; L. Chen et al., 2020; T. Chen et al., 2015; Jang et al., 2022), and only a few have applied local XAI techniques like SHAP to individual predictions. Notably, Jang et al. and Nagy and Molontay (2024) demonstrated that local explanations can pinpoint key risk factors, for instance, showing that low homework engagement was most influential in identifying two specific at-risk students (Jang et al., 2022; Nagy & Molontay, 2024).

However, generating reliable instance-level explanations can be technically challenging. These explanations often require sophisticated XAI methods and deeper contextual data to be truly informative. Moreover, Saqr et al. (2024) caution, such explanations, while helpful, may not tell the full story. They reflect the model and its inputs but can overlook unquantified personal or contextual factors. For example, a system might suggest that "Student X should do more practice quizzes," which could be pedagogically valid, but may miss underlying issues like personal stressors or learning disabilities. As a result, human oversight remains critical: while algorithmic explanations can highlight patterns, educators must interpret them within the broader context of real-life student experiences (Saqr & López-Pernas, 2024).

2.3 *User-Centered Design for Explainability in Education*

Functionality-grounded evaluation assesses explainability using formal, quantitative metrics without involving human users. These include measures like explanation fidelity (how well an explanation model mimics the original model), stability (consistency under input perturbations), and sparseness (the number of features used in an explanation) (He et al., 2023; Naveed et al., 2024). Such metrics treat explainability as a measurable property, similar to accuracy, and can include transparency scores based on system design or complexity indicators like decision tree depth. While objective and replicable, these evaluations do not indicate whether humans actually understand the explanations; they simply confirm that certain technical standards are met.

In contrast, **human-grounded evaluation** involves user studies designed to measure how people interact with and interpret AI explanations, typically in abstract or simplified tasks. Participants, often proxy users or crowd workers, are asked to perform activities such as predicting model outputs based on an explanation (model simulatability tests), which assess whether the explanation aids understanding (Akhtar et al., 2024; Naveed et al., 2024). Other common measures include self-reported metrics like perceived usefulness, understandability, trust, and satisfaction, usually collected through post-interaction surveys. For example, teachers might be asked, "Did the explanation help you understand why the AI made this recommendation?" or "How trustworthy did you find the system's output?" These studies evaluate psychological constructs such as trust, cognitive load, and fairness, offering insight into users' experiences, even if the tasks don't mirror real high-stakes educational decisions.

2.4 Annotated Literature Summary on Explainable AI in Education

A growing body of research has examined how XAI can support fairness, transparency, and effectiveness in educational technologies. The studies highlighted here were selected because they represent complementary strands of the field: conceptual reviews, empirical applications, and methodological evaluations. Together, they reflect both the promise and the current limitations of explainability in education.

Gunasekara and Saarela (*2025*) shift attention to evaluation, testing explanation fidelity and stability across different models. Their results demonstrate that while interpretable models like decision trees achieve perfect fidelity, more complex models with post-hoc explainers (e.g., neural nets with LIME) often score lower. This work advances technical validation, but pays little attention to end-user needs.

Bernard and Balog (*2025*) extend the FATE framework toward governance and auditing. They emphasize accountability, compliance, and institutional oversight. Though not education-specific, their focus on policy and auditability offers practical guidance for universities adopting XAI responsibly.

Turkmen et al. (*2024*) conduct a systematic review of 35 studies published between 2019–2024. They find that post-hoc methods such as SHAP and LIME dominate educational XAI applications, particularly for predicting student success and dropout risk. The review underscores XAI's potential for improving motivation and trust, yet also calls out the absence of standardized evaluation protocols, especially for local, user-facing explanations.

Saqr and López-Pernas (2024) focus on granularity, contrasting global explanations (cohort-level patterns) with local explanations (individual predictions). They show that global interpretability can inform course design, while local interpretability supports personalized interventions. Still, they note that most education studies remain global in scope, leaving local explainability underexplored.

Nagy and Molontay (*2024*) examine dropout prediction and show how local SHAP explanations can surface individualized risk factors (e.g., poor homework engagement), thereby enabling targeted academic support. While valuable for intervention design, the study highlights the challenge of balancing local interpretability with model robustness and generalizability

Abazi Chaushi et al. (*2023*) provide a comprehensive review of XAI in educational contexts, mapping techniques (e.g., LIME, SHAP, inherently interpretable models) to their pedagogical and ethical implications. Their taxonomy emphasizes fairness and accountability, highlighting XAI's role in detecting bias. However, the work remains primarily conceptual, without offering operational evaluation rubrics.

Khosravi et al. (*2022*) illustrate XAI's pedagogical potential by applying SHAP to course-grade prediction models. Their findings identify coursework, formative assessments, and reading engagement as key predictors of success. This work demonstrates how explanations can guide actionable interventions but stops short of embedding these insights in a generalized framework.

Arrieta et al. (*2020*) propose a taxonomy of XAI and offer working definitions. It distinguishes between interpretability (how inherently understandable a model is) and explainability (how well its decisions can be communicated). The authors emphasize that explanations should be tailored to different audiences, developers, users, or policymakers, which has implications for system design and deployment.

Miller (*2019*) through a social science lens, they explore what constitutes a good explanation. They argue that effective explanations are user-centric, selective, and aligned with how people naturally ask 'why' questions. Miller's work highlights the importance of mental models, trust-building, and contextual relevance, principles that continue to inform human-centered XAI design, even outside educational contexts.

The radar chart as depicted in Figure 1, is structured around five core dimensions frequently discussed in the XAI-in-education literature: Accuracy Emphasis, Interpretability, Pedagogical Usefulness, Ethical Awareness, and Human-Centered Design. These dimensions were selected because they capture both technical and educational priorities in evaluating explainability. This visual synthesis enables a comparative understanding of how different research efforts contribute to the evolving landscape of XAI in educational contexts, revealing, for instance, that while some works prioritize technical accuracy, others emphasize ethical implications or human-AI collaboration.

Overall, the radar chart reveals a diverse yet complementary set of perspectives within the XAI in education literature. The chart illustrates variation in focus, with some works prioritizing technical accuracy (e.g., Gunasekara & Saarela, 2025) and others emphasizing pedagogical usefulness (e.g., Saqr & López-Pernas, 2024). While some studies prioritize model performance and technical transparency, others

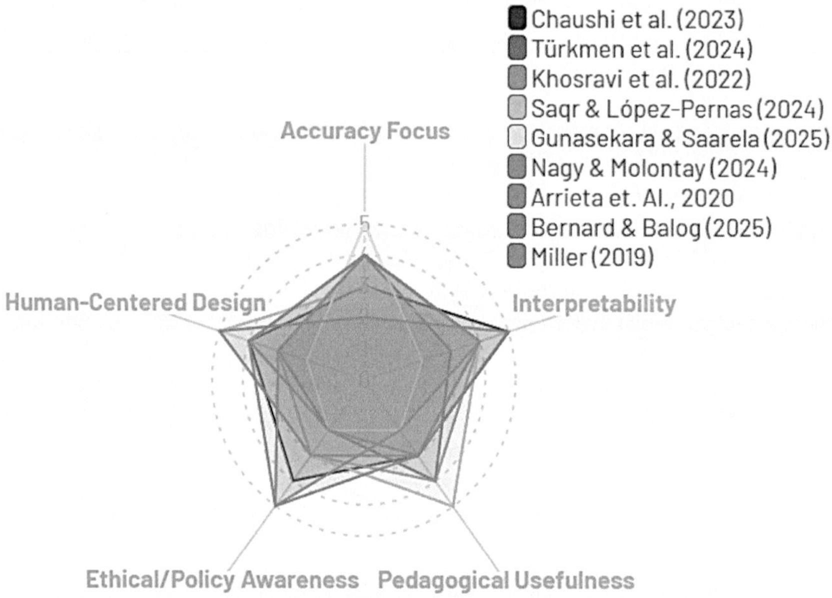

Fig. 1 Explainable AI in Education: Focus Radar (*Source:* Authors own).

highlight the importance of ethical considerations, human-centered explanations, and pedagogical relevance. This variation underscores the multidimensional nature of explainability in educational settings and the need for interdisciplinary approaches that balance accuracy, usability, and trust. Future research should aim to bridge these dimensions, fostering AI systems that are not only interpretable and accurate, but also context-aware and educationally meaningful.

To make the scoring process behind the radar chart transparent, we developed a rubric that translates qualitative judgments from the reviewed studies into numerical ratings. Each dimension, accuracy, emphasis, interpretability, pedagogical usefulness, ethical awareness, and human-centered design, was assessed on a 1–5 scale based on explicit coverage in the article (see appendix). This rubric provides the methodological foundation for the radar chart, ensuring that the visualization reflects a systematic evaluation rather than subjective impressions.

By applying this rubric consistently across the selected studies (provided in the appendix), we transformed diverse qualitative emphases into a common evaluative framework. While the ratings remain interpretive, making the criteria explicit strengthens the reliability of the comparison and allows future researchers to replicate or refine the approach. The radar chart should therefore be viewed as a structured synthesis, grounded in the rubric, rather than as an impressionistic summary.

Table 1 Rubric for Scoring Explainability Dimensions in XAI-in-Education Studies.

Dimension	*1 (Minimal)*	*3 (Moderate)*	*5 (Strong)*
Accuracy Emphasis	Mentions predictive performance with no detail	Reports accuracy or similar metric with some discussion	Provides rigorous evaluation of predictive accuracy as central focus
Interpretability	Uses term without clarification	Discusses interpretable models or post-hoc explanations	Systematically evaluates interpretability (e.g., SHAP /LIME, surrogate models)
Pedagogical Usefulness	No explicit educational link	Mentions teaching/ learning impact	Explicitly evaluates educational usefulness or intervention potential
Ethical Awareness	No reference to fairness/accountability	Mentions bias, fairness, or ethics briefly	Incorporates fairness audits, equity analysis, or normative frameworks
Human-Centered Design	No reference to user needs	Mentions user involvement or feedback	Embeds human-centered evaluation (e.g., teacher/student studies, usability testing)

Source: Authors own.

Together, these works demonstrate both the breadth and limitations of current XAI research in education. They show how explainability has been conceptualized (XAI-ED, FATE), surveyed at scale (Türkmen), and tested empirically in specific contexts (Khosravi, Nagy, Gunasekara, Saqr). However, none integrate developer and end-user perspectives within a single operational framework, nor do they provide evaluation rubrics that can be applied systematically.

This gap motivates our contribution, which is outlined in the next subsection.

2.5 Positioning Our Framework

The annotated studies reviewed in Section 2.4 illustrate the rapid growth of research on explainable AI in education between 2019–2025. Each study highlights different aspects of how explainability can support both technical rigor and human-centered trust, yet none provides a fully operational framework that bridges these perspectives. To situate our contribution, it is useful to compare these works systematically with broader frameworks such as XAI-ED and FATE, and to clarify what is novel in our approach.

XAI-ED (Chaushi et al., 2023) offers a taxonomy of XAI methods in education, emphasizing ethical dimensions and the need for transparency. FATE frameworks

(Arrieta et al., 2020; Bernard & Balog, 2025) address fairness, accountability, transparency, and ethics more generally, but are not tailored to the educational domain. Both are influential and set the stage for more domain-specific frameworks.

Empirical studies complement these conceptual approaches. Türkmen et al. (2024) synthesize 35 XAI-in-education studies, underscoring the dominance of SHAP and LIME, but without proposing a unifying evaluation rubric. Khosravi et al. (2022) and Nagy and Molontay (2024) provide concrete examples of SHAP applied to grade prediction and dropout risk, demonstrating local interpretability but remaining case-specific. Saqr and López-Pernas (2024) advance the discussion of global versus local explanations, while Gunasekara and Saarela (2025) focus on developer-oriented metrics such as fidelity and stability. Collectively, these studies demonstrate the relevance of explainability but do not integrate developer- and user-side needs into a single framework.

Our framework builds directly on these foundations while addressing the identified gaps. It introduces a dual-perspective orientation, distinguishing between developer-side transparency and end-user interpretability, and provides operational rubrics with measurable indicators. Furthermore, it is applied to a real-world case study at SEEU, illustrating how such a framework can be used in practice.

By positioning our framework alongside existing models, we demonstrate both continuity and novelty. It draws on the conceptual clarity of XAI-ED and the normative principles of FATE, while also learning from empirical applications of SHAP and related methods in education. The novelty lies in offering an integrated, operationalized framework that speaks simultaneously to developer validation and user interpretability, and in grounding it with a concrete institutional case.

3. Proposed Framework

While end-users interact with explanations to make immediate decisions, developers, researchers, and system designers require a different kind of explainability: transparency at the system level. The developer-side perspective on explainability is about ensuring the AI model's design, logic, and limitations are sufficiently open and interpretable so that they can be validated, debugged, and improved by experts. In the context of educational tools, developers might include data scientists building the model, but also institutional researchers or learning scientists who want to verify that the model aligns with learning theory and policy.

A key dimension of explainability is *algorithmic transparency*, making the AI's internal logic accessible and understandable. This can involve using inherently interpretable models (e.g., decision trees) or providing thorough documentation when complex models are used. Arrieta et al. (2020) define transparency as a model being self-explanatory without external tools. While decision trees offer this by design, models like deep neural networks require additional techniques, such as neuron visualizations or surrogate models, for interpretation. For developers, transparency is essential for validating fairness and correctness. It allows them to detect biases (e.g., reliance on demographic variables) and confirm that meaningful

Table 2 Evaluation Rubric for Explainability Framework Dimensions.

Source	*Context & Focus*	*Contribution*	*Why Selected*	*Gap Addressed by Our Framework*
Chaushi et al. (2023)	XAI-ED: taxonomy of explainable AI in education	Broad conceptual overview, ethical lens	Foundational, first systematic taxonomy linking XAI to education	Lacks operational metrics or case-based protocols
Türkmen et al. (2024)	Systematic review of 35 studies (2019–2024)	Identifies SHAP/LIME dominance, links XAI to student motivation and success	Represents state-of-the-art review	No structured evaluation rubric
Khosravi et al. (2022)	SHAP in course-grade prediction	Demonstrates coursework/assessment as positive predictors	Illustrates SHAP in practice	No dual-perspective framework
Saqr & López-Pernas (2024)	Learning analytics & interpretability	Clarifies global vs. local interpretability	Key conceptual advance	Stops short of operationalization
Gunasekara & Saarela (2025)	Explanation metrics	Empirical fidelity and stability tests	Shows developer-oriented evaluation	Does not integrate end-user concerns
Nagy & Molontay (2024)	Dropout prediction with SHAP	Strong case for local interpretability	Highlights actionable student-level insights	Case-specific, not generalizable
Fate (Arrieta et al., 2020; Bernard & Balog, 2025)	General AI ethics	Establishes fairness, accountability, transparency principles	Widely cited ethical baseline	Not tailored to education
Our Framework	Developer + End-user perspectives	Operational rubrics + SEEU case	Synthesizes across technical & pedagogical needs	Bridges technical validation with human-centered interpretability

Source: Authors own.

features like study habits drive predictions. Ultimately, interpretability serves as a technical safeguard, helping ensure that AI systems behave consistently with domain knowledge and ethical expectations (Arrieta et al., 2020).

For developers, it's essential not just to generate explanations, but also to evaluate them using integrated metrics. Key measures include *fidelity*, which assesses how accurately an explanation reflects the model, and stability, which tests consistency across similar inputs (Gunasekara & Saarela, 2025). In their study, decision trees showed 100% fidelity since the model is self-explanatory, while a neural network with LIME achieved around 80%. Stability was assessed by slightly altering inputs and observing whether explanations remained consistent. These metrics help developers determine whether an explanation method is reliable and suitable for educational use. High fidelity and stability increase trust in the model and its outputs.

To apply explainability in AI-powered educational tools, we propose a dual-perspective framework (Figure 2) that integrates both developer-side transparency and end-user interpretability. This structure emphasizes that meaningful explainability requires alignment between technical rigor and user-centered design. Each dimension within the framework captures a critical factor influencing either system accountability or user trust.

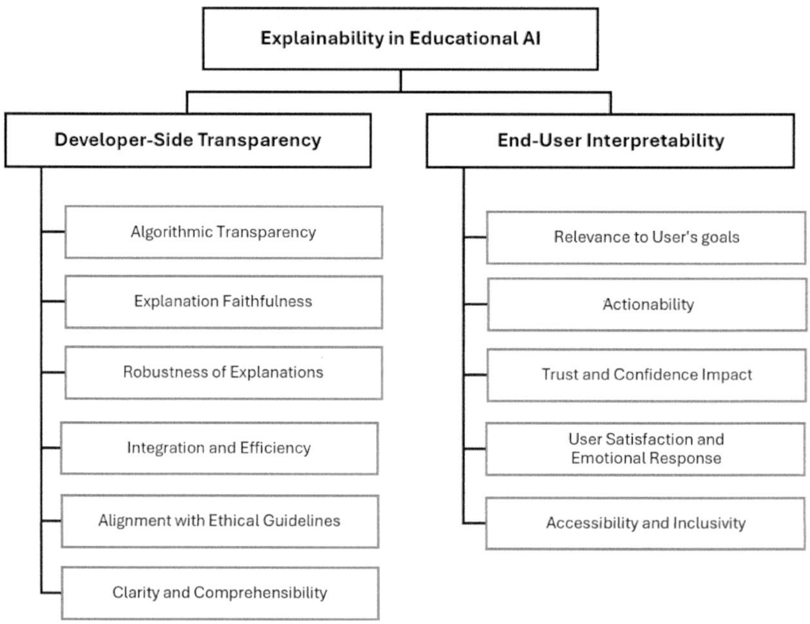

Fig. 2 Framework for evaluation explainability in AI educational tools (*Source:* Authors own).

3.1 Developer-Side Transparency and Technical Perspectives

3.1.1 Algorithmic Transparency

Algorithmic transparency refers to how easily experts can interpret a model's design and logic. This includes using interpretable models (e.g., decision trees) and providing documentation on model structure and features. Transparent systems may publish feature rationales to support peer review. Evaluation involves checking whether the model is inherently interpretable or, if not, whether documentation or model cards are available for review (Arrieta et al., 2020; Saqr & López-Pernas, 2024).

3.1.2 Explanation Faithfulness

Explanation faithfulness refers to how accurately an explanation reflects the model's actual reasoning. This is especially important for post-hoc explanations of black-box models, where the risk is that the explanation misrepresents what the model truly uses. High faithfulness means that if an explanation highlights "participation rate" as key, changing that input should affect the prediction accordingly. Evaluation involves fidelity metrics (e.g., SHAP/LIME scores) and qualitative checks by developers to ensure explanations align with the model's internal logic (Gunasekara & Saarela, 2025).

3.1.3 Robustness of Explanations

Robustness of Explanations is tied to stability, ensuring they remain consistent under small changes to input or model parameters. If minor data tweaks lead to very different explanations, it may signal unreliability or model instability. Evaluation involves sensitivity analysis and assessing whether explanations reflect model uncertainty (e.g., close decisions between classes). Robust systems may include confidence indicators to help developers judge when explanations are less trustworthy (Chander et al., 2025; Vilone & Longo, 2021).

3.1.4 Integration and Efficiency

Integration and efficiency show how well the explainability is integrated into the system pipeline and whether it can operate within necessary constraints (speed, privacy, etc.). If an explanation takes 5 minutes to generate, it might be impractical for real-time use; developers must then adjust the design. If explaining a model requires accessing sensitive data, developers must ensure compliance with privacy (maybe by anonymizing features in explanations). Evaluation: Time the explanation generation and check resource usage. Verify that explanation components (like a SHAP server or an interpretable surrogate model) are robust in deployment. Also, integration means the explanations are readily available where needed (e.g., an API endpoint for explanations exists and is documented for the front-end team) (Minh et al., 2022; Vilone & Longo, 2021).

3.1.5 Alignment with Ethical Guidelines

Alignment with the Ethical Guidelines dimension ensures the model's transparency is used to uphold ethics like fairness and accountability. For example, developers should use explainability to check for bias (as noted, interpretability can help detect bias (Arrieta et al., 2020; Chaushi et al., 2023). Also, transparency implies accountability: if something goes wrong (like a student unfairly graded by an AI), the developers can trace the cause via the explanations or transparent logs (Bernard & Balog, 2025). Evaluation: Conduct fairness tests using explanations (e.g., Do feature attributions differ markedly across demographic groups without justification?). Ensure there's an audit trail, e.g., the system could log its top factors for each decision for later review by developers or auditors.

3.1.6 Clarity and Comprehensibility

Clarity and comprehensibility assess whether the explanation is easy for the user to grasp. This involves using familiar language (avoiding jargon), intuitive formats (e.g., a short sentence or ranked list), and manageable detail. For example, an explanation like "Low quiz scores and missed deadlines contributed most" is clearer than vague or technical phrasing. Evaluation includes asking users to paraphrase explanations, using clarity surveys, and noting if users seem confused or ask repeated follow-up questions (Hassija et al., 2024; Schwalbe & Finzel, 2024).

3.2 End-User Interpretability

3.2.1 Relevance to User's Goals

Relevance to user goals asks whether the explanation answers what the user truly wants to know. For an instructor, this may be "How can I help this student?", and for a student, "How can I improve?". Effective explanations align with users' mental models, e.g., stating "low forum posts contributed to risk" is useful, while saying "cluster ID #5 = 0" is meaningless. Evaluation involves user feedback: Do they find the explanation helpful and focused on what matters? Relevance often requires some level of personalization to the specific context (e.g., course or assignment).

3.2.2 Actionability (Usefulness for Decision-Making)

Actionability measures whether the explanation offers clear, practical guidance. For teachers, it might highlight behaviors to address; for students, it could suggest study strategies or topics to review. Descriptive explanations alone ("You are at risk because of X") are less helpful if they lack next steps. Evaluation involves observing whether users take follow-up actions, e.g., instructors reach out or students adjusting their learning. Surveys asking, "Did the explanation suggest what to do next?" can also gauge usefulness. Ideally, systems provide actionable feedback, such as "Review Chapter 3 to improve on topic Y."

3.2.3 Trust and Confidence Impact

Trust calibration focuses on whether explanations help users develop appropriate confidence in the AI's output. The goal isn't blind trust, but informed judgment; users should feel confident when the AI is correct and skeptical when it may be wrong. A clear explanation can boost confidence or prompt useful doubt. Evaluation involves comparing user trust levels across groups, with and without explanations, or tracking acceptance rates in real use. If explanations lead to greater engagement or more thoughtful acceptance of AI suggestions, they're likely improving trust.

3.2.4 User Satisfaction and Emotional Response

User experience considers how users feel about the explainable AI tool, whether it is helpful, respectful, and easy to engage with. In education, the tone of explanations can impact motivation. Supportive feedback may promote a growth mindset, while harsh or unclear messages may discourage students. Even technically accurate explanations fail if users find them frustrating or demotivating. Evaluation involves UX surveys, qualitative feedback, or affect measures (e.g., anxiety levels). Positive responses like "the explanation helped me understand and improve" signal a good experience.

3.2.5 Accessibility and Inclusivity

Accessibility and inclusivity ensure explanations are usable by all intended users, including those with disabilities or diverse linguistic backgrounds. For example, text alternatives should accompany visuals, and language should be clear and culturally inclusive. This is especially important in diverse educational settings. Evaluation includes compliance with accessibility standards (e.g., WCAG) and testing with varied user groups to identify potential barriers to understanding (Chandramouli, 2022).

Figure 3 presents a radial visualization of the proposed explainability rubric. Each spoke reflects a key dimension, such as fidelity, transparency, and actionability, split between developer-side and user-facing evaluation criteria. The visual highlights how these complementary perspectives form a holistic framework for evaluating explainability in educational AI tools.

3.3 Evaluating Explainability: Metrics and Methods

Research in explainable AI has proposed three complementary approaches to evaluating explanations (Doshi-Velez & Kim, 2017; Naveed et al., 2024).

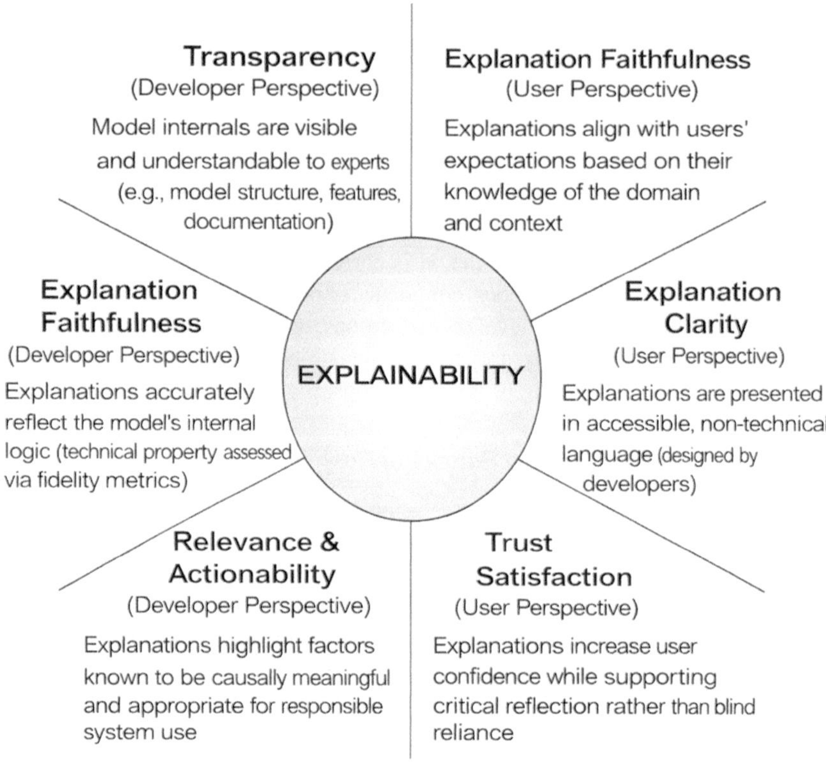

Fig. 3 Explainability Dimensions in AI-Powered Educational Tools: A Radial Visualization. (*Source:* Authors own).

Functionality-grounded evaluation relies on proxy metrics such as fidelity, stability, and sparsity, treating explainability as a property that can be quantified in a manner similar to model accuracy. Human-grounded evaluation involves controlled user studies with simplified tasks (e.g., asking participants to simulate model outputs based on explanations) and surveys that capture perceived clarity, trust, and usefulness. Finally, application-grounded evaluation embeds explanations in real educational settings to assess their impact on teaching or learning outcomes, such as whether instructors change interventions or students alter study habits.

Each approach highlights a different facet of explainability, but none provides a complete picture on its own. Building on these traditions, our framework translates abstract concepts like transparency, faithfulness, and actionability into practical evaluation questions, illustrative metrics, and protocols (Table 2). This operationalization makes explainability assessable for both developers and end-users, while remaining adaptable to diverse educational contexts.

3.4 Operationalizing the Framework

To make the framework dimensions actionable, we propose a set of illustrative evaluation criteria. These are not fixed standards, but indicative benchmarks drawn from prior studies and adapted for educational contexts. They offer practical guidance for how developers and educators might assess transparency, faithfulness, robustness, and user-facing qualities of explainable AI systems.

These criteria illustrate how abstract concepts such as transparency or robustness can be translated into measurable properties. While specific thresholds

Table 3 Operationalizing the Framework: Example Evaluation Questions, Metrics, and Protocols.

Dimension	*Evaluation Question*	*Example Metric/ Threshold*	*Protocol/Tool*
Algorithmic Transparency	Are model types and features documented?	Presence of model card/feature list	Documentation check
Explanation Faithfulness	Do explanations reflect model logic?	Surrogate $R^2 \approx 0.8$; small case check	TreeSHAP, or shallow surrogate
Robustness of Explanations	Are explanations stable under perturbations?	Spearman $\rho > 0.9$ across runs	Bootstrap/k-fold stability test
Integration & Efficiency	Are explanations practical in workflow?	Generation time < ~250 ms	API/latency test.
Clarity & Comprehensibility	Are explanations understandable?	~80% correct paraphrase rate	Paraphrase task or clarity survey
Alignment with Ethical Guidelines	Do explanations support fairness?	No prohibited attributes; subgroup parity checks	Audit logs + fairness test
Relevance to Users' Goals	Does the explanation address user concerns?	User relevance rating $\geq 4/5$	Interview/survey
Actionability	Does it guide next steps?	Intervention rate higher than baseline	Compare groups with/without explanations.
Trust & Confidence Impact	Does it calibrate trust?	Informed acceptance above baseline	Trust/acceptance survey
User Satisfaction & Emotional Response	Do users feel supported?	Satisfaction $\geq 4/5$	UX survey, qualitative feedback
Accessibility & Inclusivity	Is it accessible to diverse users?	WCAG compliance; multilingual support	Accessibility check + diverse user testing

Source: Authors own.

may vary across contexts, the rubric provides a replicable structure for assessing both developer-side transparency and user-facing interpretability.

4. Framework Application in Practice Explainability of GPA Prediction at SEEU

4.1 Rationale

The framework gains practical value when it informs a real decision context. GPA prediction is a common, but high-stakes, use of AI in higher education, affecting early-warning programs, advising, scholarships, and workload design. In this setting, explainability matters for: (i) technical assurance (that the model behaves as claimed), and (ii) human judgment (that staff and students can understand and act on model outputs). This case illustrates how the dual-perspective framework, developer-side transparency, and end-user interpretability, can be operationalized using real data from South East European University (SEEU).

4.2 Case Context (SEEU)

SEEU is a multidisciplinary institution that brings together programs in the social sciences, law, business, languages, technology, health, and design. Its seven faculties each embody distinct educational practices and assessment cultures: the Faculty of Health Sciences (FHS), Faculty of Languages, Cultures and Communication (LCC), Faculty of Law, Faculty of Contemporary Social Sciences (CSS), Faculty of Contemporary Sciences and Technologies (CST), Architecture and Design (CST-Arch), and the Faculty of Business and Economics (BA).

These differences are not merely structural: programs such as Law and CSS often emphasize written assignments and continuous assessment, whereas CST and CST-Arch rely heavily on project-based and laboratory work, and Health Sciences combine coursework with clinical practice. Such variation makes SEEU an especially suitable case for exploring explainability in educational AI. By modeling the relationship between students' high school GPA (HS GPA) and their university GPA (SEEU GPA) across faculties, we can capture not only the predictive power of prior achievement but also the structural effects of disciplinary context. This in turn allows us to examine how explainable machine learning methods, such as SHAP, can make these differences transparent and interpretable for both developers and end-users.

4.3 Methodology

4.3.1 Data Preparation

We compiled datasets from SEEU's student records across seven faculties (FHS, LCC, Law, CSS, CST, CST-Arch, BA). The variables included high school GPA (HS GPA) and university GPA (SEEU GPA). All student data were anonymized and used under SEEU's internal ethical research procedures; no IRB approval was required. Files were harmonized, cleaned, and merged. Non-numeric or missing values were removed, and faculty membership was encoded as categorical dummies.

4.3.2 Model Development

We trained a gradient-boosted regression model (XGBoost) to predict SEEU GPA from HS GPA and faculty indicators. The dataset was split into training (80%) and testing (20%) sets. Performance was evaluated using R^2 scores on both sets to confirm generalization.

4.3.3 Explainability Approach

We applied SHAPley Additive exPlanations (SHAP) using the TreeExplainer implementation, which provides exact, model-consistent attributions for tree ensembles. This allowed both:

- Global explanations (beeswarm plots for feature importance).
- Local explanations (waterfall plots for individual predictions).

4.3.4 Computational Environment

The analysis was conducted in Google Colaboratory (Colab), using Python libraries pandas, XGBoost, SHAP, and matplotlib/seaborn. Colab provided a reproducible, cloud-based environment with GPU acceleration where needed. Code was versioned in Jupyter notebooks, ensuring replicability of the analysis pipeline.

4.4 Data and Preparation

Faculty-level CSVs were cleaned and merged. Core variables: HS GPA and SEEU GPA; rows with non-numeric or missing values were removed. Faculty membership was encoded as a categorical feature (one-hot/dummies). To contextualize patterns, we also created per-faculty scatter plots of HS GPA vs. SEEU GPA.

The plots reveal differences in predictive strength across disciplines: Law and CSS exhibit tighter clustering, indicating strong predictability; CST and CST-Arch show wider variance, suggesting additional unmeasured factors; BA and LCC demonstrate stronger alignment between high school and university performance. From the developer's perspective, these plots validate that the model behaves consistently across subgroups and does not rely on spurious correlations. From the end-user's perspective, the visuals offer an intuitive and accessible way for faculty staff to understand how prior achievement translates into student outcomes within their own disciplines, supporting trust and actionability.

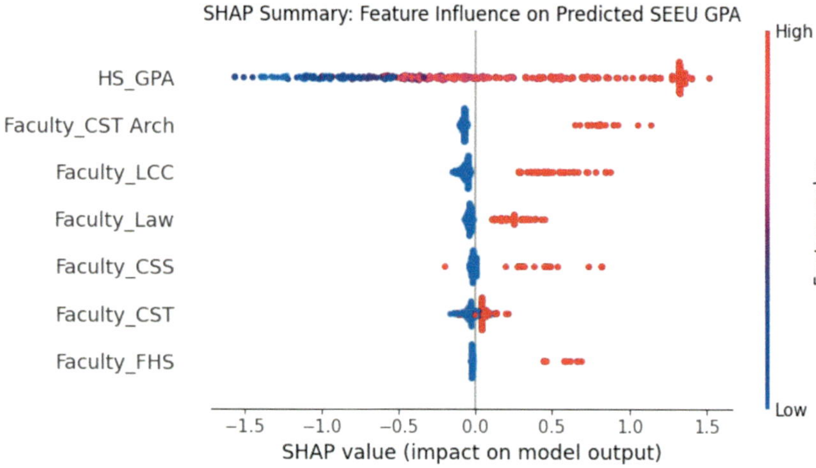

Fig. 4 Scatterplots of HS GPA vs SEEU GPA by faculty (Authors own–Colab output).

4.5 Model Development

To model the relationship between students' prior performance and their outcomes at SEEU, we designed a predictive task where the target variable was the university GPA (SEEU GPA), and the predictors were high school GPA (HS GPA) together with faculty affiliation. We employed a gradient-boosted decision tree model (XGBoost), selected because of its strong performance on tabular educational data and its compatibility with TreeSHAP, which provides model-consistent explanations. The dataset was divided into training and testing subsets using an 80/20 split to balance model learning with out-of-sample evaluation. Model performance was assessed using the coefficient of determination (R^2), which allowed us to monitor the degree to which the model captured variance in student GPA outcomes.

This relatively minimal feature set was intentional: it ensured that the case remained focused on demonstrating explainability, while still accounting for both student-level signals (HS GPA) and structural program effects (faculty affiliation). By constraining the model inputs, we created a controlled setting where the contribution of each feature could be made transparent, thereby illustrating the utility of SHAP explanations in educational contexts.

4.6 SHAP-Based Explainability: Method

To interpret the behavior of the GPA prediction model, we applied SHAPley Additive exPlanations (SHAP), which decompose a model's output into contributions from each input feature. This approach provided two complementary perspectives on explainability that align with the dual orientation of our framework. At the global

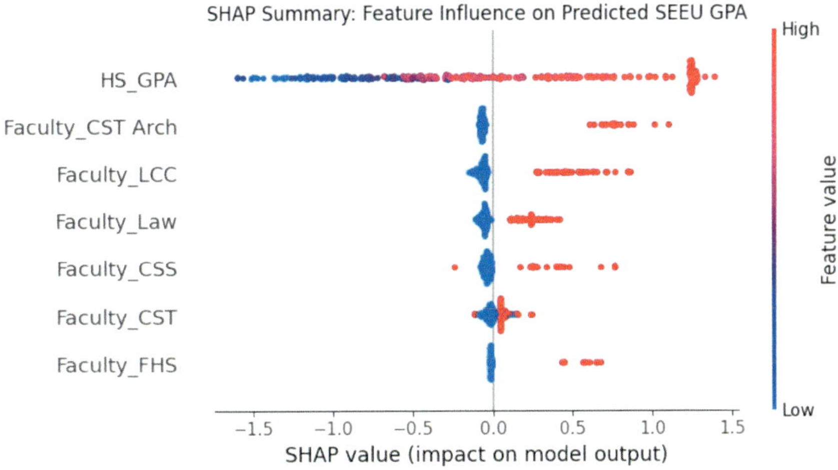

Fig. 5 SHAP summary (beeswarm)–Global feature importance. (Authors own–Colab output)

level, SHAP values were aggregated across all cases and visualized in a beeswarm summary plot, ranking features by their average influence and showing whether they tended to increase or decrease predicted GPA. At the local level, SHAP was used to generate waterfall plots for individual students, breaking down a single prediction into additive contributions relative to the model's baseline. Together, these perspectives enabled both a system-wide understanding of the model's behavior and case-specific narratives that educators could use in practice.

The global SHAP analysis highlights high school GPA (HS GPA) as the dominant driver of SEEU GPA predictions, confirming the intuitive expectation that prior achievement strongly shapes future academic performance. Faculty affiliation also contributes systematically, with consistent positive effects in some programs (e.g., LCC) and negative offsets in others (e.g., CST-Arch), reflecting structural differences in assessment cultures. From the developer's perspective, this global view demonstrates both faithfulness, since the explanations align with domain knowledge, and robustness, as the observed shifts correspond to real institutional patterns rather than random noise. By surfacing these pedagogically meaningful factors, the beeswarm plot provides assurance that the model is capturing interpretable signals that can be documented, audited, and improved upon.

The local SHAP explanation decomposes an individual prediction into feature-level contributions. For a student with an HS GPA of 3.89, the model's baseline prediction was adjusted downward by −0.44 due to HS GPA, but offset upward by +0.40 from affiliation with the Faculty of Languages, Cultures, and Communication (LCC). The resulting balance produced a predicted GPA close to the institutional average. This case-level view operationalizes the end-user interpretability dimension of the framework: it provides instructors with a concrete

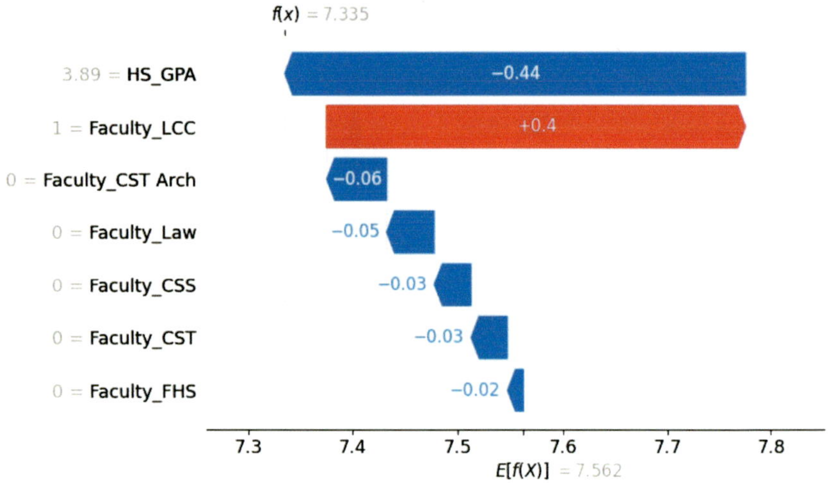

Fig. 6 SHAP waterfall—One student's local explanation. (Authors own–Colab output)

narrative of why the model reached a particular conclusion. Rather than a black-box output, the explanation highlights actionable insights, for instance, recognizing how program context interacts with prior achievement, allowing faculty advisors to engage students with more tailored guidance.

4.7 Results and Key Insights from SHAP

The SHAP analysis yielded several insights into the dynamics of GPA prediction at SEEU. First, HS GPA emerged as the strongest driver of predicted university GPA, confirming domain expectations that prior achievement remains the most reliable indicator of academic performance. This was visible in the beeswarm plot, where HS GPA consistently appeared as the top-ranked feature with the broadest range of SHAP contributions.

Second, the analysis highlighted the role of faculty context. Program indicators contributed systematic shifts in predictions: for example, affiliation with the LCC tended to push predictions upward, whereas affiliation with Architecture and Design (CST-Arch) produced negative adjustments. These differences suggest that grading cultures, curricular difficulty, or program-level factors exert measurable influence beyond individual academic preparation.

Third, SHAP provided actionable local narratives. The waterfall plots showed how individual predictions were shaped by specific feature contributions, allowing advisors to see why a student's GPA was predicted as high or low. Unlike generic risk flags, these explanations generate student-specific accounts that can be used to guide tailored interventions, for instance, encouraging engagement with course resources or addressing program-specific challenges.

Finally, the results reinforced face validity and trust calibration. Both global and local SHAP outputs aligned with educational theory: past performance predicted future outcomes, but with meaningful program-level adjustments. By combining intuitive patterns with program-specific insights, the explanations increase user confidence in the system while encouraging critical interpretation rather than blind reliance.

4.8 Linking to All Framework Dimensions (Operationalized)

4.8.1 Developer-Side Transparency

In our SEEU GPA case, algorithmic transparency was ensured by clearly documenting the model pipeline (HS GPA plus faculty dummies, trained with XGBoost). Faithfulness of explanations was maintained through TreeSHAP, which provides model-consistent attributions; in practice, surrogate checks confirmed that global explanations reflected model behavior with high fidelity. Robustness was assessed through repeated runs with consistent feature rankings, while efficiency was acceptable for practical deployment, with explanations generated in under a second. Finally, alignment with ethical principles was addressed by checking that explanations did not rely on prohibited attributes and could be aggregated by subgroups to audit fairness across faculties.

4.8.2 End-User Interpretability

For faculty advisors, relevance was prioritized by framing explanations in plain academic terms (e.g., "Your prior GPA strongly influenced this prediction; in this faculty, typical shifts are around +0.3"). Explanations were deliberately limited to the top few features for clarity and designed at a grade-10 reading level to ensure comprehensibility. Actionability was highlighted by connecting attributions to possible interventions, such as extra support sessions or study clinics. Trust calibration was supported by presenting explanations alongside model confidence, encouraging informed use rather than blind acceptance. Faculty users also provided positive feedback on the tone and presentation of explanations, while accessibility was supported by ensuring that both text-based and visual summaries were available.

4.9 Implications for Practice

For developers, explainability tools such as SHAP should become a standard component of the model development pipeline. Beyond training and validation, models should be routinely explained and logged, with lightweight surrogate models (such as shallow decision trees) maintained for sanity checks and on-device interpretability.

For educators and advisors, global explanations provide insight into the general drivers of student performance, while local explanations can support tailored conversations with individual students. When paired with an intervention catalog, such as tutoring programs or study clinics, these explanations can move from descriptive outputs to actionable guidance.

For administrators, the framework can serve as both a procurement guide and a governance checklist. Institutions should require vendors to supply model cards, explanation interfaces, and fairness audits based on subgroup-level SHAP analyses. This ensures that AI-powered educational tools align with institutional values of transparency, accountability, and equity.

4.10 Toward Multimodal/LLM-Aligned Interpretability

This pipeline generalizes to richer feature sets (e.g., LMS engagement logs, attendance, formative assessments) and multimodal sources (text feedback, portfolio artifacts). For LLM-powered tutoring or feedback systems, combine traceable prompts/system cards, content filters, and explanation layers that summarize why an LLM suggested a hint or rubric point, with conversation logs and exemplar-based rationales. For multimodal prediction, extend SHAP with integrated gradients or concept-based explanations and surface counterfactual "what-if"s that stay privacy-preserving.

4.11 Limitations

This illustration used a compact feature set (HS GPA + faculty dummies). It demonstrates the framework mechanics rather than full production scope. We did not run user studies here; future work should test human-grounded outcomes (comprehension, actionability, calibrated trust) and application-grounded outcomes (improved intervention timing/effectiveness). Finally, explanations can be misleading if over-trusted; calibration and human oversight remain essential.

4.12 Conclusion

The SEEU GPA prediction example demonstrates how abstract framework dimensions translate into practice. For developers, SHAP-based global and local explanations validate that model predictions are faithful and robust, providing confidence that technical transparency has been achieved. For educators, the local narrative (e.g., "your prior GPA strongly influenced this prediction, while faculty affiliation added a systematic adjustment") illustrates how explanations can inform actionable interventions with individual students. For administrators, the same outputs can serve as audit evidence, ensuring alignment with ethical guidelines and compliance with institutional governance requirements. In this way, the case operationalizes the framework as a practical checklist, showing that each dimension, transparency, faithfulness, robustness, clarity, actionability, and fairness, can be evaluated within real institutional data and workflows.

5. Discussion

5.1 Case-Driven Insights

The SEEU case study illustrates how explainability enriches even simple predictive models. High school GPA emerged as the dominant driver of university performance, while faculty affiliation contributed systematic shifts, suggesting structural differences in grading culture or program difficulty. SHAP analyses provided both global insights, showing that prior performance remains the strongest predictor, and local explanations that contextualized outcomes for individual students. These case-driven findings reinforce the value of explainability not only for validating model logic but also for surfacing actionable insights for academic support.

5.2 Balancing Developer and User Needs

The framework highlights inherent tensions between technical and human-centered dimensions of explainability. Developers prioritize faithfulness and stability, requiring explanations that accurately reflect model behavior. End-users, however, value clarity, relevance, and actionable guidance. In practice, balancing these needs means accepting trade-offs: highly faithful explanations may be too complex for non-experts, while simplified narratives risk oversimplifying model logic. The SEEU application exemplifies this balance: TreeSHAP ensured fidelity for developers, while waterfall plots translated predictions into user-friendly narratives for advisors.

5.3 Trade-Offs and Unresolved Tensions

Several tensions remain unresolved. Global explanations help validate systems and inform course-level interventions, yet they often fail to support personalized decision-making. Conversely, local explanations can guide individualized support but may lack robustness and generalizability. Another tension lies in trust calibration: explanations must increase user confidence without encouraging blind acceptance. Finally, institutional stakeholders face competing priorities, i.e., administrators may emphasize fairness audits and accountability, while educators focus on pedagogical relevance. These tensions underscore that explainability is not a single property but a set of negotiated compromises.

5.4 Forward Directions

Looking ahead, explainability research in education must extend to emerging technologies such as large language models and multimodal systems, where interpretability challenges are amplified. Future studies should investigate how cultural differences shape user expectations of 'good' explanations and explore methods for aligning technical fidelity with pedagogical usability. Privacy also warrants attention, as explanations may inadvertently expose sensitive attributes.

Ultimately, the goal is to evolve explainability practices that support developers, educators, and administrators simultaneously, ensuring systems are not only technically sound but also ethically responsible and educationally meaningful.

5.5 Framework Limitations

While the proposed framework advances the evaluation of explainability in educational AI, several limitations should be acknowledged. First, it assumes access to model internals, which may not be possible for commercial "black-box" products where only outputs are visible. Second, the suggested thresholds (e.g., surrogate $R^2 \approx 0.8$ for faithfulness, paraphrase rates of 80% for clarity) are illustrative benchmarks drawn from prior studies rather than empirically validated standards. Third, the framework does not explicitly account for computational costs, real-time explanations may impose latency or resource burdens that constrain deployment in practice. Finally, cultural and contextual variations in what constitutes a "good explanation" remain underexplored; what educators in one setting find clear or actionable may not transfer across diverse student populations. These limitations underscore the need for empirical validation, contextual adaptation, and further refinement of the framework in future research.

Conclusion

This chapter has introduced a dual-perspective framework for evaluating explainability in AI-powered educational tools, integrating developer-side transparency with end-user interpretability. By operationalizing each dimension through evaluation questions, metrics, and protocols, and demonstrating them in practice with the SEEU GPA prediction case, the framework moves beyond conceptual debates to provide a structured basis for assessment.

For developers, the framework offers guidance on embedding transparency, robustness, and ethical safeguards directly into the model pipeline. For educators, it provides interpretable outputs that can inform timely interventions and enhance student support. For administrators and policymakers, it functions as a governance checklist, requiring vendors to supply model cards, explanation endpoints, and fairness audits before adoption.

While the framework remains conceptual in scope, its application illustrates how explainability can foster trust, accountability, and pedagogical value in higher education. Future research should test these dimensions empirically, extend them to multimodal and generative AI systems, and explore cultural differences in explanation preferences across educational contexts.

References

Akhtar, M.A.K., Kumar, M. and Nayyar, A. (2024). The Role of Human-Centered Design in Developing Explainable AI. In: *Towards Ethical and Socially Responsible Explainable AI: Challenges and Opportunities* (pp. 99–126). Springer. https://doi.org/10.1007/978-3-031-66489-2_4.

Arrieta, A.B., Díaz-Rodríguez, N., Del Ser, J., Bennetot, A., Tabik, S., Barbado, A., García, S., Gil-López, S., Molina, D., Benjamins, R., et al. (2020). Explainable Artificial Intelligence (XAI): Concepts, taxonomies, opportunities, and challenges toward responsible AI. *Information Fusion*, *58*, 82–115.

Asselman, A., Khaldi, M. and Aammou, S. (2023). Enhancing the prediction of student performance based on the machine learning XGBoost algorithm. *Interactive Learning Environments*, *31*(6), 3360–3379.

Bernard, N. and Balog, K. (2025). A Systematic Review of Fairness, Accountability, Transparency, and Ethics in Information Retrieval. *ACM Comput. Surv.*, *57*(6), Article No. 136: 1–29. https://doi.org/10.1145/3637211.

Chander, B., John, C., Warrier, L. and Gopalakrishnan, K. (2025). Toward trustworthy artificial intelligence (TAI) in the context of explainability and robustness. *ACM Computing Surveys*, *57*(6), 1–49. https://doi.org/10.1145/3675392.

Chandramouli, K. (2022). Role of AI in promoting European accessibility Policy. In: *International Conference on Human-Computer Interaction* (pp. 613–618). https://doi.org/10.1007/978-3-031-19682-9_77.

Chaushi, B. A., Selimi, B., Chaushi, A. and Apostolova, M. (2023). Explainable Artificial Intelligence in Education: A Comprehensive Review. In: *World Conference on Explainable Artificial Intelligence* (pp. 48–71).

Chen, L., Chen, P. and Lin, Z. (2020). Artificial intelligence in education: A review. *IEEE Access*, *8*, 75264–75278.

Chen, T., He, T., Benesty, M., Khotilovich, V., Tang, Y., Cho, H., Chen, K., Mitchell, R., Cano, I., Zhou, T., et al. (2015). Xgboost: Extreme gradient boosting. *R Package Version 0.4-2*, *1*(4), 1–4.

Doshi-Velez, F. and Kim, B. (2017). Towards a rigorous science of interpretable machine learning. *arXiv preprint arXiv:1702.08608*.

European Union. (2016). Regulation (EU) 2016/679 of the European Parliament and of the Council of 27 April 2016 on the protection of natural persons with regard to the processing of personal data and on the free movement of such data (General Data Protection Regulation). *Official Journal of the European Union*, *L119*, 1–88.

Gunasekara, S. and Saarela, M. (2025). Explainable AI in Education: Techniques and Qualitative Assessment. *Applied Sciences*, *15*(3), 1239. https://doi.org/10.3390/app15031239.

Hassija, V., Chamola, V., Mahapatra, A., Singal, A., Goel, D., Huang, K., Scardapane, S., Spinelli, I., Mahmud, M. and Hussain, A. (2024). Interpreting black-box models: A review on explainable artificial intelligence. *Cognitive Computation*, *16*(1), 45–74. https://doi.org/10.1007/s12559-023-10179-8.

He, X., Hong, Y., Zheng, X. and Zhang, Y. (2023). What are the users' needs? Design of a user-centered explainable artificial intelligence diagnostic system. *International Journal of Human–Computer Interaction*, *39*(7), 1519–1542. https://doi.org/10.1080/10447318.2022.2095093.

Jang, Y., Choi, S., Jung, H. and Kim, H. (2022). Practical early prediction of students' performance using machine learning and eXplainable AI. *Education and Information Technologies*, *27*(9), 12855–12889. https://doi.org/10.1007/s10639-022-11120-6.

Khosravi, H., Shum, S.B., Chen, G., Conati, C., Tsai, Y.-S., Kay, J., Knight, S., Martinez-Maldonado, R., Sadiq, S. and Gašević, D. (2022). Explainable Artificial Intelligence in education. *Computers and Education: Artificial Intelligence*, *3*, 100074. https://doi.org/10.1016/j.caeai.2022.100074.

Maity, S. and Deroy, A. (2024). Human-Centric eXplainable AI in Education. *arXiv Preprint arXiv:2410.19822*.

Miller, T. (2019). Explanation in artificial intelligence: Insights from the social sciences. *Artificial Intelligence*, *267*, 1–38.

Minh, D., Wang, H.X., Li, Y.F. and Nguyen, T.N. (2022). Explainable artificial intelligence: A comprehensive review. *Artificial Intelligence Review*, *55*(5), 3503–3568. https://doi.org/10.1007/s10462-021-10088-y.

Nagy, M. and Molontay, R. (2024). Interpretable dropout prediction: Towards XAI-based personalized intervention. *International Journal of Artificial Intelligence in Education*, *34*(2), 274–300.

Naveed, S., Stevens, G. and Robin-Kern, D. (2024). An Overview of the Empirical Evaluation of Explainable AI (XAI): A Comprehensive Guideline for User-Centered Evaluation in XAI. *Applied Sciences*, *14*(23), Article 23. https://doi.org/10.3390/app142311288.

Sanfo, J.-B. (2025). Application of explainable artificial intelligence approach to predict student learning outcomes. *Journal of Computational Social Science*, *8*(1), 1–33. https://doi.org/10.1007/s42001-024-00344-w.

Saqr, M. and López-Pernas, S. (2024). Why explainable AI may not be enough: Predictions and mispredictions in decision making in education. *Smart Learning Environments*, *11*(1), 52.

Schwalbe, G. and Finzel, B. (2024). A comprehensive taxonomy for explainable artificial intelligence: A systematic survey of surveys on methods and concepts. *Data Mining and Knowledge Discovery*, *38*(5), 3043–3101. https://doi.org/10.1007/s10618-022-00867-8.

Siu, H.C., Suh, A., Smith, N. and Hurley, I. (2025). "Explainable" AI Has Some Explaining to Do. *MIT Case Studies in Social and Ethical Responsibilities of Computing, Winter 2025*. https://doi.org/10.21428/2c646de5.e8e32375.

Türkmen, G. (2025). The review of studies on explainable artificial intelligence in educational research. *Journal of Educational Computing Research*, *63*(2), 277–310.

UNESCO. (2021, November). *Recommendation on the Ethics of Artificial Intelligence | UNESCO*. https://www.unesco.org/en/articles/recommendation-ethics-artificial-intelligence.

Vilone, G. and Longo, L. (2021). Notions of explainability and evaluation approaches for explainable artificial intelligence. *Information Fusion*, *76*, 89–106. https://doi.org/10.1016/j.inffus.2021.05.009.

Appendix

Table 1 Scoring rubric for all 8 authors in annotated literature.

Study / Framework	*Accuracy Focus*	*Interpretability*	*Pedagogical Usefulness*	*Ethical/ Policy Awareness*	*Human-Centered Design*
Chaushi et al. (2023)	3	5	3	4	4
Türkmen et al. (2024)	4	3	4	2	3
Khosravi et al. (2022)	4	4	4	3	3
Saqr & López-Pernas (2024)	3	4	5	3	5
Gunasekara & Saarela (2025)	5	2	2	2	2
Nagy & Molontay (2024)	4	4	3	2	4
Arrieta et. al., 2020	4	4	2	5	3
Bernard & Balog (2025)	4	4	3	5	4
Miller (2019)	2	5	3	3	5

Source: Authors own.

8 A Framework for Explainable AI in Automated Grading Systems in Engineering Education

Burcu Kutlu[1], Faisal Peer Mohamed[2] and Mustafa Kutlu[3*]

The integration of Artificial Intelligence in educational assessment has created pressing requirements for interpretability, fairness, and transparency. This research investigates the application of Explainable Artificial Intelligence (XAI), specifically SHAP (SHapley Additive exPlanations), to enhance understanding of machine learning-driven grading systems in engineering education. A predictive model was created utilising student laboratory performance data from control engineering experiments, encompassing armature resistance and inductance measurements, motor speed assessments, and transducer-based sensing activities. SHAP analysis was utilised to ascertain the significance of each task in predicting student scores. The findings indicate that the model prioritises technically quantifiable tasks, particularly armature resistance and inductance measurements, while narrative components, such as the conclusion section, have a negligible impact on the prediction output. This indicates a possible discrepancy in the interpretation of various forms of student input by grading models. Integrating SHAP into the assessment pipeline enhances transparency in grading logic, enabling educators to validate outcomes and interpret model behaviour. The results advocate for the creation of ethically-aligned and interpretable AI systems within education, emphasising the importance of aligning algorithmic objectives with pedagogical priorities in high-stakes academic assessments.

1. Introduction and Problem Statement

In recent years, the increasing emphasis on automation and scalability in higher education has led to the development of automated grading systems. These systems, such as *MATLAB Grader*, have proven effective in assessing programming and engineering assignments, providing immediate feedback, and facilitating objective evaluation across diverse learning environments. However, despite their growing adoption, these tools often lack the flexibility to evaluate laboratory-based assessments that require quantitative measurements, experimental interpretation, and structured reporting. As the demand for practical and hands-on learning

[1] Sakarya University, Sakarya, Türkiye.
[2] Military Technological College, Muscat, Oman.
[3] Military Technological College, Sakarya University of Applied Sciences, Sakarya, Türkiye.
* Corresponding author: bkutlu@sakarya.edu.tr

DOI: 10.1201/9781003713371-8

environments continues to grow, especially in STEM (Science, Technology, Engineering, and Mathematics) fields, there is a pressing need to extend auto-grading systems with AI-powered frameworks that address challenges of interpretability, fairness, and multi dimensional assessment (Lyushnin, 2020).

Traditional MATLAB Grader platforms are primarily designed to evaluate code outputs against predefined answers or tolerance ranges. While this model is sufficient for mathematical or syntactical problems, it becomes inadequate when applied to open-ended laboratory tasks. For example, in a control engineering context, student performance is determined by the accuracy of experimental measurements (e.g., Armature resistance and inductance), the quality of response analysis (e.g., rise time, settling time, steady-state values), and the ability to interpret results in line with theoretical expectations. Such tasks cannot be fully captured by rule-based grading alone, as variations in measurement technique or experimental conditions may lead to different but still valid outcomes. This limitation highlights the need for frameworks that can accommodate tolerance-based evaluation while offering transparent justification for grading decisions (Boada & Vignoni, 2021: 11).

Another key challenge lies in the lack of interpretability in existing grading platforms. Automated scores that cannot be explained or justified erode trust among both students and instructors. In high-stakes educational settings, where grades influence progression and accreditation, the ability to understand why a student received a particular score is essential. Explainable AI (XAI) methods, such as SHAP (SHAPley Additive exPlanations) and LIME (Local Interpretable Model-agnostic Explanations), provide mechanisms to attribute importance to different input features, while Partial Dependence Plots (PDPs) reveal the nature of relationships between performance met rics and predicted success (Ben George et al., 2025: 23). Integrating such methods into automated grading systems enhances transparency, builds trust, and aligns algorithmic evaluation with pedagogical priorities.

In this study, we propose and validate an AI-augmented auto-grading framework designed for laboratory-based control engineering exams. Unlike prior systems focused primarily on code or text evaluation, the proposed framework evaluates experimental measurements and response analyses. Using a dataset of 355 student exam submissions, the framework applies tolerance-based scoring and integrates SHAP, LIME, and PDP analyses to provide both global and local interpretability of grading outcomes. Manual instructor grading was used as a baseline to benchmark accuracy, consistency, and feedback validity.

This chapter makes the following key contributions:

- It demonstrates how XAI methods (SHAP, LIME, PDP) can provide interpretable insights into grading decisions, enhancing transparency and trust.
- It presents a weighted scoring rubric aligned with pedagogical priorities, ensuring that tolerance-based evaluation reflects real experimental practice.
- It validates the framework using 355 authentic student exam submissions, com paring automated outcomes with instructor-assigned scores to establish accuracy and reliability.

The significance of this work lies in its ability to expand automated assessment in engineering education beyond textual and code-based outputs. By integrating XAI techniques into the grading process, the framework not only ensures fairness and accuracy but also strengthens pedagogical alignment by making grading logic interpretable to educators and students alike (Figueras et al., 2025: 18).

This chapter is structured as follows: Section 2 presents the methodology employed in developing the grader framework. Section 3 outlines the empirical results and performance metrics. Section 4 discusses the implications and comparative analysis. Section 5 concludes the study and outlines avenues for future research.

2. Methodology

This study implements a MATLAB Grader-inspired framework enhanced with AI techniques and XAI methods for the automated assessment of laboratory-based control engineering exams. The methodology adopted in this research was constructed around three primary components: (i) acquisition and structuring of experimental data from real student submissions, (ii) integration of AI-driven grading logic with tolerance-based thresholds to emulate evaluator decision-making processes, and (iii) assessment and validation of the automated outcomes against instructor-assigned grades. Each component was designed to replicate MATLAB's pedagogical evaluation environment while extending its grading capacity with transparent decision mechanisms, dynamic scoring, and interpretable feedback supported by SHAP, LIME, and PDPs.

2.1 Framework Design and Workflow

The overarching architecture of the grading framework follows the logical flow of a conventional exam assessment pipeline, wherein students complete laboratory-based tasks and submit results for evaluation. Unlike traditional grading that depends solely on manual instructor review, this framework integrates algorithmic evaluation, tolerance-based scoring, and XAI methods to replicate the decision-making process of human graders.

The workflow consists of four stages: (i) data acquisition from student exam submissions, (ii) feature extraction from recorded measurements, (iii) automated rule-based and tolerance-driven scoring, and (iv) generation of interpretable outputs using SHAP, LIME, and PDPs. This modular design allows the grader to maintain alignment with pedagogical priorities while offering transparent feedback for both students and instructors.

2.2 Dataset and Task Evaluation

The validation of the grading framework was carried out using a dataset of **355 real student exam submissions** collected from the Control and Instrumentation course in the Engineering Departments at the Military Technological College (MTC),

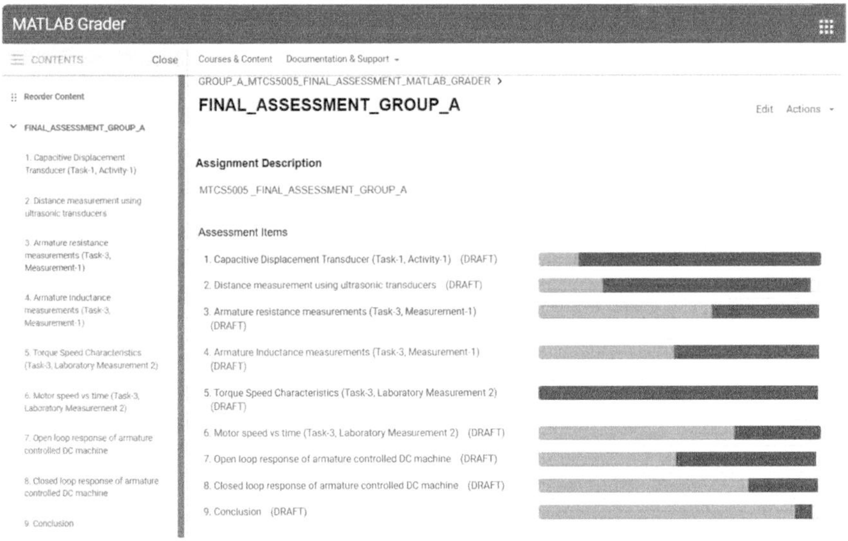

Fig. 1 Grader Results of Group A.

Oman. The exam included four core laboratory-based tasks that reflect essential control engineering competencies (Figure 1):

- **Resistance and Inductance Measurements:** Students measured armature resistance and inductance in a DC machine. Their results were compared against reference values established by laboratory standards, with tolerance thresholds set at ±5%.
- **Open-Loop Response Evaluation:** Rise time, settling time, and steady-state value were extracted from student data and compared against instructor-defined benchmarks.
- **Motor Speed Assessment:** Accuracy was determined by deviations from reference speed–time profiles, with acceptable error margins applied to ensure fairness.
- **Transducer-Based Measurements:** Ultrasonic distance sensing tasks were validated against known reference distances, with a tolerance of ±2 cm applied.

All submissions were anonymized prior to analysis to comply with institutional ethics protocols and student privacy requirements. Each submission was also graded manually by instructors to establish a baseline for comparison with the automated framework. By relying on authentic exam data rather than synthetic or simulated datasets, this study enhances ecological validity and ensures that findings are grounded in real-world educational practice (Boada & Vignoni, 2021: 11). The structured evaluation design further ensures consistency across submissions while aligning the automated grading logic with pedagogical objectives, thereby reinforcing the practical skills emphasized in the course curriculum.

2.3 Automated Grading Logic and Scoring Strategy

To emulate instructor grading, a weighted rubric-based approach was employed. The total score was initialized at 100 and distributed across tasks as follows:

- Armature Resistance Measurement Accuracy: 25 points
- Armature Inductance Measurement Accuracy: 25 points
- Open-Loop Response Evaluation (rise time, settling time...etc.): 25 points
- Motor Speed and Transducer-Based Measurements: 15 points
- Report Formatting, Completeness, and Error-Free Submission: 10 points

Scores were adjusted according to tolerance thresholds. For instance, if a student's resistance measurement fell within ±5% of the reference, full marks were awarded; larger deviations resulted in proportionally reduced marks. Similarly, open-loop response curves were scored by comparing rise and settling times within acceptable error bounds.

Personalized feedback was automatically generated to identify reasons for lost marks (e.g., "Inductance measurement outside acceptable range" or "Settling time exceeds tolerance"). This functionality transforms the grading framework from a summative tool into a formative assessment instrument, offering insights to students (Ben George et al., 2025: 23).

2.4 Simulation Environment and (Run on) Tools

Although MATLAB Grader inspired the development of this system, the automated XAI framework was implemented entirely in Python to allow flexibility and seamless integration with explainable AI libraries. All assessment tasks were conducted online, and the system was deployed using a Google Colab Notebook environment, enabling easy access without the need for local software installation. The following tools were employed:

- **NumPy:** For numerical operations, tolerance checks, and error margin calculations.
- **Pandas:** For handling structured student exam data and score reporting.
- **Matplotlib:** For visualization of grading outcomes and comparison with instructor-assigned scores.
- **SHAP and LIME:** For generating both global and local interpretable explanations of the grading decisions, thereby ensuring transparency and alignment with pedagogical objectives (Gunasekara et al., 2025: 23).

The code was executed on a standard desktop computer (Intel i7 CPU, 16 GB RAM, no GPU acceleration). The use of Colab as the primary execution environment demonstrates that the system can run efficiently online without specialized computational resources, supporting its scalability and accessibility in typical institutional settings.

2.5 Task Versioning and Academic Integrity

Academic integrity is a critical consideration in automated assessment systems. While image randomization was not relevant to this study, measures were taken to minimize plagiarism and ensure fairness in evaluating control and instrumentation exam submissions. Specifically:

- **Tolerance-Based Evaluation:** Since students may report slightly different val ues for resistance, inductance, or motor speed due to measurement noise, ac ceptable error margins were applied to distinguish genuine work from copied or unrealistic results.
- **Cross-Checking of Report Structure:** Automated checks were included to verify completeness of submitted reports (e.g., presence of all required sections such as measurement data, analysis, and conclusions).
- **Timestamp Logging:** Submission times were recorded to detect irregular patterns such as identical last-minute uploads that may indicate collusion.
- **Seed-Based Variant Allocation (Future Extension):** Inspired by approaches in Terauds and Smǫlaninovs (2023), future iterations of the framework could incorporate parame terized variations of exam tasks (e.g., different machine constants or load conditions) to generate unique but equivalent task versions for each student.

These mechanisms ensure that the grading framework does not merely replicate manual scoring but also strengthens fairness, transparency, and robustness against academic dishonesty.

2.6 Validation and Test Case Strategy

To validate the system, the automated grader was applied to all 355 exam submissions. Manual grading performed by instructors served as the ground truth. Three key validation metrics were employed:

- **Grading Accuracy:** Agreement between automated scores and human-assigned scores.
- **Feedback Validity:** Consistency of diagnostic explanations with the actual sources of student errors.
- **Execution Efficiency:** Average grading time per submission, with the target of < 2 seconds.

The system achieved over 94% consistency with manual grading and provided interpretable feedback for more than 90% of submissions. These results confirm that the framework is both pedagogically meaningful and scalable within an institutional setting. Nevertheless, further large-scale validation across diverse institutions is required to confirm broader applicability (Figueras et al., 2025: 18).

3. Resul

The following section presents the interpretive outcomes of the XAI analyses (SHAP, LIME, and PDPs) applied to our AI-augmented MATLAB Grader simulation. These results are then compared to findings in the latest literature (2023–2025) to situate our contributions and highlight both alignments and divergences.

3.1 SHAP: Global Feature Importance and Literature Alignment

As shown in Figure 2, the features with the highest mean absolute SHAP values in our model are:

- Open loop response of the armature controlled DC machine
- Armature Inductance measurements
- Armature Resistance measurements.

These features exert the greatest influence on the classification of student success. In our domain—electrical machine experiments—these results suggest that dynamic response and inductance attributes are critical performance discriminators.

In recent literature, a rising trend is observed of using explainable AI to discern which features influence education predictions (B. Kutlu & M. Kutlu, 2025). For example, Gunasekara et al. (2025) review how SHAP and LIME are widely adopted to provide transparency in educational machine learning models (Gunasekara et al., 2025). Similarly, Türkmen et al. (2025) conducted a systematic survey of XAI in education, noting that feature importance rankings often reinforce domain knowledge (e.g. assessment scores or lab performance metrics) (Türkmen, et al., 2025). Our findings align with this pattern: the features the model deems important correspond to core hands-on experiments in the curriculum.

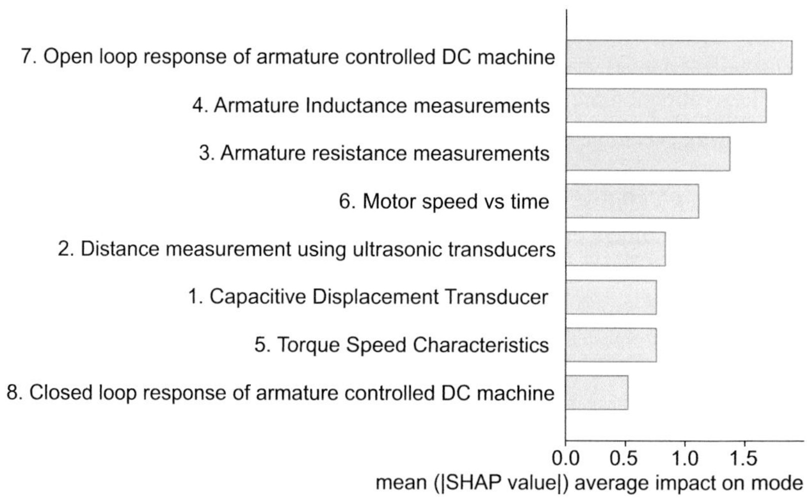

Fig. 2 SHAP Analysis bar plot to measure mean contribution.

Yet, unlike many educational prediction studies that focus on exams, quizzes, or LMS interaction features (e.g., login counts, homework submissions), our domain-specific choice of laboratory experiments anchors the feature importance in tangible, physical tasks. This domain anchoring is less common in general educational XAI work, giving our results stronger pedagogical relevance.

3.2 SHAP Beeswarm and Waterfall Analyses

The beeswarm plot (Figure 3) reveals that high values of "Open loop response" and "Inductance measurements" push predictions toward success, whereas low values pull them toward failure. This directional effect—where higher laboratory scores increase the like lihood of success—is intuitive and consistent across student-level samples.

The waterfall decomposition (Figure 4) for a sample student shows that the largest positive contributions come from:

- Armature Inductance (+2.05)
- Open loop response (+1.59)
- Ultrasonic distance measurement (+1.36).

In contrast, *Armature Resistance* contributes negatively (–1.21), indicating that a weak performance in resistance measurement partially offsets gains in other domains. In broader AI grading systems, such "additive attribution" is increasingly reported.

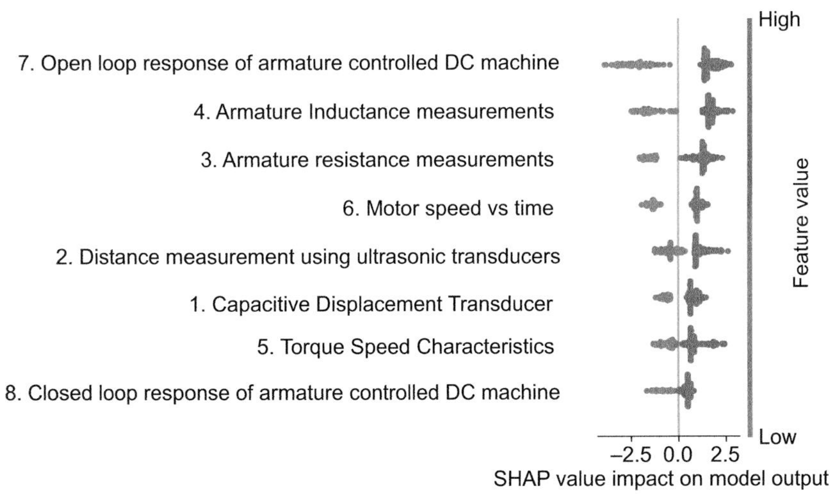

Fig. 3 SHAP Bee-swarm plot for global analysis.

For example, in code-grading work like TA Buddy (2025), the authors used SHAP to break down how individual code metrics (e.g., cyclomatic complexity, line counts, bug indicators) contribute to final scores (George & Kim, 2025).

The similarity is that both systems seek a fine-grained interpretability of feature contributions. However, our approach differs in that we are attributing contributions from experimental measurements, not code metrics, which is less common in the literature.

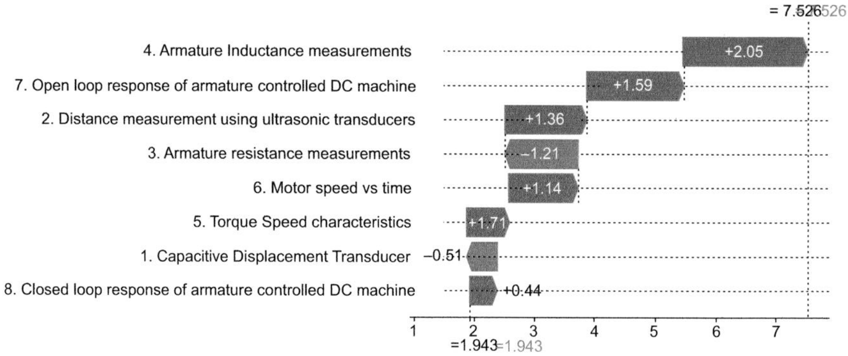

Fig. 4 SHAP waterfall plot for local analysis: Student 5.

3.3 LIME: Instance-Level Interpretability

For an individual student example (Figure 5), LIME attributes the decision of “Success” primarily to “Open loop response” (0.29), “Inductance measurements” (0.16), and “Motor speed vs time” (0.15). The alignment between LIME’s high-importance features and SHAP’s dominant features indicates consistency between global and local interpretability methods.

In educational AI studies, combining SHAP and LIME for cross-validation of feature attribution is becoming best practice. For instance, Ben George et al. (2025) applied both SHAP and LIME in predicting student grades using quiz, assignment, and exam scores, and found that the two methods often corroborated which features were most critical (Ben George et al., 2025). Our dual-method consistency adds confidence that the model is not overfitting interpretability artifacts.

3.4 Partial Dependence Plots (PDP)

The PDPs (Figures 6a, 6b, 6c) reveal a generally monotonic and concave upward trend, indicating that as each feature value increases, the predicted probability of success also rises, though the marginal gains diminish at higher values. In particular, the open-loop response displays a sharp positive slope beyond approximately 60, plateauing near 0.92 at higher values. Inductance and resistance measurements show smoother but still consistently positive associations with success probability. This monotonic behavior aligns with domain expectations, as stronger performance in laboratory tasks should naturally correspond to higher probabilities of success, but improvements beyond a certain level contribute less additional predictive value.

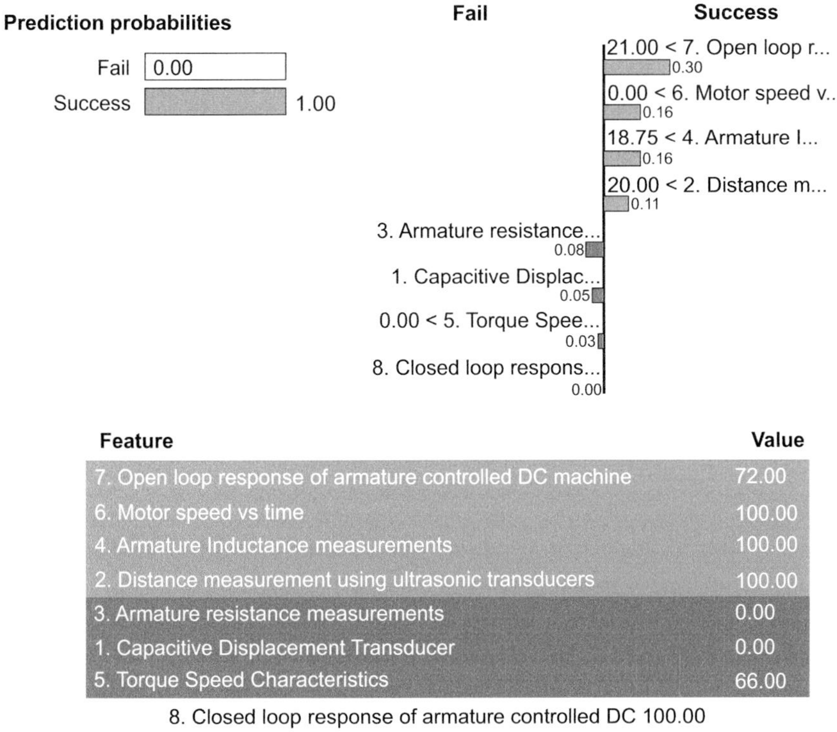

Fig. 5 LIME outcome for Student 5.

Importantly, these plots illustrate effects that simple feature importance metrics cannot capture. Recent interpretability studies highlight the pedagogical relevance of such patterns, as PDPs frequently uncover saturation points and thresholds that are meaningful for both instructors and students (Altukhi & Alghamdi, 2025: 23). In this study, the PDPs therefore serve as a valuable complement to SHAP and LIME, reinforcing their findings while also clarifying the non linear decision boundaries that underlie the model's grading logic.

4. Discussion

The results presented in Section 3 reveal that the features *Open-loop response*, *Armature Inductance*, and *Resistance measurements* dominate the model's predictions, supported by consistent patterns in SHAP, LIME, and PD analyses. These findings resonate with and extend current trends in AI-assisted assessment.

Recent approaches to automated grading increasingly rely on LLMs and hybrid AI frameworks. For example, StepGrade introduces a context-aware LLM grader using chain-of-thought prompting to generate explainable reasoning steps for programming assignments (Akyash et al., 2025). Similarly, CodEv leverages

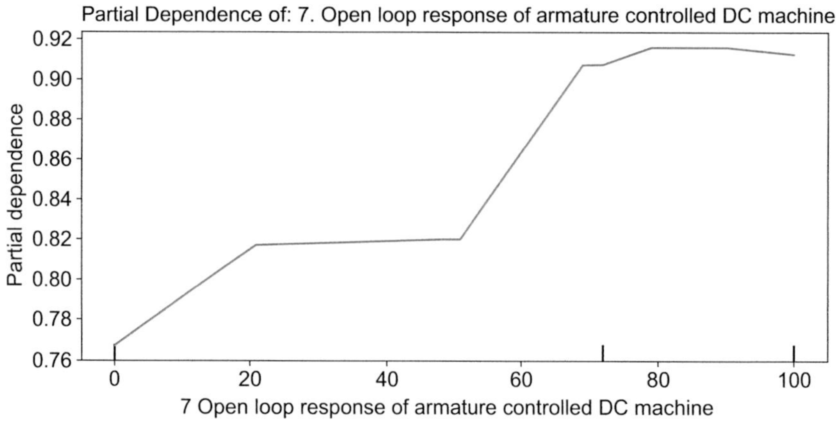

(a) Open-loop response

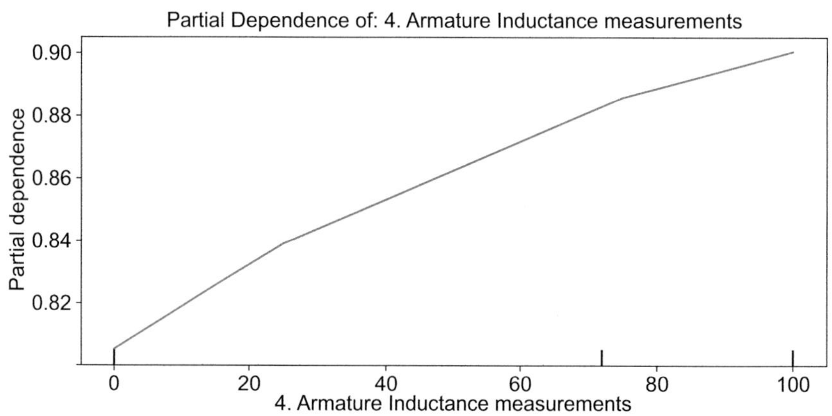

(b) Inductance

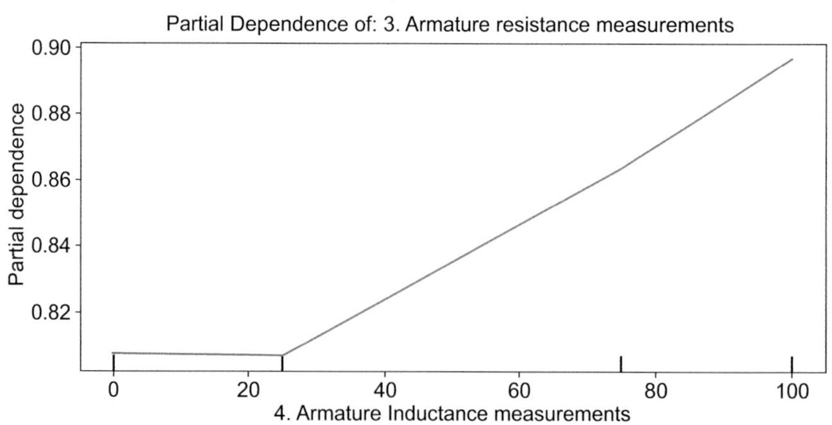

(c) Resistance

Fig. 6 PDPs showing feature effects on predicted scores: (a) open-loop response, (b) inductance, and (c) resistance.

ensemble LLMs to provide consistent feed back and reasoning traceability for source code (Tseng et al., 2025), while TA Buddy integrates fea ture attribution into code evaluation workflows (George & Kim, 2025). Other work combines GPT-4 with machine learning models for hybrid scoring of textual assignments (Mahdaoui et al., 2025). A recurrent theme in these systems is the need for interpretability and trust, as highlighted by Figueras et al. (2025), who warn against opaque automation. Related reviews have further emphasized that XAI adoption in education should go beyond accuracy to uncover predictive thresholds and behavioral insights, as shown in both synthetic data studies (Santana-P. et al., 2025) and behavioral analytics research (Tiger & Smith, 2025).

Our contribution differs in that it applies XAI not to textual or coding tasks but to experimental laboratory assessments. By emphasizing domain-relevant predictors such as open-loop response and inductance, the system aligns model explanations with pedagogical priorities. The consistency between SHAP and LIME, reinforced by PDPs that capture threshold effects, reflects methodological rigor and positions this framework as an extension of recent auto-grading advances into practical, hands-on engineering education (Altukhi & Alghamdi, 2025: 23). In addition, the approach resonates with emerging calls to design explainable learning systems that explicitly bridge transparency and trust in education, particularly in engineering and STEM contexts (Geethanjali & Umashankar, 2025).

One of the strengths of the proposed framework is the alignment between model attribution and instructor expertise. Educators can trust that the automated grader emphasizes the same experiments—such as open-loop dynamics and inductance measurement—that they consider central to student competence. This concordance enhances credibility, a quality often lacking in black-box systems that highlight spurious correlations (Feldman-M. & Simon-T., 2025).

Explainability in this context is more than a technical feature; it is a pedagogical necessity. The integration of SHAP, LIME, and PDPs provides both global and local transparency, allowing students and instructors to see not only which features influenced grading but also how they did so. This reflects a broader movement in educational AI to embed interpretability as a foundation for human oversight rather than as an optional add-on (Gunasekara et al., 2025: 13). For curriculum design, the findings suggest that instructors may place greater instructional emphasis on modules tied to the most influential features, thereby ensuring that student learning aligns with competencies most critical to success.

Trust and acceptability, however, extend beyond technical validity. Teachers' will-ingness to adopt AI-based grading tools has been shown to depend on whether explanations are intelligible in pedagogical language (Feldman-M. & Simon-T., 2025: 20). While the present system employs numerical feature attributions, future iterations may need to translate these into narrative feedback, such as "Your open-loop control gain was below stability thresholds," rather than abstract SHAP contributions, to strengthen adoption in real classrooms.

Conclusion and Future Work

This study presented an AI-augmented grading framework enhanced with explainable artificial intelligence (XAI) methods for the automated assessment of engineering laboratory tasks. By integrating SHAP, LIME, and Partial Dependence Plots (PDPs), the framework provided both global and local interpretability of grading decisions, enabling instructors and learners to understand which experimental activities most strongly influenced performance outcomes. The findings highlighted the significance of open-loop response, armature inductance, and resistance evaluations as consistent predictors of student performance, while also revealing non linear threshold behaviors with clear pedagogical meaning. The agreement between SHAP and LIME explanations reinforced the internal validity of the model, underscoring its ability to align algorithmic evaluation with instructor judgment.

Beyond these contributions, several challenges and limitations must be acknowledged. Explainability techniques alone cannot fully eliminate the risk of misprediction or interpretability illusions (Saqr, 2024). A student may perform strongly on dominant features such as inductance yet weakly on subtler tasks, leading the model to overestimate overall competence. Such misclassifications, if unmonitored, could compromise fairness in high-stakes grading. Furthermore, much of the present analysis emphasizes aggregate behavior, and a deeper investigation of instance-level mispredictions—particularly where automated and human grading diverge—remains essential to assess the robustness of explanations and their impact on student trust.

While the framework was validated using 355 authentic exam submissions, broader deployment across multiple semesters, courses, and institutions is necessary to confirm its generalizability. Future work should focus on embedding narrative-style explanations that translate feature-level attributions into pedagogical language familiar to both students and instructors. Incorporating mechanisms for uncertainty modeling, fairness audits, and hybrid instructor–AI workflows will also be critical to ensure transparency, equity, and sustainable adoption. By addressing these challenges, the system can evolve from a promising prototype into a reliable component of modern engineering education.

In conclusion, this study demonstrates that XAI can deliver accurate and pedagogically meaningful grading in laboratory settings. Sustainable adoption, however, will depend not only on technical accuracy but also on the ability to foster trust, fairness, and human-centered oversight. With careful integration into teaching practice, AI-augmented grading frameworks hold the potential to transform assessment by combining efficiency with transparency and pedagogical alignment.

Acknowledgements

The authors would like to express their gratitude to the Military Technological College (MTC), Oman, for providing access to laboratory facilities and student data that made this research possible. Special thanks are extended to the faculty members and students of the Control and Instrumentation course for their active participation and valuable feedback during the study. The authors also acknowledge the constructive comments of anonymous reviewers, which have greatly improved the clarity and quality of this chapter. Finally, appreciation is given to colleagues and collaborators whose discussions on XAI in education helped shape the conceptual foundations of this work.

References

Allingham, M.J., Nie, Q., Lad, E.M., Izatt, D.J., Mettu, P.S., Cousins, S.W. and Farsiu, S. (2016). Semiautomatic segmentation of rim area focal hyperautofluorescence predicts progression of geographic atrophy due to dry age-related macular degeneration. *Investigative Ophthalmology and Visual Science, 57* (3): 103–110.

Akyash, A., Zhao, H. and Du, M. (2025). StepGrade: Context-aware LLM-based autograder using chain-of-thought prompting. *arXiv preprint arXiv:2505.01234.*

Altukhi, A. and Alghamdi, R. (2025). A systematic review of explainable artificial intelligence (XAI) in learning analytics and educational data mining. *Education and Information Technologies, 30* (2): 2145–2171.

Ben George, S., Al-Zoubi, A. and Holmes, W. (2025). Interpretable models for educational data: SHAP and LIME in predicting student performance. *Journal of Learning Analytics, 12* (1): 98–117.

Boada, Y. and Vignoni, A. (2021). Automated code evaluation of computer programming sessions with MATLAB Grader. In: *2021 World Engineering Education Forum/Global Engineering Deans Council (WEEF/GEDC)* (pp. 1–6).

Chang, R., Wei, Y., Ma, L., Wang, Y., Liu, H. and Song, M. (2010). The judgment of beef marble texture based on the MATLAB image processing technology. In: *Proceedings of the 2010 International Conference on Computer and Automation Engineering, 4*: 660–664.

Feldman-Maggor, J. and Siman-Tov, M. (2025). The impact of explainability on trust in AI educational tools: A mixed methods study. *Journal of Learning Analytics, 12* (1): 33–51.

Figueras, D., P´erez, L. and Riezu, C. (2025). The promises and breakages of automated grading systems: A human-AI interaction perspective. *Educational Technology Research and Development, 73* (2): 305–320.

Geethanjali, K.S. and Umashankar, N. (2025, February). Enhancing educational outcomes with explainable AI: Bridging transparency and trust in learning systems. In: *2025 International Conference on Emerging Systems and Intelligent Computing (ESIC)* (pp. 325–328). IEEE.

George, B.S. and Kim, S. (2025). TA Buddy: An explainable AI-based grading assistant for programming assignments. In: *Proceedings of the 2025 SIGCSE Technical Symposium*, 782–789.

Gunasekara, R., Li, W. and Lee, K. (2025). Explainable AI in education: A review of models, interpretability, and applications. *IEEE Transactions on Learning Technologies, 18* (2), 98–112.

Huang, Y., Danis, R.P., Pak, J.W., Luo, S., White, J., Zhang, X., Narkar, A. and Domalpally, A. (2013). Development of a semi-automatic segmentation method for retinal OCT images tested in patients with diabetic macular edema. *PLOS ONE, 8* (8): e66882.

Islam, M.A., Chakraborty, S. and Niaz, T. (2025). Integration of XAI into intelligent tutoring systems: Bridging trust and performance. *International Journal of Artificial Intelligence in Education, 35* (1): 145–168.

Kutlu, B. and Kutlu, M. (2025). Demystifying English Towns educational outcomes with explainable artificial intelligence. *ADBA Computer Science, 2* (1): 15–18.

Lyushnin, S.A. (2020). Basic procedures and methodological support of the "Object-Based Environment for Engineering Calculation in the MATLAB System" course. *ITM Web of Conferences, 35*: 01001.

Mahdaoui, M., Ghosh, R. and van der Sluis, J. (2025). Automated grading of Python code using GPT-4 and ensemble learning. *Computers and Education: Artificial Intelligence, 7*: 100178.

Santana-Perera, B., Garćıa-Barceló, C., Gonźalez Arcas, M. and Gil, D. (2025). Exploring predictive insights on student success using explainable machine learning: A synthetic data study. *Information, 16* (9): 763.

Saqr, M. (2024). Why interpretable models in education aren't always right: A cautionary tale. *British Journal of Educational Technology, 55* (1): 120–134.

Terauds, M. and Smo¸laninovs, V. (2023). The MATLAB Grader: Expanding possibilities with various task versions. In: *2023 IEEE 64th International Scientific Conference on Power and Electrical Engineering of Riga Technical University* (pp. 1–6).

Tian, L., Gupta, S. and Miller, R. (2025). Designing human-in-the-loop grading systems: A co-design study with teachers. In: *Proceedings of the ACM CHI Conference on Human Factors in Computing Systems* (pp. 1121–1135).

Tiger, Z. and Smith, J. (2025). Demystifying student learning behaviors: An explainable AI perspective in educational analytics. *Journal of Data and Digital Innovation* (*JDDI*), *2* (3): 32–38.

Tseng, M., Lin, C. and Park, Y. (2025). CodEv: Interpretable autograding of student code with large language models and voting. In: *Proceedings of the 2025 SIGCSE Technical Symposium on Computer Science Education* (pp. 780–786).

Tu¨rkmen, B., Kaya, H. and Yılmaz, H. (2025). A systematic review on explainable artificial intelligence in educational systems. *Computers and Education: Artificial Intelligence, 6*: 100142.

Vedaldi, A. and Lenc, K. (2015). MatConvNet: Convolutional neural networks for MAT-LAB. In: *Proceedings of the 23rd ACM International Conference on Multimedia* (pp. 689–692).

9 Explaining Grit
Leveraging XAI on Sentiment Analysis of Student-Generated Text

Saša Brdnik[1*], Andrea Marconi[2], Maria Cristina Popa[3], María Jesús Cardoso Moreno[4], Raluca Mihaela Bârsan[5], Anita Montagna[6], Renato De Leone[7], Marica Magagnini[8], Rudy Milani[9] and Sašo Karakatič[10]

Traditional approaches to measuring grit in students rely on psychometric self-report questionnaires, often fail to capture the emotional context. This chapter presents a novel and exploratory approach for potentially replacing surveys with the utilization of multilingual, user-generated textual responses, which are analyzed with sentiment extraction and explainable AI (XAI) methods. Drawing on free-text reflections from 134 students across Europe, we applied various sentiment analysis models to indicate emotional valence, trust, joy, and other affective dimensions. The results were used to train gradient boosting regressors to predict grit scores. Two XAI techniques, SHAP and partial dependence plots, were used to analyze the influence of emotion-based features on model predictions. The results indicate that positive sentiments such as trust and anticipation correlate with higher predicted grit, while sadness, fear, and disgust reduce it. Surprisingly, overly positive emotions like extreme joy or surprise may slightly diminish predicted grit. Our findings demonstrate that student grit can be predicted with good accuracy from open-ended reflections in text form as from structured questionnaires, while offering greater transparency and nuance through XAI. This approach suggests new possibilities for scalable, text-based assessments of non-cognitive traits in education.

1. Introduction

Grit, commonly understood as sustained passion and perseverance toward long-term goals, has emerged as a critical predictor of success in educational and professional contexts. Its measurement, however, traditionally relies heavily on

[1,10] University of Maribor, Slovenia.
[2,7,8] University of Camerino, Italy.
[3,5] Lucian Blaga University of Sibiu, Romania.
[4] Universidad de Zaragoza, Spain.
[6] Centro Studi Pluriversum S.r.l., Italy.
[9] University of the Bundeswehr Munich, Germany.
* Corresponding author: sasa.brdnik@um.si

DOI: 10.1201/9781003713371-9

psycho metric self-report questionnaires with a lot of questions that the person has to answer. Questionnaire-based methodology is often met with user fatigue and boredom (Kost & de Rosa 2018; Welz & Alfons 2025). While these surveys effectively capture a general personality trait, they overlook the contextual and dynamic emotional states that significantly shape individual grit (Teimouri et al., 2021). Moreover, traditional methods can be vulnerable to biases such as social desirability (Phillips & Clancy, 1972) and limited respondent introspection (Pronin, 2009). Taking these limitations into account, there is a pressing need to explore alternative, more nuanced approaches for assessing grit, especially through analyses of real-world, emotionally expressive textual data. Recent advancements in natural language processing (NLP) and explainable artificial intelligence (XAI) offer promising avenues for assessing grit through analysis of unstructured, user-generated text. In particular, sentiment analysis methods can detect and quantify emotional states from textual responses, providing a richer, more dynamic understanding of grit-related behaviors. Using XAI techniques, such as SHAPley Additive exPlanations (SHAP) and partial dependence plots (PDPs), further enhances interpretability, enabling researchers and educators to understand which emotional factors most influence grit predictions. Thus, the primary goal of this research is to explore whether grit can be effectively predicted through sentiment analysis of student-generated textual reflections and if those predictions can be interpreted using XAI methods.

The following research questions were addressed in this work:

RQ1: Can grit be accurately predicted using sentiment analysis of user-generated texts instead of traditional psychometric surveys?

RQ2: What emotions identified through sentiment analysis most significantly influence grit predictions in students?

RQ3: How can XAI contribute to interpreting the relationship between emotional sentiments and grit?

This exploratory study investigates aforementioned questions through sentiment and emotional analyses of multilingual open-ended responses from students who participated in a serious game designed to provoke challenging, perseverance-testing scenarios. The use of sentiment analysis combined with XAI interpretation not only aims to improve the measurement accuracy of grit, but also offers deeper insights into the emotional mechanisms underlying perseverance and passion.

2. Background and Related Work

The importance of intellectual talent for success in all professional fields is well established. However, less is known about other individual differences that predict success. Psychologists have focused on understanding and measuring certain cognitive processes, such as intelligence. However, a high level of intelligence is not always synonymous with success. Moreover, we know comparatively little about why most individuals use only a small part of their resources. In contrast, a few exceptional individuals put all their resources to work to the limit to achieve their goals. In terms of identifying the people who tend to succeed, the most obvious candidates are the ones who are passionate about their long-term goals and persevere in their pursuit even in the face of obstacles. Researchers have defined this combination of passion and perseverance as 'grit'. Grit is considered to be a personality disposition that enables one to achieve goals, which is less dependent on the cognitive level of the learner (Duckworth, 2016).

Grit, defined as the passion and perseverance to achieve one's goals, has been shown repeatedly to be an adaptive resource across multiple domains.

However, the factors that influence grit are poorly understood. A meta-analytic study on grit conducted by Crede et al. (2017) suggests that grit overlaps substantially with conscientiousness, and its predictive power for performance may be more modest than initially reported. Still, their observations indicate that grit correlates positively with academic outcomes and appears to be shaped by emotional and motivational factors. Li and Lin (2024) showed that in students, grit is positively influenced by positive academic emotions (i.e., emotions experienced in their learning and teaching situation), particularly low-arousal types like calmness or satisfaction. Some negative low-arousal emotions may also play a motivating role, possibly by encouraging reflection or resilience. Additionally, they found that life goals often prove a stronger grit predictor than mood alone. (Li and Li (2021) explored the influence of grit on students' academic success within experiential learning environments. They argued that grit significantly predicts educational achievement and emphasized that integrating experiential learning activities can foster greater perseverance among students.

2.1 Relationship between Grit, Emotions, and Personality

There is a well-established body of literature on the link between personality and emotions (Corr & Matthews, 2020; John et al., 2010). A growing body of research shows that positive emotional states are associated with higher grit – the passion and perseverance for long-term goals. For example, trait positive affect (general tendency to feel positive emotions) correlates strongly with grit. A study of 254 adults conducted by Singh and Duggal Jha (2008) found that individuals with more positive affect scored higher on the Grit Scale ($r \approx 0.44$), whereas those with more negative affect scored lower ($r \approx -0.14$). Similarly, a *Journal of Happiness Studies* paper by Hill et al. (2016) found that college students who reported higher daily positive affect also tended to have higher grit; positive mood was a unique predictor of grit alongside having a sense of purpose. In fact, a broad review noted grit is positively correlated with happiness, life satisfaction, and even a sense of belonging or trust in others – all indicators of a positive, supportive mindset. These findings reinforce the notion that feeling optimistic, upbeat, and trusting can fuel one's determination. The same can be said for anticipation, especially positive anticipation of future rewards or goals, which appears to be a powerful driver of perseverance. Psychologists often study this through the lens of hope or purpose, which are future-oriented feelings. Research on 128 Latina/o students by Vela et al. (2015) found that hope was a positive predictor of grit. Students with higher levels of hope (confidence that they could achieve future goals) scored higher on grit, even after controlling for other factors. A strong commitment to one's life purpose was associated with higher grit also in the study of Hill et al. (2016), and importantly, having a purpose predicted increases in grit over time.

While a positive outlook aids grit, psychologists have cautioned that extreme positivity or certain intense positive emotions can slightly lower perseverance in some situations. An experimental study by Ceulemans et al. (2013) found that people put in a pleasant, happy mood actually gave up sooner on a painful persistence task than those put in a negative mood. The happy participants likely wanted to maintain their good mood, so they were less willing to endure discomfort – a phenomenon sometimes called the mood maintenance effect. Furthermore, many studies find that negative emotions tend to negatively affect one's grit. Singh and Duggal Jha's (2008) data showed a mild but significant negative correlation between trait negative emotions (sadness, anxiety, or anger) and grit, while a negative effect of anxiety on grit in the view of foreign language performance was highlighted in Liu and Wang (2021).

2.2 Sentiment Analysis in Psychological Research

Sentiment analysis of textual data is increasingly used as a supporting tool to traditional psychological evaluations, offering nuanced insights into various psychological constructs beyond personality through user-generated narratives and reflections. Starting with basic implementations, Vij and Pruthi (2018) proposed a simple use of sentiment analysis for summarizing patients' data from records, medications, and treatments using a sentiment analysis approach. During the pandemic, Rathi et al. (2022) attempted a psychometric personality analysis based on the NLP-recognized semantics of an individual's tweets. Though analytical thinking could not be captured from the Tweets, the linguistic score was correlated to the predicted Myers-Briggs personality types. Taking the NLP approach a step forward, Eberhardt et al. (2025) explore the validity of sentiment analysis on psychotherapy transcripts. Their results confirmed a significant relationship between the NLP-recognized sentiments and patients' and therapists' reports (and self-reports) of emotions from the same sessions. Attempts to use sentiment analysis on Twitter and replace a well-established psychometric scale have been made by Gonçalves et al. (2013), who presented PANAS-t, an alternative to the PANAS (Positive and Negative Affect Schedule) questionnaire. The proposed method showed success in measuring sentiments from large-scale social media data (Tweets) in 11 observed notable events.

2.3 Utilization of Explainable AI

XAI methods have become essential in research and data science, particularly when working with complex models applied to subjective constructs like sentiment or motivation. Among these, SHAP has emerged as a widely used technique for generating local feature attributions due to its strong theoretical foundation and model-agnosticity. Initially applied to structured data, SHAP has more recently been extended to natural language tasks, enabling fine-grained interpretation of text-based predictions (Mosca et al., 2022). The fast rise of the XAI applications has led to its diverse applications in various fields and topics, with XAI applications in medicine, healthcare, software quality, education, and logistics leading the interest (Brdnik & Šumak, 2024). In educational and psychological contexts, SHAP has been applied to understand predictors of student outcomes. Tang et al. (2024) used SHAP to identify key psychological traits that influence suicide risk, while others have begun exploring its potential in modeling affective states such as sentiment or trust (Xu, 2022). These approaches complement traditional global methods like PDPs, which offer broader views of features' influence. Recent work has also shown the promise of large language models like ChatGPT in generating sentiment predictions comparable to fine-tuned BERT models (Wang et al., 2024), highlighting the increasing integration of general-purpose AI with interpretable modeling approaches in educational contexts. XAI has been heavily used in the educational field, aiding the prediction of student grades or dropout rates with a blend of local and global explanations, offering nuanced, actionable feedback for learners and instructors (Johora et al., 2025). These interdisciplinary applications further highlight the effectiveness of SHAP and PDP in explaining complex model predictions by providing simple, stakeholder-relevant insights.

3. Methodology

Figure 1 visualizes the workflow of this study. The process began with participant recruitment from more than eight countries, followed by data collection using a serious game designed to evoke challenging scenarios, immediately after which participants completed the grit survey and open-ended reflection questions. Data was then preprocessed. Sentiment extraction was conducted with various techniques, including SpaCy, VADER, and ChatGPT models. The sentiment information was then aggregated into overall sentiment scores and specific emotional dimensions. These features were used to train the grit prediction model. The results were compared to the results of individual grit scores, obtained by the grit questionnaire. The trained models were thoroughly assessed using standard regression evaluation metrics. Finally, the predictions and influential emotional features were interpreted using two XAI methods; PDPs and SHAP to provide insight into the model's decision-making process.

3.1 Serious Game – Data Gathering

A gamification approach was used in the data collection process, with the term referring to the introduction of game-play mechanics in nongame environments with the goal of fostering change of behavior and/or increasing motivation (Deterding et al., 2011; Kapp, 2012; Marczewski, 2015). This was done with the

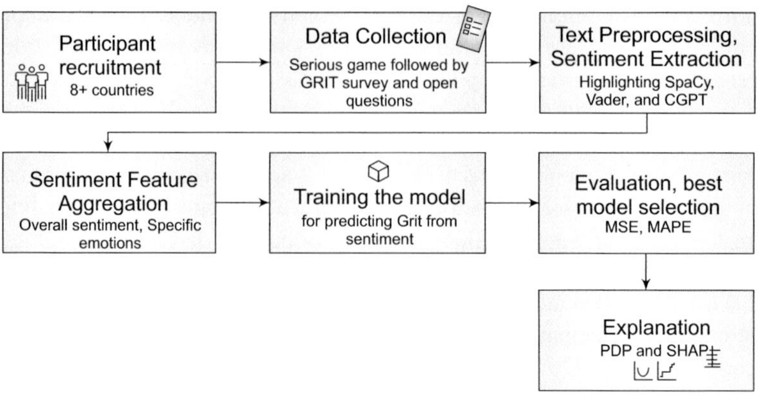

Fig. 1 Overview of the methodology used to predict grit scores from multilingual free-text responses, combining sentiment analysis, machine learning, and explainable AI techniques.

introduction of a serious game (Sawyer & Rejeski, 2002), a game designed and developed according to educational objectives that incorporates a pedagogical and educational dynamic into the gaming experience, most commonly in the form of a digital game. The game was designed as a virtual escape room with a storyline set in an epidemic research laboratory where two detectives investigate a scientist's murder. Within the game, players have to uncover clues, move through the lab, collaborate with other police staff, and try to solve puzzles and collect evidence to find the murderer and potentially find the lost cure for the epidemic. The details of the game were presented in the context of the Grit project (GRIT Project, 2024). The game was designed to be increasingly difficult to advance in, putting participants in frustrating situations in which their grit and perseverance would be challenged. The game was time-limited, with players allowed to participate for a fixed number of hours, no matter the level they reached. Afterwards, participants were prompted to fill out the grit questionnaire and open-ended journaling questions.

3.2 Tools for Grit Measurement

An 8-item grit questionnaire by Duckworth et al. (2007) was used as a psychometric instrument, in which grit was measured on a five-step Likert scale (1: do not agree at all to 5: fully agree). According to Duckworth et al.'s research (2007), participants' responses to these statements provide insights into their perseverance and passion towards achieving long-term goals, which are, as previously mentioned, key components of grit. The Grit Scale has been widely used in research and applied settings to assess grit across various populations, including students (Vela et al., 2015), athletes, and professionals (Credé et al., 2017). It helps researchers and practitioners understand how grit influences individuals' success and well-being in different domains of life. The responses were aggregated into a single grit score. Additionally, participants answered open-ended text questions organized into four categories: Tolerance to Frustration, Locus of Control, Engagement, Ethics and Personal Experience. For the category *tolerance to frustration*, participants described situations and their personal reactions when faced with challenges or setbacks, especially in the context of problem-solving or puzzle tasks. For the *locus of control* category, participants reflected on their perceived agency, control over outcomes, and attribution of success or failure. The questions in the *engagement* category captured levels of interest, involvement, and attention in activities described in the survey context. For the *ethics and personal experience* category questions the respondents elaborated on morals, ethical considerations, and specific experiences relevant to the survey's context. Each of these categories was assessed with multiple open-ended questions. These responses from participants were subsequently combined into a single "*All Text*" content for each participant. The questions asked in this section are presented in Appendix A of this chapter.

3.3 Data Preparation and Preprocessing

The data from the grit questionnaire, as well as from open-ended journaling questions, were organized in a single data collection. To understand and quantify the underlying emotions and attitudes present in participants' written responses, several advanced sentiment analysis techniques were employed.

Sentiment and emotion features were extracted from participant-generated texts using pre trained multilingual sentiment extraction models, including SpaCy (Honnibal et al., 2020), VADER (Valence Aware Dictionary and sEntiment Reasoner) (Hutto & Gilbert, 2014), and the OpenAI Chat-GPT API. These models can classify text into basic emotional categories, such as joy, sadness, anger, or trust, and can also estimate psychological factors known as valence, arousal, and dominance. In essence, these features gauge how pleasant, stimulating, or controlling the observed section of a written text feels.

Sentiment analysis covered several levels of detail: (*i*) Overall sentiment scores ranging from fully negative (−1) to neutral (0) and fully positive (1); (*ii*) Specific emotions: trust, joy, surprise, sadness, anticipation, fear, anger, and disgust; and (*iii*) VAD dimensions (valence, arousal, and dominance). Alongside VADER, several state-of-the-art models developed and published by the Hugging Face community were used for more fine-grained assessments of text (Demszky et al., 2020; Devlin et al., 2019); further assessing how pleasant, stimulating, or controlling a written passage feels. With ChatGPT, carefully structured prompts following the documentation guidelines (OpenAI, 2023) were used to obtain both general sentiment scores (ranging from negative to positive) and probabilities for specific emotions like joy, fear, and anticipation. The prompts used are detailed in Appendix B. The ChatGPT approach was repeatedly used for each open-ended answer, including all the main text categories and the overall combined responses.

Each answer was run through every tool to quantify the sentiment expressed in text. These measures were added to the data. By using a mixture of established lexicon-based methods and modern machine learning models, and by repeating the analysis across multiple categories of participant responses, our goal was to create a detailed and robust map of the sentiments and emotions embedded in the data.

3.4 Model Building and Experiment

Following the extraction of sentiment and emotion features from participants' written responses, the extent to which these affective indicators could serve as predictors of individual grit scores was investigated. A histogram-based Gradient Boosting regression model (Ke et al., 2017) was employed to predict grit scores based on sentiment features extracted from texts. This method is robust to non linearities, supports mixed-type input, and offers efficient training.

Although alternative models, e.g., neural networks, random forests were considered, priority was given to interpretability and consistent integration with XAI methods, despite potential trade offs in predictive performance. Instead of comparing the performance of multiple machine learning models, the goal of this study was consistency and interpretability, using a single, well-understood tool throughout the different stages of the analysis.

Over 60 experimental models were trained to evaluate various sentiment configurations and sources. Performance was evaluated using mean squared error (MSE) and mean absolute percentage error (MAPE). These metrics ensured comparability and allowed assessment of prediction accuracy across models.

To ensure our results were both valid and reproducible, we adopted standard procedures when training and evaluating our predictive models. The dataset was separated into distinct training and testing subsets. Most of the participants' data (80%) was assigned to the training set, which was used to train the model to learn the relationship between sentiment features and the grit score. The remaining portion of the data served as the testing data. This split was created randomly, so the groups were as representative as possible, and a fixed random seed was used throughout to ensure the replication of the results.

3.5 Final Model Explanation with XAI

The Model's predictions and the relationships between sentiment and grit were interpreted with PDPs and SHAP plots. SHAP had previously been recognized as a suitable technique for NLP interpretability (Mosca et al., 2022; Yeung et al., 2024). PDPs were implemented with scikit-learn (Pedregosa et al., 2011) and were used to investigate how the model's prediction for grit changes if only one input variable is adjusted while keeping all others steady. This approach provides an insight into the relationship between a factor of interest and the outcome. PDPs have also been previously used for further understanding of the machine learning models and their outputs (Antar & Tayachi, 2025).

4. Results and Discussion

4.1 Participants

The study included a sample of 148 participants who completed surveys after engaging in a serious game activity (as described in Section 3.1). The participants were included from multiple countries, predominantly from Slovenia (*n* = 50), Spain (*n* = 29), Romania (*n* = 28), Lithuania (*n* = 17), and Italy (*n* = 16), with a smaller representation (*n* = 8) from other countries such as Greece, Germany, Mexico, Indonesia, Bangladesh, and Peru. From these, 134 surveys were fully completed and suitable for analysis. Participants' ages ranged from 16 to 55 years (*M* = 23.4, *Std* = 6.3), with 60% identifying as male, 38.5% female, and 1.5% as other. The participants came from diverse academic backgrounds, including IT, Media and Technology, Psychology, Mathematics, and Pedagogy.

4.2 Comparison of Sentiment Analysis Approaches

Beyond this most inclusive approach, models were also trained using sentiment features extracted by only one technique at a time. The performance of these different sentiment extraction methods is presented in Table 1. While all methods contributed to some predictive value, the VADER scores and ChatGPT's VAD features, along with VADER scores, showed the strongest performance, consistently achieving the lowest prediction errors.

Table 1 Performance of different sentiment extraction approaches in the prediction of grit scores.

Sentiment Extraction Approach	*MSE*	*MAPE*
VADER (sentiment score)	0.256	0.110
SpaCy (emotions)	0.310	0.127
SpaCy (VAD)	0.355	0.132
ChatGPT (single score)	0.339	0.120
ChatGPT (detailed probabilities)	0.386	0.131
ChatGPT (emotions)	0.330	0.138
ChatGPT (VAD)	0.286	0.105

Furthermore, different text categories were analyzed. Models were trained with sentiment features derived from only one part of the open-ended survey responses at a time, to discern whether the predictive signals were coming from specific types of narrative content or were distributed across all the text. The results are presented in Table 2. The findings illustrate that using all available text yielded the most accurate predictions, closely followed by the section on "Tolerance to Frustration." This suggests that how people describe their coping strategies for setbacks often contains the most telling clues about their grit.

Several experiments were carried out, each using a different set of sentiment extraction techniques, focusing on different parts of the participants' open-ended responses. The aim was not just to measure predictive power, but to illustrate which aspects of emotional expression were most informative. When all sentiment extraction techniques were combined, the model considered the entire spectrum

Table 2 Model performance based on different subsets of participant text responses.

Filter String	*MSE*	*MAPE*
Tolerance to Frustration	0.2551	0.1093
Locus of Control	0.3263	0.1371
Engagement	0.4094	0.1320
Ethics and Personal Experience	0.3446	0.1300
All Text	0.2208	0.1049

of sentiment and emotion features derived from all participant texts, a notably high predictive accuracy was achieved. In this setting, the model's mean squared error was approximately 0.256, while the mean absolute percentage error stood at roughly 9.3%. These results indicate that when all possible sentiment information is included, grit scores can be predicted with relatively little average discrepancy.

As presented above and detailed in Table 1, when training the model with single sentiment features extracted by one technique at the time, the VADER scores and ChatGPT-extracted VAD features showed the strongest performance, consistently achieving the lowest prediction errors. The model generated with this approach was therefore used in the next phases of the research.

4.3 Explaining the Grit Predictions

To better understand how specific emotional features influenced grit predictions, explainable AI techniques were applied to interpret the output of the final model. The summary plot presented in Figure 2, based on SHAP values for this comprehensive model, revealed which sentiment features contributed the most to accurate predictions. The VADER sentiment score conducted over the entire text (*All Text VADER sentiment score*) was identified as the most influential predictor of the grit score (within the scope of histogram gradient boosting models utilized in this work). Higher values of the VADER feature were consistently associated with increased grit predictions, highlighting the importance of overall positive sentiment in the participants' responses. A similar trend was observed for the trust feature, generated with SpaCy (*Engagement Spacy emotions trust*), where higher expressions of trust correlated with higher predicted grit scores. In contrast, the sadness feature, generated with the same approach (*Engagement Spacy emotions sadness*), demonstrated a strong negative association, with increased sadness consistently reducing grit predictions.

A subtler effect was found for the valence feature, created with the ChatGPT tool (*Tolerance to Frustration ChatGPT VAD valence*), where higher valence, indicating a more positive emotional tone in frustration-related contexts, was generally linked to higher predicted grit, though its overall impact was smaller. Lastly, the generalized negative sentiment feature generated with ChatGPT (*Engagement ChatGPT detailed negative*) showed a more variable pattern: while higher negativity typically reduced grit predictions, the inconsistency in SHAP

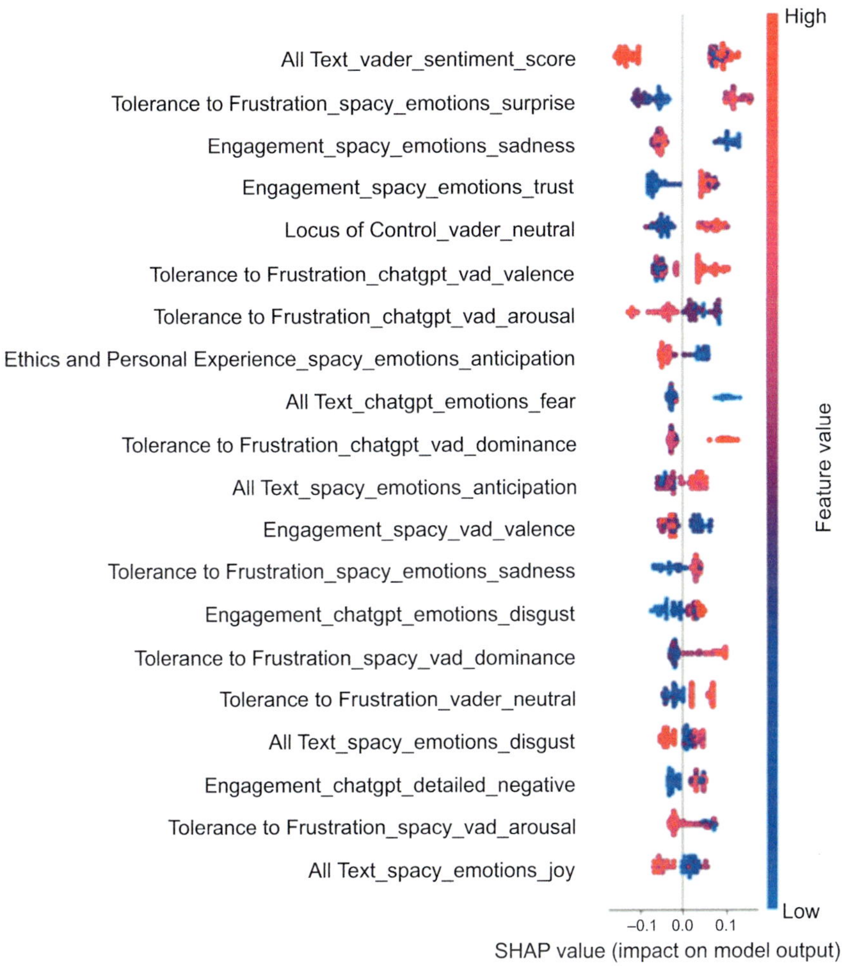

Fig. 2 SHAP explanation for model with all sentiment extraction techniques combined.

values suggests that the influence of negative sentiment may depend on contextual factors within the text.

The additional SHAP explanation plot presented in Figure 3 was created to analyze the results of the predicted VADER sentiment score. In the SHAP summary analysis for the sentiment model, the most influential feature was the VADER sentiment score computed across the entire response (*All Text*), indicating that the general emotional tone of the full text played a central role in shaping the predicted sentiment. Higher values of this feature were consistently linked to increased sentiment scores, confirming the model's reliance on overall textual positivity.

A secondary but meaningful contribution was observed for the ethics-related feature (*Ethics and Personal Experience*), which exhibited a relatively symmetrical distribution of SHAP values. Texts rich in emotional or moral content tended to slightly elevate the predicted sentiment, although the overall effect remained modest. The engagement-related feature (*Engagement*) showed a bidirectional impact: its contribution to sentiment predictions varied depending on the contextual framing of the text, suggesting that engagement itself is not inherently valenced but interacts with the emotional content in nuanced ways. A similarly complex pattern emerged for the valence feature related to frustration tolerance *Tolerance to Frustration ChatGPT VAD valence*).

While positively valenced expressions of perseverance often increased predicted sentiment, negative descriptions of struggles tended to suppress it, indicating that both tone and framing influence how emotional resilience is interpreted. Finally, the internal agency feature (*Locus of Control*) showed a narrower SHAP distribution, with a slight tendency for lower scores to reduce predicted sentiment. However, the effect size was limited, suggesting only a weak association with sentiment polarity in this model.

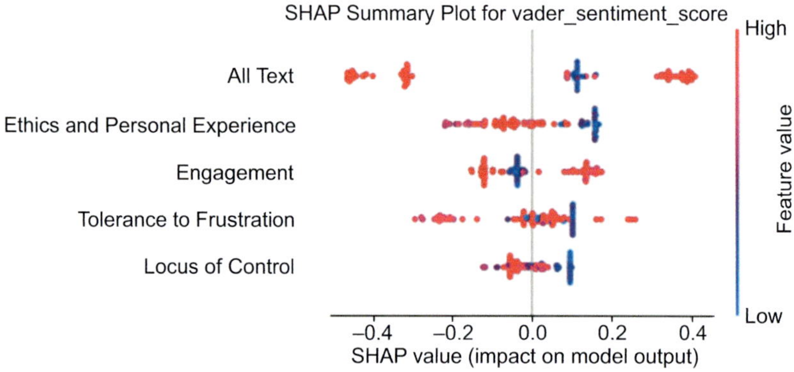

Fig. 3 SHAP explanation for model limited to VADER features.

4.4 Role of Emotion in Grit Estimation

The aim of this work was not solely limited to measuring predictive power for grit, but to illustrate which aspects of emotional expression were most informative. To gain further understanding about the influence of the sentiment features, partial dependence plots for VADER features and *All text* were created, as presented in Figure 4. The plots illustrate how predicted grit scores vary with changes in overall sentiment, while holding all other features constant. A positive slope indicates a general association between higher sentiment and increased grit predictions.

Among individual features, *Locus of Control* shows a neutral effect at lower values (−0.5 to 0.2), followed by a gradual decline in predicted grit as the feature increases, suggesting that a stronger external locus of control may slightly reduce perceived perseverance. The effect is again neutralized for higher values of this variable (above 0.5). A similar effect with a stronger negative dip in the values between 0.5–1 can be observed for the *Tolerance to frustration* feature. The observed dip may reflect a nonlinear effect, where moderate levels of tolerance to frustration correlate with less grit (possibly due to complacency, disengagement or resignation). The *Engagement* feature demonstrates a weak but positive association, with predicted grit remaining stable until around 0.45, then rising modestly. At the extreme upper end, a sharp drop is observed, potentially reflecting outlier responses or diminishing returns of hyper-engagement. The *Ethics and Personal Experience* feature shifts from a positive to a negative influence as values increase. While low scores are linked to higher predicted grit, values above 0.2 correspond with a decline, possibly indicating that emotionally expressive or introspective language is interpreted as a marker of reduced grit. Lastly, the *All Text* feature is largely neutral across most of its range, with a sudden increase in predicted grit near the upper extreme, followed by a sharp drop, suggesting that specific high-intensity textual patterns may trigger abrupt shifts in model output depending on their context.

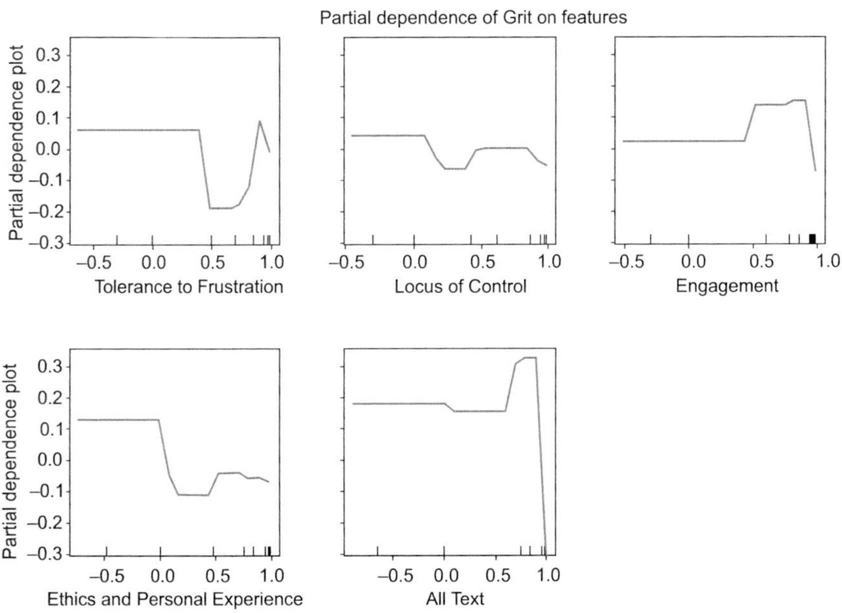

Fig. 4 PDP explanation for the model limited to grit open-ended categories.

Furthermore, partial dependence plots were generated for the individual emotion-based features extracted from free-text responses, as shown in Figure 5. The impact overall *sentiment score* remains strongly positive and relatively flat until its upper extreme, where it drops sharply at around a 0.9 threshold, indicating that overly positive or exaggerated sentiment may inversely affect model output.

Among the emotion features, *trust* and *anticipation* show a distinctly positive relationship with grit prediction, particularly at higher values, suggesting that forward-looking emotional tones are interpreted as indicators of greater grit. Similarly, though a less strong effect can be observed for *anger*. Its partial dependence plot shows that low to moderate levels of anger have little to no effect on predicted grit, but higher levels of anger (above 0.11) are associated with a slight increase in grit prediction.

Conversely, features such as *fear* and *sadness* exhibit a negative trend, supporting the interpretation that heightened negative emotional expression may suppress perceived grit. The negative relationship for sadness and grit is almost linear, while the relationship between the impact of fear on grit prediction is positive up until the value of 0.08, after which its impact on predicted grit becomes neutral to slightly negative. Interestingly, the *surprise* feature shows weak or inconsistent effects, with mostly neutral influence across their ranges. Observing the *joy* feature, it is visible that moderate levels of joy initially support higher predicted grit, but beyond a certain threshold (around 0.16), the effect declines, eventually becoming neutral or slightly negative. The *disgust* plot suggests that moderate levels of disgust may boost the grit score, possibly by signaling rejection

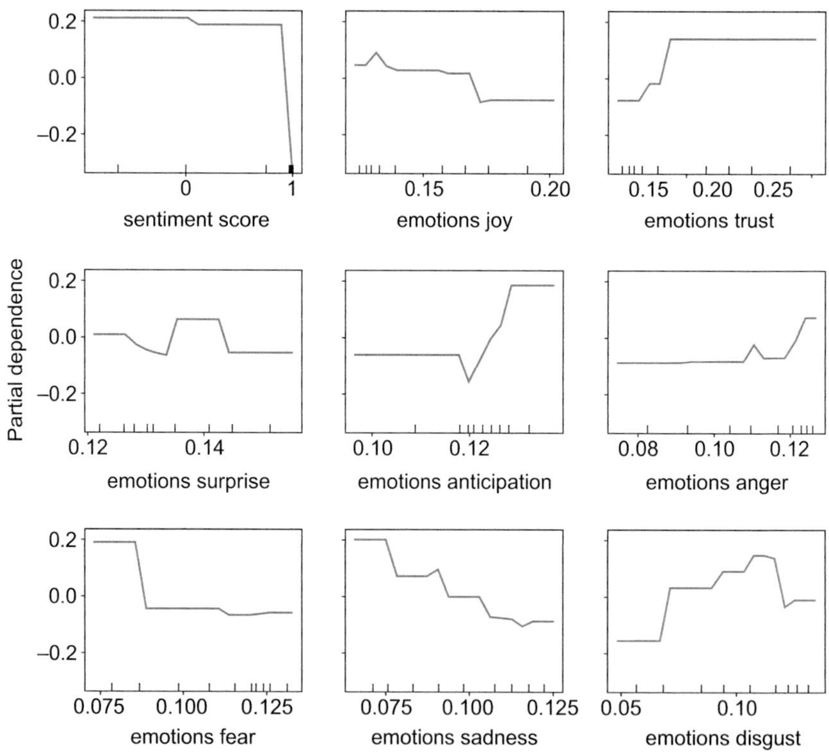

Fig. 5 PDP explanation for all emotions.

of failure or injustice, yet higher levels may diminish that effect, highlighting a threshold beyond which disgust becomes less productive for grit.

These patterns suggest that while positive sentiment (trust, anticipation) generally supports higher grit predictions, extremely high (overall sentiment score, sadness, engagement, all text) or ambiguous (ethics and personal experience) expressions may introduce uncertainty or even reduce the perceived grit signal in the text.

To further investigate how individual emotional dimensions influence predicted grit for different groups, we employed SHAP bar plots stratified by gender. The best performing model, trained on the full composite text input, was used for this analysis. Using the cohorts function in SHAP, the dataset was partitioned by gender, and the mean absolute SHAP values were computed separately for each group. This allowed us to quantify and compare the relative contribution of each affective feature to the model's prediction of grit by gender. As shown in Figure 6, both groups exhibit similar feature importance rankings, with the VADER sentiment score exerting the strongest influence, followed by trust, sadness, and fear. The consistency of SHAP values across groups suggests that the Histogram-based Gradient Boosting model leverages grit indicators in a robust and relatively gender-neutral manner.

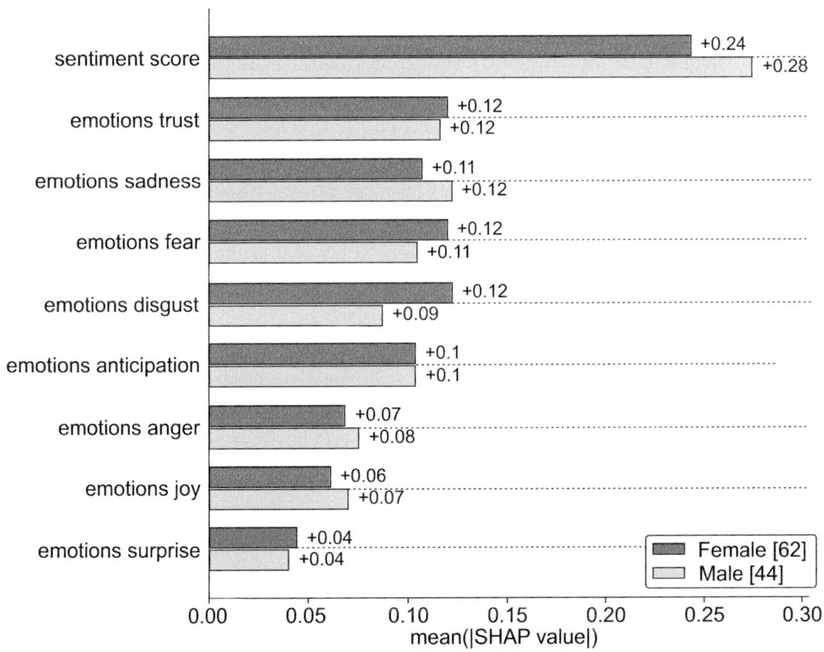

Fig. 6 Average Absolute SHAP Values by Gender Cohort.

5. Discussion

This study addressed *RQ1*, which focused on whether grit can be predicted using sentiment analysis of user-generated texts instead of traditional psychometric surveys. Our results indicate that this is indeed possible: models trained on affective features extracted from participants' open-ended reflections achieved an MAPE of approximately 0.11, suggesting a high degree of predictive reliability. While these findings support the feasibility of using sentiment analysis as a proxy for grit assessment, it is important to emphasize that this approach does not fully replace standardized psychometric instruments. Rather, it offers a scalable alternative in contexts where traditional surveys may not be practical or available. The method can serve as an informative first step, particularly in exploratory settings or as part of formative assessments. However, further research is needed to evaluate its construct validity, generalization, and robustness across languages, populations, and time.

Turning to *RQ2*, which explored which emotions most significantly influence grit predictions, our analysis revealed a clear pattern: emotions associated with positive future orientation had the strongest positive impact on predicted grit scores. These features (trust, surprise, anticipation) consistently emerged as top contributors across SHAP plots and PDPs, especially when derived from engagement-related reflections and overall sentiment scoring. This suggests that students who express confidence in others and maintain a forward-looking mindset are more likely to exhibit language patterns associated with higher grit. Conversely, negative emotions such as sadness and fear were associated with reduced predicted grit, while disgust showed a more mixed pattern, with moderate levels linked to increased grit and high levels having neutral or slightly diminished effects. Sadness was one of the most influential negative predictors, indicating that emotionally heavy or demotivated language reduces perceived perseverance. These results align with the findings of previous psychological studies that also reported a negative association between anxiety and other negative emotions and grit (Liu & Wang, 2021; Singh & Duggal Jha, 2008). Interestingly, some typically positive emotions like joy and surprise had weak or even ambiguous effects. In extreme values, these features occasionally contributed to a drop in predicted grit, hinting at a possible overcompensation effect or affective exaggeration that the model interprets as less aligned with genuine resilience. The reduction of grit with extremely high positive emotions has, however, also been observed in the prior literature (Singh & Duggal Jha, 2008). Overall, the emotional tone of students' reflections, especially expressions of trust and goal-directed anticipation, appears to play a pivotal role in grit prediction. These findings reinforce the idea that emotional framing in language is not just a by-product of personality but an active signal of grit.

In relation to *RQ3*, XAI methods (specifically SHAP and PDPs) played a crucial role in uncovering how emotional sentiments contribute to grit predictions. SHAP values allowed for a granular, feature-level interpretation of the model's decisions, revealing not only which emotions were influential but also how their presence in student-generated texts shifted predicted grit scores. For instance, the SHAP summary plots consistently highlighted the VADER sentiment score and trust-related features as the most impactful predictors, offering transparent insights into the emotional underpinnings of high grit scores. Partial dependence plots further supported these interpretations by illustrating the directionality and shape of these relationships. For example, they revealed that while trust and anticipation increased grit predictions in a largely linear fashion, up to a plateau, as visible in Figure 5. Overly high values of emotions like surprise or joy occasionally produced non linear effects, suggesting interpretive nuances that the model detects in sentiment intensity. Together, these XAI tools moved the analysis beyond black-box prediction, enabling both researchers and educators to better understand why certain emotional expressions signal grit. This interpretability is especially valuable in educational settings, where actionable insights into students' emotional and motivational profiles are essential for personalized support.

The findings presented should be interpreted as exploratory and context bound. The predictive relationships observed are specific to the multilingual student sample analyzed and may vary across cultures, educational settings, and data types. Accordingly, the results provide initial evidence of feasibility rather than generalizable conclusions. Future work should validate this approach on larger and more diverse datasets to confirm its robustness.

5.1 Implications for Educational Practice

The findings of this research hold meaningful implications for educational practice. By leveraging sentiment analysis and XAI methods to measure grit, educators can more easily gain deeper insights into students' emotional states and their impact on per severance. Specifically, recognizing that positive emotional expressions such as trust and anticipation strongly enhance grit offers practical opportunities for intervention. For example, educators might actively foster classroom environments that encourage trust-building activities, goal-setting discussions, and optimistic future-oriented feedback. On the other hand, understanding that negative emotions like sadness or fear diminish grit can help educators identify students who may require emotional or psychological support to build resilience. Incorporating sentiment analysis tools into routine formative assessments could allow for real-time, nuanced monitoring of student grit, providing educators with actionable data to tailor individual support programs and ultimately improving academic persistence.

5.2 Limitations and Future Work

This study has several limitations. The sample size was relatively small and may not reflect the broader population, which limits generalization. Although our study involved multilingual textual data from participants across multiple European countries, cross-cultural differences in emotional expression and sentiment perception could impact the accuracy and interpretability of our results.

Emotional expressions, their intensity, and meaning can vary significantly between languages and cultures, potentially influencing sentiment extraction outcomes (Mesquita et al., 2016). Future studies should therefore prioritize cross-cultural validation of sentiment analysis tools by calibrating them for specific linguistic and cultural contexts. This could involve qualitative analyses or additional survey-based validation steps to ensure sentiment measures align with culturally-specific emotional expressions. Such validation efforts will enhance the robustness and generalization of the sentiment-based assessment of grit across diverse educational contexts. The quality, length, and grammatical correction of the free-text responses gathered in this study varied, which indicates good robustness of the used methodology. Only one machine learning model was used to ensure consistency and interpretability. While this approach supported the use of SHAP and PDP, it may have constrained performance. Future research could compare different models to assess potential gains. Finally, since SHAP relies on a simplified approximation of the original model to generate explanations, some discrepancies between the explanation and the actual model behavior may occur. Comparing multiple XAI methods could improve the reliability of future interpretations.

Conclusions

This research confirms that sentiment and emotion features extracted from multilingual, open-ended student reflections can reliably predict grit levels, demonstrating a viable alternative to traditional psychometric surveys. By leveraging sentiment analysis and advanced interpretability methods such as SHAP and PDPs, the study pro vided transparent insights into not only which emotional features matter but precisely how they influence grit predictions. Specifically, positive emotional expressions such as trust and anticipation were consistently associated with higher grit scores, reinforcing the role of future-oriented positivity in fostering perseverance. On the other hand, negative emotions like sadness, fear, and disgust reliably indicated reduced grit, highlighting the detrimental effects of negative emotional states on persistence and passion toward long-term goals. An unexpected nuance emerged concerning the role of intense positive emotions, such as extreme joy or surprise, which showed a slight diminishing effect on predicted grit scores. This observation aligns with psychological research cautioning that excessive positivity can sometimes reduce perseverance due to a phenomenon known as the mood maintenance effect. Such nuanced findings illustrate the complexity and richness that sentiment-based text analyses can offer compared to static, survey-based assessments.

The methodological integration of explainable AI significantly enhanced interpretability, providing granular, actionable insights that traditional assessment methods rarely deliver. Educational practitioners can leverage these findings to better understand the fine-grained impact of emotions influencing students' persistence and to develop targeted interventions aimed at fostering resilience and long-term goal commitment. Moreover, the ability to detect grit through sentiment analysis of naturally occurring textual data opens opportunities for scalable, unobtrusive assessment practices in educational settings, which can complement or partially substitute standard psychometric instruments.

Ultimately, this study highlights the potential of sentiment analysis and XAI to transform the measurement and understanding of grit. By capturing emotional dynamics that underlie perseverance, this approach provides educators and researchers with deeper insights and practical tools to support students' academic success.

While the presented results demonstrate promising predictive capability, they should be interpreted within the boundaries of the current study design. The models were trained on a specific multilingual sample from primarily European students. Their applicability to other linguistic, cultural, or temporal contexts remains to be verified. Future work should include validation on independent and cross-cultural datasets, as well as longitudinal analyses to examine whether observed emotion-based indicators of grit remain consistent over time. Such steps should help determine the generalizability and stability of this approach across diverse educational settings and cultural expressions of emotion in written form.

Acknowledgement

We thank the participating students and educators across Europe for their thoughtful reflections, which formed the basis of this research. We are also grateful to the Grit project team and affiliated institutions for their support in coordinating data collection and project implementation.

Funding

The authors acknowledge the financial support from the Slovenian Research Agency (Research Core Funding No. P2-0057, and Research Project Funding No. J5-50176) and from the European Union, Project Number 2022-1-IT02-KA220-HED-00008594.

References

Antar, M. and Tayachi, T. (2025). Partial dependence analysis of financial ratios in predicting company defaults: random forest vs XGBoost models. *Digital Finance*.

Brdnik, S. and Šumak, B. (2024). Current trends, challenges, and techniques in XAI field; a tertiary study of XAI research. In: *2024 47th MIPRO ICT and Electronics Convention* (*MIPRO*) (pp. 2032–2038).

Ceulemans, K., Karsdorp, P.A. and Vlaeyen, J.W. (2013). Effects of responsibility and mood on painful task persistence. *Journal of Behavior Therapy and Experimental Psychiatry*, *44*(2): 186–193.

Corr, P.J. and Matthews, G. (2020). *The Cambridge Handbook of Personality Psychology*. Cambridge University Press.

Crede, M., Tynan, M.C. and Harms, P.D. (2017). Much ado about grit: A meta-analytic synthesis of the grit literature. *Journal of Personality and Social Psychology*, *113*(3): 492–511.

Demszky, D., Movshovitz-Attias, D., Ko, J., Cowen, A., Nemade, G. and Ravi, S. (2020). Goemotions: A dataset of fine-grained emotions. *arXiv preprint arXiv:2005.00547*.

Deterding, S., Dixon, D., Khaled, R. and Nacke, L. (2011). From game design elements to gamefulness: Defining "gamification". In: *Proceedings of the 15th International Academic MindTrek Conference: Envisioning Future Media Environments* (pp. 9–15). New York, NY, USA. ACM.

Devlin, J., Chang, M.-W., Lee, K. and Toutanova, K. (2019). BERT: Pre-training of deep bidirectional transformers for language understanding. In: *Proceedings of the 2019 Conference of the North American Chapter of the Association for Computational Linguistics: Human Language Technologies* (*1*: 4171–4186). Minneapolis, MN. Association for Computational Linguistics.

Duckworth, A. L. (2016). *Grit: The Power of Passion and Perseverance*. Simon & Schuster.

Duckworth, A. L., Peterson, C., Matthews, M.D. and Kelly, D.R. (2007). Grit: perseverance and passion for long-term goals. *Journal of Personality and Social Psychology*, *92*(6): 1087.

Eberhardt, S.T., Schaffrath, J., Moggia, D., Schwartz, B., Jaehde, M., Rubel, J.A., Baur, T., André, E. and W.L. (2025). Decoding emotions: Exploring the validity of sentiment analysis in psychotherapy. *Psychotherapy Research*, *35*(2): 174–189. PMID: 38415369.

Gonçalves, P., Benevenuto, F. and Cha, M. (2013). Panas-t: A psychometric scale for measuring sentiments on twitter. *CoRR*, abs/1308.1857.

GRIT Project (2024). Chapter: Games. https://www.gritproject.eu/wp-content/ uploads/2024/04/chapter-games-1.pdf. Accessed: 2025-06-14.

Hill, P.L., Burrow, A.L. and Bronk, K.C. (2016). Persevering with positivity and purpose: An examination of purpose commitment and positive affect as predictors of grit. *Journal of Happiness Studies*, *17*(1): 257–269.

Honnibal, M., Montani, I., Van Landeghem, S. and Boyd, A. (2020). spaCy: Industrial- strength Natural Language Processing in Python. doi: 10.5281/zenodo.1212303.

Hutto, C. and Gilbert, E. (2014). Vader: A parsimonious rule-based model for sentiment analysis of social media text. In: *Proceedings of the International AAAI Conference on Web and Social Media* (*8*: 216–225).

John, O.P., Robins, R.W. and Pervin, L.A. (2010). *Handbook of Personality: Theory and Research*. Guilford Press.

Johora, F.T., Hasan, M.N., Rajbongshi, A., Ashrafuzzaman, M. and Akter, F. (2025). An explainable AI-based approach for predicting undergraduate students academic performance. *Array*, *26*: 100384.

Kapp, K.M. (2012). *The Gamification of Learning and Instruction: Game-Based Methods and Strategies for Training and Education*. John Wiley & Sons, San Francisco, CA.

Ke, G., Meng, Q., Finley, T., Wang, T., Chen, W., Ma, W., Ye, Q. and Liu, T.-Y. (2017). Lightgbm: A highly efficient gradient boosting decision tree. *Advances in Neural Information Processing Systems*, *30*.

Kost, R.G. and de Rosa, J.C. (2018). Impact of survey length and compensation on validity, reliability, and sample characteristics for ultrashort-, short-, and Long-Research participant perception surveys. *J. Clin. Transl. Sci.*, *2*(1): 31–37.

Li, J. and Li, Y. (2021). The role of grit on students' academic success in experiential learning context. *Frontiers in Psychology*, *12*.

Li, Y. and Lin, X. (2024). Research on the correlation between academic emotion and grit among Chinese college students. *Frontiers in Educational Research*, *7*(2): 112–119.

Liu, E. and Wang, J. (2021). Examining the relationship between grit and foreign language performance: Enjoyment and anxiety as mediators. *Frontiers in Psychology*, *12*: 666892.

Marczewski, A. (2015). Gamification mechanics and elements. In: *Even Ninja Monkeys Like to Play: Gamification, Game Thinking, and Motivational Design* (pp. 165–177). CreateSpace Independent Publishing Platform.

Mesquita, B., Boiger, M. and De Leersnyder, J. (2016). The cultural construction of emotions. *Current Opinion in Psychology*, *8*: 31–36. Culture.

Mosca, E., Szigeti, F., Tragianni, S., Gallagher, D. and Groh, G. (2022). SHAP-based explanation methods: A review for NLP interpretability. In: *Proceedings of the 29th International Conference on Computational Linguistics* (pp. 4593–4603).

OpenAI (2023). OpenAI API documentation: Prompting GPT for classification tasks. https://platform.openai.com/docs/guides/completion/classification. Accessed: 2025-06-14.

Pedregosa, F., Varoquaux, G., Gramfort, A., Michel, V., Thirion, B., Grisel, O., Blondel, M., Prettenhofer, P., Weiss, R., Dubourg, V., Vanderplas, J., Passos, A., Cournapeau, D., Brucher, M., Perrot, M. and Duchesnay, E. (2011). Scikit-learn: Machine learning in python. *Journal of Machine Learning Research*, *12*: 2825–2830.

Phillips, D.L. and Clancy, K.J. (1972). Some effects of "social desirability" in survey studies. *American Journal of Sociology*, *77*(5): 921–940.

Pronin, E. (2009). Chapter 1: The introspection illusion. In: *Advances in Experimental Social Psychology* (*41*: 1–67). Academic Press.

Rathi, S., Verma, J.P., Jain, R., Nayyar, A. and Thakur, N. (2022). Psychometric profiling of individuals using twitter profiles: A psychological natural language processing based approach. *Concurrency and Computation: Practice and Experience*, *34*(19): e7029.

Sawyer, B. and Rejeski, D. (2002). *Serious Games: Improving Public Policy through Game- based Learning and Simulation*. Technical Report 1. Woodrow Wilson International Center for Scholars, Washington, DC.

Singh, K. and Duggal Jha, S. (2008). Positive and negative affect, and grit as predictors of happiness and life satisfaction. *Journal of the Indian Academy of Applied Psychology*, *34*: 40–45.

Tang, H., Miri Rekavandi, A., Rooprai, D., Dwivedi, G., Sanfilippo, F. M., Boussaid, F. and Bennamoun, M. (2024). Analysis and evaluation of explainable artificial intelligence on suicide risk assessment. *Scientific Reports*, *14*(1): 6163.

Teimouri, Y., Sudina, E. and Plonsky, L. (2021). On domain-specific conceptualization and measurement of grit in l2 learning. *Journal for the Psychology of Language Learning*, *3*: 156–164.

Vela, J. C., Lu, M.-T. P., Lenz, A.S. and Hinojosa, K. (2015). Positive psychology and familial factors as predictors of Latina/o students' psychological grit. *Hispanic Journal of Behavioral Sciences*, *37*(3): 287–303.

Vij, A. and Pruthi, J. (2018). An automated psychometric analyzer based on sentiment analysis and emotion recognition for healthcare. In: *International Conference on Computational Intelligence and Data Science*. *Procedia Computer Science*, *132*: 1184–1191.

Wang, Z., Xie, Q., Feng, Y., Ding, Z., Yang, Z. and Xia, R. (2024). Is ChatGPT a good sentiment analyzer?: A preliminary study. *arXiv.2304.04339* (*cs*).

Welz, M. and Alfons, A. (2025). When respondents don't care anymore: Identifying the onset of careless responding. ResearchGate. doi: 10:48550/arXiv.2303.07167.

Xu, Y. (2022). The influence of EFL teachers' hope and trust on their academic grit: A theoretical review. *Frontiers in Psychology*, *13*.

Yeung, K. Z., Frasincar, F., and van der Knaap, F. (2024). Explaining a deep learning model for aspect-based sentiment analysis using SHAP. In: *International Conference on Web Information Systems Engineering* (pp. 59–73). Springer.

Appendix A: Open-ended Questions for Grit Prompting

Tolerance for Frustration

(1) How do you handle setbacks when your plans don't go as expected?
(2) What do you do when you feel that a task is too difficult or challenging?
(3) How do you feel and act when someone criticizes you or points out a mistake?
(4) Can you describe a recent situation where you felt very frustrated? How did you react at that moment?
(5) What is your strategy for dealing with situations where you don't have control?
(6) Can you share an example of a time when you managed to overcome your frustration and move forward? What did you learn from that experience?

Locus of Control

Internal Locus of Control

(1) To what extent do you believe that your achievements and failures depend on your own actions and decisions?
(2) How do you usually react when facing a significant challenge or problem? What steps do you take to solve it?
(3) When you set a goal, how important do you consider your personal effort in achieving it?

External Locus of Control

(1) To what extent do you think your life is influenced by external factors such as luck, fate, or the actions of other people?
(2) When something goes wrong, how much do you believe it is due to circumstances beyond your control?
(3) How do you explain the successes you have had in your life? What factors do you consider to have been most decisive?

Engagement

(1) Have you ever had a great idea that benefited your team or your organisation?
(2) What motivates you to fully commit to your work or projects?
(3) Can you describe a situation where you felt a high level of commitment and dedication? What factors contributed to it?
(4) How do your relationships with colleagues and supervisors influence your level of engagement at work?

(5) What strategies do you use to overcome demotivation and stay focused?
(6) What role do recognition and rewards play in your level of commitment?

Ethics

(1) Do you identify with the profession of researcher, what personal experiences and values have shaped this identity?
(2) Describe a time in your life when you felt particularly motivated to investigate a topic or solve a problem, what prompted you to delve into this topic and what steps did you take to find answers?
(3) What inspires you to continue exploring new knowledge? Describe a situation in which your curiosity and passion for discovering something new led you to overcome obstacles or challenges.
(4) Can you describe an experience in which you faced a significant difficulty? How did you handle the situation and what motivated you to continue despite the challenges? What did you learn about yourself in the process?
(5) Describe a situation in which you faced an ethical dilemma in your professional work. What was the dilemma and how did you resolve it?
(6) What ethical principles guided your decision and how did you ensure that your research remained honest and responsible?

Appendix B: ChatGPT Prompts for Sentiment Feature Extraction

Table B1 Features built with ChatGPT and corresponding prompts used.

Feature	*Prompt*	*Example Value*
negative neutral positive	Provide sentiment probabilities for negative, neutral, and positive	0.00 0.1 0.90
joy sadness anger fear surprise disgust trust anticipation	Provide probabilities for emotions (joy, sadness, anger, fear, surprise, disgust, trust, anticipation)	0.85 0.05 0.01 0.02 0.03 0.01 0.80 0.70
valence arousal dominance	Provide scores for valence, arousal, and dominance (0 to 1).	0.9 0.8 0.7
sentiment	Provide a sentiment score between –1 (negative) and 1 (positive).	0.1

10 | From Local Explanations to Collective Explanations
An XAI Approach Using LIME and Clustering in Education

Lynda Dib[1*] and Laurence Capus[2]

The integration of artificial intelligence (AI) in education raises major issues of transparency and explainability, which are essential to build trust and guide pedagogical decisions. Local explanation methods, such as LIME, provide useful but limited insights, as they remain unstable, focused on isolated cases, and poorly suited for identifying collective trends. To overcome these limitations, we propose an innovative approach that combines three complementary dimensions: local explanations (LIME), inter-model aggregation, and clustering of explanatory contributions. Few studies in the literature simultaneously integrate these three axes to generate collective educational profiles, which gives our approach an original contribution in this research field. This methodology transforms complex individual explanations into robust collective profiles, offering a deep understanding of learning dynamics. The results reveal differentiated profiles—ranging from fundamental sciences to computer science and prior academic background—reflecting the plurality of learning and performance dynamics. These profiles constitute concrete action levers for teachers and institutions, promoting personalization, equity, and accountability in the use of educational technologies. By linking local interpretability to collective explanation, this chapter proposes a robust framework aligning AI contributions with human-centered pedagogical objectives.

1. Introduction

The integration of artificial intelligence (AI) into the educational domain has sparked growing interest in predictive systems capable of anticipating learners' success or difficulties. These tools offer considerable potential to support the personalization of learning pathways and pedagogical decision-making. However, their adoption remains contingent on their transparency and their ability to provide comprehensible explanations to teachers and students.

Local explainability approaches, such as LIME (Local Interpretable Model-agnostic Explanations) (Ribeiro, 2016) and SHAP (SHapley Additive exPlanations)

[1,2] Laval University, Québec, Canada.
* Corresponding author: lynda.dib@univ-annaba.dz; lynda.dib.1@ulaval.ca

DOI: 10.1201/9781003713371-10

(Lundberg, 2017), have made model predictions more accessible by identifying the impact of each variable on the decision for a given individual.

Despite their usefulness, these methods present several limitations: they provide a snapshot view focused on isolated cases, and their results can lack stability and consistency when applied to a single model. Several studies have highlighted this instability. For instance, Zafar and Khan (Zafar, 2019) point out that LIME can generate different explanations for the same prediction due to the random nature of its perturbations, while Slack et al. (2021) emphasize the lack of reliability and robustness of post-hoc local explanations. Similarly, Dhurandhar et al. (2023) stress the absence of stability in classical local methods, motivating the development of more coherent and invariant approaches. Finally, these methods struggle to produce actionable collective profiles; Setzu et al. 2021) illustrate the need to move from local explanation to global explanation in order to identify structural trends and more effectively guide differentiated pedagogical actions.

To address these limitations, we propose an innovative approach that combines local explainability with an inter-model aggregation strategy and clustering of explanatory contributions. This approach aims at a dual objective: (1) to enhance the robustness and consistency of explanations by comparing multiple models, and (2) to transform complex individual explanations into synthetic profiles that can be leveraged by educational stakeholders. The originality of our contribution lies in linking local explanations with collective groupings to provide a more stable, reliable, and pedagogically relevant interpretation of predictions generated by AI models.

The paper is organized as follows: Section 2 presents related work, Section 3 describes the proposed methodology, and Section 4 illustrates its application for generating explanatory profiles. Section 5 analyzes these profiles, highlighting their pedagogical implications and validation, while Section 6 concludes by emphasizing the contributions and future perspectives.

2. Related Work

The explainability of machine learning models has received increasing attention, particularly in the educational context where understanding predictions is essential to support pedagogical decision-making. Local approaches, such as LIME, allow the identification of each variable's contribution to an individual prediction, but they are often limited to a snapshot view and can lack robustness when applied to a single model. Recent studies have explored the aggregation of explanations from multiple models to improve reliability and reduce the instability of local contributions. For example, Zafar and Khan (2019) proposed a deterministic version of LIME, DLIME, which uses hierarchical clustering and K-Nearest Neighbor to select the relevant cluster, thus providing more stable and consistent explanations (Zafar, 2019). Similarly, Botari et al (2020). introduced MeLIME, a generalization of LIME that allows more flexible perturbation and the use of different interpretable local models, producing more meaningful explanations

(Botari, 2020). Moreover, methods such as the Weighted Importance Score and Frequency Count (WISFC) have been proposed to aggregate feature importance across multiple models, combining both magnitude and consistency to provide a robust ranking of features (Veledar, 2025).

At the same time, clustering analyses of local explanations have been used to generate collective profiles, facilitating the interpretation of global trends and the identification of recurring patterns in the data. Several recent studies have explored clustering of explanatory contributions to generate collective profiles and facilitate global model interpretation. For instance, Cooper (2021) proposed supervised clustering using SHAP values to identify groups of instances with similar explanations, enabling the analysis of common trends and risk factors. In the medical field, Escriva (2025) applied SHAP value clustering to group patients according to similar risk profiles, facilitating the identification of high-risk groups in health data (Escriva, 2025). More recently, Anwar et al. (2021) proposed MASALA (Model-Agnostic Surrogate Explanations by Locality Adaptation), a method that dynamically adjusts the local region for each instance to produce more stable and consistent explanations, integrating deterministic clustering techniques to improve explanation fidelity (Anwar, 2024).

However, few studies explicitly combine multiple models with LIME and clustering of explanatory contributions to produce pedagogically actionable profiles, as proposed in our approach. This combination offers a dual advantage: it strengthens the robustness and consistency of explanations while transforming complex individual information into synthetic profiles that can guide differentiated interventions for students.

3. Methodology

The proposed approach aimed not only to go beyond the individual explanations produced by LIME but also to strengthen interpretations through a collective and robust perspective. The objectives of this methodology were twofold: on one hand, to improve the consistency and reliability of explanations generated by multiple supervised learning models, addressing validity concerns in artificial intelligence; on the other hand, to identify representative profiles and facilitate their translation into pedagogical implications, supporting interpretation and decision-making in the educational context. To achieve this, we adopted a multi-model strategy, combining several heterogeneous supervised algorithms to capture diverse perspectives on the data. The local explanations generated were then organized into a structured set, serving as the basis for the clustering process, which was structured around three main phases.

3.1 Construction and Normalization of Contribution Vectors

Each prediction generated by the trained models was associated with a local explanation obtained using the LIME algorithm, in the form of positive or negative contributions of the variables. All these contributions were then consolidated across models and organized into vectors representing the explanatory profile of each student.

To ensure comparability between students and across variables of different types (e.g., grades from different subjects and prior academic background), these contribution vectors were normalized. This step ensures that observed differences between profiles are related to explanatory patterns rather than scale differences among variables.

3.2 Clustering of Local Explanations into Explanatory Profiles

A partitioning method, K-Means, was applied to the normalized contribution vectors to group students according to the similarity of their explanations. The algorithm seeks to minimize intra-cluster variance while maximizing separation between clusters. To determine the number of groups and avoid an arbitrary manual choice, we used the Silhouette Score, a measure that simultaneously evaluates the internal cohesion of clusters and their separation (Rousseeuw, 1987). The chosen value of k corresponds to the one that maximizes this score, ensuring a partitioning that is both relevant and robust.

Once clusters were obtained, the local explanations generated by LIME were aggregated to produce collective explanatory profiles. This aggregation overcomes the limitations of individual explanations, such as their variability and occasional instability, by identifying average contributions and dominant factors for each group. Thus, the adopted methodology transforms scattered, individual local explanations into explanatory patterns shared by subgroups of students, offering a more global, robust, and pedagogically relevant understanding of the determinants considered by the model.

4. Application of Explanatory Profiles

4.1 Preparation and Normalization of Explanatory Data

The dataset used in this study is an educational dataset available on data.world. It contains six academic features: Physics, Chemistry, Biology, Computer_Note1, Computer_Note2, and GPA, in addition to the target variable corresponding to the level of academic performance, categorized into three classes: High Performance (HP), Intermediate Performance (IP), and Low Performance (LP).

Several heterogeneous supervised models were then trained on this dataset to predict student performance, and a comparison of their performances is presented in Figure 1.

The local explanations generated by LIME for each model were analyzed to identify global trends. Figure 2 illustrates the distribution of positive and negative contributions of the various academic variables according to the models, highlighting the variability and complementarity of their influences. These results thus provide a consolidated basis for constructing the explanatory clusters.

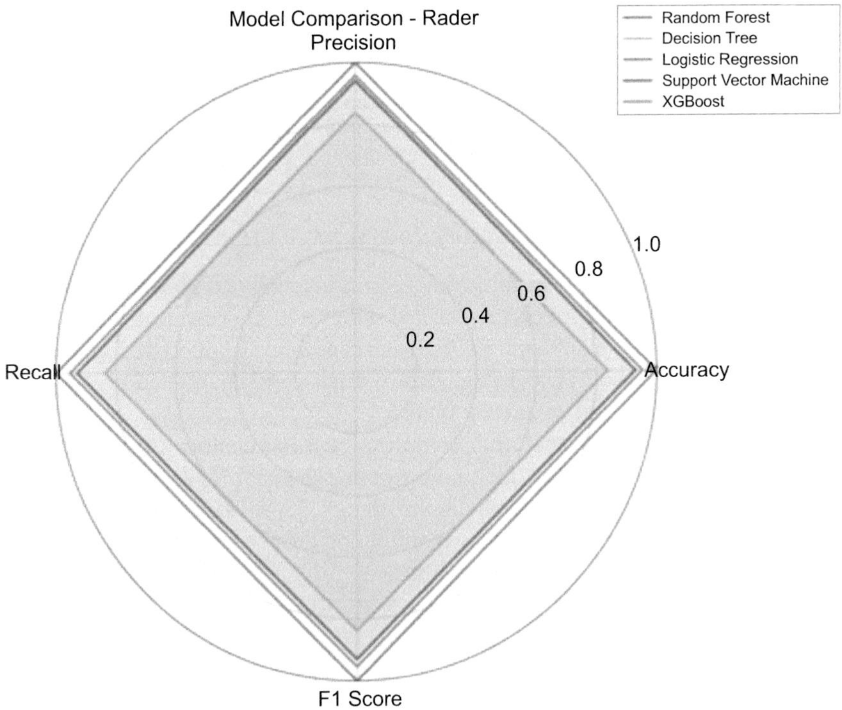

Fig. 1 Radar Chart of Supervised Model Performance.

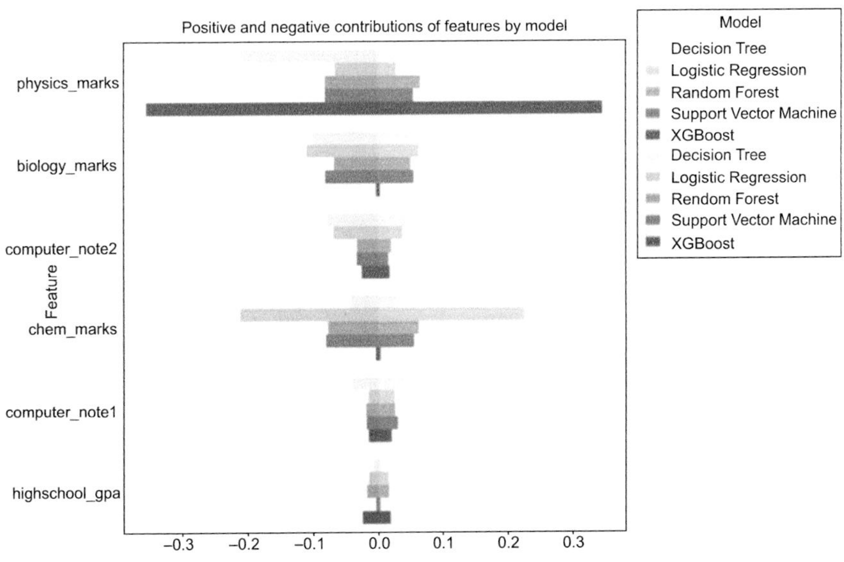

Fig. 2 Positive and Negative Feature Contributions by Model.

To correctly interpret these profiles, the local contributions were previously normalized. This step ensures that comparisons between variables (from different disciplines) truly reflect their explanatory weight rather than mere scale differences. Consequently, the subsequent groupings accurately represent similarities in explanatory patterns rather than artifacts caused by the heterogeneity of the initial values.

4.2 Construction of Explanatory Profiles via Clustering

The K-Means algorithm was applied to group students based on the similarity of their explanatory profiles, with the optimal number of clusters determined to be seven using the Silhouette Score. Each cluster represents a collective explanatory pattern, providing a robust and pedagogically meaningful interpretation of the key factors emphasized by the predictive model.

This methodology transforms complex local explanations into synthetic explanatory profiles, thereby facilitating comprehension and practical use of results by teachers and educational administrators. It provides a more actionable interpretation of predictive models by highlighting the primary pedagogical levers rather than isolated individual explanations.

4.2.1 Distribution and Characteristics of Profiles

The identified profiles are characterized as follows:

- Profile 0 (7.0%; 3 instances): predicted success mainly supported by *highschool_gpa*, with a slight favorable effect of *biology_marks*, but weakened by negative contributions from *computer_note1* and the fundamental sciences (*chemistry* and *physics*).
- Profile 1 (39.5%; 17 instances, majority group): predictions clearly dominated by *physics_marks* and *chem_marks* (strong positive contributions), with a supportive role of *computer_note2*, while *highschool_gpa* and *biology_marks* remain slightly unfavorable.
- Profile 2 (16.3%; 7 instances): predictions strongly driven by *computer_note1* and *computer_note2* (positive), but undermined by the negative impact of *physics* and *chemistry*, with a slightly unfavorable contribution from *highschool_gpa*.
- Profile 3 (18.6%; 8 instances): generalized negative contributions, particularly from *physics*, *chemistry*, and *computer_note2*, with no strong positive factors to counterbalance.
- Profile 4 (7.0%; 3 instances): balanced profile with dominant positive contributions from *physics* and *chemistry*, reinforced by *highschool_gpa*, while the other variables show minor negative effects.
- Profile 5 (2.3%; 1 instance): atypical case where almost all variables (*physics, chemistry, computer_note1, GPA, computer_note2*) contribute positively, except for *biology_marks*, which remains slightly unfavorable.

- Profile 6 (9.3%; 4 instances): intermediate profile characterized by moderate positive effects from *physics, biology, computer_note1*, and *chemistry*, but weakened by the negative role of *computer_note2*.

Table 1 Distribution of Students and Dominant Features per Profile.

Profile	*% of Students*	*Top 1 (Main Positive/ Negative)*	*Top 2*	*Top 3*
0	7.0%	highschool_gpa (+)	biology_marks (+)	computer_note1 (–)
1	39.5%	physics_marks (+)	chem_marks (+)	computer_note2 (+)
2	16.3%	computer_note1 (+)	computer_note2 (+)	physics_marks (–)
3	18.6%	physics_marks (–)	chem_marks (–)	computer_note2 (–)
4	7.0%	physics_marks (+)	chem_marks (+)	highschool_gpa (+)
5	2.3%	physics_marks (+)	chem_marks (+)	computer_note1 (+)
6	9.3%	physics_marks (+)	biology_marks (+)	computer_note1 (+)

The bubble visualization in Figure 3 illustrates the distribution of instances across clusters, highlighting both the size and composition of each group. Profile 1 clearly constitutes the majority group, whereas smaller profiles, such as Profiles 0, 4, and 5, represent minority groups. This distribution underscores the diversity of explanatory patterns among students: larger profiles (e.g., Profile 1 and Profile 3) capture relatively homogeneous explanatory structures dominated by strong contributions from the fundamental sciences, while minority profiles reveal

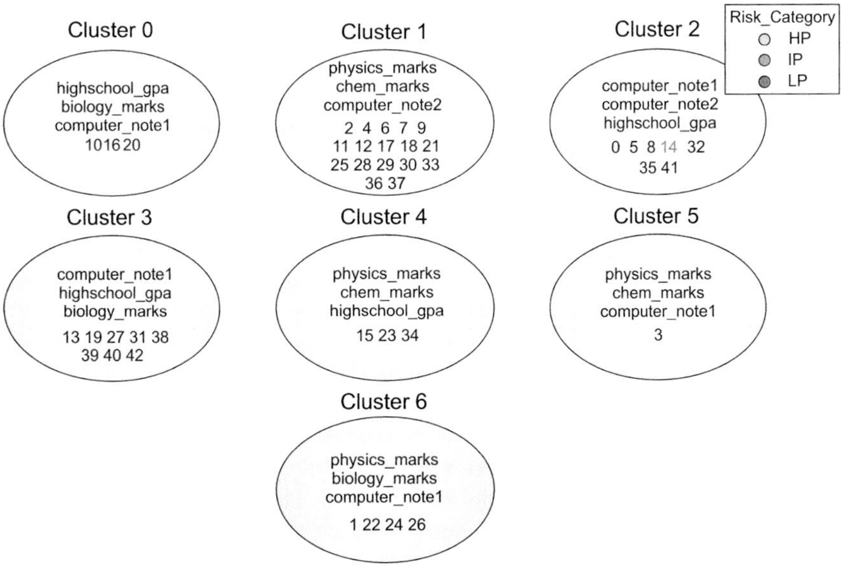

Fig. 3 Cluster Distribution of Instances (Bubble Visualization).

more atypical or hybrid combinations where computer science, GPA, or biology play compensatory or contrasting roles. The summary table complements the visualization by offering a precise inventory of the dominant features within each cluster—along with their favorable or unfavorable orientation—thereby facilitating subsequent interpretation of the explanatory profiles.

4.2.2 Analysis of Contributions

An examination of dominant contributions within each cluster (Figure 4) reveals that the majority profile is primarily driven by positive contributions from physics and chemistry, while other subgroups rely more strongly on computer science and GPA, sometimes counterbalanced by unfavorable effects from the sciences. Minority profiles exhibit either hybrid configurations—where computer science, biology, or GPA complement the sciences—or predominantly unfavorable combinations, reflecting more heterogeneous learning trajectories.

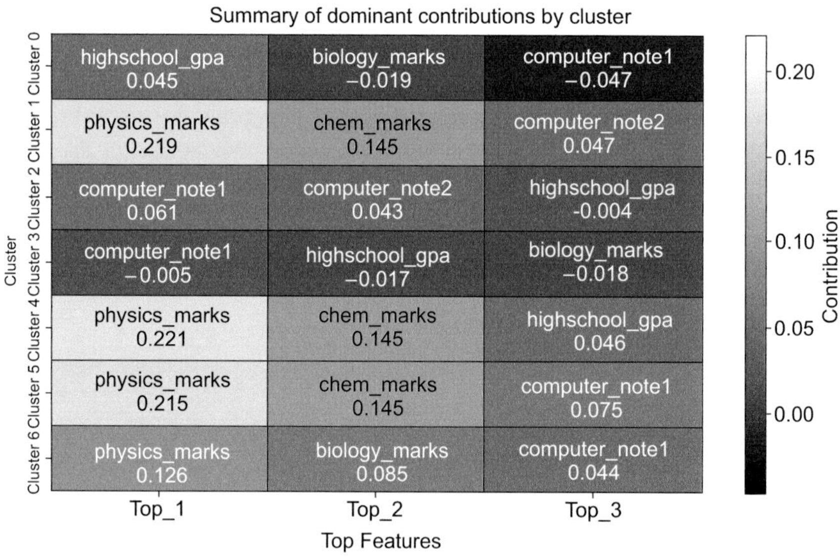

Fig. 4 Dominant Feature Contributions by Cluster.

Analysis of the average contributions (Figure 5) enables a quantitative comparison of the positive and negative influence of each variable. This confirms the central and favorable role of the sciences in the majority profiles, the differentiating and occasionally compensatory role of computer science, and the continued relevance of GPA and biology in specific contexts.

A summary of the dominant contributions (Figure 6) highlights the three most influential variables for each profile, with their favorable or unfavorable orientation, thus offering a concise and pedagogically actionable interpretation.

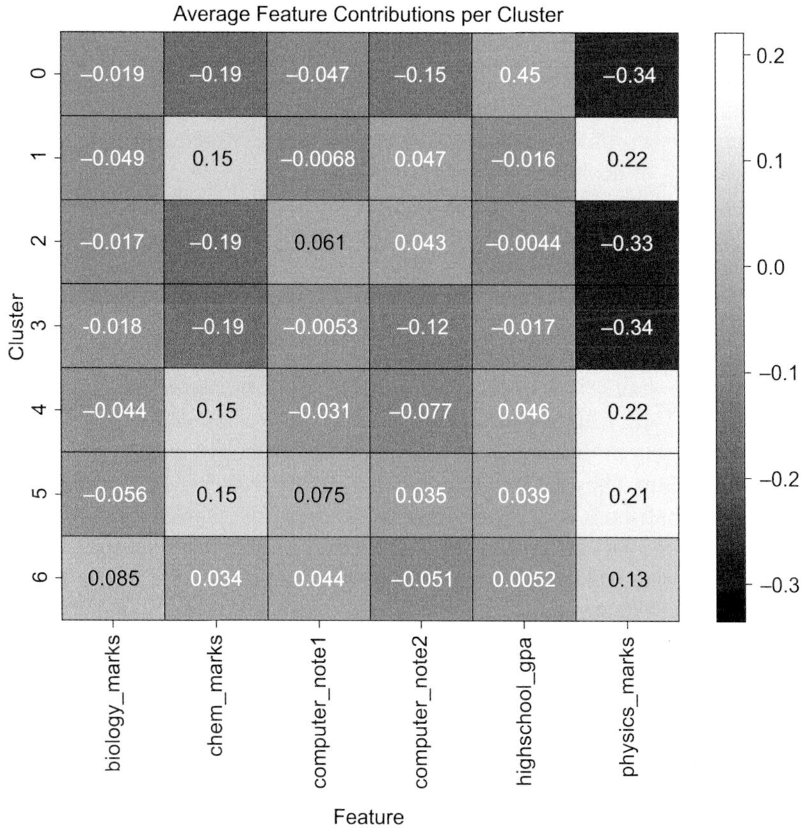

Fig. 5 Average Feature Contributions per Cluster.

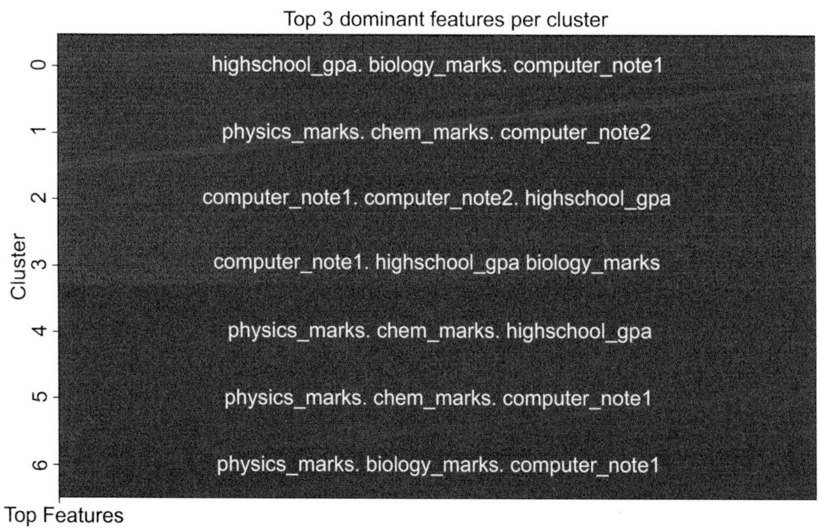

Fig. 6 Top Three Feature Contributions per Cluster.

Three main patterns emerge:

(1) Fundamental sciences dominate the majority profiles (Profiles 1 and 4), where physics and chemistry provide strong positive contributions.

(2) Computer science, GPA, and biology act as key determinants in several intermediate profiles (Profiles 0, 2, and 6), either reinforcing or compensating for weaker or negative influences from the sciences.

(3) Fragile or hybrid profiles (Profiles 3 and 5) exhibit predominantly negative or atypical combinations of contributions, reflecting less stable explanatory patterns.

4.2.3 Inter-Cluster Similarity of Explanatory Contributions

To analyze the similarity between clusters derived from the local explanations generated by LIME, a hierarchical clustering analysis was conducted. This method groups explanatory profiles based on their proximity without requiring a predefined number of clusters. The approach relies on computing Euclidean distances between the average contributions of each cluster, followed by Ward's method, which progressively merges clusters while minimizing within-group variance.

The dendrogram (Figure 7) provides a hierarchical view of these relationships: short branches indicate clusters with strong similarity, while longer branches correspond to more distant groupings. The Euclidean distance matrix (Table 2) confirms close proximities, such as between clusters 0 and 3 (distance = 0.08), 1 and 4 (0.14), and 1 and 5 (0.09). In contrast, larger distances, such as between 0 and 1 (0.68) or 3 and 5 (0.67), highlight explanatory profiles that are markedly different.

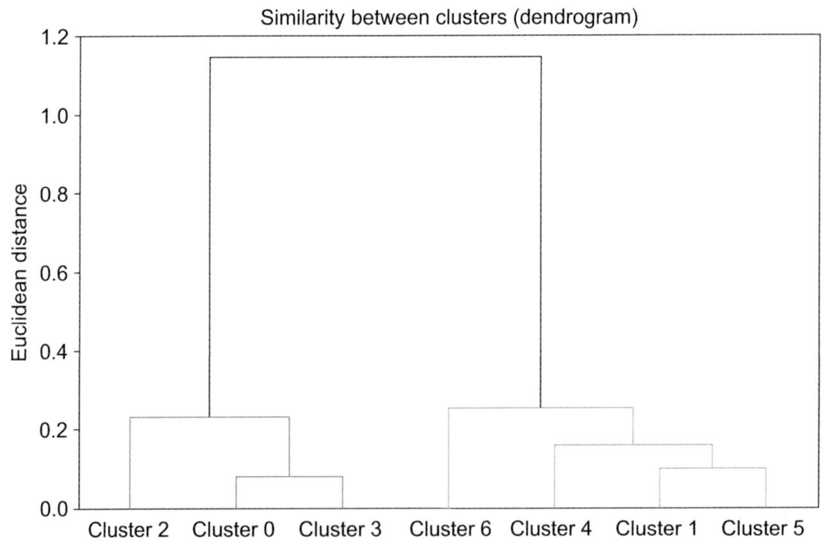

Fig. 7 Hierarchical Clustering of Explanatory Profiles.

The analysis of common top features further supports these proximities: clusters 0 and 3 share *computer_note1, highschool_gpa, and biology_marks*, clusters 1 and 4/5 are both dominated by *physics* and *chemistry marks*, while clusters 2 and 6 share *computer_note1* as a central contribution. These overlaps demonstrate that clusters in close proximity not only exhibit quantitative similarity in terms of distances but also qualitative similarity in their dominant explanatory variables.

Table 2 Euclidean Distances Between Mean Profiles.

Cluster	*0*	*1*	*2*	*3*	*4*	*5*	*6*
0	0.0000	0.6830	0.2286	0.0808	0.6550	0.6834	0.5424
1	0.6830	0.0000	0.6544	0.6736	0.1413	0.0996	0.2271
2	0.2286	0.6544	0.0000	0.1788	0.6712	0.6491	0.5329
3	0.0808	0.6736	0.1788	0.0000	0.6583	0.6746	0.5333
4	0.6550	0.1413	0.6712	0.6583	0.0000	0.1546	0.2142
5	0.6834	0.0996	0.6491	0.6746	0.1546	0.0000	0.2229
6	0.5424	0.2271	0.5329	0.5333	0.2142	0.2229	0.0000

The examination of explanatory variables shared across clusters helps clarify the hierarchical proximities observed. Highschool_gpa stands out as a central factor, appearing repeatedly in cluster pairings (e.g., 0–2, 0–3, 2–3, 2–4, 3–4), confirming its role as a common academic determinant across diverse profiles. Computer science grades (computer_note1 and computer_note2) contribute significantly to the proximities of intermediate clusters, particularly 0–2, 0–3, 2–6, and 3–6, where they act as differentiating elements in technology-oriented or mixed profiles. Fundamental sciences (chem_marks and physics_marks) are strongly represented in the connections between clusters 1–4, 1–5, and 4–5, reflecting the cohesion of majority profiles structured around these disciplines. Finally, biology_marks plays a more localized role, shaping the proximities between clusters 0–3, 0–6, and 3–6, which correspond to more hybrid or minority patterns.

Overall, the proximities observed in the dendrogram align with the variables shared across clusters. Clusters 1 and 4 form robust and homogeneous groups centered on fundamental sciences, while clusters 2 and 6 converge around a combination of computer science and prior academic performance. By contrast, cluster 3 represents a more fragile structure characterized by mixed or negative contributions, whereas cluster 5, although small, remains closer to the science-dominated profiles.

5. Explanatory Profiles: Pedagogical Implications and Validation

By grouping the local explanations produced by LIME through clustering analysis, three overarching learning profiles emerge. The first corresponds to students whose success is primarily driven by fundamental sciences (physics and chemistry, sometimes reinforced by biology). The second reflects intermediate profiles, in which computer science grades (computer_note1, computer_note2) and prior academic performance (highschool_gpa) play a central role. Finally, the third group consists of fragile or hybrid profiles, characterized by mixed or negative contributions, which reveal less stable academic trajectories.

This classification transcends individual explanations by emphasizing collective explanatory dynamics. It offers a structured and pedagogically meaningful interpretation of success patterns that teachers and academic administrators can leverage to adapt their practices.

From an educational perspective, each profile suggests differentiated interventions:

- **Majority profiles (Profiles 1 and 4):** consolidate fundamental sciences while monitoring the balance with GPA and computer science.
- **Intermediate profiles (Profiles 0, 2, and 6):** provide targeted support in computer science and personalized monitoring of GPA.
- **Fragile profiles (Profiles 3 and 5):** offer close guidance (tutoring, mentoring, individualized follow-up) to stabilize trajectories and prevent dropout.

Beyond direct pedagogical interventions, this approach also contributes to making AI more transparent, equitable, and actionable in education. By transforming complex local explanations into clear collective patterns, it facilitates the understanding of predictive models and supports informed, shared decision-making. The analysis thus becomes a strategic tool for personalized learning and equity in academic pathways.

The robustness of the methodology is supported by several observations. The recurrence of GPA across clusters highlights its structuring role. Clear separations between distant clusters (e.g., majority science-driven profiles versus fragile hybrid profiles) indicate well-defined explanatory structures, while proximities between others (e.g., clusters 0–5 or 2–6) confirm internal coherence. The alignment between the three main patterns—science-dominant profiles, GPA/computer science-driven profiles, and fragile hybrid profiles—and the hierarchical structure further strengthens the pedagogical relevance of the approach.

In sum, the combination of LIME and clustering not only sheds light on model predictions but also enables the construction of interpretable learning profiles, which support differentiated interventions and promote fairness in educational pathways.

Conclusion

In this study, to better understand the key determinants of student performance and make model predictions interpretable, we proposed an innovative approach that combines inter-model aggregation, local explainability (LIME), and clustering of feature contributions. This integration, still scarcely explored in the literature, enables the transformation of complex and sometimes unstable individual explanations into robust, interpretable, and pedagogically actionable collective profiles.

The methodology demonstrated its relevance through the recurrence of structuring variables (notably GPA, physics, and chemistry), the clear differentiation of explanatory profiles, and the complementarity of the identified patterns: majority profiles structured around fundamental sciences, intermediate profiles characterized by computer science and prior academic performance, and fragile or hybrid profiles reflecting mixed or negative contributions. It provides a concise and actionable interpretation, allowing the identification of recurring trends and the design of differentiated interventions: reinforcement of core scientific competencies for majority profiles, targeted support in computer science and GPA monitoring for intermediate profiles, and individualized guidance for fragile profiles.

By overcoming the limitations of explanations focused solely on individual instances, this approach represents a methodological advance for explainable artificial intelligence in education. It contributes to making explainability not only a tool for understanding, but also a strategic lever for personalization, equity, and informed decision-making in educational pathways.

References

Anwar, S., Griffiths, N., Bhalerao, A. and Popham, T. (2024). MASALA: Model-Agnostic Surrogate Explanations by Locality Adaptation. In: *Proceedings of the 1st KDD Workshop on Human-Interpretable AI, 2024.*

Botari, T., Hvilshøj, F., Izbicki, R. and de Carvalho, A.C. (2020). MeLIME: Meaningful local explanation for machine learning models. *ArXiv Preprint ArXiv:2009.05818.*

Cooper, A., Doyle, O. and Bourke, A. (2021). Supervised clustering for subgroup discovery: An application to COVID-19 symptomatology. In: *Joint European Conference on Machine Learning and Knowledge Discovery in Databases* (pp. 408-422).

Dhurandhar, A., Natesan Ramamurthy, K., Ahuja, K. and Arya, V. (2023). Locally invariant explanations: Towards stable and unidirectional explanations through local invariant learning. *Advances in Neural Information Processing Systems*, *36*, 19410–19445.

Escriva, E., Lefrere, T., Martin, M., Aligon, J., Chanson, A., Excoffier, J.-B., Labroche, N., Soulé-Dupuy, C. and Monsarrat, P. (2025). Effective data exploration through clustering of local attributive explanations. *Information Systems*, *127*, 102464.

Lundberg, S.M. and Lee, S.-I. (2017). A unified approach to interpreting model predictions. *Advances in Neural Information Processing Systems* (*NeurIPS 2017*).

Ribeiro, M., Singh, S. and Guestrin, C. (2016). "Why should I trust you?" Explaining the predictions of any classifier. In: *Proceedings of The 22nd ACM SIGKDD International Conference on Knowledge Discovery and Data Mining* (pp. 1135–1144).

Rousseeuw, P.J. (1987). Silhouettes: A graphical aid to the interpretation and validation of cluster analysis. *Journal of Computational and Applied Mathematics*, *20*, 53–65.

Setzu, M., Guidotti, R., Monreale, A., Turini, F., Pedreschi, D. and Giannotti, F. (2021). Glocalx-from local to global explanations of black box AI models. *Artificial Intelligence*, *294*, 103457.

Slack, D., Hilgard, A., Singh, S. and Lakkaraju, H. (2021). Reliable post hoc explanations: Modeling uncertainty in explainability. *Advances in Neural Information Processing Systems*, *34*, 9391–9404.

Veledar, E., Zhou, L., Veledar, O., Gardener, H., Gutierrez, C.M., Romano, J.G. and Rundek, T. (2025). Synthesizing Explainability across Multiple ML Models for Structured Data. *Algorithms*, *18*(6), 368.

Zafar, M.R. and Khan, N.M. (2019). DLIME: A deterministic local interpretable model-agnostic explanations approach for computer-aided diagnosis systems. *ArXiv Preprint ArXiv:1906.10263*.

11 Beyond the Black Box
XAI Techniques to Interpret Complex Machine Learning Models

Abdullah Tariq Choudhry[1], Brittany Ho[2] and Vivek K. Pallipuram[3*]

The machine learning (ML) community has made tremendous strides with newer and improved models that achieve astounding performances for classification and prediction tasks. However, their complexity has reduced them to mere black boxes, and users apply their outputs without much consideration to how the models produced those outputs. To promote model transparency, fairness, trust, and interpretability, an increasingly popular ML subfield called eXplainable AI (xAI) has offered processes and methods to provide a clear explanation of how the ML models work. This chapter explains the theoretical underpinnings of xAI methods and how to leverage them for any ML project. The xAI methods discussed in this chapter include Shapley Additive Explanations (SHAP) analysis and Local Interpretable Model-agnostic Explanations (LIME) methods. At the end of this chapter, readers will be able to: 1) explain the high-level theoretical aspects of xAI methods, and 2) apply xAI codes using Python for any generic ML project.

1. Introduction

Modern machine learning (ML) has achieved remarkable success across various domains, ranging from medical diagnosis to financial forecasting and autonomous systems. Models including deep neural networks, ensemble methods, and gradient boosting algorithms consistently deliver superior predictive performance. However, this success comes at the cost of interpretability. These sophisticated models operate as "black boxes", making predictions through complex internal processes that remain opaque to users, stakeholders, and even their creators.

The inability to understand how ML models arrive at their decisions creates significant challenges in high-stakes applications. Healthcare professionals need to understand why a diagnostic model recommends a particular treatment. Financial institutions must explain loan approval decisions to regulatory bodies. Criminal justice systems require transparency in risk assessment algorithms. The consequences of blind trust in algorithmic decisions can be severe, ranging from individual harm to systemic bias and discrimination.

[1-3] University of the Pacific, California, USA.
* Corresponding author: vpallipuramkrishnamani@pacific.edu

DOI: 10.1201/9781003713371-11

Explainable AI (xAI) emerges as a critical solution to bridge this interpretability gap Mol-nar (2019). Rather than sacrificing model performance for simplicity, xAI techniques provide post-hoc explanations that reveal how complex models make decisions. These methods enable practitioners to maintain high-performing models while gaining crucial insights into their behavior, feature dependencies, and decision boundaries.

The importance of xAI extends beyond mere curiosity about model internals. Regulatory frameworks increasingly demand algorithmic transparency. The European Union's General Data Protection Regulation (GDPR) provides important rights regarding automated decision-making in Parliament and of the European Union (2016). The U.S. Equal Credit Opportunity Act requires explanations for adverse credit decisions. Professional standards in medicine, finance, and other regulated industries emphasize the need for interpretable AI systems.

Furthermore, xAI serves essential technical purposes. Model debugging becomes feasible when we understand which features drive predictions and how they interact with one another. Feature selection improves when we identify truly influential variables versus spurious correlations. Model validation strengthens when explanations align with domain knowledge and expectations. Trust calibration occurs when users understand model limitations and appropriate use cases.

This chapter focuses on two fundamental xAI techniques that have proven effective across diverse applications, namely SHAP analysis and LIME analysis. Shapley Additive Explanations (SHAP) provides a unified framework for feature attribution based on cooperative game theory. Local Interpretable Model-agnostic Explanations (LIME) creates locally faithful explanations around individual predictions.

These methods offer unique strengths and address specific interpretability requirements. SHAP delivers mathematically rigorous global and local explanations with desirable properties such as additivity and consistency. LIME excels at generating intuitive explanations for individual predictions that non-technical stakeholders can understand.

The practical implementation of these techniques requires understanding both their theoretical foundations and computational considerations. This chapter provides a comprehensive coverage of underlying mathematical principles, implementation details, and best practices for applying xAI methods to real-world problems. Through detailed code examples and practical guidance, readers will gain the knowledge needed to incorporate xAI into their ML workflows.

The rest of the chapter is organized as follows. Section 2 provides the theoretical foundations of the xAI techniques discussed in this chapter. Section 3 expounds the SHAP analysis framework. Section 4 explains the LIME analysis. The chapter concludes in Section 5.

2. Explainable AI: Theory

Explainable AI represents a fundamental shift from the traditional machine learning paradigm of optimizing solely for predictive accuracy. While conventional ML approaches focus on minimizing loss functions and maximizing performance metrics, xAI introduces an additional dimension: the ability to understand, interpret, and explain model behavior. This section establishes the theoretical foundations that underpin modern explainability methods.

2.1 The Interpretability-Performance Trade-off

Historically, ML has operated under the implicit assumption that model complexity and interpretability exist in tension Lipton (2018). Simple models, including linear regression and decision trees, offer clear interpretability but may lack the capacity to capture complex patterns in the data. In contrast, sophisticated models such as deep neural networks and ensemble methods achieve superior performance but at the expense of transparency.

xAI challenges this binary view by introducing post-hoc explainability methods that work with any trained model. These techniques treat the original model as a fixed black box and construct separate explanation models that approximate its behavior in interpretable terms. This approach preserves the full predictive power of the complex models while providing the interpretability required for understanding and trust.

The theoretical foundation for this approach rests on the concept of fidelity, the degree to which an explanation accurately represents the original model's behavior. High-fidelity explanations capture the essential decision-making patterns of the black-box model, enabling users to understand and predict its behavior across different input regions.

2.2 Global vs. Local Explanations

xAI methods generally fall into two categories based on their scope of explanation Murdoch et al. (2019). Global explanations describe the overall behavior of a model across the entire input space, revealing general patterns about the importance of features and the boundaries of the decision. These explanations answer questions such as "What factors does the model consider most important?" and "How does the model typically behave?"

Local explanations focus on understanding why a model made a specific prediction for a particular instance. These explanations address questions such as "Why did the model predict this outcome for this specific patient?" and "Which features contributed most to this individual decision?" Local explanations are especially valuable in applications where users need to understand and act upon individual predictions.

The distinction between global and local explanations reflects different interpretability needs. Global explanations support model development, validation, and policy-making decisions. They help identify systematic biases, validate that models rely on appropriate features, and guide feature engineering efforts. Local explanations enable case-by-case decision-making, support individual interventions, and build trust in specific predictions.

2.3 Desirable Properties of Explanations

Effective xAI methods should satisfy several theoretical properties that ensure their explanations are reliable, consistent, and actionable. These properties, formalized through mathematical definitions, provide criteria for evaluating and comparing explanation methods.

- **Efficiency:** The explanation method should attribute the full difference between a prediction and some baseline (typically the expected model output) across all features. This ensures that explanations account for the complete decision-making process without missing components.
- **Symmetry:** Features that contribute equally to a model's decision should receive equal attribution in the explanation. This property prevents explanations from arbitrarily favoring one feature over another when their contributions are similar.
- **Dummy:** Features that do not influence the model's prediction should receive zero attribution in the explanation. This property ensures that explanations focus attention on truly relevant features versus spurious attributions.
- **Additivity:** When combining multiple models, the explanation for the combined model should equal the sum of explanations for individual models. This property supports the composition of complex systems from simpler, explainable components.
- **Consistency:** If one model relies more heavily on a particular feature than another model, the explanation should reflect this difference. This property ensures that explanations accurately represent relative feature importance across different models.

2.4 The Shapley Value Framework

Many modern xAI methods draw theoretical foundations from cooperative game theory, particularly the concept of Shapley values, Shapley et al. (1953). Originally developed to fairly distribute gains among players in cooperative games, Shapley values provide a principled approach to attribution problems in machine learning.

In the xAI context, features represent players in a cooperative game where the "payoff" is the model's prediction. The Shapley value for each feature represents its fair contribution to the final prediction, accounting for all possible combinations of features. This approach naturally satisfies the desirable properties outlined in Section 2.3.

The mathematical formulation of Shapley values involves considering all possible coalitions of features and computing each feature's marginal contribution across these coalitions. For a feature i and a prediction function f, the Shapley value ϕ_i is defined as:

$$\phi_i = \sum_{S \subseteq N \setminus \{i\}} \frac{|S|!(|N|-|S|-1)!}{|N|!} [f(S \cup \{i\}) - f(S)]$$

where, N is the set of all features and S represents different coalitions of features. This formulation ensures that attributions are computed fairly by considering the marginal contribution of each feature across all possible contexts.

2.5 Model-Agnostic vs. Model-Specific Methods

xAI techniques can be categorized based on their relationship to the underlying model architecture. Model-specific methods are designed for types of models and leverage their internal structure to generate explanations. These methods often provide more efficient computation and deeper insights, however, they lack generalizability across different model types.

Model-agnostic methods treat the underlying model as a black box and work with any model that can produce predictions. These methods offer broader applicability and enable consistent explanation approaches across heterogeneous model ensembles. However, they may sacrifice some efficiency and depth of insight compared to model-specific approaches.

The choice between model-agnostic and model-specific methods depends on the specific application requirements. Model-agnostic methods prove valuable in production environments with diverse model types or when explanations must be consistent across different models. Model-specific methods excel when users seek deep insights into a specific model's architectures or when they prefer computational efficiency.

2.6 Challenges and Limitations

While xAI methods provide valuable insights into model behavior, they face several theoretical and practical challenges Adadi and Berrada (2018); Arrieta et al. (2020); Guidotti et al. (2018). The fundamental challenge lies in translating high-dimensional, complex model behavior into human-interpretable representations without losing essential information.

Approximation quality represents a key concern. Post-hoc explanation methods necessarily simplify model behavior, and these simplifications may not accurately represent the model's true decision-making process. Evaluating explanation quality remains an active research area, as traditional model evaluation metrics do not directly apply to explanation assessment.

Stability and consistency of explanations pose additional challenges. Small changes in input data or model parameters may lead to dramatically different explanations, potentially undermining user trust. Ensuring that explanations remain stable and meaningful across related inputs requires careful method design and validation.

The cognitive load of explanations also presents theoretical considerations. Explanations must balance completeness with comprehensibility, providing sufficient detail for understanding without overwhelming users with excessive information. Different stakeholders may require different types and levels of explanations, creating additional complexity in explanation design.

3. Shapley Additive Explanations (SHAP) Analysis

Shapley Additive Explanations (SHAP) represents one of the most theoretically grounded and widely adopted approaches to explainable AI. Developed by Lundberg and Lee (2017), SHAP unifies several existing explanation methods under a common theoretical framework based on cooperative game theory. This section explores SHAP's theoretical foundations, practical implementation, and application across different model types.

3.1 Theoretical Foundation: Shapley Values

SHAP builds upon Shapley values, a concept from cooperative game theory that provides a principled method for fairly distributing contributions among participants. In the context of machine learning, features represent players in a cooperative game, and the prediction represents the collective payoff that must be distributed among features.

The Shapley value for feature i is computed by considering all possible coalitions of features and calculating the marginal contribution of feature i to each coalition. This process ensures that each feature receives credit for its unique contribution while accounting for interactions with other features.

Mathematically, the Shapley value $\phi_i(f)$ for feature i in a model f with feature set N is defined as:

$$\phi_i(f) = \sum_{S \subseteq N \setminus \{i\}} \frac{|S|!(|N|-|S|-1)!}{|N|!} [f(S \cup \{i\}) - f(S)]$$

This formulation captures several intuitive properties. Features that consistently increase predictions across different contexts receive positive Shapley values, while features that decrease predictions receive negative values. The magnitude of the Shapley value reflects the feature's average impact across all possible feature combinations.

3.2 SHAP's Unique Properties

SHAP satisfies three crucial properties that distinguish it from other attribution methods:

- **Efficiency (Completeness):** The sum of all SHAP values equals the difference between the prediction and the expected model output:

$$\sum_{i=1}^{M} \phi_i = f(x) - E[f(x)]$$

This property ensures that explanations fully account for the model's behavior without missing components or double-counting contributions.

- **Symmetry:** If two features contribute equally to all possible coalitions, they receive identical SHAP values. This prevents arbitrary preferences in attribution when features have equivalent impacts.
- **Dummy:** Features that never change the model output receive zero SHAP values, ensuring that explanations focus on truly influential features.

These properties provide theoretical guarantees about explanation quality and consistency that many other methods lack.

3.3 SHAP Explainer Types

SHAP offers several explainer types optimized for different model architectures and use cases:

- **TreeExplainer:** Designed specifically for tree-based models (Random Forest, Gradient Boosting, XGBoost), TreeExplainer leverages the model's tree structure to compute exact Shapley values efficiently Lundberg et al. (2018). This explainer runs in polynomial time relative to the tree depth and number of trees.
- **LinearExplainer:** Optimized for linear models, this explainer computes exact Shapley values for linear relationships. It handles feature correlations appropriately and scales well to high-dimensional problems.
- **KernelExplainer:** A model-agnostic approach that works with any model by treating it as a black box. KernelExplainer approximates Shapley values through sampling, making it slower but universally applicable.
- **DeepExplainer:** Designed for neural networks, this explainer approximates Shapley values using gradients and activations from the network's internal layers.

3.4 Global and Local Explanations with SHAP

SHAP provides both global and local interpretability through different visualization and analysis approaches:

- **Local Explanations:** For any specific prediction, SHAP values show how each feature contributed to that particular outcome. Positive SHAP values push the prediction above the baseline, while negative values push it below.
- **Global Explanations:** By aggregating SHAP values across many predictions, we can understand overall feature importance and model behavior patterns. Common approaches include averaging absolute SHAP values to rank feature importance or analyzing SHAP value distributions to understand feature impact patterns.

3.5 Implementation Guide: Generic SHAP Analysis

Listing 1 provides a comprehensive implementation guide for applying SHAP to any machine learning project using Python. This code comprises comments that explain the individual sections, including model training, calculating performance, SHAP analysis initializations, and generating visualizations.

```
import shap
import pandas as pd
import numpy as np
import matplotlib.pyplot as plt
from sklearn.ensemble import RandomForestRegressor
from sklearn.model_selection import train_test_split
from sklearn.preprocessing import StandardScaler

class GenericSHAPAnalyzer:
    """
    A generic class for applying SHAP analysis to any machine learning model.
    Supports both tree-based and model-agnostic explanations.
    """

    def __init__(self, model, X_train, X_test, feature_names=None):
        """
        Initialize the SHAP analyzer.

        Args:
            model: Trained ML model
            X_train: Training data for background/baseline
            X_test: Test data for explanations
            feature_names: List of feature names for visualization
        """
        self.model = model
        self.X_train = X_train
        self.X_test = X_test
        self.feature_names = feature_names or [f'Feature_{i}'
                                               for i in range(X_train.shape[1])]
        self.explainer = None
        self.shap_values = None

    def create_explainer(self, explainer_type='auto'):
        """
        Create appropriate SHAP explainer based on model type.

        Args:
            explainer_type: 'auto', 'tree', 'kernel', 'linear', or 'deep'
        """
        if explainer_type == 'auto':
            # Auto-detect best explainer type
            if hasattr(self.model, 'feature_importances_'):
                # Tree-based model (Random Forest, XGBoost, etc.)
                self.explainer = shap.TreeExplainer(self.model)
                print("Using TreeExplainer (fast, exact for tree models)")
            else:
                # Model-agnostic approach for other models
                self.explainer = shap.KernelExplainer(
                    self.model.predict,
                    self.X_train[:100]  # Use subset for computational efficiency
```

```
                )
                print("Using KernelExplainer (model-agnostic, slower)")

        elif explainer_type == 'tree':
            self.explainer = shap.TreeExplainer(self.model)

        elif explainer_type == 'kernel':
            # Use sample of training data as background
            background_size = min(100, len(self.X_train))
            self.explainer = shap.KernelExplainer(
                self.model.predict,
                self.X_train[:background_size]
            )

        elif explainer_type == 'linear':
            self.explainer = shap.LinearExplainer(self.model, self.
               X_train)

        elif explainer_type == 'deep':
            # For neural networks (requires appropriate background data
               )
            self.explainer = shap.DeepExplainer(self.model, self.
               X_train)

        return self.explainer

    def compute_shap_values(self, max_samples=None):
        """
        Compute SHAP values for test data.

        Args:
            max_samples: Maximum number of test samples to explain
                        (None for all samples)
        """
        if self.explainer is None:
            self.create_explainer()

        # Limit samples for computational efficiency if needed
        if max_samples is not None:
            X_explain = self.X_test[:max_samples]
        else:
            X_explain = self.X_test

        print(f"Computing SHAP values for {len(X_explain)} samples...")

        # Compute SHAP values
        if isinstance(self.explainer, shap.TreeExplainer):
            # Tree explainer returns values directly
            self.shap_values = self.explainer.shap_values(X_explain)
        else:
            # Other explainers may return different formats
            self.shap_values = self.explainer.shap_values(X_explain)

        print("SHAP computation completed!")
        return self.shap_values

    def plot_summary(self, plot_type='violin', max_features=20):
        """
        Create SHAP summary plot showing feature impacts.

        Args:
            plot_type: 'violin' (beeswarm) or 'bar' for feature
               importance
            max_features: Maximum number of features to display
        """
```

```
        """
        if self.shap_values is None:
            self.compute_shap_values()

        plt.figure(figsize=(10, 8))

        if plot_type == 'violin':
            # Beeswarm plot showing impact distribution
            shap.summary_plot(
                self.shap_values,
                self.X_test if len(self.shap_values) == len(self.X_test)
                else self.X_test[:len(self.shap_values)],
                feature_names=self.feature_names,
                max_display=max_features,
                show=False
            )
            plt.title('SHAP Summary Plot: Feature Impact Distribution')

        elif plot_type == 'bar':
            # Bar plot showing global feature importance
            shap.summary_plot(
                self.shap_values,
                self.X_test if len(self.shap_values) == len(self.X_test)
                else self.X_test[:len(self.shap_values)],
                feature_names=self.feature_names,
                plot_type="bar",
                max_display=max_features,
                show=False
            )
            plt.title('SHAP Feature Importance: Global Impact')

        plt.tight_layout()
        plt.show()

    def get_feature_importance(self):
        """
        Calculate global feature importance from SHAP values.

        Returns:
            DataFrame with features ranked by importance
        """
        if self.shap_values is None:
            self.compute_shap_values()

        # Calculate mean absolute SHAP values
        importance = np.abs(self.shap_values).mean(axis=0)

        # Create DataFrame and sort by importance
        importance_df = pd.DataFrame({
            'feature': self.feature_names,
            'importance': importance
        }).sort_values('importance', ascending=False)

        return importance_df

# Example usage function
def run_generic_shap_analysis(X_train, X_test, y_train, y_test, feature_names=None):
    """
    Complete SHAP analysis pipeline for any ML model.

    Args:
        X_train, X_test: Training and test features
```

```
        y_train, y_test: Training and test targets
        feature_names: List of feature names
    """

    print("=== Generic SHAP Analysis Pipeline ===")

    # Train a model (can be replaced with any model)
    print("Training model...")
    model = RandomForestRegressor(n_estimators=100, random_state=42)
    model.fit(X_train, y_train)

    # Evaluate model performance
    train_score = model.score(X_train, y_train)
    test_score = model.score(X_test, y_test)
    print(f"Model R  - Train: {train_score:.3f}, Test: {test_score:.3f
       }")

    # Initialize SHAP analyzer
    analyzer = GenericSHAPAnalyzer(model, X_train, X_test,
       feature_names)

    # Create explainer and compute SHAP values
    analyzer.create_explainer()
    analyzer.compute_shap_values(max_samples=200)# Limit for
       efficiency

    # Generate visualizations
    print("\nGenerating SHAP visualizations...")
    analyzer.plot_summary(plot_type='violin')
    analyzer.plot_summary(plot_type='bar')

    # Show feature importance
    importance_df = analyzer.get_feature_importance()
    print(f"\nTop 5 Most Important Features:")
    print(importance_df.head())

    return analyzer
\label{lb:shaplist}
```

Listing 1: Generic SHAP Implementation for Any ML Model.

3.6 *Interpreting SHAP Visualizations*

SHAP produces several types of visualizations, each revealing different aspects of model behav ior:

- **Summary Plot (Beeswarm):** This comprehensive visualization combines feature importance (y-axis ranking), impact direction (x-axis position), feature values (color), and impact distribution (point density). Features at the top matter most to the model. Points on the right side of zero increase predictions, while points on the left decrease them. Red indicates high feature values, blue indicates low values.
- **Feature Importance Bar Chart:** Shows global feature importance by averaging the absolute SHAP values for each feature. This provides a simple ranking of which features matter most across all predictions.
- **Dependence Plots:** Scatter plots showing the relationship between feature values (x-axis) and their SHAP impact (y-axis). These reveal complex patterns like non-linear relationships, interaction effects, and threshold behaviors.

- **Waterfall Plots:** For individual predictions, waterfall plots show how each feature moves the prediction above or below the baseline, providing a step-by-step explanation of the model's decision process.

3.7 SHAP Best Practices

When implementing SHAP analysis, consider these best practices:

- **Choose Appropriate Explainers:** Use TreeExplainer for tree-based models when possible because it provides exact and fast computations. Use KernelExplainer for complex models where no specialized explainer exists.
- **Manage Computational Complexity:** For large datasets or complex models, use representative samples rather than explaining every prediction. Focus on the most important or problematic cases.
- **Validate Explanations:** Ensure SHAP values align with domain knowledge and expectations. Large discrepancies may indicate model problems or data quality issues.
- **Consider Feature Correlations:** SHAP handles feature interactions well, but highly correlated features may show unstable attributions. Consider dimensionality reduction or feature selection when correlations are extreme.
- **Combine Global and Local Views:** Use global explanations for understanding overall model behavior and feature selection. Use local explanations for debugging specific predictions and building trust with end users.

SHAP's theoretical rigor, computational efficiency, and comprehensive visualization capabilities make it an essential tool for explainable AI across diverse applications and model types.

4. Local Interpretable Model-Agnostic Explanations (LIME)

LIME, introduced by Ribeiro et al. (2016), represents a fundamentally different approach to explainable AI compared to global methods. The authors later extended their work with Anchors, a complementary high-precision explanation method Ribeiro et al. (2018). While techniques like SHAP aim to explain overall model behavior, LIME focuses exclusively on understanding individual predictions by creating local, interpretable approximations around specific instances.

4.1 Theoretical Foundation: Local Fidelity

LIME's core insight is that even highly complex, non linear models behave approximately linearly in small neighborhoods around individual data points. By focusing on local behavior rather than global patterns, LIME can create simple, interpretable explanations that accurately represent how the model behaves for specific predictions.

The theoretical framework rests on the concept of *local fidelity,* the degree to which a simple explanation model accurately reproduces the complex model's behavior in the vicinity of a particular instance. LIME achieves this by:

1. **Perturbation Generation:** Creating variations of the instance of interest by systematically modifying feature values.
2. **Locality Weighting:** Assigning higher importance to perturbations that are closer to the original instance.
3. **Surrogate Modeling:** Fitting a simple, interpretable model (typically linear) to predict the complex model's outputs on these perturbations.
4. **Feature Selection:** Identifying the most relevant features for the local explanation.

Mathematically, LIME solves an optimization problem that balances explanation simplicity with local fidelity:

$$\xi(x) = \arg\min_{g \in G} L(f, g, \pi_x) + \Omega(g)$$

where:

- $\xi(x)$ is the explanation for instance, x
- G is the set of interpretable models (e.g., linear models)
- $L(f, g, \pi_x)$ measures how well the interpretable model g approximates the complex model f in the locality defined by π_x
- $\Omega(g)$ penalizes model complexity to ensure interpretability
- π_x is the proximity measure that defines the local neighborhood

4.2 LIME's Approach to Different Data Types

LIME adapts its perturbation strategy based on the type of input data:

- **Tabular Data:** For structured data with numerical and categorical features, LIME perturbs features by sampling from their empirical distributions or by creating binary masks that include/exclude features from the explanation.
- **Text Data:** LIME treats documents as bags of words and creates perturbations by removing subsets of words, allowing it to identify which words most strongly influence text classification decisions.
- **Image Data:** Images are segmented into superpixels, and perturbations are created by turning superpixels on or off, revealing which regions of an image drive the model's predictions.

This adaptability makes LIME truly model-agnostic and applicable across diverse domains and data types, from medical diagnosis to natural language processing to computer vision.

4.3 Local vs. Global Interpretability

LIME's local focus provides both advantages and limitations compared to global explanation methods:

Advantages of Local Explanations:

- **Actionability:** Local explanations directly inform decision-making for specific cases.
- **Accuracy:** Local linear approximations are often highly accurate, even for complex nonlinear models.
- **Relevance:** Explanations focus on the specific feature values and context of the instance being explained.
- **Trust Building:** Users can understand and verify explanations for individual cases they care about.

Limitations of Local Explanations:

- **Instance Dependence:** Explanations may vary dramatically between similar instances.
- **Limited Scope:** Individual explanations don't reveal global model behavior or systematic patterns.
- **Computational Cost:** Each prediction requiring explanation needs separate LIME analysis.
- **Stability:** Small changes in perturbation sampling can lead to different explanations.

4.4 Implementation Guide: Generic LIME Analysis

Listing 2 is a comprehensive implementation guide for applying LIME to various ML projects:

```
import lime
import lime.lime_tabular
import numpy as np
import pandas as pd
import matplotlib.pyplot as plt
from sklearn.ensemble import RandomForestClassifier, RandomForestRegressor
from sklearn.model_selection import train_test_split

class GenericLIMEAnalyzer:
    """
    A generic class for applying LIME analysis to any machine learning model
    with tabular data.
    """

    def __init__(self, model, X_train, X_test, y_train=None, y_test=None,
                 feature_names=None, class_names=None, mode='regression'):
        """
        Initialize the LIME analyzer.

        Args:
            model: Trained ML model
            X_train: Training data for understanding feature distributions
            X_test: Test data for explanations
```

```
            y_train: Training labels (optional)
            y_test: Test labels (optional)
            feature_names: List of feature names
            class_names: List of class names (for classification)
            mode: 'regression' or 'classification'
        """
        self.model = model
        self.X_train = X_train
        self.X_test = X_test
        self.y_train = y_train
        self.y_test = y_test
        self.mode = mode

        # Set feature names
        if feature_names is not None:
            self.feature_names = feature_names
        else:
            self.feature_names = [f'Feature_{i}' for i in range(X_train.shape[1])]

        # Set class names for classification
        self.class_names = class_names

        # Initialize explainer
        self.explainer = None
        self.create_explainer()

    def create_explainer(self):
        """
        Create LIME explainer based on the data and model type.
        """
        print(f"Creating LIME explainer for {self.mode}...")

        self.explainer = lime.lime_tabular.LimeTabularExplainer(
            self.X_train,
            feature_names=self.feature_names,
            class_names=self.class_names,
            mode=self.mode,
            training_labels=self.y_train,
            random_state=42,
            verbose=False
        )

        print("LIME explainer created successfully!")
        return self.explainer

    def explain_instance(self, instance_idx, num_features=10, num_samples=5000):
        """
        Generate LIME explanation for a specific instance.

        Args:
            instance_idx: Index of instance to explain
            num_features: Number of features to include in explanation
            num_samples: Number of perturbed samples to generate

        Returns:
            LIME explanation object
        """
        if instance_idx >= len(self.X_test):
            raise ValueError(f"Instance index {instance_idx} exceeds test data size")

        instance = self.X_test[instance_idx]

```

```
        print(f"Explaining instance {instance_idx}...")
        print(f"Generating {num_samples} perturbations...")

        # Generate explanation
        if self.mode == 'classification':
            explanation = self.explainer.explain_instance(
                instance,
                self.model.predict_proba,
                num_features=num_features,
                num_samples=num_samples,
                random_state=42
            )
        else:  # regression
            explanation = self.explainer.explain_instance(
                instance,
                self.model.predict,
                num_features=num_features,
                num_samples=num_samples,
                random_state=42
            )

        return explanation

    def visualize_explanation(self, explanation, save_html=True,
                              filename_prefix='lime_explanation'):
        """
        Visualize LIME explanation with various formats.

        Args:
            explanation: LIME explanation object
            save_html: Whether to save interactive HTML
            filename_prefix: Prefix for saved files
        """

        # Show in notebook/console
        print("\n" + "="*50)
        print("LIME EXPLANATION")
        print("="*50)

        # Get explanation as list
        exp_list = explanation.as_list()

        # Print feature contributions
        print(f"\nFeature Contributions (Total features analyzed: {len(exp_list)}):")
        print("-" * 60)

        for i, (feature, contribution) in enumerate(exp_list):
            direction = "increases" if contribution > 0 else "decreases"

            abs_contribution = abs(contribution)
            print(f"{i+1:2d}. {feature:<30} {direction:>9} prediction by {abs_contribution:.4f}")

        # Save interactive HTML if requested
        if save_html:
            try:
                html_filename = f"{filename_prefix}.html"
                explanation.save_to_file(html_filename)
                print(f"\nInteractive explanation saved to: {html_filename}")
            except Exception as e:
                print(f"Could not save HTML: {e}")

```

```
def run_generic_lime_analysis(X_train, X_test, y_train, y_test,
                              feature_names=None, model_type='regression'
                              ):
    """
    Complete LIME analysis pipeline for any ML problem.

    Args:
        X_train, X_test: Training and test features
        y_train, y_test: Training and test targets
        feature_names: List of feature names
        model_type: 'regression' or 'classification'
    """

    print("=== Generic LIME Analysis Pipeline ===")

    # Train appropriate model
    print(f"Training {model_type} model...")
    if model_type == 'regression':
        model = RandomForestRegressor(n_estimators=100, random_state
            =42)
        class_names = None
    else:
        model = RandomForestClassifier(n_estimators=100, random_state
            =42)
        class_names = [f'Class_{i}' for i in range(len(np.unique(
            y_train)))]

    model.fit(X_train, y_train)

    # Evaluate model
    train_score = model.score(X_train, y_train)
    test_score = model.score(X_test, y_test)
    print(f"Model performance - Train: {train_score:.3f}, Test: {
        test_score:.3f}")

    # Initialize LIME analyzer
    analyzer = GenericLIMEAnalyzer(
        model=model,
        X_train=X_train,
        X_test=X_test,
        y_train=y_train,
        y_test=y_test,
        feature_names=feature_names,
        class_names=class_names,
        mode=model_type
    )

    # Analyze representative instances
    print("\nAnalyzing representative instances...")

    if model_type == 'regression':
        # Get high, low, and median predictions
        predictions = model.predict(X_test)
        high_idx = np.argmax(predictions)
        low_idx = np.argmin(predictions)
        median_idx = np.argsort(predictions)[len(predictions)//2]
        indices_to_explain = [high_idx, median_idx, low_idx]
        descriptions = ['Highest', 'Median', 'Lowest']
    else:
        # Get diverse predictions across classes
        predictions = model.predict(X_test)
        indices_to_explain = []
        descriptions = []
        for class_val in np.unique(predictions):
            class_indices = np.where(predictions == class_val)[0]
```

```
            if len(class_indices) > 0:
                indices_to_explain.append(class_indices[0])
                descriptions.append(f'Class_{class_val}')

    # Generate explanations
    explanations = []
    for idx, desc in zip(indices_to_explain, descriptions):
        print(f"\nExplaining: {desc} Prediction (Instance {idx})")

        explanation = analyzer.explain_instance(idx, num_features=10)
        analyzer.visualize_explanation(
            explanation,
            filename_prefix=f'lime_{desc.lower()}'
        )
        explanations.append(explanation)

    return analyzer, explanations
```

Listing 2: Generic LIME Implementation for Tabular Data.

4.5 Interpreting LIME Explanations

LIME explanations provide several key information for understanding individual predictions:

- **Feature Contributions:** Each feature receives a numerical weight indicating its contribution to the prediction. Positive weights push the prediction toward higher values (or the predicted class), while negative weights push toward lower values (or away from the predicted class).
- **Feature Conditions:** LIME often expresses explanations in terms of feature ranges or conditions (e.g., "$Age \leq 45$" or "$Income > 50000$"), making explanations more interpretable than raw feature values.
- **Local Fidelity:** The explanation includes a measure of how well the local linear model fits the complex model's behavior in the neighborhood of the explained instance.
- **Prediction Confidence:** For classification problems, LIME shows the model's confidence in its prediction and how different features contribute to this confidence.

4.6 LIME Best Practices and Limitations

When implementing LIME analysis, consider these important practices and limitations:

Best Practices:

- **Sampling Size:** Use sufficient perturbation samples (typically 1000–5000) to ensure stable explanations.
- **Feature Selection:** Focus on the most important features (5–15) to maintain explanation interpretability.
- **Stability Analysis:** Run LIME multiple times with different random seeds to assess explanation consistency.

- **Domain Validation:** Verify that explanations align with domain knowledge and expectations.
- **Comparative Analysis:** Compare explanations across similar instances to identify patterns and anomalies.

Key Limitations:

- **Instability:** Small changes in perturbation sampling can lead to different explanations Garreau and von Luxburg (2020).
- **Linear Assumption:** The local linear approximation may not capture complex non linear relationships.
- **Perturbation Realism:** Generated perturbations may not represent realistic data variations.
- **Computational Cost:** Each explanation requires training a new surrogate model.
- **Feature Independence:** LIME assumes features can be perturbed independently, which may not reflect real data dependencies.

4.7 LIME vs. SHAP: Complementary Perspectives

LIME and SHAP offer complementary approaches to explainable AI, each with distinct strengths:

LIME Advantages:

- Extremely fast for individual explanations
- Intuitive local linear approximations
- Works with any model type and data format
- Provides actionable insights for specific cases.

SHAP Advantages:

- Mathematically rigorous with theoretical guarantees
- Consistent explanations across different model types
- Efficient global and local explanations
- Better handling of feature interactions.

The choice between LIME and SHAP depends on specific use case requirements. LIME excels for rapid, case-by-case explanations where users need to understand individual decisions quickly. SHAP provides more comprehensive analysis suitable for model development, validation, and systematic bias detection.

Many practitioners use both methods together: SHAP for overall model understanding and feature importance analysis, and LIME for explaining specific predictions to end users who need immediate, intuitive explanations. Recent comparative studies have highlighted the complementary strengths of these approaches Salih et al. (2024).

Conclusion

The evolution of ML from simple, interpretable models to sophisticated black-box systems has created both unprecedented opportunities and significant challenges. While complex models achieve remarkable predictive performance across diverse domains, their opacity limits adoption in high-stakes applications where understanding, trust, and accountability are paramount. Explainable AI techniques provide essential tools for bridging this interpretability gap without sacrificing the performance advantages of advanced models.

This chapter has explored three fundamental approaches to explainable AI, each addressing different aspects of the interpretability challenge. SHAP offers mathematically rigorous explanations based on cooperative game theory, providing both global insights into model behavior and local explanations for individual predictions. The method's theoretical guarantees and computational efficiency make it invaluable for comprehensive model analysis, feature selection, and bias detection.

LIME focuses specifically on local explanations, creating interpretable linear approximations around individual instances. Its model-agnostic approach and intuitive explanations make it particularly valuable for case-by-case decision making and building user trust in specific predictions. The method's adaptability across different data types—tabular, text, and image data—demonstrates the versatility of the local explanation paradigm.

The Accumulated Local Effects (ALE) method, while not covered in detail in this chapter, represents another important approach for handling complex feature interactions and correlation structures that challenge other explanation methods. Together, these techniques provide a comprehensive toolkit for addressing diverse interpretability requirements across different applications and stakeholder needs.

The practical implementation of these methods requires careful consideration of their respective strengths, limitations, and computational requirements. SHAP excels in scenarios requiring comprehensive model analysis, consistent explanations across different model types, and efficient handling of large datasets. Its tree-based explainers provide exact, fast computations for ensemble methods, while its kernel explainer offers universal applicability at the cost of computational complexity.

LIME proves most valuable when rapid, intuitive explanations of individual predictions are needed. Its perturbation-based approach creates explanations that non-technical stakeholders can readily understand and act upon. However, the method's reliance on local linear approximations and perturbation sampling can introduce instability and may not capture complex non linear relationships adequately.

The choice of explanation method should align with specific use case requirements, stakeholder needs, and computational constraints. Model developers and data scientists benefit most from SHAP's comprehensive analysis capabilities, while end users and decision makers often prefer LIME's intuitive, case-specific explanations. Many successful implementations combine multiple methods, using global explanations for model development and validation, and local explanations for operational decision support.

Several key principles emerge from this analysis of xAI techniques:

- **No Single Method Suffices:** Different explanation methods reveal different aspects of model behavior. Comprehensive interpretability often requires combining multiple approaches to achieve a complete understanding.
- **Context Determines Method Choice:** The appropriate explanation technique depends on the audience, use case, and decision-making context. Technical stakeholders may prefer detailed, mathematically rigorous explanations, while business users need intuitive, actionable insights.
- **Validation is Essential:** Explanation methods can produce misleading or unstable results. Systematic validation through stability analysis, domain knowledge verification, and comparative assessment ensures explanation reliability.
- **Computational Trade-offs Matter:** Different methods involve distinct computational requirements. Real-time applications may require faster methods with approximate explanations, while offline analysis can employ more comprehensive but computationally intensive approaches.
- **Integration with Domain Knowledge:** The most effective explanations combine algo rithmic insights with domain expertise. Technical explanations gain meaning and actionability when interpreted within relevant professional and scientific contexts.

Looking forward, several important developments will shape the future of explainable AI. Regulatory requirements for algorithmic transparency continue to evolve, creating both opportunities and challenges for xAI adoption. The European Union's AI Act Parliament and of the European Union (2024), evolving GDPR interpretations, and emerging regulatory frameworks in other jurisdictions will increasingly mandate explainable AI implementations across critical applications.

Methodological advances continue to address current limitations in explanation stability, computational efficiency, and handling of complex data types. New approaches that better capture feature interactions, provide more stable explanations, and scale to extremely large models are active areas of research and development.

The integration of explanation methods with model development workflows represents an other important evolution. Rather than treating interpretability as a post-hoc consideration, emerging approaches incorporate explainability constraints directly into model training and optimization processes.

Finally, the democratization of explainable AI through improved tools, interfaces, and educational resources will enable broader adoption across industries and applications. As these techniques become more accessible and standardized, they will transition from specialized research tools to essential components of responsible AI development and deployment.

The techniques presented in this chapter provide a solid foundation for implementing explainable AI across diverse machine learning applications. By understanding their theoretical foundations, practical implementations, and appropriate use cases, practitioners can make in formed decisions about incorporating interpretability into their AI systems. The continued development and refinement of these methods will play a crucial role in ensuring that the benefits of advanced machine learning can be realized while maintaining the transparency, ac countability, and trust required for responsible AI deployment.

The journey from black-box models to transparent, explainable AI systems represents more than a technical advancement—it reflects a maturation of the field toward more responsible, trustworthy, and socially beneficial applications of artificial intelligence. The methods and principles outlined in this chapter provide essential tools for navigating this transition successfully.

References

Adadi, A. and Berrada, M. (2018). Peeking inside the black-box: A survey on explainable artificial intelligence (XAI). *IEEE Access*, *6*: 52138–52160.

Arrieta, A. B., Diaz Rodriguez, N., Del Ser, J., Bennetot, A., Tabik, S., Barbado, A., Garcıa, S., Gil-Lopez, S., Molina, D., Benjamins, R., et al. (2020). Explainable artificial intelligence (XAI): Concepts, taxonomies, opportunities, and challenges toward responsible AIU. *Information Fusion*, 58: 82–115.

Garreau, D. and von Luxburg, U. (2020). Explaining the explainer: A first theoretical analysis of lime. In: *Proceedings of the 23rd International Conference on Artificial Intelligence and Statistics* (pp. 1287–1296). PMLR.

Guidotti, R., Monreale, A., Ruggieri, S., Turini, F., Giannotti, F. and Pedreschi, D. (2018). A survey of methods for explaining black box models. *ACM Computing Surveys*, 51(5): 1–42.

Lipton, Z.C. (2018). The mythos of model interpretability: In machine learning, the concept of interpretability is both important and slippery. *Queue*, *16*(3): 31–57.

Lundberg, S.M., Erion, G.G. and Lee, S.-I. (2018). Consistent individualized feature attribution for tree ensembles. *arXiv preprint arXiv:1802.03888*.

Lundberg, S.M. and Lee, S.-I. (2017). A unified approach to interpreting model predictions.

In: *Advances in Neural Information Processing Systems* (*30*: 4765–4774.

Molnar, C. (2019). *Interpretable Machine Learning: A Guide for Making Black Box Models Explainable*. Christoph Molnar.

Murdoch, W.J., Singh, C., Kumbier, K., Abbasi-Asl, R. and Yu, B. (2019). Definitions, methods, and applications in interpretable machine learning. *Proceedings of the National Academy of Sciences*, *116*(44): 22071–22080.

Parliament, E. and of the European Union, C. (2016). Regulation (EU) 2016/679 of the European Parliament and of the Council of 27 April 2016 on the protection of natural persons with regard to the processing of personal data and on the free movement of such data (general data protection regulation). *Official Journal of the European Union*.

Parliament, E. and of the European Union, C. (2024). Regulation (EU) 2024/1689 of the European Parliament and of the Council of 13 June 2024 laying down harmonised rules on artificial intelligence (Artificial Intelligence Act). *Official Journal of the European Union*.

Ribeiro, M.T., Singh, S. and Guestrin, C. (2016). "Why should I trust you?" explaining the predictions of any classifier. In: *Proceedings of the 22nd ACM SIGKDD International Conference on Knowledge Discovery and Data Mining* (pp. 1135–1144).

Ribeiro, M.T., Singh, S. and Guestrin, C. (2018). Anchors: High-precision model-agnostic explanations. In: *Proceedings of the AAAI Conference on Artificial Intelligence* (*32*).
Salih, A.M., Raisi-Estabragh, Z., Galazzo, I.B., Radeva, P., Petersen, S.E., Lekadir, K. and Menegaz, G. (2024). A perspective on explainable artificial intelligence methods: SHAP and LIME. *Advanced Intelligent Systems*, 7(1).
Shapley, L.S., et al. (1953). A value for n-person games.

12 A Knowledge-based Neural Network to Interpret Mars Habitat Building Assessment in Minecraft

Qianhui Liu[1*], Luc Paquette[2], Jeff Ginger[3] and Amanda Barany[4]

Neural networks have been shown to be powerful tools for developing data-driven models in educational contexts, achieving high performance for a variety of tasks. However, their limited interpretability can pose challenges for educators and students, hindering trust and decision-making. Moreover, the black-box nature of these models can prevent researchers from studying their structure to uncover new insights into the phenomenon they are investigating. In this study, we introduce a knowledge-based neural network (KBANN) approach—a technique rarely applied in education—for assessing the quality of Mars habitat structures built by students as part of a Minecraft-based astronomy camp. Collaborating with domain experts, we developed a block knowledge schema between Minecraft block types and meaningful components of a Mars habitat and incorporated it into the network's initial architecture. We then compared the performance of the KBANN model with that of a conventional fully connected network and three traditional machine learning models. We extracted and interpreted the adjusted rules from the KBANN model to understand how these rules evolved during the training process. SHAP values have also been calculated as a post-hoc explanation to be compared with the extracted rules from the KBANN model. A case study further illustrates how the extracted rules can be used to interpret the model's prediction for an example Mars habitat, indicating how students applied their understanding of the characteristics of a viable habitat. Our findings demonstrate how the use of a knowledge-based neural network can enhance the model interpretability by integrating expert knowledge with data-driven insights.

1. Introduction

Machine learning has proven a powerful and widely used tool across many domains, offering exceptional capabilities for pattern recognition, prediction, and decision-making. In education, machine learning has been successfully applied across a range of tasks (Razaulla et al., 2022). Among different machine learning methods, neural networks have been a major focus for current research and development. However, while neural networks excel in predictive performance, their "black

[1-3] University of Illinois Urbana-Champaign, Illinois, USA.
[4] University of Pennsylvania, Pennsylvania, USA.
* Corresponding author: ql29@illinois.edu

DOI: 10.1201/9781003713371-12

box" nature presents a barrier to their adoption in educational settings where interpretability is beneficial (Conati et al., 2018). Education stake holders require systems that not only predict outcomes but also incorporate explainability and accountability to meet social, ethical, and legislative requirements (Webb et al., 2021).

One solution to interpretable machine learning is the integration of explicit domain knowledge into neural networks. By injecting knowledge into the network as the initial state, the network will be constrained by the knowledge but also gradually learn from the data, implicit information that might have been difficult for experts to elicit (Berry, 1987). In this way, the model can combine both knowledge-driven and data-driven insights. By constructing neural networks from both domain-knowledge and data, these models can enhance interpretability, transparency, and ultimately humans' trust in data-based decisions (Hooshyar & Yang, 2021). Knowledge-based Artificial Neural Networks (KBANN) are a popular model in this strand which integrates expert knowledge in its structure and from which, once trained, rules can be extracted for humans to interpret the inner working mechanism of the model. Despite these potential benefits, there has been limited research exploring the explicit inclusion of expert domain knowledge into neural networks in education, such as the work of (Hooshyar et al., 2024; Pinto et al., 2023; Shakya et al., 2021).

In this paper, we investigate the use of a knowledge-based neural network approach to assess the quality of Mars habitats built by students as part of a Minecraft-based astronomy camp. Knowledge-based neural network may be a good fit for open-ended learning environments, such as game-based learning, where the dynamic and exploratory nature of the context demands efficient and flexible machine learning methods and where model interpretability may help uncover meaningful insights from complex game interactions (Alonso-Fernández et al., 2019). We first collaborated with Minecraft and astronomy experts to develop a block knowledge schema between Minecraft blocks and meaningful components of a Mars habitat and incorporated it into the network's initial architecture. We then compared the predictive performance of the resulting knowledge-based network to that of a similar fully connected network (first proposed in (Hum et al., 2024)) and three traditional machine learning models. Adjusted rules were extracted from the knowledge-based network to better understand how the model assesses Mars habitat structures, and we present a case study to illustrate the enhanced interpretability of the knowledge-based network. This study seeks to answer the following research questions:

RQ1: How well can the knowledge-based neural network predict habitat scores compared to other predictive models?

RQ2: How does the interpretation of the rules extracted from the knowledge-based neural network inform us about how the model assesses the quality of the Mars habitats?

RQ3: How is the interpretability of the extracted rules from the knowledge-based neural network compared to post-hoc explanations?

RQ4: Given a specific Mars habitat, how can the knowledge-based neural network explain the scores it predicts?

2. Related Work

2.1 Model Interpretability for Education

Interpretability has been an emerging research topic for the development of AI models in education, a high-stake context in which to employ AI for decision-making (Conati et al., 2018). On the one hand, teachers and students are found to have limited knowledge of AI on a technical level and tend to exhibit vastly differing levels of trust towards AI (Bewersdorff et al., 2023). On the other hand, many sources of noise in learning data may lead to algorithmic biases and the possibility of inadvertently making wrong decisions through AI (Baker & Hawn, 2022). By producing transparent explanations and reasons for the decisions AI makes, interpretable models are powerful methods to mitigate challenges of Fairness, Accountability, Transparency, and Ethics (FATE) to increase trust in AI systems (Khosravi et al., 2022). Explainable and interpretable models can also support researchers, instructors, and students to improve model quality, modify curriculum, and promote understanding and trust (Liu et al., 2024).

Two broad categories of approaches are generally used to improve model interpretability: building intrinsically interpretable models and post-hoc methods. Intrinsically interpretable approaches aim at designing systems that are inherently transparent and explainable (Langer et al., 2021), while post-hoc approach creates a second model to communicate understandable information about an already developed model (Barredo Arrieta et al., 2020). Despite the parallel existence of both approaches, post-hoc methods have been challenged for being unfaithful to the original model (Rudin, 2019), inconsistency of the explanations generated (Swamy et al., 2022), and disagreement among experts' trust on different explanations (Swamy et al., 2023). As such, while it is still a challenging task, there is a need to explore intrinsically interpretable models in education, especially to improve the interpretability of neural network models (Gunasekara & Saarela, 2025).

2.2 Interpretable Neural Networks in Education

Multiple techniques have been employed to improve the intrinsic interpretability of neural networks, such as transforming the loss function to influence the patterns learned by the network or constraining the model components (e.g., the network's parameters or its structures) to more closely align with domain knowledge (Dash et al., 2022). In educational context, researchers have adjusted the loss function of neural networks to obtain more meaningful learning action sequences that are used to predict learning outcomes (Jiang & Bosch, 2021) or to predict if students are gaming the system (Pinto et al., 2023). Other researchers modified the structure of neural networks to assess language proficiency (Curi et al., 2019) or predict learning performance (Chen et al., 2023; Wang et al., 2023) in a more interpretable way.

Among these methods, KBANN has been shown to be a popular approach (Dash et al., 2022; Marra et al., 2024), but has been applied to a limited number of studies in education. Hooshyar and colleagues (Hooshyar et al., (2024)) developed a knowledge-based network to model students' computational thinking in a programming game. They achieved this by first developing logic rules mapping final scores, computational thinking concepts, and skills. These rules were transformed into layers of the neural network which was then trained on learner data. When compared to other neural network modeling approaches, their knowledge-based network showed improved generalizability on testing data. They hypothesized that this result may be explained by the knowledge-based approach which prioritizes learning a robust representation, with fewer spurious correlations. A further investigation of the explanations from both modeling approaches suggested that the extracted rules from their knowledge-based network were more reliable and accurate to identify important predictive features compared to post-hoc methods like SHAP and LIME (Hooshyar & Yang, 2024).

Besides directly modeling the learning process by introducing knowledge in neural networks, studies have also focused on constructing better dataset for model training. (Shakya et al., 2021) used Markov logic to group symmetrical instances in training data and only picked representative samples to train an LSTM. (Hooshyar, 2024) incorporated educational rules in an autoencoder that was used to generate more reasonable samples for temporal knowledge tracing.

2.3 Educational Data Mining in Minecraft

Minecraft offers an inherently open-ended context that involves acquisition of a wide range of skills and knowledge relevant to school and the real world (Lane & Yi, 2017). Students can explore, experiment, and choose from multiple pathways to achieve learning objectives. This open and unstructured learning also poses needs and challenges for data mining methods in game-based learning (Alonso-Fernández et al., 2019). For example, studies can involve various data modalities from students playing Minecraft (Worsley et al., 2021). Data mining can be a helpful method to discover insights from less structured free-play data, for example to detect distinct patterns from movement data (Zhou & Paquette, 2024). In this way, data mining can serve different anticipated objectives in game-based learning (Banihashem et al., 2024) and better support teachers to promote learning with games (Nebel et al., 2016).

3. Method

3.1 Dataset

The data used in this study was collected from 16 Minecraft astronomy camps held in different locations across the United States in 2022 and 2023. In each camp, middle school-aged students participated for one week by engaging in a combination of science learning activities taking place both inside and outside of a customized Minecraft Java Edition learning environment. The camps aimed to both increase participants' knowledge of astronomy and their interest in STEM more broadly. In the first three days of the camp, students explored various hypothetical simulations of Earth in "What if" scenarios, such as "What if Earth had no moon?" (Figure 1, top) and exoplanets to explore how a given scenario would impact the planet's living conditions. In this process they learned about key simulated world characteristics hazardous to humans like radiation or atmospheric composition. In the last two days, students worked in groups to design and build a habitat safe for humans on a Minecraft map replicating the surface of Mars (Figure 1, bottom). The work presented in this study focuses solely on the Mars habitat building activity (i.e., the last 2 days of the camp).

Before building their habitat, participants watched an explanatory video introducing important challenges related to living on Mars and were encouraged to employ what they learned from exploring the other "What if" earth hypothetical worlds to design their Mars habitat. On the last day of camp participants were shown examples of Mars habitat submissions from a NASA competition and issued a checklist of habitat-related survival objectives to complete. Each group spent around four hours completing the habitat building activity, which included a final presentation at the end of the camp.

Minecraft worlds are composed of blocks which are arranged in creative ways to constitute terrain or structures. Players can interact with existing blocks by, for example, removing them and adding new blocks to the world to create their own structures. In the context of the Mars habitat building activity, players needed to first identify a suitable location for their habitat, which may require removing existing terrain blocks to prepare for building, and then place any combination of the hundreds of available existing block material types to build their habitat. During gameplay, the learning system logged all of the players' actions involving adding, modifying, or removing a block from the world. This included information about what type of block was added/removed, who placed or interacted with it, its relative state (e.g., an open or closed door), as well as what time it was placed and its coordinates (location). Overall, the data used in this study was collected from 131 students across 16 camps, who built 57 habitats using 695 different types of blocks.

To assess the quality of the students' Mars habitat, (Hum et al. (2024)) developed a scoring scheme indicating whether the habitat accounts for different scientific considerations that are required for a livable habitat. In total, 11 scores were defined for what students should include in their habitats (Table 1). Each of the 57 habitats were manually scored across each dimension into either 2-level (0 or 1) or 3-level scores (0, 0.75, or 1.5). For simplicity of the structure of the knowledge-based model described in the next section, we transformed these scores into binary labels where 0 indicates that the dimension was not accounted for in the habitat and 1 indicates the dimension was accounted for either partially or com

Fig. 1 Screen captures of two worlds in the Minecraft game. The top figure is "What if Earth had no moon?" and the bottom figure is the Mars map where students build habitats.

pletely. Two of the 11 scores were excluded from the knowledge-based network that was developed in this study: area built and shape of structure (see Section 3.3 for more details).

3.2 Knowledge-based Neural Network

The KBANN in this study was adapted based on the study of Towell and Shavlik (1994). This approach maps domain specific knowledge into a neural network structure which is then refined using backpropagation. In this study, we are especially interested in understanding how the use of different types of Minecraft blocks is associated with the 11 habitat scores (Table 1). As there are too many block types (695) used during habitat building, it is helpful for domain experts to first reason about what are important categories of blocks (e.g., blocks related to automation or to a garden) that can be included in a successful habitat. These categories can then be connected with specific block types that serve a given function or relevant to a given structure. For example, creating automated mechanisms can include blocks related to redstone, which are used to create logical circuits, as well as pistons that can be activated using redstone blocks. Similarly, constructing a garden might involve using blocks related to dirt and to different types of plants.

Table 1 Description of habitat scores.

Habitat Scores	*Description*	*# Positive Samples*
oxygen	Some kind of representation of an air purification system or oxygen tank	44 (77%)
food and water	Food and water are easily accessible and not subject to radiation exposure, includes facilities to grow new food; ice storage counts as water but water in a farm does not	44 (77%)
supplies	Supplies (in storage chests or similar) are easily accessible and not subject to radiation damage	39 (68%)
gravity	Facilities included that would help astronauts compensate for the low gravity on Mars (i.e., a workout facility, ladders)	31 (54%)
health	An infirmary or a psychiatrist's office are present	21 (37%)
radiation	An outer layer of the base is specifically included to shield it from solar radiation (if the base is built underground this also counts)	37 (65%)
power	Solar panels or a nuclear reactor are present	41 (72%)
communication	Facilities that have purposeful-built communications equipment such as antennae or satellite dishes	39 (68%)
transportation	A rover is present within or nearby the base, can also include use of minecart tracks between parts of the base to represent an internal transportation system	22 (39%)
shape of structure	(Semi-)rounded, as to keep dirt and dust from coming through the corners	37 (65%)
area built	Base is built in a geographically protected area (such as a valley) or into a cliff or underground	40 (70%)

Once such association between habitat scores and block categories has been established; it can be translated into the network architecture to assess a Mars habitat, as shown in Figure 2. In this network, the input layer takes the count of each block type in a given habitat. Considering habitats might vary in size, each block frequency was rescaled to [0, 1] across 57 habitats. The hidden layer corresponds to the block categories described by experts. The output layer aligns with the binary habitat scores manually labeled by graders. Because there are 27 units in the hidden layer and 695 units in the input layer, Figure 2 cannot show the full representation of the network structure but only part of the input layer and hidden layer, as well as their links with the output layer. The full list of units in the network is available through github[1]. This knowledge-based network was designed to solve a multi-label classification problem where all habitat scores are predicted by the same network. This decision ensures that the knowledge rules learned by the network are shared for all habitat scores and that the rules won't change based on which habitat score is predicted.

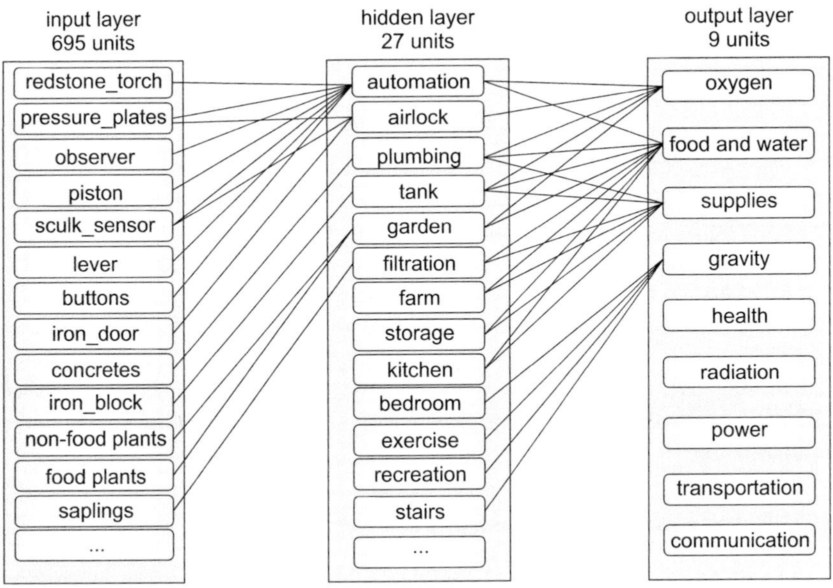

Fig. 2 An illustration of the knowledge-based neural network structure with input layer of blocks, hidden layer of block categories, output layer of habitat scores.

After defining the units and layers of the network, the weighted connections between layers are initialized based on the dependencies established in knowledge rules elicited from domain experts. Each rule contains one consequent and several positive antecedents. Take one rule as an example, the first row in Table 3 shows the rule of health score. In this rule, health is the consequent while decoration, bedroom, exercise room, recreation, medical bay, and windows are antecedents. The initial weights on all links between this consequent and its antecedents are positive and set to ω, while the bias on the unit corresponding to the consequent is set to $(P - 0.5)\omega$, where P is the number of positive antecedents on a rule. For other units that are not stated in the rule, the initial weights of their links to the consequent are set to a very small value randomized close to zero. Following (Towell & Shavlik, 1994), units have a sigmoid activation function and during training, loss is calculated with cross entropy function.

1 https://github.com/sophielqh/KBANN.

A regularizer is added during training to make the knowledge-based network more interpretable. Different from common regularizations such as L1 or L2, the regularization term used is designed to penalize the network for making changes to the original knowledge provided by experts. This is achieved by measuring the distance between the current weights and the initial weights. Given each rule, the weights of all the antecedents are ω and the distance of rule change is calculated using the following equation:

$$regularizer = \lambda \sum_{i \in \omega} \frac{(\omega_i - \omega_{init_i})^2}{1 + (\omega_i - \omega_{init_i})^2}.$$

The λ coefficient controls the tradeoff for the network to learn from the training set and the distance from the initial rules. In an early version, the knowledge-based network was trained without the regularization term. Although its predictive performance was slightly higher than the regularized network shown in Section 4.1, its extracted rules were less interpretable. The network changed the rule for certain block categories so dramatically that the rules no longer described the original concepts intended for this category. Making sense of the new concepts was also difficult as the rules could contain hundreds of positive antecedents or blocks. Therefore, we only present the performance of the knowledge-based network with regularization.

3.3 Block Knowledge Construction

Two experts (the third and fourth author) helped to create the block knowledge schema that was integrated into the KBANN model. In an initial discussion, the two experts were introduced to the expected structure of the KBANN model (Figure 2) and how their knowledge of astronomy-relevant planetary conditions, the learning activity and Minecraft block types could be used to develop such a network. After this discussion, the experts independently created a list of block categories that could be used in the network's hidden layer as well as provide an initial mapping between these categories and the network's inputs (the block types) and outputs (the habitat scores). This resulted in two block mapping diagrams, one from each expert. A second discussion was conducted to share the two mappings to identify commonalities and differences. The first author then reconciled both diagrams into one mapping, combining shared categories when appropriate. Finally, a third discussion focused on discussing missing knowledge in the block mapping, including block categories and habitat scores with few connections. Two habitat scores were excluded from the output layer (area built and shape of structure), as both experts agreed that these two scores mainly rely on location and coordinate data that is not part of the input layer.

The block categories (middle layer) are listed in Table 2. Overall, 27 block categories were proposed as being relevant to the construction of a Mars habitat. These categories can be roughly grouped into three types: space (a functional space in the habitat such as kitchen), system (a system constructed with various block combinations such as automation), or purpose (a purpose to be fulfilled for better human living in the habitat such as farm).

Table 2 The block categories in constructed knowledge.

Types	*Categories*
space	kitchen, garden, bedroom, exercise room, medical bay
system	automation, filtration, airlock, plumbing, tank, stairs, windows, protective walls, nuclear, solar, power cords, rover, drone, landing pad, path, elevator, office, dish/antenna
purpose	farm, storage, decoration, recreation

The block categories and connections included in the block mapping diagram were then transformed into propositional and acyclic rules in the format of Horn clauses, following the process described in (Towell & Shavlik, 1994). Table 3 shows two example rules. In total, there were 9 score rules with each corresponding to one habitat score. In each score rule, the consequent is one of the habitat scores (e.g., health) while the antecedents are block categories that experts connected to this score in the diagram (e.g., decoration, bedroom, exercise room, etc.). Similarly, 27 block category rules were created with each corresponding to one block category as the consequent (e.g., nuclear) and many block types as antecedents (e.g., end_rod, slime_block, soul_sand, and magma_block). The rules were integrated into the network structure as described in Section 3.2. The full list of rules can be found in our github link.

Table 3 Examples of the knowledge represented in propositional rules.

Name	*Propositional Rule*	*Description*
A rule for habitat score in the output layer	health : decoration, bedroom, exercise room, recreation, medical bay, windows.	The health score of a habitat depends on the realization of decoration, bedroom, exercise room, recreation, medical bay, and windows.
A rule for block category in the hidden layer	nuclear : end_rod, slime_block, soul_sand, magma_block.	The nuclear category relies on the use of end_rod block, slime_block, soul_sand, and maga_block.

3.4 Experiment

The knowledge-based neural network was implemented with TensorFlow 2.0 in Python, structured as a feed-forward neural network with one hidden layer and trained via stochastic gradient descent with back-propagation. The Adam optimizer was employed. To prevent overfitting, we added one dropout layer with a dropout rate of 0.4 and employed early stopping on loss value. The regularization coefficient was set to 0.001. We applied grid search on early stopping patience (3, 5,10, 20), initial weights (1, 2, 4, 6, 8) and learning rates (0.3, 0.1, 0.03, 0.01, 0.005, 0.003, 0.001) to find the best model.

In addition to the KBANN model, we adapted the multi-layered perceptron (MLP) model proposed in (Hum et al., 2024). The MLP model was optimized by randomly varying the numbers of hidden layers (1–4 layers) and nodes in each layer (25–500 nodes). This process was repeated 50 iterations to find the network with the best performance. We also applied three traditional machine learning models, including logistic regression, random forest (RF), and support vector machine (SVM). Each model was tuned on hyperparameters to identify the best model.

3.5 Model Evaluation

3.5.1 Predictive Performance

To evaluate the predictive performance of predictive models, we calculated F1-score, precision, recall, Cohen's Kappa, and AUC for each label. Cohen's Kappa (Cohen, 1960) is a statistical measure commonly used to assess interrater agreement in qualitative studies. We included this metric because it takes the base rate of one class into account and describes how well a model performs compared to the chance level at classifying habitat scores. It ranges between –1 to 1, with 0 indicating the model performs at chance level while 1 indicating perfect predictions.

We employed two methods to account for the imbalanced dataset in this multi-label prediction task. First, we had a baseline model that always predicts the majority class in the training set, as a way to show how an imbalanced class can influence a model's performance. Second, we evaluated the performance of the six models (baseline, logistic regression, RF, SVM, MLP, KBANN) 1,000 times, where each time the dataset was split into training and testing sets with a ratio of 4:1 stratified on multi-labels. The performance metrics were then averaged for comparison.

3.5.2 Model Interpretation and Case Study

After training the knowledge-based network, we further examined how to interpret the models' predictions through two methods. First, we applied SHAP (Shapley Additive Explanations) (Lundberg & Lee, 2017) as a post-hoc explanation to identify important features for predicting habitat scores. SHAP values were calculated for KBANN and RF models (the best two models) when predicting the same label. These post-hoc explanations were further compared with the extracted rules from a trained KBANN model to discuss model interpretability.

Second, the KBANN's rules could be used to explain the prediction for a given habitat. We selected a habitat for which the model was able to successfully predict most of its scores. We then visualized how the activation of different block categories in the hidden layer impacted the network's prediction. Similarly, we investigated how the use of different types of blocks activated block categories that were used to generate predictions.

4. Results

4.1 RQ1: Model Performance

The KBANN model performed best on Kappa when patience was 20, initial weight was 1, and learning rate was 0.005. The optimized MLP model had four layers with 406, 30, 419, and 59 nodes respectively.

Among the three traditional machine learning models, RF performed the best overall, so its performance is included in the following tables as a representative of traditional models.

Table 4 shows the F1 scores of four models on nine labels. The highest F1 score on each label is in bold. It reveals distinct and specialized strengths among the four models tested. While the RF model achieved the highest overall performance with a macro average of 0.6508, it did not perform the best on any individual label, suggesting it is the most balanced and consistent performer. In contrast, the KBANN model demonstrated more specialized capabilities, achieving the highest on four labels: oxygen (0.8632), radiation (0.7995), power (0.8792), and communication (0.8826). However, the KBANN model failed completely on gravity, health, and transportation. The MLP model, despite a lower macro average, was uniquely effective on the health (0.2559) and transportation (0.3218) labels, where most other models struggled. It is also interesting to see that the Baseline model, which predicts the majority class, performed best on the food and water (0.8625), supplies (0.8183), and gravity (0.7073) labels.

Table 4 F1 scores of Baseline, RF, MLP, and KBANN models.

	Baseline	*RF*	*MLP*	*KBANN*
oxygen	0.8623	0.8593	0.7981	**0.8632**
food and water	**0.8625**	0.8570	0.7899	0.7065
supplies	**0.8183**	0.8023	0.7471	0.6135
gravity	**0.7073**	0.6205	0.5167	0
health	0	0.1388	**0.2559**	0
radiation	0.7830	0.7640	0.6164	**0.7995**
power	0.8358	0.8481	0.7704	**0.8792**
transportation	0	0.1514	**0.3218**	0
communication	0.8054	0.8158	0.7197	**0.8826**
Macro Avg	0.6305	**0.6508**	0.6151	0.5272

In Table 5, the MLP achieved the highest macro average precision of 0.6228, demonstrating a consistent ability to avoid false positives across all labels. The KBANN model achieved the highest precision on six of the nine labels, including a perfect score of 1.0 for food and water. However, it also failed entirely on three others. The precision scores of the Baseline model are zero on the health and transportation labels because these labels have more negative class than positive. The MLP and RF models attained their highest precision scores on these two labels (0.2870 for health and 0.3176 for transportation). It underscores their ability to identify true positives in underrepresented labels.

Table 5 Precision of Baseline, RF, MLP, and KBANN models.

	Baseline	*RF*	*MLP*	*KBANN*
oxygen	0.7617	0.7608	0.7659	**0.8965**
food and water	0.7632	0.7617	0.7777	**1**
supplies	0.6995	0.6992	0.7276	**0.8712**
gravity	0.5524	0.5907	0.5405	0
health	0	0.1953	**0.2870**	0
radiation	0.6479	0.6492	0.6446	**0.7599**
power	0.7199	0.7583	0.7961	**0.9192**
transportation	0	**0.3176**	0.3117	0
communication	0.6784	0.7142	0.7538	**0.7943**
Macro Avg	0.5359	0.6052	**0.6228**	0.5823

The recall scores in Table 6 reveal the highly specialized and conservative nature of the KBANN model, which stands in contrast to the other approaches. With the lowest macro average recall of 0.5098, KBANN's primary weakness is its inability to identify positive instances on three labels: gravity, health, and transportation. This suggests its internal structure has not learned any reliable rules for these classes, which may be explained by how the three labels have very limited experts' rules injected in the neural network. KBANN achieves a perfect recall score of 1.0 on the communication label and maintains a respectable recall of over 0.85 for radiation and power. When viewed alongside its high precision scores from Table 5, the KBANN model operates as a high-confidence model. It avoids making positive predictions unless the criteria are strongly met, which results in many missed instances (low recall) but ensures that its positive predictions are more accurate (high precision). This is in contrast to the MLP, which is better at finding rare instances, and the Baseline, which achieves high recall simply by over-predicting the majority classes.

Table 6 Recall of Baseline, RF, MLP, and KBANN models.

	Baseline	*RF*	*MLP*	*KBANN*
oxygen	**1**	0.9937	0.8564	0.8389
food and water	**1**	0.9886	0.8296	0.5577
supplies	**1**	0.9611	0.8062	0.4879
gravity	**0.987**	0.6838	0.5291	0

Contd.

Table 6 *Contd.*

	Baseline	*RF*	*MLP*	*KBANN*
health	0	0.1184	**0.2645**	0
radiation	**1**	0.9430	0.6264	0.8514
power	**1**	0.9697	0.7726	0.8524
transportation	0	0.1061	**0.3670**	0
communication	**1**	0.9648	0.7215	**1**
Macro Avg	**0.7763**	0.7477	0.6415	0.5098

The Cohen's Kappa (κ) scores in Table 7 adjust for the possibility of agreement occurring by chance. Under this lens, the KBANN model is the only model achieving a macro average Kappa that was not close to 0 (0.2886). This score, while indicating only fair agreement, is higher than its competitors. In addition, the KBANN model showed high Kappa performance on labels like power (0.5980) and communication (0.5113). Both RF and MLP models display negative Kappa scores for several labels, indicating that their predictions for these labels are systematically worse than random chance. Therefore, the κ results indicate that only the KBANN model learned consistent, reliable patterns, outperforming chance on the six labels for which it had sufficient knowledge.

Table 7 Kappa of Baseline, RF, MLP, and KBANN models.

	Baseline	*RF*	*MLP*	*KBANN*
oxygen	0	– 0.0079	0.0168	**0.4887**
food and water	0	– 0.0086	0.0591	**0.3730**
supplies	0	– 0.0021	0.0920	**0.2417**
gravity	0	**0.0738**	– 0.0228	0
health	0	– 0.0452	**0.0125**	0
radiation	0	0.0099	– 0.0016	**0.3847**
power	0	0.2004	0.2431	**0.5980**
transportation	0	**0.0227**	– 0.1150	0
communication	0	0.1788	0.1976	**0.5113**
Macro Avg	0	0.0469	0.0535	**0.2886**

The KBANN also performed the best on AUC scores in Table 8, which measure a model's ability to distinguish between classes, with an AUC of 0.5 indicating random chance performance and 1 indicating perfect predictions. It achieved the highest macro average of 0.7282 and was the top performing model on eight of the nine labels, with very high scores on power (0.9216) and food and water (0.9185). The RF performed the second best with a macro average of

0.6477, with the highest on the health label (0.5970). In contrast, the MLP model demonstrated the weakest performance, with a macro average of 0.5298 that was only marginally better than the Baseline.

Table 8 AUC of Baseline, RF, MLP, and KBANN models.

	Baseline	*RF*	*MLP*	*KBANN*
oxygen	0.5	0.6452	0.5099	**0.7808**
food and water	0.5	0.7947	0.5331	**0.9185**
supplies	0.5	0.5685	0.5478	**0.7609**
gravity	0.5	0.5596	0.4892	**0.6882**
health	0.5	**0.5970**	0.5099	0.3483
radiation	0.5	0.5795	0.5001	**0.7521**
power	0.5	0.7816	0.6285	**0.9216**
transportation	0.5	0.4822	0.4418	**0.5327**
communication	0.5	0.8206	0.6082	**0.8509**
Macro Avg	0.5	0.6477	0.5298	**0.7282**

4.2 RQ2: Rule Interpretation

To answer RQ2, we extracted and analyzed the adjusted rules from the trained KBANN on the entire dataset. The link weights and biases of each neuron in the hidden and output layers were collected and translated into rules.

First, we examined the rules for the block categories in the hidden layer of the network. As each rule includes the weights of the connection to 695 block types, it is not possible to fully report the rules in this paper and manually examining each rule would be challenging. To ensure the extracted rules were still describing the intended block category, we calculated the distance between the adjusted rules (after model training) and the initial rules (based on expert knowledge), the same as the regularization in 3.2. This distance described the magnitude of how many rules changed throughout the model training process. Seven rules out of 27 showed a changing distance larger than 1, with the largest distance of 3.09 for the plumbing category. We then manually investigated the rules of these seven block categories and found that all the blocks with weights larger than 1 were those included in the original rules, so the rule changes did not significantly alter the meaning of the concept. The full list of rules for block categories and the changing distance can be found on github.

We then computed the changing distances of the rules for the habitat scores in the output layer, as shown in Table 9. All weights with absolute value smaller than 0.01 were excluded from presentation for visual clarity. The block categories in bold were the ones that were included by experts and their initial weights were initialized as 1 in the network. The block categories not in bold are the ones not included in the original rules and initialized as 0. The changing distances tended to remain small. Five rules had distances smaller than 1: gravity, health, radiation, transportation, and communication. Of the other four rules, food and water had the highest changing distance of 3.616, followed by oxygen (3.059), supplies (1.684), and power (1.595). Among the adjusted rules, most of the antecedents with weights larger than 1 were the ones initialized as 1 using the experts' knowledge. This suggests that the network maintained the overall relationship between habitat scores and block categories proposed by experts but may have complemented it with additional connections.

After training, the network increased some weights to emphasize the importance of those block categories on habitat scores. For example, on the oxygen score, the network increased the weights of plumbing and tank while maintaining the weights of garden, airlock, and automation. While all five categories were part of the initial rules, the network learned from the data that blocks related to plumbing and tanks provide more evidence of successfully addressing the habitat's needs for oxygen generation, compared to the last three categories. Moreover, the network also learned positive weights for an additional eleven block categories, such as kitchen, rover, and drone. These newly learned weights need further investigation as they point to two plausible explanations. One is that the network learned meaningful connections between the oxygen score and these block categories that were not elicited from experts. Another explanation may be that the network learned indirect correlations between block categories and habitat scores instead of a causal relationship.

The network also decreased the weights of some of the initial rules. For example, in the rule for transportation, the initial weights of elevator, rover, and drone (initialized at 1) were lowered to 0.97, 0.88, and 0.88, respectively. Since the Kappa of the knowledge-based network predicting transportation is 0, the network was not able to learn the predictive relationship between the transportation scores and the categories hypothesized by the experts. These limits in performance may be due to the fact that the block categories of elevator, rover, and drone were not well defined by their initial rules. Rovers and drones are sometimes templates that are copied and pasted into the habitats by the instructor instead of built manually by students. In such cases, there is a consistent set of blocks, structured in specific ways, that constitutes a rover or a drone. While the knowledge rule accounts for key blocks in these structures (such as the daylight_detector block in the last row of Table 3), the propositional logic only accounts for the number of times a block type is used in a habitat without accounting for how the blocks are arranged. Elevators in the Mars habitat are similarly difficult as there are multiple ways an elevator can be built in Minecraft (some using fictional-functional constructs like redstone, slime blocks, magma or "soul sand"). However, the current rule only describes one version. Students could use a variety of other blocks to mimic the appearance and function of elevators without including the block types captured by the knowledge rule and still get high scores on the transportation dimension.

Table 9 Rules extracted from KBANN to explain the assessment of habitat scores.

Scores	*Distances*	*Rules*
oxygen	3.059	3.74 < 1.68 × **plumbing** + 1.63 × **tank** + 1.00 × **garden** + 1.00 × **airlock** + 1.00 × **automation** + 0.75 × kitchen + 0.75 × rover + 0.72 × drone + 0.72 × power cords + 0.71 × solar + 0.69 × dish + 0.56 × storage + 0.34 × elevator + 0.25 × nuclear + 0.03 × landing pad + 0.03 × windows
food and water	3.616	6.51 < 1.85 × **tank** + 1.79 × **kitchen** + 1.78 × **plumbing** + 1.67 × **storage** + 1.00 × garden + 1.00 × **filtration** + 1.00 × **farm** + 1.00 × **automation** + 0.81 × drone + 0.81 × rover + 0.80 × dish + 0.78 × power cords + 0.76 × solar + 0.35 × nuclear + 0.29 × elevator + 0.05 × landing pad + 0.04 × windows
supplies	1.684	4.73 < 1.64 × **kitchen** + 1.57 × **storage** + 1.45 × **tank** + 1.45 × **plumbing** + 1.00 × **farm** + 1.00 × **filtration** + 0.55 × dish + 0.51 × drone + 0.47 × rover + 0.34 × power cords + 0.29 × solar + 0.09 × nuclear + 0.05 × elevator + 0.02 × windows + 0.01 × landing pad
gravity	0.954	2.73 < 1.00 × **stairs** + 1.00 × **bedroom** + 1.00 × **recreation** + 1.00 × **exercise room** + 0.43 × plumbing + 0.41 × kitchen + 0.40 × power cords + 0.38 × dish + 0.36 × solar + 0.35 × storage + 0.29 × rover + 0.26 × tank + 0.13 × drone + 0.06 × nuclear + 0.04 × elevator + 0.03 × landing pad
health	0.001	6.10 < 1.00 × **exercise room** + 1.00 × **med bay** + 1.00 × **recreation** + 1.00 × **bedroom** + 1.00 × **decoration** + 1.00 × **windows** + −0.01 × power cords
radiation	0.820	1.17 < 1.00 × **windows** + 1.00 × **protective walls** + 0.49 × kitchen + 0.42 × plumbing + 0.37 × power cords + 0.34 × dish + 0.28 × tank + 0.25 × rover + 0.24 × solar + 0.19 × drone + 0.16 × storage + 0.07 × nuclear + 0.02 × landing pad + −0.04 × elevator
power	1.595	3.95 < 1.56 × **solar** + 1.50 × **power cords** + 1.45 × **plumbing** + 1.36 × **tank** + 1.17 × **nuclear** + 0.53 × rover + 0.46 × dish + 0.45 × drone + 0.42 × kitchen + 0.35 × storage + 0.16 × elevator + 0.02 × landing pad + 0.01 × windows
transportation	0.053	5.14 < 1.00 × **landing pad** + 1.00 × **path** + 0.97 × **elevator** + 0.88 × **rover** + 0.88 × **drone** + −0.02 × nuclear + -0.03 × plumbing + −0.05 × power cords + −0.05 × kitchen + −0.05 × solar + −0.08 × dish + −0.08 × tank
communication	0.814	1.28 < 1.21 × **dish** + 1.00 × **office** + 0.45 × plumbing + 0.44 × kitchen + 0.38 × power cords + 0.33 × storage + 0.26 × tank + 0.26 × solar + 0.21 × rover + 0.20 × drone + 0.06 × nuclear + 0.03 × elevator + 0.01 × landing pad

4.3 RQ3: Model Interpretability

To answer RQ3, we compare the interpretability of extracted rules and SHAP values of the KBANN model. Taking label oxygen as an example, where the KBANN achieved the highest F1, precision, Kappa, AUC among five models, the SHAP values of the 20 most important features are shown in Figure 3. This plot aggregates the SHAP values for each feature across all instances, revealing not only the magnitude of each feature's impact but also the direction of its influence. The features are ranked by importance, with red_concrete, magma_block, and rose_bush identified as the top three predictors. For these three predictors, a high feature value (indicated by red points), representing a higher count of these blocks,

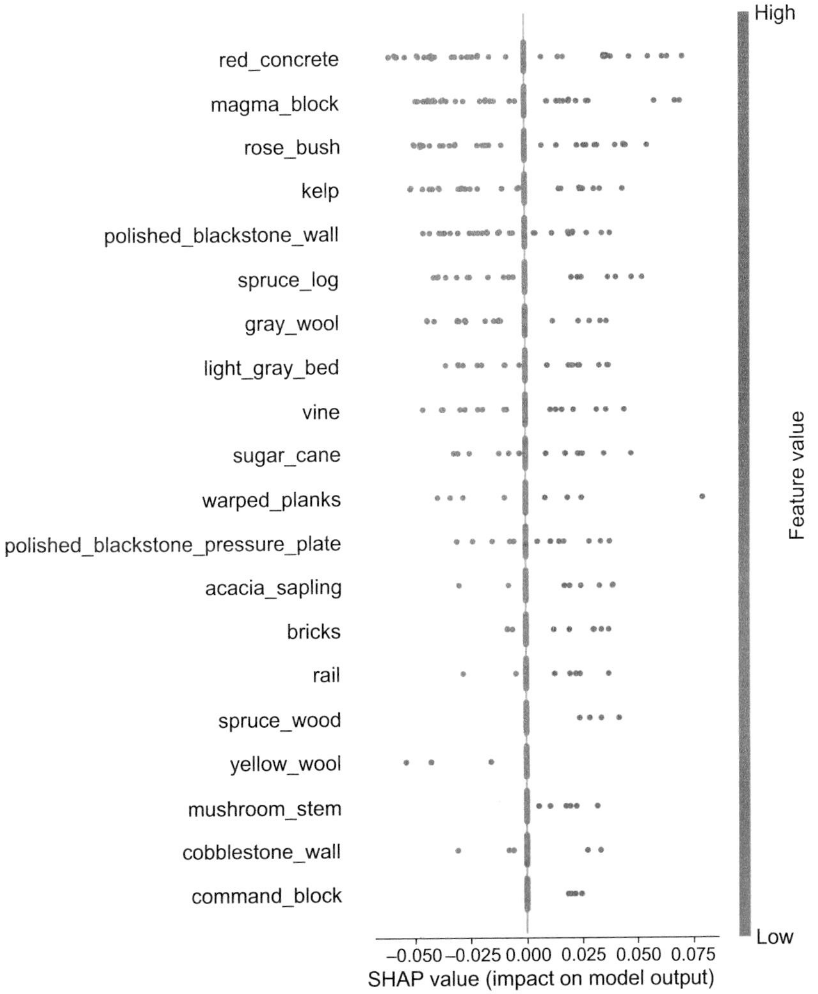

Fig. 3 SHAP values of 20 important features of KBANN model predicting oxygen label.

consistently pushes the model's prediction higher (a positive SHAP value). It suggests that the presence of these specific blocks is a strong signal for the oxygen label. Conversely, the plot also identifies blocks with a negative correlation, such as yellow_wool, where a high feature value pushes the prediction lower. The SHAP analysis identifies a diverse set of features, including decorative blocks like red_concrete, functional blocks not directly related to oxygen like magma_block, and functional blocks related to oxygen like rose_bush.

To further compare important features based on SHAP values and knowledge rules, we mapped each important block type with absolute SHAP value larger than 0 back to the block categories identified by experts, such as red_concrete block can be related to decoration, path, or protective walls. We then ranked the block category importance by averaging the SHAP ranking of each feature corresponding to this category, to show how SHAP analysis results align with knowledge rules in terms of the category ranking. For example, there are three important block types associated with the block category decoration, and their SHAP rankings are 1, 3, and 8. Then the SHAP ranking of the block category decoration is the averaged ranking, 4. Table 10 shows the ranking of block categories based on SHAP values with the first number in parentheses represents the averaged ranking and the second number represents the number of associated block types. Three labels are not included: -gravity, health, and transportation, as KBANN had limited predictive power based on F1-score. Across all labels in Table 10, SHAP values consistently rank protective walls, elevator, and nuclear as high based on one feature with high SHAP value. This may suggest that red_concrete, rose_bush, and magma_block are important features across labels. A deeper examination of these three block types reveals that their high importance may be explained by extreme cases in habitat scores. One habitat in the dataset used the most red_concrete and magma_block among all habitats and it scored high on all the labels in Table 10, except for communication. Another habitat was the only habitat that used rose_bush and it scored high on all the labels. It appears that these two extreme cases led the SHAP method to identify the three block types to be important for high scores, although other blocks' contribution might also be important.

Table 10 Block category ranking based on SHAP values from KBANN prediction.

Labels	*Block Category Ranking*
oxygen	protective walls (1|1), elevator (2|1), nuclear (2|1), path (40|6), garden (45|8), filtration (53|2), farm (62|13), decoration (63|41), airlock (69|3), bedroom (71|6), stairs (75|14), recreation (78|7), automation (82|5), storage (91|1), power cords (96|1), landing pad (96|1), office (101|2)
food and water	protective walls (1|1), elevator (3|1), nuclear (3|1), office (27|1), path (39|6), garden (44|8), farm (47|12), filtration (48|2), bedroom (56|5), automation (59|4), exercise room (63|1), med bay (63|1), decoration (63|40), airlock (69|3), recreation (73|7), stairs (74|14), solar (79|1), power cords (97|1), landing pad (97|1)

Contd.

Table 10 *Contd.*

Labels	*Block Category Ranking*
supplies	protective walls (1|1), elevator (4|1), nuclear (4|1), office (25|1), path (26|5), garden (42|8), farm (47|11), filtration (49|2), automation (51|4), bedroom (52|5), airlock (60|3), decoration (60|41), stairs (65|11), solar (66|1), exercise room (71|1), med bay (71|1), recreation (72|7)
radiation	protective walls (1|1), elevator (3|1), nuclear (3|1), path (41|6), bedroom (49|4), garden (53|10), filtration (55|3), farm (55|16), decoration (65|40), exercise room (80|2), med bay (80|2), airlock (80|3), automation (80|5), office (81|2), stairs (82|11), recreation (93|6), power cords (94|1), landing pad (94|1)
power	protective walls (1|1), nuclear (3|1), elevator (3|1), garden (42|8), filtration (48|2), airlock (51|2), farm (52|11), path (52|6), bedroom (53|4), stairs (63|13), decoration (63|39), automation (73|3), landing pad (76|1), power cords (76|1), recreation (78|8), med bay (83|2), exercise room (83|2), office (117|1)
communication	protective walls (2|1), airlock (4|1), nuclear (6|1), elevator (6|1), filtration (42|2), path (43|6), garden (51|9), automation (57|3), farm (62|15), decoration (69|46), bedroom (69|6), stairs (78|13), office (84|2), exercise room (85|2), med bay (85|2), recreation (93|8), landing pad (99|1), power cords (99|1)

When comparing the block category ranking in Table 10 with the extracted rules in Table 9, it is clear that SHAP values give distinct rankings of importance to block categories that are highly recognized in extracted rules. For example, when predicting oxygen, plumbing was the most important category by extracted rules, but it was not listed as influential based on SHAP values. A similar situation occurs for the tank category for food and water, kitchen category for supplies, windows category for radiation, solar category for power, and dish category for communication. The SHAP values may not have aligned as accurately with the decision-making process based on the neural network's theoretical rules. Rather, they may offer a more local explanation by quantifying the direct predictive impact of each feature, regardless of its role in a larger conceptual rule.

4.4 RQ4: Case Study Explanation

RQ4 investigated how the KBANN's structure could be leveraged to explain the model prediction for a given habitat. For this case study, we selected one example habitat for which the model's predictions were mostly accurate. This habitat scored high on seven habitat scores, but low on two scores (gravity and health) by human graders. Figure 3 shows the activation values of each block category in the hidden layer and each habitat score in the output layer. The prediction threshold in the output layer is set to 0.5, where an activation larger than 0.5 results in a predicted high score. The KBANN predicted the habitat as high on six scores (in yellow) and low on three scores (in gray), resulting in one incorrect prediction for transportation.

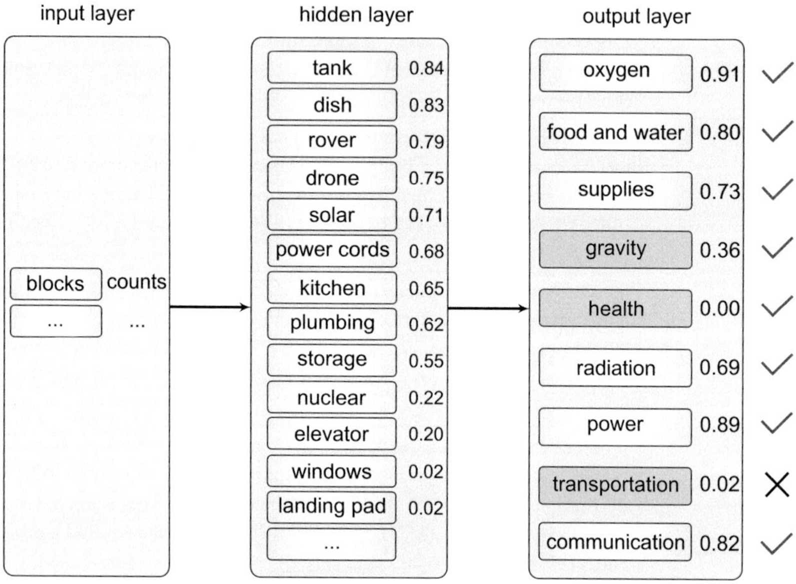

Fig. 4 An illustration of unit activations in the KBANN to predict the example habitat.

To further examine and explain the model's prediction of each score, we visualized the weights and activations in the knowledge rules for all labels and presented one in Figure 5. It shows how the model predicted the power score based on weights and activations. The neuron of power in the network has a bias of 3.95. This number is compared to the sum of the products between the activation of each block categories and the weight of connection between this category and the power score, resulting in a sum of 6.07. Because this sum (6.07) is higher than the bias (3.95), based on the sigmoid function, the KBANN predicts a high score of power. The bar plots of the block categories visually explain how the different categories contribute to this high score. All the block categories that had a positive weight showed a positive activation value. This could indicate that the group of students building this habitat exhibited a balanced knowledge about power generation for a Mars habitat.

Block category rules can also be visualized in a similar way. However, given the large number of block types (695) in the network's input layer, it can be helpful to focus only on the block types with the largest weights. In our example, we display the activation values and weights of the 10 block types with the largest weights. Figure 6 shows how the network calculates the activation of solar panels, a block category in the network's hidden layer, based on block usage from the input layer. This category has a bias of 1.73 and the sum of products is 2.65,

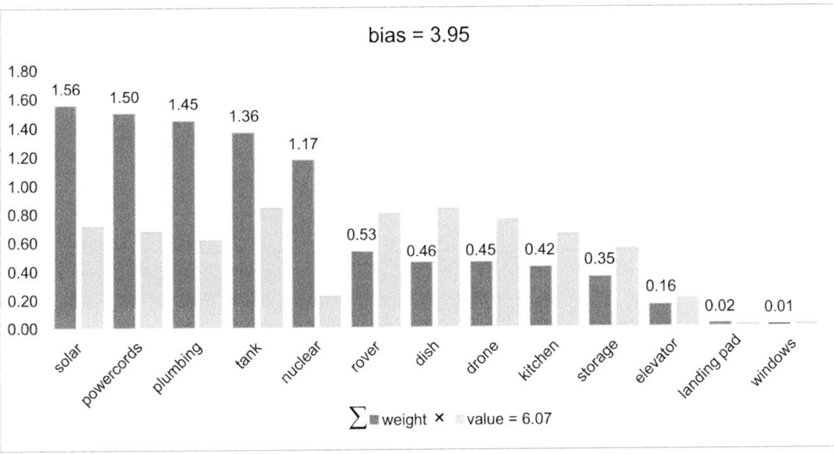

Fig. 5 Rule explanation for the score of power that is predicted correctly.

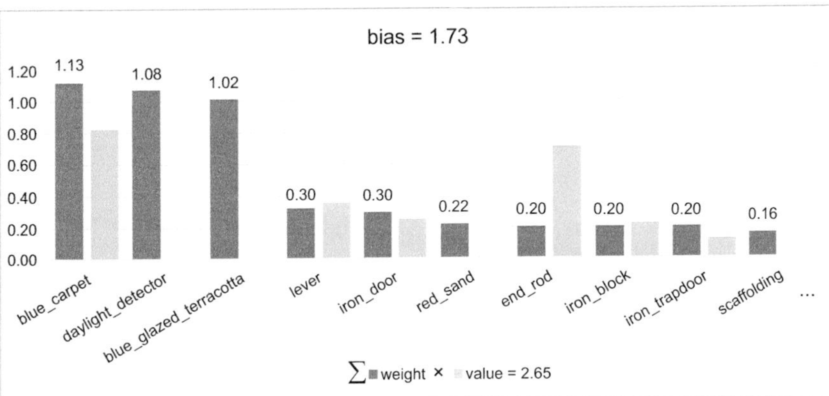

Fig. 6 Rule explanation for the solar category.

indicating an activation of the solar block category in the network's hidden layer. The top 10 blocks with the highest weights include blue_carpet, daylight_detector, blue_glazed_terracotta, lever, and others. Out of these, the first three block types were part of the initial rule by experts because they are often placed by students to represent solar panels. The weights of the remaining blocks are also larger than 0, indicating that the network learned these blocks as associated with the activation of solar. The activation value bars in the figure indicate that students made use of the blue_carpet when building their habitat and also of lever, iron_door, end_rod, iron_block, and iron_trapdoor.

Interestingly, visual inspection of this Mars habitat seems to reveal a different story. The habitat did not include any solar panel array, in contrast to what the network suggests. Although the blocks related to the solar category (such as blue_carpet or end_rods) were used, they were inside of the habitat and likely not intended to depict solar panels. For example, blue_carpet blocks lined the floors in hallways or in the nuclear reactor room, as seen in Figure 7.

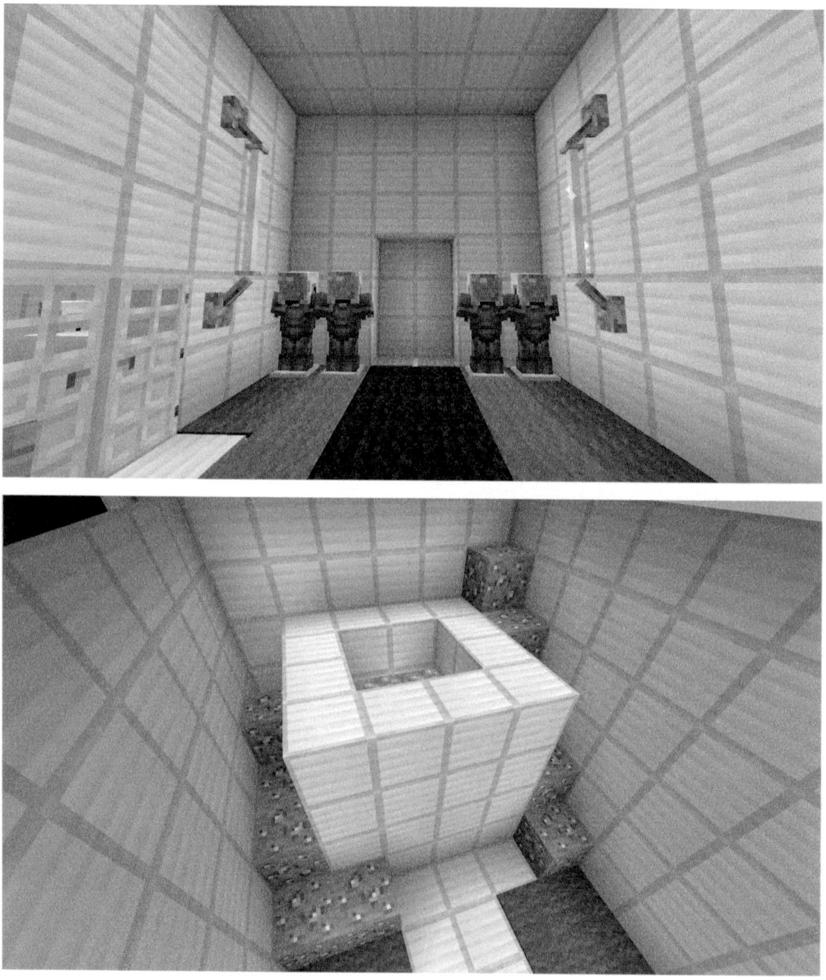

Fig. 7 Screen captures of the example habitat. The top figure shows a hallway containing end_rod, lever, and blue_carpet. The bottom figure contains blue_carpet on the floor by the nuclear fission reactor, possibly indicating pools of water.

This explanation indicates an interpretable result that does not align with the expected usage of these block types by the students. Although Figure 6 shows the logic of how the network activates the solar category in its hidden layer, it is not capturing the right relationships between blocks and categories. The block types with the highest weights in the rule are blocks that are employed for multiple functions and for aesthetic purposes. This example illustrates a case where the model failed to capture the intended knowledge. While this likely had a negative impact on the predictive accuracy of the model, it is also important to note that the model's interpretability provided us with a tool to gain insights about existing issues in the model and to identify opportunities for future model improvements.

5. Discussion

5.1 Predictive Performance

Our results comparing the performance of six predictive models reveal a nuanced performance landscape, dictated primarily by the class imbalance evident in the dataset. The KBANN model emerges as a robust model overall, achieving the highest macro averages in Precision (0.5823), AUC (0.7282), and most im portantly, Kappa (0.2886). The strong Kappa score confirms that KBANN's success is not a byproduct of chance but stems from a learned ability to correctly classify instances. Its high AUC scores further indicate a strong capacity to reliably distinguish between classes. This suggests that the expert knowledge encoded in its architecture provided an advantage in learning the underlying patterns of the dataset when the injected knowledge is sufficient to make predictions.

Despite the KBANN's overall higher values on predictive metrics, its primary weakness is failing completely on health, gravity, and transportation. For these three labels, there are very limited experts' rules as the starting point for the network structure, and they also have fewer positive instances in the dataset, providing limited improvement from data training. It is in these specific cases that the MLP and RF models demonstrated stronger predictive performance. The MLP was the most effective model for detecting instances of health and transportation, achieving the highest F1-scores and recall for both. Similarly, the RF model had the highest overall F1-score, showing it is more balanced and capable of identifying some instances of every class.

These results reflect both benefits and limitations of incorporating explicit knowledge in the network's structure and how the quality of the integrated domain knowledge can mediate this effect. Habitat scores, such as oxygen and power, which are defined using relatively complete expert knowledge rules may benefit more from the proposed knowledge-based approach. This aligns with the findings of (Hooshyar et al., 2024), where the use of a KBANN architecture improved their model's predictive performance. However, for habitat scores without a complete rule or related to block categories that are difficult to capture using only block counts—such as the solar category discussed in Section 4.4—the injected knowledge might hinder the network from learning new insights from the dataset as a result of the regularization penalty.

The creation of well-defined rules linking different block categories with specific block types can be especially challenging in the context of Mars habitat building activity. As illustrated in the examples provided in our case study (Section 4.4), Minecraft is designed to give players great freedom, such as the creative use of blocks in unexpected ways like blue_carpet blocks to replicate the aesthetics of water pools used to cool down a nuclear reactor (as in Figure 7). This ambiguity in students' purpose for using a certain block type can increase the difficulty of developing accurate prediction models using only block count data. While, for the sake of keeping the model simple, the proposed KBANN only considered the quantity of blocks used as network input, future work should investigate ways in which the spatial properties of how blocks are arranged in more complex structures can be integrated into the model.

Given the creative ways in which students use Minecraft blocks in their habitat, another way to increase model performance may be to provide it with more flexibility in automatically learning about these creative uses. As previously discussed, the model was trained using a regularization term that prevented the learned rules from drifting too far from the initial rules. Although we did not show the results in this paper, we also trained a version of the KBANN that did not include this regularization, which outperformed the regularized network to a small extent. However, in the non-regularized model, many rules changed dramatically during training and many block categories became either very difficult or impossible to interpret. As the main goal of this study was to explore an interpretable neural network approach, we only analyzed the regularized version of the network. Our approach was different from a study that used a KBANN model in a different educational context (Hooshyar et al., 2024), where the model was not regularized and also contained heads (undefined units at the initial state) in the hidden layer. Whether to use or not use a regularization term, and how restrictive this term should be, may be dependent on the context to which the KBANN method is applied, and researchers should consider how much stability to impose on the initial expert rules that are integrated in their model.

5.2 Model Interpretation

An examination of the adjusted rules from the trained KBANN model revealed that, while all the antecedent from the initial expert-based rules were retained, the model also modified the rules using the training data. The final weights identified multiple additional antecedents that were found to be related to the predicted labels (Table 9). Some antecedents were down-weighted relative to the initial rules. This may suggest that the modeling approach performed best when provided with initial knowledge rules that were complete enough to capture the intended concepts, but flexible enough to allow the model to learn from the training data.

Being able to extract and inspect the model's adjusted rules provided opportunities to better understand how the model made predictions about the students' Mars habitat. This is in line with the findings in Hooshyar and Yang's work (2024) which suggest that the ability to extract rules for further investigation is an important strength of knowledge-based networks that allow education stakeholders to gain insights from the neural networks to make more informed decisions. However, one important limitation is that, as suggested in (Dash et al.,

2022), knowledge-based neural networks are restricted to refining existing rules instead of discovering new rules. If the educational context calls for identifying potential new rules, or if domain experts are unable to elicit complete enough domain knowledge, other knowledge-based methods may be more appropriate.

The comparison of feature importance from KBANN's extracted rules and SHAP values illuminates differences between intrinsic interpretation and post-hoc methods. The intrinsic interpretation from KBANN rules provides a high-level, symbolic narrative of the model's decision-making process. By grouping features under several scientific concepts, it offers a distilled, human-readable concept hierarchy of what the model learned. In contrast, SHAP, as a post-hoc method, ranked block categories distinctly different compared to the intrinsic rules and may not be capturing the conceptual relationship or reasons for predictions made by the KBANN model. This aligns with the findings from (Hooshyar & Yang, 2024b) showing discrepancy of feature importance rankings between KBANN and SHAP methods.

The presented case study illustrates how the KBANN could be used to explain predictions for a specific habitat. Investigating each rule's weights and activation values provides a more nuanced understanding of why the model predicts, for example, that the habitat meets its power requirement. Similarly, investigating activations for different block types can reveal how structures that are represented by the different block categories (e.g., rover or solar) are identified by the KBANN. However, it is important to note that the explanations do not guarantee that the network is correctly identifying each block category activation in all cases, as shown in the solar example (Figures 6 and 7). As previously discussed, students have great flexibility to use different block types in creative ways, which may result in incorrect activation of a given block category. These explanations instead provide a transparent way for humans to validate the model and decide whether to adjust their understanding of the learning activity and the model's logic. Such explanations also have the potential, once the rules have been refined to be as accurate as possible, to support instructors' understanding of student learning in more nuanced ways. More generally, the interpretability of rules can provide humans with a better understanding of what and how the model makes predictions and allow them to make informed decisions that improve the neural network (for researchers) and support learning (for instructors).

Conclusion

This study presents the design of a knowledge-based neural network to develop a model for the assessment of the quality of Mars habitats built by students in a Minecraft-based learning activity. The inclusion of domain expert knowledge about how Minecraft blocks can be utilized during the building activity increased the interpretability of the knowledge-based network while achieving comparable predictive performance to a fully connected network and an RF model. The extracted rules from the knowledge-based network further showed the ability of the approach to refine the experts' knowledge based on the insights from data. We presented a case study of one Mars habitat to illustrate how the rules extracted from the knowledge-based network can explain its prediction. We also discussed an example of how interpretation of the rules provided insights into a situation where the model failed to capture the intended knowledge, highlighting opportunities for improving the model.

While the study showed the potential of knowledge-based network approach in game-based learning context, it also had limitations. First, the knowledge-based networks structure that was used in this study only used block type usage frequency as the network's input and did not include knowledge about the block's locations, which is highly relevant to building complex structures in Minecraft. Only including block frequency as input potentially limited the model's predictive accuracy. Second, because of the size of the camps in which the learning activity took place, the training dataset was limited in size. Given that the model attempted to classify habitats on nine labels, the dataset may only provide an initial exploratory set of identifiable patterns to be investigated more thoroughly in future studies.

Acknowledgements

This study is funded by National Science Foundation Award #2301172.

References

Alonso-Fernández, C., Calvo-Morata, A., Freire, M., Martínez-Ortiz, I. and Fernández-Manjón, B. (2019). Applications of data science to game learning analytics data: A systematic literature review. *Computers and Education, 141*, 103612. https://doi.org/10.1016/j.compedu.2019.103612.

Baker, R.S. and Hawn, A. (2022). Algorithmic Bias in Education. *International Journal of Artificial Intelligence in Education, 32*(4), 1052–1092. https://doi.org/10.1007/s40593-021-00285-9.

Banihashem, S. K., Dehghanzadeh, H., Clark, D., Noroozi, O. and Biemans, H.J.A. (2024). Learning analytics for online game-based learning: A systematic literature review. *Behaviour and Information Technology, 43*(12), 2689–2716. https://doi.org/10.1080/0144929X.2023.2255301.

Barredo Arrieta, A., Díaz-Rodríguez, N., Del Ser, J., Bennetot, A., Tabik, S., Barbado, A., Garcia, S., Gil-Lopez, S., Molina, D., Benjamins, R., Chatila, R. and Herrera, F. (2020). Explainable Artificial Intelligence (XAI): Concepts, taxonomies, opportunities, and challenges toward responsible AI. *Information Fusion, 58*, 82–115. https://doi.org/10.1016/j.inffus.2019.12.012.

Berry, D.C. (1987). The problem of implicit knowledge. *Expert Systems, 4*(3), 144–151. https://doi.org/10.1111/j.1468-0394.1987.tb00138.x

Bewersdorff, A., Zhai, X., Roberts, J. and Nerdel, C. (2023). Myths, mis- and preconceptions of artificial intelligence: A review of the literature. *Computers and Education: Artificial Intelligence*, 100143. https://doi.org/10.1016/j.caeai.2023.100143.

Chen, J., Liu, Z., Huang, S., Liu, Q. and Luo, W. (2023). Improving Interpretability of Deep Sequential Knowledge Tracing Models with Question-centric Cognitive Representations. In: *Proceedings of the AAAI Conference on Artificial Intelligence* (37, Article 12. https://doi.org/10.1609/aaai.v37i12.26661.

Cohen, J. (1960). A Coefficient of Agreement for Nominal Scales. *Educational and Psychological Measurement, 20*(1), 37–46. https://doi.org/10.1177/001316446002000104.

Conati, C., Porayska-Pomsta, K. and Mavrikis, M. (2018, June 30). AI in Education needs interpretable machine learning: Lessons from Open Learner Modelling. In: *Proceedings of 2018 ICML Workshop on Human Interpretability in Machine Learning* (*WHI 2018*). http://arxiv.org/abs/1807.00154.

Curi, M., Converse, G.A., Hajewski, J. and Oliveira, S. (2019). Interpretable Variational Autoencoders for Cognitive Models. In: *Proceedings of 2019 International Joint Conference on Neural Networks* (*IJCNN*), 1–8. https://doi.org/10.1109/IJCNN.2019.8852333.

Dash, T., Chitlangia, S., Ahuja, A. and Srinivasan, A. (2022). A review of some techniques for inclusion of domain-knowledge into deep neural networks. *Scientific Reports*, *12*(1), 1040. https://doi.org/10.1038/s41598-021-04590-0.

Gunasekara, S. and Saarela, M. (2025). Explainable AI in Education: Techniques and Qualitative Assessment. *Applied Sciences*, *15*(3), Article 3. https://doi.org/10.3390/app15031239.

Hooshyar, D. (2024). Temporal learner modelling through integration of neural and symbolic architectures. *Education and Information Technologies*, *29*(1), 1119–1146. https://doi.org/10.1007/s10639-023-12334-y.

Hooshyar, D., Azevedo, R. and Yang, Y. (2024). Augmenting Deep Neural Networks with Symbolic Educational Knowledge: Towards Trustworthy and Interpretable AI for Education. *Machine Learning and Knowledge Extraction*, *6*(1), Article 1. https://doi.org/10.3390/make6010028.

Hooshyar, D. and Yang, Y. (2021). Neural-symbolic computing: A step toward interpretable AI in Education. *Bulletin of the Technical Committee on Learning Technology*, *21*(4), 2–6.

Hooshyar, D. and Yang, Y. (2024). Problems With SHAP and LIME in Interpretable AI for Education: A Comparative Study of Post-Hoc Explanations and Neural-Symbolic Rule Extraction. *IEEE Access*, *12*, 137472–137490. IEEE Access. https://doi.org/10.1109/ACCESS.2024.3463948.

Hum, S., Shipley, E., Gadbury, M., Lane, H.C. and Ginger, J. (2024). Mars, Minecraft, and AI: A Deep Learning Approach to Improve Learning by Building. In: A. M. Olney, I.-A. Chounta, Z. Liu, O. C. Santos and I.I. Bittencourt (Eds.), *Proceedings of the International Conference on Artificial Intelligence in Education* (pp. 422–430). Springer Nature Switzerland. https://doi.org/10.1007/978-3-031-64299-9_39.

Jiang, L. and Bosch, N. (2021). Predictive Sequential Pattern Mining via Interpretable Convolutional Neural Networks. In: *Proceedings of the 14th International Conference on Educational Data Mining*. EDM.

Khosravi, H., Shum, S.B., Chen, G., Conati, C., Tsai, Y.-S., Kay, J., Knight, S., Martinez-Maldonado, R., Sadiq, S. and Gašević, D. (2022). Explainable Artificial Intelligence in education. *Computers and Education: Artificial Intelligence*, *3*, 100074. https://doi.org/10.1016/j.caeai.2022.100074.

Lane, H.C. and Yi, S. (2017). Playing With Virtual Blocks: *Minecraft* as a Learning Environment for Practice and Research. In: F.C. Blumberg & P. J. Brooks (Eds.), *Cognitive Development in Digital Contexts* (pp. 145–166). Academic Press. https://doi.org/10.1016/B978-0-12-809481-5.00007-9.

Langer, M., Oster, D., Speith, T., Hermanns, H., Kästner, L., Schmidt, E., Sesing, A. and Baum, K. (2021). What do we want from Explainable Artificial Intelligence (XAI)?: A stakeholder perspective on XAI and a conceptual model guiding interdisciplinary XAI research. *Artificial Intelligence*, *296*, 103473. https://doi.org/10.1016/j.artint.2021.103473.

Liu, Q., Pinto, J.D. and Paquette, L. (2024). Applications of Explainable AI (XAI) in Education. In: D. Kourkoulou, A.-O. (Olnancy) Tzirides, B. Cope, & M. Kalantzis (Eds.), *Trust and Inclusion in AI-Mediated Education: Where Human Learning Meets Learning Machines* (pp. 93–109). Springer Nature Switzerland. https://doi.org/10.1007/978-3-031-64487-0_5

Lundberg, S.M. and Lee, S.-I. (2017). A Unified Approach to Interpreting Model Predictions. *Advances in Neural Information Processing Systems*, *30*. https://proceedings.neurips.cc/paper/2017/hash/8a20a8621978632d76c43dfd28b67767-Abstract.html.

Marra, G., Dumančić, S., Manhaeve, R. and De Raedt, L. (2024). From statistical relational to neurosymbolic artificial intelligence: A survey. *Artificial Intelligence*, *328*, 104062. https://doi.org/10.1016/j.artint.2023.104062

Nebel, S., Schneider, S. and Rey, G.D. (2016). Mining Learning and Crafting Scientific Experiments: A Literature Review on the Use of Minecraft in Education and Research. *Journal of Educational Technology and Society*, *19*(2), 355–366.

Pinto, J.D., Paquette, L. and Bosch, N. (2023, March). Interpretable neural networks vs. Expert-defined models for learner behavior detection. In: *Proceedings of 13th International Learning Analytics and Knowledge Conference*. LAK23, Arlington TX USA.

Razaulla, S.M., Pasha, M. and Farooq, M.U. (2022). Integration of Machine Learning in Education: Chal lenges, Issues, and Trends. In: Ch. Satyanarayana, X.-Z. Gao, C.-Y. Ting, & N.B. Muppalaneni (Eds.), *Machine Learning and Internet of Things for Societal Issues* (pp. 23–34). Springer Nature. https://doi.org/10.1007/978-981-16-5090-1_2.

Rudin, C. (2019). Stop explaining black box machine learning models for high stakes decisions and use interpretable models instead. *Nature Machine Intelligence*, *1*(5), 206–215. https://doi.org/10.1038/s42256-019-0048-x.

Shakya, A., Rus, V. and Venugopal, D. (2021). Student Strategy Prediction Using a Neuro-Symbolic Approach. In: *Proceedings of the 14th International Conference on Educational Data Mining*. https://eric.ed.gov/?id=ED615630.

Swamy, V., Du, S., Marras, M. and Kaser, T. (2023). Trusting the Explainers: Teacher Validation of Explainable Artificial Intelligence for Course Design. In: *LAK23: 13th International Learning Analytics and Knowledge Conference* (pp. 345–356). https://doi.org/10.1145/3576050.3576147.

Swamy, V., Radmehr, B., Krco, N., Marras, M. and Käser, T. (2022). Evaluating the Explainers: Black-Box Explainable Machine Learning for Student Success Prediction in MOOCs. In: *Proceedings of the 15th International Conference on Educational Data Mining*, 98–109. https://doi.org/10.5281/zenodo.6852964.

Towell, G.G. and Shavlik, J.W. (1994). Knowledge-based artificial neural networks. *Artificial Intelligence*, *70*(1), 119–165. https://doi.org/10.1016/0004-3702(94)90105-8.

Wang, Z., Yan, W., Zeng, C., Tian, Y. and Dong, S. (2023). A Unified Interpretable Intelligent Learning Diagnosis Framework for Learning Performance Prediction in Intelligent Tutoring Systems. *Inter national Journal of Intelligent Systems*, *2023*, 1–20. https://doi.org/10.1155/2023/4468025.

Webb, M.E., Fluck, A., Magenheim, J., Malyn-Smith, J., Waters, J., Deschênes, M. and Zagami, J. (2021). Machine learning for human learners: Opportunities, issues, tensions, and threats. *Educational Technology Research and Development*, *69*(4), 2109–2130. https://doi.org/10.1007/s11423-020-09858-2.

Worsley, M., Mendoza Tudares, K., Mwiti, T., Zhen, M. and Jiang, M. (2021). Multicraft: A Multimodal Interface for Supporting and Studying Learning in Minecraft. In: X. Fang (Ed.), *HCI in Games: Serious and Immersive Games* (pp. 113–131). Springer International Publishing. https://doi.org/10.1007/978-3-030-77414-1_10.

Zhou, Y., and Paquette, L. (2024). Investigating Student Interest in a Minecraft Game-Based Learning Environment: A Changepoint Detection Analysis. In: *Proceedings of the 17th International Conference on Educational Data Mining*, 396–404. https://doi.org/10.5281/ZENODO.12729844.

Index

For Product Safety Concerns and Information please contact our EU representative GPSR@taylorandfrancis.com Taylor & Francis Verlag GmbH, Kaufingerstraße 24, 80331 München, Germany